RESTAGING THE SIXTIES

RESTAGING THE SIXTIES

Radical Theaters and Their Legacies

EDITED BY

James M. Harding & Cindy Rosenthal

THE UNIVERSITY OF MICHIGAN PRESS   ANN ARBOR

Copyright © by the University of Michigan 2006
All rights reserved
Published in the United States of America by
The University of Michigan Press
Manufactured in the United States of America
∞ Printed on acid-free paper

2009   2008   2007   2006   4   3   2   1

A CIP catalog record for this book is available from the British Library.

Library of Congress Cataloging-in-Publication Data

Restaging the sixties : radical theaters and their legacies / edited
    by James M. Harding and Cindy Rosenthal.
      p.   cm.
    Includes index.
    ISBN-13: 978-0-472-09954-2 (cloth : alk. paper)
    ISBN-10: 0-472-09954-X (cloth : alk. paper)
    ISBN-13: 978-0-472-06954-5 (pbk. : alk. paper)
    ISBN-10: 0-472-06954-3 (pbk. : alk. paper)
      1. Theater—United States—History—20th century.   2. Theater—Political aspects—
    United States—History—20th century.   I. Harding, James Martin, 1958–
    II. Rosenthal, Cindy, 1954–

    PN2266.5.R47   2007
    792.0973'09046—dc22   2006021890

Cover: photos (left to right): John O'Neal and Gil Moses in *Ghetto of Desire* (Free Southern
Theater) © Herbert Randall, McCain Library and Archives, University of Southern Mississippi; *La Carpa de los Rasquachis* (El Teatro Campesino) © Theodore Shank; *Paradise Now*
(Living Theater) courtesy Living Theater Archive; *Raped* (At the Foot of the Mountain) Performing Arts Archives, University of Minnesota.

In memory of Bevya Rosten

PREFACE

This anthology primarily addresses an audience of beginning and advanced theater students, although we expect it to have a broader appeal. Balancing theoretical and historical inquiry, it is structured with undergraduate and graduate courses in mind. It provides a critical survey of the rise of radical collective theaters in the United States, and its diverse scholarly perspectives on their legacies will be of significant interest to scholars of experimental theater as well. Of particular interest will be the book's historiographic concerns, which center around a dynamic interpretation of the question of legacy.

At the undergraduate level, the book will be particularly suitable for upper division courses concentrating on the history, theory, and practice of mid-twentieth-century theater. It may also prove useful in beginning courses where students first learn to conceptualize dramatic literature in terms of its performance history and in terms of theatre historiography. At the advanced undergraduate and graduate levels, it promises to become a crucial text for seminars on theater in the sixties, on the blurring of activism and theater, on text and performance, on performance theory, or on the radical redefinition of theatrical spaces. We hope the volume will also find a place in interdisciplinary and cultural studies courses examining political activism and political culture in the United States during the sixties and seventies. Because of its focus on "the turbulent decade," this will be an appealing text for courses in comparative cultural history, where the social and cultural upheavals of those years are considered within an international context. Indeed, the collective theaters examined here invite precisely such an approach because many of them (e.g., the Living Theatre, the Open Theatre, and Bread and Puppet) rose to international status.

Acknowledgments

The idea for this anthology was born out of the energy, collegiality, and caffeine buzz of conversations during session breaks at the American Society for Theatre Research Conferences in 2000 and 2001. At ASTR, Performance Studies International, and Association for Theatre in Higher Education conferences, our ongoing dialogues with colleagues, some of whom became contributors to this book, have sparked and inspired this project. It's been a wonderful experience to work with and learn from each of our contributors, and we are tremendously grateful to them, especially those who were with us from the first and have been patient throughout this long process, and those, like Roger Babb, Carol Martin, Martin Puchner, and Charlotte Canning who joined us late in the day and delivered terrific essays in limited time. We are also grateful to Taylor Ball for his diligent work on the preparation of this manuscript. One could not ask for a better editorial assistant.

We owe huge thanks to our families—to Friederike Eigler and sons Lukas and Daniel, and to Emanuel Levy and daughters Anya and Adin—who put up with our endless phone conversations and evenings hunched over the computer screen, even during family vacations.

We are much indebted to LeAnn Fields for her immediate interest in, and keen excitement about, this project. We are most grateful to Richard Schechner for his support for and sage advice about the anthology. And finally we will forever be indebted to all the Group Theatre's members—some of whom passed away while this book was in process—for leaving us an extraordinary, fascinating, living legacy that is the heart and soul of the book.

This anthology is dedicated to the memory of Bevya Rosten, a gifted scholar, teacher, and director, who left us too soon to complete her essay on the Open Theatre for the anthology. We wish we could have had the opportunity to work with her and know her as well as we've come to know our other contributors. She is much missed.

CONTENTS

INTRODUCTION

Between Characteristics, Continuities, and Change—
Theorizing the Legacy of Radical Theaters

James M. Harding & Cindy Rosenthal

In the latter half of the 1990s, the reissue of seminal texts like Arthur
Sainer's *The New Radical Theatre Notebook* and Richard Schechner's *Environmental Theatre* signaled two realities in theater scholarship. First, there
was a resurgence of interest in the political theater groups that sought in
the 1960s to radically reconceptualize activist theater. Second, there was
a growing demand for scholarly material on theater in the 1960s that
could easily find its way into the classroom. Yet the fact that both of these
texts were not merely reissued but rather appeared in revised editions
tells us much about the competing demands that they attempted to meet.
Caught between their own status as invaluable historical documents and
a recognition of the profoundly different scholarly landscape of the late
1990s, the revised *New Radical Theatre Notebook* and *Environmental Theatre*
implicitly acknowledged a demand that they could not meet, a demand
for a theoretically informed, critical history of the radical collectives from
the 1960s that have had a major impact on our understanding of political
theater today. The present volume provides that history, and does so at a
moment when political activism in the United States is once again on the
rise. Consequently, a fundamental rethinking of the *histories* and *legacies* of
group theaters can cultivate a valuable political dialogue among artists,
scholars, and students in and beyond the theater community.

Looking beyond a basic goal of documentation, this anthology responds to the need for a critically informed analysis of the pivotal political collective theaters during the 1960s, an analysis that offers us theoretical paradigms for understanding their individual contributions to the history of experimental theater and that offers us theoretical strategies for conceptualizing the legacies of these contributions. In this respect, there is no direct existing alternative to the scholarship in the pages that follow. While works like Arthur Sainer's *The New Radical Theatre Notebook* may be important to our understanding of theater in the turbulent period of the 1960s—since it offers an enthusiastic insider account of the time and of a number of theater collectives, as well as a selection of primary source materials (script and journal fragments, interviews, photographs, and drawings)—it nonetheless constitutes part of the very history that *Restaging the Sixties* interrogates. From a theoretical perspective, similar limitations beset Theodore Shank's more recently reissued *Beyond the Boundaries: American Alternative Theatre,* a book that is as informative as it is frustrating. Indeed, we have a great deal of admiration for the detailed historical overviews that Shank provides of major American collectives in his book.[1] But while *Beyond the Boundaries* is certainly less subjective than Sainer's book, unfortunately it is no more theoretical. In fact, like the reissued version of Sainer's book, the most recent version of Shank's *Beyond the Boundaries* is fashioned as a historical document as well. By Shank's own admission, the sections that his book offers on group theaters are dated. Despite the continued work of any number of the groups discussed in his study, he openly admits to having decided not to revise the discussions of them that he first provided in 1982. Whatever the reason for this decision, its consequence is twofold: first, it sidesteps the wide array of theoretical perspectives that have emerged in the last twenty years and that can genuinely enhance our understanding of the significance of the radical collectives of the 1960s; second, it truncates the history of groups like El Teatro Campesino, the San Francisco Mime Troupe, the Bread and Puppet Theater, or the Living Theatre, all of whose legacies are at least in part manifested in the work that they continue to produce today.

It is the theoretically informed exploration of this deceptively simple question of legacy that ultimately distinguishes *Restaging the Sixties* from *The New Radical Theatre Notebook* and *Beyond the Boundaries* and from subsequent scholarship as well. While Sainer provides us with an important collection of historical documents, and while Shank documents the performance history of major American collective theaters, we have sought to provide readers with a complex, historiographical inquiry into the work of those collective theaters. We commissioned essays that would take critical stock not merely of the history of American collective theaters but of the models one uses to construct those histories, to assess their significance, and to weigh their impact on how experimental political theater is understood today. In this regard, juxtaposing studies of eight of the most important political theater collectives in the United States is a strategy for provoking sustained reflections not only on the concept of a collective theater but also on the concept of a legacy as well.

Individually, and in interaction with each other, the essays contained in the pages that follow present a dynamic image of the work and legacies of the radical collectives that emerged shortly after the middle of the twentieth century. The individual essays speak for themselves, either illuminating different nuances in the political and aesthetic forms that group theaters have embraced, or plotting the trajectory of the legacies that their work has generated. And yet much of the force of this anthology resides in the unforeseen ways that these essays interact with each other. Before delving into the particulars of those interactions, we would like to provide some perspective on the overall aims and structure of this anthology.

Aims and Structure

This volume coordinates the work of eighteen scholars, offering the first combined critical assessment of the radical collective theaters that, beginning in the 1960s and early 1970s, redefined the relationship between theater and political activism, and that as a consequence challenged the traditional foundations of theater itself. The essays examine that redefinition from a variety of perspectives, which while not always in agreement are nonetheless in dialogue with each other. Collectively, the essays thus offer a dynamic understanding of the blurring of performance and politics that was not only the defining gesture of the group theaters that emerged in the tumultuous social context of the 1960s but that continues to inform and shape activist theater today. To cite the enduring impact of these collectives is, from a historical perspective, perhaps justification enough to warrant the concerted study that *Restaging the Sixties* provides. This is, in fact, one of the book's main objectives: in mapping out the critical histories of collective theaters from the 1960s and 1970s, the anthology implicitly argues that understanding activist theater today necessitates understanding the political and aesthetic traditions that preceded and influence it. We have structured this collection with the intent of cultivating such a historical understanding in a way that it is theoretically sophisticated and rigorous, as well as systematic and accessible. With this objective in mind, we organized the book so that each collective is assessed in terms of history, theory, and legacy.

The book includes essays on the following group theaters: the Living Theatre, the Open Theatre, Bread and Puppet, San Francisco Mime Troupe, The Performance Group, El Teatro Campesino, Free Southern Theater, and At the Foot of the Mountain. Three complementary essays are devoted to each theater, and the book is thus divided into eight structurally similar sections. Each section opens with a historical overview of the group, followed by a critical essay and then a discussion of the theater's legacy. The goal of those essays is as follows:

Historical overviews. The historical overviews provide students and scholars with a factual, chronological narrative of the collectives' beginnings, their production histories, the context of their activities, and a rough sketch of their members. The historical overviews are intended to ensure that readers have a baseline of knowledge about the collectives, enabling the two essays that follow to delve deeper into theoretical concerns and into the collectives' legacies.

Critical essays. The critical essays build upon the historical overviews by providing readers with a theoretical framework with which to understand the dynamics and significance of a given collective. They posit, specify, and define a critical discourse that they argue is crucial to conceptualizing the significance (and potentially the problems) of a given collective. Although the contributors pursue this goal with some variation, each essay grounds its discussion and focus on the major individual productions of a given collective. This grounding ensures continuity between the historical overviews as well.

Legacy essays. These essays discuss the legacy of a particular collective. They examine how its theatrical practices have affected or are reflected in more recent theaters, movements, and notions of performance. Because some of the collectives continue to thrive while others have disbanded, the question of legacy varies from collective to collective and consequently produces a variety of approaches, but each essay anchors its discussion with a clear connection with a specific theater.

This threefold assessment in terms of history, theory, and legacy is more than a reflection of the anthology's commitment to a complex understanding of the radical collectives that renegotiated the relationship of politics and theater in the 1960s. It provides an important response to a generational shift. With no systematic study of group theaters available and with a new generation of students and scholars entering into theater studies, the anthology provides a constructive response to the growing lack of firsthand knowledge of this fascinating but sorely underexplored aspect of avant-garde performance history. In practical terms, *Restaging the Sixties* appeals to an audience largely unfamiliar with the larger contexts of the collective theaters, while simultaneously satisfying the critical demands of theater historians who know the work of these groups from their own experience.

Authority, Activism, and Radical Collectives

Above and beyond their value as specific studies of individual theaters, the essays in this book speak to each other. Not only is there dialogue between the paired essays, that is, between a critical essay and its corresponding legacy essay, but the discussions of different collectives and different types of legacies also generates a dialogue across the entire volume from which we can cull a sense of the more general characteristics of the radical collective theaters that first came to prominence in the 1960s and from which, furthermore, we can garner a more dynamic understanding of the notion of a legacy as such. We will return to that question momentarily, but first it is worth looking at what the group theaters from the 1960s had in common. The essays assembled here indicate that the radical collective theaters of the 1960s coalesced around responses to issues of authority and community, both as these issues related to their position vis-à-vis society at large and vis-à-vis theatrical practice in particular. Obviously the responses differed. Even within a single collective, the members frequently found themselves at odds with each other and/or entangled in the contradictory tendencies of espousing a militant antiauthoritarian ideology while simultaneously embracing—indeed, at times begrudgingly submitting to—a charismatic figure of authority from within their own ranks.

Across the spectrum of the theaters represented in this anthology, we find instances in which, as collectives, they defined themselves in opposition to the perceived authoritarian underpinnings of mainstream society. As Erika Munk notes regarding the Living Theatre, for example, "the essence of their project" can be found "in the way they externalized— made theater of—their anarcho-pacifist politics." While among the collectives of the 1960s the Living Theatre was the most openly anarchistic in its political expression, a revolutionary challenge to the existing hierarchies of Western political authority echoes through every group. Two groups in particular stand out in this regard: the Bread and Puppet Theater and the

San Francisco Mime Troupe. The antiwar pieces that played such a definitive role in shaping early Bread and Puppet work not only challenged the
militaristic foreign policies and the heavy-handed authoritarianism of the
U.S. political establishment, but, as Sonja Kuftinec reminds us, in works
like *The Cry of the People for Meat,* Bread and Puppet accentuated the "anarchist and socialist elements" of biblical narratives as a strategy for shifting
their audience's allegiance "from authoritative power to individual human
potential." Much of that shift pivoted on techniques and strategies that
challenged the political establishment from within the subversive and anarchistic irreverence of popular folk traditions. Similar strategies have long
been at the core of what Claudia Orenstein characterizes as the San Francisco Mime Troupe's "festive revolutionary" embrace of "commedia del-
l'arte, vaudeville, puppetry, mime, minstrel shows, and circus clowning."

The combination of popular folk traditions and leftist politics in the
work of Bread and Puppet and the Mime Troupe underscores the crucial
role that class consciousness played in the antiauthoritarian politics of the
radical collective theaters of the 1960s. Moreover, for groups like the
Mime Troupe, class consciousness inevitably dovetailed with civil rights issues, and as it evolved as a collective, so too did the members' awareness
of how the structures of authority that regulate class divisions also foster
institutionalized racism in America. The Mime Troupe challenged these
structures, in part, through a conscious commitment to diversifying its
own ranks, a commitment that also surfaced in At the Foot of the Mountain's evolving feminist critique of patriarchal society. In the attention they
gave to diversifying their membership, both groups offer good examples
of the way that the political convictions of group theaters were enacted
within the structures of their own community as a collective. It is important to note that with regard to the combined questions of race and class,
the Mime Troupe and At the Foot of the Mountain followed a precedent
set by El Teatro Campesino and the Free Southern Theater, both of which,
from their very inception, were engaged in political activism that challenged the racist underpinnings of class divisions in the United States.

Born out of the labor politics of the United Farm Workers, El Teatro
Campesino is a particularly important group not only because of its close
affiliation with migrant workers and the larger Latino community but also
because its embrace of popular folk traditions undercut the cultural chauvinism of a Eurocentric conceptualization of performance. Indeed, the
political activism of El Teatro Campesino and the Free Southern Theater
not only challenged exploitative labor practices on the West Coast and
the sanctioned racism of segregation in the South, but also questioned
long-standing assumptions about Western cultural authority. Yolanda

Broyles-González centers much of her essay on El Teatro Campesino around this very point, noting that "the Teatro's collective functioning was culturally and aesthetically rooted in the indigenous Mesoamerican (i.e., Native American) cultural/social matrix." This grounding in non-hegemonic cultures was evident in many collectives, including the Free Southern Theater. Although Free Southern did not gesture as directly as El Teatro Campesino toward a recovery of repressed cultural traditions, it was equally critical of Western cultural hegemony and, as Annemarie Bean points out, Free Southern only really came to "artistic fruition" when in the latter part of the 1960s it "rejected the integrationist platform [of white liberal patronage] in favor of the multiplicity of the black experience espoused by the Black Arts Movement." In both instances, El Teatro Campesino and the Free Southern Theater tackled the racist proclivities of the American cultural mainstream by bringing political theater to the most disenfranchised of any ethnic community: to the poor, the exploited, and the barely educated. In fact, Free Southern, living literally up to its name, never charged admission. For collectives like El Teatro Campesino and the Free Southern Theater, the struggle against authority was always already a struggle against the social and cultural economies of racism.

Part of that struggle involved a direct challenge to the normative cultural values of bourgeois society, a challenge that overlapped with a tendency among all group theaters to question the traditional structures of mainstream theater and the authority of the literary dramatic text. Bringing theater to those who would otherwise not have access to it was an attempt to effect social and political change; it was also an attempt to wrestle theater from the "deadly" commercial mainstream,[2] an attempt evident in the political street theater of groups like the Living Theatre, Bread and Puppet, and the San Francisco Mime Troupe. Perhaps most important, the collective theaters acknowledged models of performance on which bourgeois theater had thrown a disdainful eye. If El Teatro Campesino and Free Southern brought theater to the disenfranchised, the point was not to "educate" them (in the traditional sense of the term) into an appreciation of high bourgeois culture but rather to subvert the high/low cultural distinctions that selectively legitimized only specific traditions and subordinated theatrical practice to Western literary culture. In his essay on the Performance Group, Martin Puchner speaks to this very issue, particularly in his discussion of interculturalism and the Performance Group's trip to India, where members hoped (somewhat naively) that an encounter with local theater would challenge the Western mind-set of their own notions of performance. In this respect, the embrace of diverse folk traditions,

which challenged the primacy of Western literature and theater, participated in a general tendency among collectives that links the more activist
group theaters like El Teatro Campesino and Free Southern with other
collectives like the Performance Group and the Open Theatre, whose
work, while frequently quite political in content (e.g., The Open's *America
Hurrah* and *Viet Rock*), was nonetheless removed from the front lines of
labor politics, the civil rights movement, and the public streets and parks.

Two aspects of that link are especially noteworthy: a rejection of theater's traditional deference to the authority of the literary text and a rejection of the traditional boundaries separating performers and spectators. Both had implicit political ramifications that echoed in throughout
the aesthetics of virtually every collective. There is little need, in this regard, to rehearse the argument that much of the reputation of the Performance Group rests on the provocative liberties they took with the texts
of *The Bacchae* and *Macbeth* in their productions of *Dionysus in 69* and *Makbeth,* both of which, with the group's seminal use of environmental theater
techniques, deliberately drew audiences into the performances. Certainly, both productions, with their emphasis on immediacy and actuality
over subservience to literary authority, echoed Artaud's famous adage,
"No More Masterpieces." But the politics of that immediacy, with its lack
of deference to the authority of the literary text, was arguably also linked
to a belief that theater could circumvent the rarified abstractions of literary expression and thus, in its own enactment of a radical actuality, heed
the admonishment in Marx's assertion, "The philosophers have only *interpreted* the world, in various ways; the point, however, is to *change* it."[3] In
their shift from a literary theater to a theater of radical actuality, the collectives thus evinced a belief, first, that the change of which Marx spoke
could begin in the immediacy of the performance itself and, second, that
the changes enacted in performances—especially those that blurred the
boundaries between performers and spectators—could be carried out
into society at large.

Leading audiences out into the street at the end of *Dionysus in 69* was
part of this belief that theater, as an event that enveloped the audience
and made them active agents in the performance, could effect social, political, and cultural change more generally. This same conviction was
echoed in the Living Theatre's repeated refrain at the end of their performances to leave the theater and make revolution. That refrain was, in
fact, a call to carry forward the revolution that the members were convinced they had already enacted in the organization of their group as a
collective and in performances of works like *Paradise Now* that were a
product of both the calculated creative collaboration among the mem-

bers of the theatre and the unpredictable dynamics of audience participation. Even if only by virtue of having created an experience that stood in dramatic political contrast to the structures of daily experience in the social mainstream, such moments of collaboration mark the utopian, countercultural aspirations of the radical collective theaters of the sixties and seventies—both within the collectives themselves and in their relation to audiences. Nowhere was this intense commitment to collaboration better evident than in the work of the Open Theatre, which "more than any other theatre in the late 1960s . . . furthered the concept of collective creation" and which was formed in order "to provide a workshop for theatre exploration rather than" performances as the end product of rehearsal.[4] In these collaborative endeavors, theater and theater-making frequently blurred into a process of investigation and experimentation that became an end in itself and thus provided a viable, enacted counter—indeed, an embodied counterexample—to the cultural and political offerings of bourgeois society.

In many respects, the countercultural aspirations of that blurring were directly tied to the goal of reorganizing the means of production: first of theater itself and, by logical extension, of society at large. When Carol Martin argues that for the Open Theatre, "theater was the means for both a critical vision of the world and a proposal for different possibilities," the theater to which she refers was one already situated outside of dominant conventions and located at the point where the concept of collaboration and the idea of a collective met in uncharted artistic and political terrain. Indeed, it is hard to overstate, in this regard, how closely related the terms *collaboration* and *collective* are in the history of group theaters in the latter part of the twentieth century. Primarily, these two terms converged in a radical democratization of the creative processes of making theater, and it is worth pausing momentarily to reflect on how this convergence affected the internal structures of the collectives themselves. Substantial effort was made to allow creation to emerge from a largely nonhierarchical distribution of labor among collective members. Making theater was in this respect as much an experiment in the practice of radical democracy as it was an exploration of the possibilities of theater as such. Challenging not only boundaries of theater, collective creation was thus intended to model the sociopolitical ideals espoused by the collectives themselves.

The form that such modeling took varied from collective to collective, some opting for what we might characterize as a community structure, while others tended toward a full-fledged communal structure, and others still fell somewhere between community and commune. For groups like the Open Theatre and the Performance Group, the collective functioned as a community. Members convened and organized an alternative cultural space in the public sphere (the Open Theatre used a New York loft on West Fourteenth Street; the Performance Group, a renovated garage on Wooster Street) where the creative decisions about their work were the product of collective consensus rather than what in the early seventies Karen Malpede Taylor, echoing Herbert Marcuse, called "the logic of domination."[5] This approach stood in marked contrast to the reified strictures of commercial theater and had radical implications for the organization of labor more generally since, in the case of the Open Theatre, for example, the community model was conceived as "a cooperative venture where all would be equal and no one would be leader."[6] Yet, for all the artistic accomplishments of the community model of collective creation, cultural critics were ambivalent about its political efficacy[7] since the approach tended to privilege art over politics at a time when many group theaters were placing the highest premium not just on a blurring of art and politics but on a complementary blurring of art and life as well.

Perhaps the most famous example of this tendency to unite art, politics, and life is in the work of the Living Theatre, which Erika Munk so aptly describes as "a wandering anarchist commune that had lost its outward community" and that was organized around the principle of "self-governing consensus." As a commune, the Living Theatre not only extended this principle to the practice of their art but to the practice of their daily lives as well. Few if any of the collectives achieved the level of synthesis between art and life that has been practiced by the Living Theatre for over four decades, but it would be a mistake to assume that no other collective theaters attempted to unify art, politics, and life along communal lines. In the early days of the Free Southern Theater's participation in the civil rights movement, for example, their travels from community to community within the larger context of a dangerously hostile racist South necessitated a communal structure, as local activists provided food, shelter, and haven to the collective's five black and three white members. In a very literal sense, the communal structure of these trips allowed the members of Free Southern to enact the antisegregationist politics that they advocated in their theater. El Teatro Campesino faced similar situations in its activism on behalf of the United Farm Workers, and in the early seventies the members of the Teatro "lived and worked communally" on the lands that they purchased just outside of San Juan Bautista.[8] More loosely communal structures were evident in the Bread and Puppet Theater, especially during its stay at Goddard College, and, at one level, there is even a plausible argument to be made that At the Foot of the Mountain had communal elements in its organization during the period in which Martha Boesing and Phyllis Jane Rose were lovers.

Regardless of where one places the individual collectives within the spectrum of possibilities offered by community or communal organization, the idea of collective collaboration was almost uniformly conceptualized as a strategy for radicalizing audiences. Nowhere was that strategy better evident than in workshops that became ends in themselves. The workshops exposed the means of theatrical production and disrupted the spectators' role as passive consumers by presenting them not with a finished product but with an open-ended process (e.g., the Open Theatre) in which they were frequently expected to play an active part (e.g., the Performance Group) and which, because it was open-ended, could not be passively consumed as a prepackaged product of commercial entertainment. Such moments of collective collaboration, combined as they often were with a subversion of the boundaries separating performers from spectators, were widely believed to contain the seeds of a radical transformation of Western bourgeois culture. Some forty years later, it is difficult for us to capture this profound sense of revolutionary exploration or the confident belief in the possibility of unrealized alternatives to the status quo. But that sense and that belief permeate productions like the Performance Group's *Commune* or the Open Theatre's *The Serpent* and *The Mutation Show.*

These were collaborative pieces that emerged out of workshops in which, to follow Carol Martin's discussion of Joseph Chaikin a bit further, the "goal was to create techniques for a physical and vocal theatrical expression capable of conveying a different realm of content; one that could speak to what people knew but were forbidden to say." How this sense of transgression, this sense of speaking the forbidden, played out varied from collective to collective. If in "conveying a different realm of content" the workshops served as a harbinger for the new, as they did with the Open Theatre, for other collectives they were also an outlet for voices and experiences otherwise suppressed in American cultural discourse. Such was the impetus behind the Free Southern Theater's gradual embrace of the Black Arts Movement. After having earlier adapted pieces like *Waiting for Godot* so it would highlight civil rights issues, Free Southern focused increasingly in the middle and late sixties on work by black artists, emphasizing black experience and giving it expression long denied in white America. Moreover, improvisational works like *The Jonesburo Story* and *The Bougalusa Story,* both from the mid-1960s, grew directly out of community-based workshops that Free Southern conducted in an effort to provide a critical expression of neglected local history. Not just for

Free Southern but for collectives more generally, workshops quickly became a model for giving a voice to the marginalized and silenced in American society. As Lynne Greeley reminds us in her essay on At the Foot of the Mountain, workshops often blurred into the performances themselves with the result that pieces like *Story of a Mother* and *Story of a Mother II* were constructed out of narratives contributed by members of the audience. Even the adaptation of Brecht's *Exception and the Rule,* which At the Foot of the Mountain's retitled *RAPED: A Woman's Look at Bertolt Brecht's Exception and the Rule,* was structured around narratives contributed by audience members. Those narratives not only recounted the audience's experiences as women. In performances, they became part of a profoundly moving, collective chorus speaking out against, and in defiance of, the silences imposed by patriarchal society.

The internal history of group theaters is marked by such moments of speaking out against imposed silences as well. The workshop, in fact, serves as an apt metaphor for the difficult internal negotiations that group theaters undertook in an open-ended process of collectively plotting the course of their theater while simultaneously being drawn to charismatic figures of creative authority from within their own ranks. For all their idealistic promise, those negotiations often translated into bitter struggles. The San Francisco Mime Troupe's structure as a collective, for example, was largely the result of the departure of its founder, R. G. Davis, a departure that was precipitated both by the troupe's resistance to his desire to remain the company's sole director and by the women members becoming increasingly critical of their subordinate role in the decision-making process. Other examples are easy to find. Beneath the surface of the important creative innovations of the Performance Group, for instance, bitter legal battles unfolded between members as Richard Schechner took measures to consolidate his control as artistic director of the group and as managing director of the Performing Garage. Much of the controversy surrounding Yolanda Broyles-González's book *El Teatro Campesino: Theatre in the Chicano Movement* centers around the difficult question of how much undue credit Luis Valdez (an artist of amazing creative energy and courage) has received for the collective work of other members of El Teatro Campesino. Less contentious examples are to be found in the central role of Joseph Chaikin in the Open Theatre, or in the prominent, almost parental, status that Julian Beck and Judith Malina had in both the creative work and the communal structure of the Living Theatre. Indeed, the ease with which such examples can be found across the spectrum of group theaters from the sixties and seventies contributes to a plausible argument that the concerns with which Sonja Kuftinec opens her essay on the Bread and Puppet Theater—concerns that weigh the notion of a collective against the indisputably decisive role that Peter Schumann has played in all of Bread and Puppet's work, i.e., concerns that weigh collective creation against individual contribution—are more the rule than the exception and ought to be calculated in our basic understanding of group theaters more generally.

While there were certainly instances enough of counterproductive pettiness to these negotiations, the pitched battles that erupted within the San Francisco Mime Troupe when the Marxist-leaning members left in protest or within the Free Southern Theater when Gil Moses and Denise Nicholas hoped to transform the group into an all-black theater company remind us not to be naive about how messy the practice of radical democracy is. Even on the small scale of a collective theater, the stakes in those battles were genuine and significant. They were a microcosm of the battles that the members of the collectives fervently believed the public sphere required, but could only be waged within the radical democracy that they attempted to enact within the collectives themselves.

Toward a Theory of Legacy

A certain irony accompanies our shift from a general characterization of group theaters to a discussion of their legacies. With regard to the question of legacy, this anthology, indeed even this introduction, is involved in the production of the object of its own inquiry. In the broadest sense of the term, of course, a legacy constitutes something of value that is transmitted by or received from a predecessor. It suggests a bequeathal that, while intelligible enough in the realm of tangible cultural artifacts, proves far more elusive in the performing arts. For while individuals may pass treasured artifacts from one generation to the next, theatrical legacies are always a collaborative endeavor between generations. Hence the question of legacy circulates within a host of accompanying questions. As Charlotte Canning notes, for example, in her essay on At the Foot of the Mountain, even the basic notion of how one identifies a beneficiary of a theater's legacy is profoundly affected by historiographic criteria that feminist theorists and historians have challenged us to fundamentally rethink.

Inextricably bound to the ephemerality of performance, the question of a theatrical legacy is only answered by creative response, regardless of whether that response comes from the theater practitioner learning a mentor's technique and craft or from the theater historian documenting a theatrical movement and tradition. In the performing arts, those who address a legacy are those who share in its construction. A legacy is as much a product of the terms of its transference as it is of the terms of its reception—as much a product of the transferor as of the recipient. Moreover, the issue here is not merely one of who transmits to whom but of what is transmitted, what is received, and ultimately what criteria are used to assess the value of that which is received. As obvious as these questions may sound, they are seldom openly asked in discussions of legacy. Yet how one answers those questions—and there is a wide variety of legitimate answers—largely determines the legacy one produces, whether it is one's own, that of one's immediate predecessors, or that of artists whose work scholars argue is of lasting significance.

To say that there is a wide variety of answers to the unspoken questions that define how artists and scholars construct a notion of legacy is to offer only a rough compass for navigating our way beyond the sorely undertheorized notions of legacy that dominate our profession. As theater historians, we are all involved in the production of legacy, at least insofar as we assume the critical function of sifting through the traces of past performances and of deciphering from among them a path to the present. More often than not, artists beat the path before us, searching among the exercises, aesthetic techniques, and performance strategies of their predecessors for the building blocks with which to construct a contemporary theater. In such instances, the work of the historian is to provide a critical assessment of the legacy that contemporary artists excavate, (re)construct, and propagate in their own work. As a collection of scholarship, this anthology is situated somewhere between these two tasks of theater historiography. For in assembling this volume, we as editors consciously set out to place the history of group theaters in critical relief and to argue on behalf of its significance for the present moment. Transcribing that history into the discourse of scholarship and arguing that it is invaluable to our understanding of contemporary political theater, we are obviously positing a very specific type of legacy, one that shapes and is shaped by cultural criticism. At the same time, many of our contributors, particularly those who have written on the legacies of specific collectives, have explored the myriad ways in which contemporary artists have absorbed select elements of the history of group theaters for their own theatrical endeavors. Although these explorations are obviously also mediated by the discourses of criticism, they nonetheless point to a very different type of legacy than that generated by scholars addressing scholars: namely, the circulation of artistic expression among theater practitioners.

Yet the line separating these two forms of legacy is a porous border where ideas about history, performance, and politics are contested simultaneously in the arts and scholarship and where, consequently, a dynamic notion of legacy thrives. It is the site of (what for lack of a better term we can characterize as) living legacies, that is, a site where ideas and ideologies circulate in rigorous debate, where performance traditions endure in the teaching of craft and technique, and where individual theaters (like the Living, the San Francisco Mime Troupe, El Teatro Campesino and Bread and Puppet) evolved over the course of decades. The fact that many of our contributors are scholar-practitioners themselves and have often played some role in the performance legacies they discuss is but one small indication of how porous that border is. Indeed, the model of the scholar-practitioner is part of the legacy of group theaters as well. In this regard, one need only recall the influential presence that many of the artists discussed in this book—Richard Schechner, probably the most prominent among them—have had in academic institutions. It should be of little wonder, then, that an essay like Michael Vanden Heuvel's highlights the legacy of the Performance Group not, as one might expect, in the postmodern theater of the Wooster Group but in the academic debates framing the reception of works like *Dionysus in 69* and *Commune* among performance theorists and theater historians. As Vanden Heuvel notes, Schechner has played a seminal role in those debates, drawing upon his experiences both in the Performance Group (as well as in East Coast Artists) and in academia to posit "an increasingly expansive theory of 'performance' as a cross-disciplinary subject." Schechner has long cited the connection between performance theory and the avant-garde, and inasmuch as this volume is itself informed by that theory, it too falls well within the parameters of the legacy mapped out by Vanden Heuvel.

At the opposite end of that academic spectrum, the discourses of criticism are secondary to the cultivation of craft, and the workshops that were so crucial to the early history of group theaters have frequently found their way into colleges, universities, and conservatories where the tools, techniques, and methodologies of alternative, noncommercial theater are taught to a new generation of students. Significant in this regard is the legacy of Joseph Chaikin, who, together with the other members of the Open Theatre, did frequent residencies during the seventies at various universities in the State University of New York and University of California systems and later had very strong ties to Princeton and New York University.[9] Chaikin developed a somatic approach to acting, or actor-oriented theater, that is centered around a notion of presence and that has evolved into one of the most important countertraditions to the Stanislavski method to be found in American theater today. Indeed, the Open Theatre's focus on actor-oriented theater has spurred a legacy with multiple trajectories in and out of university settings. While Roger Babb, in his discussion of the Open's interest in the actor's body and the ped-agogy and exercises associated with this interest, clearly understands legacy as that which can be identified in the conscious dissemination of techniques first forged in the workshops of the Open Theatre, he is equally cognizant of the diverse application that those techniques have found in subsequent theaters where former members of the Open The-ater are active and have carved out strikingly new contexts for exploring what Chaikin called "the body in motion."[10] This too is legacy, and in the case of theater companies like the Omaha Magic Theatre and the Woman's Experimental Theatre, former Open Theater members like Jo Ann Schmidman, Megan Terry, and Roberta Sklar have successfully translated its legacy of exploration of presence and the actor's body into a feminist critique that, as Babb observes, has noteworthy metacritical overtures, addressing not only "sexism in . . . society at large but also within the Open Theatre itself."

The feminist orientation of these theaters is an important register of legacy as a site of conceptual evolution rather than of uncritical repeti-tious preservation. In many respects, that orientation tackles the prob-lems of presence that critics like Philip Auslander argue lie "behind much of the experimental theatre and performance of the 1960s" and that, ac-cording to Auslander, arise with regard to the then widespread assump-tion that the "pure presentation of performer to audience . . . [was] the best means available to the theatre to make a radical spiritual/political statement."[11] In conceptualizing the political in postmodern theater, Aus-lander notes that "the whole notion of presence" has fallen under "a sus-picion which derives from the apparent collusion between political struc-tures of authority and the persuasive power of presence,"[12] and hence he doubts the viability of the idea of presence for a politically oriented post-modern theater. Interestingly enough, the idea has proven, in the hands of feminist artists like Schmidman, Terry, and Sklar, to be far less concep-tually rigid and far more dialectically dynamic than Auslander suggests. Indeed, the legacy of presence within theaters like the Magic Theatre and the Women's Experimental Theatre is marked by a dialectic in which the very suspicion that Auslander cites is subsumed. At the very least, one of the trajectories of the Open Theatre's legacy is to be found in the feminist exploration of the body—and specifically the presence of the female per-former's body—as a locus of resistance against patriarchal authority and its repressive tools of representation. This exploration constitutes a self-conscious and introspective turn—one that is consistent with much of what Chaikin himself argued and one that thus suggests the need to con-ceptualize the legacy of the Open Theatre (and other theaters as well) in

fluid and evolving terms. If as Auslander suggests, "the postmodern theatre of resistance must . . . both expose the collusion of presence with authority and resist such collusion,"[13] that task does not move us away from
presence but rather into its legacy. Arguably, one of legacies of the Open
Theatre is to be found precisely in the feminist rethinking of presence
along the lines mentioned by Auslander, that is, in the transformation of
the actor's body and its presence into a site of exposure and resistance.

Such outcomes suggest important conceptual similarities between
the Open Theatre and At the Foot of the Mountain as described by Charlotte Canning. They also lead us to Bread and Puppet and the Living Theatre (to name only two), which have remained amazingly loyal to their
original political commitments while evolving through the course of four
and sometimes five decades. In the case of Bread and Puppet, for example, Peter Schumann (who brought it in the early seventies to Goddard College for an important period of residency) has cultivated a
legacy of workshops where theatrical craft lies, as John Bell notes, "outside the nexus of actors' theater" and in the production of puppets and
masks for politically oriented circus, folk theater, parades, and pageants.
Although the work of Bread and Puppet has led to a type of performance
very different from that which is associated with Chaikin's notion of presence (i.e., actor-oriented theater), the legacies of the Open Theatre and
Bread and Puppet coincide both in the international impact that their
productions and workshops have had on subsequent practitioners and in
a fundamental fluidity that has marked the forms that their basic concepts have assumed from generation to generation, from theater to theater, and from decade to decade.

It is not a matter of coincidence in this latter regard that John Bell in
his discussion of the legacy of the Bread and Puppet Theater entitles one
of the subsections of his essay "The Obvious Appropriateness of Avant-
Garde Traditions." That legacy-affirming title is a polemical retort to Auslander's characterization of the political aesthetics of avant-garde theater
in the 1960s as now "obviously inappropriate."[14] Bell takes particular issue
with the stagnant and universalizing conception of the activist legacy in
Auslander's claim that contemporary political theater suffers from "a widespread critical inability to conceive of aesthetic/political *praxis* in terms
other than these inherited ones," that is, in terms other than those inherited from "the historical avant-garde . . . and from the 1960s."[15] Directly
challenging Auslander's characterization of the nature of the inheritance,
Bell argues that the legacy of the Bread and Puppet Theater—and here
inheritance and legacy overlap—is marked by a coexistence "of continuity
and change." The activist impulse that characterized early productions,

especially their "low-level grassroots communication of ideas," has remained constant while nonetheless malleable enough "to respond to the
changing nature of the cultural landscape." Among other collective theaters, the legacy of such adaptability may have found its most brilliant self-
conscious articulation in the Free Southern Theater's final performance:
*A Funeral for the Free Southern Theater. A Valediction without Mourning: The
Role of the Arts for Social Change* (1986), which, as Jan Cohen-Cruz observes, "marked the death of the Free Southern Theater at the same time
that it affirmed the continuity of activist theater." At the most immediate
level, this continuity was manifested in Junebug Productions, the company that was the direct successor to the Free Southern Theater, but
much of the force of this particular performance came from the larger
legacy in which it participated. That legacy gives us some indication of
how the legacies of individual collectives are often couched within a
nexus of different legacies.

Situated as this final Free Southern Theater performance was in an orchestrated New Orleans jazz funeral, it affirmed not only the larger legacy
of activist theater to which the Free Southern Theater had made an invaluable contribution, but it did so while embracing the terms of an inherited
cultural tradition—and jazz is an avant-garde tradition—whose appropriateness as a political art strategy is directly tied to resisting a long, indeed
continuing, repression of African-American culture and community. The
legacy of an activist theater of resistance as exemplified in the Free Southern Theater and its successor, Junebug Productions, is thus the dialecti-
cal antinomy to a continuing legacy of repression. That dialectic has a
dynamic that cannot entirely be subsumed by the Eurocentric lineage implicit in Auslander's characterization of contemporary political theater.
The viability of the activist tradition within that dialectic and of the legacies
in which the Free Southern Theater was both participant and producer belong to a distinctly American activist avant-garde, one that has direct ties to
an African-American community long excluded from histories of American experimental performance. Among other things, that activism includes a radical subversion of the aesthetic boundaries regulating the relationship of theaters "to their audiences and communities," a subversion
that Cohen-Cruz argues produced "the prototype for the contemporary
community-based arts movement." Not only does this prototype establish
direct conceptual ties, for example, between the Free Southern Theater
and feminist collectives like At the Foot of the Mountain that ultimately embraced the model of the community-based arts movement, but it also suggests the need to recognize in that embrace the thriving legacy of the Free
Southern Theater.

A prototype for the community-based arts movement is hardly the only model provided by the Free Southern Theater. Its close association with SNCC (the Student Nonviolent Coordinating Committee) suggests the need to contextualize the legacy of the Free Southern Theater (or of any theater for that matter) within the legacies of the sociohistorical currents of which it was a part. With regard to the legacy of the Free Southern Theater, we need, in this respect, to speak of legacy as palimpsest, of legacy inscribed upon legacy—we need, in other words, to speak of a legacy within a larger legacy, the former intimately related to the latter and the latter the acknowledged source of perhaps the most important model of activism in the United States to emerge in the second half of the twentieth century. The legacy of the Free Southern Theater begins in the heat of the very civil rights movement that provided the "model of political rebellion" for sixties radicalism,[16] addressing injustice and inequity that remain with us still, though now fallen from the spotlight of political fashion.

Festering in the shadows, issues like the enduring presence of economic racism and the continued racist biases of our judicial system remind us that though historical moments pass, history does not necessarily progress. The political fashions of a given moment are not necessarily built upon past achievements, and there is no assurance of progressive political accomplishments. Understanding the legacy of the Free Southern Theater and the appropriateness of its inherited terms thus arguably necessitates a departure from the rigid, sequential, and linear structure so often implied by the modern/postmodern conceptual divide. It necessitates the kind of conceptual rethinking of historicity, for example, that Theodor Adorno suggested when, in *Aesthetic Theory,* he argued that while "what was once true in a work of art" might in the course of time lose its immediate validity, "it can reveal its truth a second time" when social conditions have reconfigured it such a way as to resurrect its validity once again.[17] This sense of historical events eclipsing and then reigniting a work's significance offers crucial insights into the workings of legacy.

Adorno's argument has major significance not only for the legacy of the Free Southern Theater but also for the Bread and Puppet Theater and activist theater more generally. Consider, in this regard, *A Funeral for the Free Southern Theatre.* Performed roughly at the same time that Auslander was writing on postmodern theater and, more importantly, at the same time that the neoconservative policies of the Reagan administration were systematically rolling back the hard-fought gains of the civil rights movement, *A Funeral for the Free Southern Theater* is nothing short of a call to arms and a symbolic acknowledgment that sociopolitical conditions had taken a regressive turn and hence necessitated an activist response from politically progressive artists and theater practitioners. A similar call to arms with regard to reckless military adventurism of the second Bush administration serves as the backdrop for John Bell's eloquent defense of Bread and Puppet's continued viability as an activist theater. In fact, Bell suggests that this viability is profoundly exemplified in performances of its *Insurrection Mass with Funeral March for a Rotten Idea* after September 11, 2001, which coincided with massive demonstrations protesting the United States' second war against Iraq. The historical context of these performances, Bell maintains, is compelling evidence of the continued viability of the terms of aesthetic and political praxis that Bread and Puppet first forged in the antiwar movements of the 1960s. At the very least, that context marks a constellation of historical forces that breathed new life into the discourses of radical activist theater. There is a lot to be learned from these examples with regard to the question of legacy. Drawing upon Adorno's argument, we can thus learn from the historical contexts of *A Funeral for the Free Southern Theater* and *Insurrection Mass with Funeral March for a Rotten Idea* that, among its many manifestations, a legacy can be a dormant potential, waiting for historical circumstances to call it forth once again.

Whether we speak of legacy in terms of death and continuity (Cohen-Cruz) or continuity and change (Bell), the activist tradition in the performing arts, which is a mainstay of the group theater movement, is marked by a fundamental belief that through theater we can be the active agents rather than the passive subjects of history, that we can effect social change—in short, that we can influence our world and shape the world to come. As obvious as this characterization of activist theater may be, its refrain here is intended as a reminder of how closely associated the notion of influence is with that of legacy. Such beliefs in the power of agency and influence saturate the political ideologies of the radical collective theaters of the 1960s. Related notions of influence are at the core of how scholars have conceptualized the legacies of these groups. Jorge Huerta, for example, speaks of the legacy of El Teatro Campesino not only in terms of the evolution of its progressive political agenda (from an original activism on behalf of migrant farmworkers to a larger vision of and for the entire Chicano community) but also in terms of the seminal role it played in facilitating Chicano theater. It set an influential example for groups like Teatro Urbano, Teatro Chicano, Teatro de la Esperanza, and Su Teatro. It also included the positive influence El Teatro Campesino exercised through its decisive support of TENAZ (El Teatro Nacional de Aztlán), a coalition of *teatros* that, as Huerta notes, "remained a driving force in the Chicano theater movement well into the 1980s" and that "sponsored yearly festivals and minifestivals, conferences, workshops, a newsletter, and other services dedicated to the evolution of the teatro movement." These are concrete examples of influence and of influence as legacy, especially since part of the legacy that Huerta describes is framed within an organizational structure, that is, a network of teatros that, working from a model of collectivity, was able to exert influence through direct support.

More typical and more elusive—although not necessarily less valid—are the examples of influence as legacy that surface in the San Francisco Mime Troupe the Bread and Puppet Theater. Susan Mason, like Huerta, identifies part of the Mime Troupe's legacy in the theaters it influenced: spin-off groups like the Diggers and the Artist Liberation Front, or even other collectives like El Teatro Campesino (since Luis Valdez was a member of the Mime Troupe). But in her discussion of legacy, Mason places the highest premium on the Mime Troupe's definitive contributions to the strategies of radical theater, asserting a legacy not in support extended to other theaters but in the dissemination of theatrical concepts like "guerrilla theater" and a calculated and influential rejection of boulevard theater in favor of "the street as theater." Following an established scholarly consensus, Mason attributes the origin of the term *guerrilla theater* to Mime Troupe members Peter Berg and R. G. Davis and notes that after Davis published an essay on the concept in the *Tulane Drama Review* in 1966 "the term was immediately co-opted by scholars and practitioners, and guerrilla theaters sprang up on both coasts." Commenting on the unconventional venues that the Mime Troupe selected for its performances (e.g., public streets and parks), Mason argues that "Davis's greatest contribution to the American theater was . . . to take theater away from 'the self-styled elite' and give it back to the general public." The contribution here was literal since the Mime Troupe was committed to providing free theater.

The temptation shadowing depictions such as those provided by Mason is to equate an assertion of originality and precedent with the assertion of legacy—something akin to saying that whoever coins a phrase has claim to legacy in all that it is subsequently used to describe. Yet the rhetoric of originality, which implies a notion of possession, runs counter to much of the revolutionary antibourgeois sentiment that Mason rightly associates with the Mime Troupe (at least during the decade that Davis was its most prominent member). Consequently, her discussion of influence implicitly posits an important and very different notion of legacy than her essay might initially suggest. The Mime Troupe rose to prominence at a time when there was an increasing tendency from a wide variety of sectors within the performance community to take a more radical approach to combining politics and performance and to take theater into the streets in increasingly provocative ways. It is hardly a disservice to the legacy of the San Francisco Mime Troupe, in this respect, to recognize its work as part of a shared legacy. Indeed, the discussion of influence as legacy arguably always leads to a notion of shared legacy because it always leads us back to a realm of cultural negotiations.

While the terms *influence* and *legacy* are not interchangeable as synonyms, influence is certainly an aspect of legacy, and much of the difficulty that scholars historically have had with pinpointing influence has to do with the complex and not always transparent negotiations that inevitably accompany it. Such negotiations tend frequently to steer discussions of influence into the sphere of legacy, and thus we return once again to legacy as a collaborative endeavor. As we have seen, the terms of that collaboration vary widely. They are subject to constant renegotiation: between artists, between scholars, between generations, and between cultures as well. It is this last sphere that occupies a significant place in John Bell's discussion of influence as legacy, marked by an impressive catalog of theaters throughout the world that have been influenced by Bread and Puppet's work and hence participate in the living construction of its legacy. As a consequence of Peter Schumann's extensive touring, many of the artists from those theaters have collaborated with him directly either in workshops or in Bread and Puppet productions. Here a legacy is grounded in joint creation, collective experience, and shared sense of purpose. Bread and Puppet is not alone in this regard. Most of the collectives mentioned in this anthology have toured internationally and have cultivated strong international ties with other performers and theaters, and thus it is worth offering some concluding thoughts on how the legacy of group theaters has played out on the world stage.

As a point of departure, we recognize the uneven histories that populate that stage. This is not to assert that one culture or society is more advanced than another. Rather it is to acknowledge that neither histories nor cultures move in uniformity, that the changing political landscape in one culture hardly implies substantial change in another, and, finally, that the resonance of an artistic expression derives from the culture in which expression occurs as well as from the culture where it originated. On the international stage, a work's resonance, in short, is contingent upon a negotiation between multiple, concurrent, and yet distinct political and cultural realities. In this regard, there is ample room for theatrical projects of seemingly diminished significance to find revival and new validity not just, as Adorno argues, in a new temporal setting but also within a different cultural context. Given the tendency in the performing arts to think in terms of living legacies, such moments of revival constitute a crucial aspect of the legacies of group theaters. Not only do they breathe new life into aesthetic forms that critics (for a variety of ideological reasons) might otherwise dismiss as predictable, but the intercultural negotiations involved in doing so highlight the collective, constructive nature of legacy itself.

Such an understanding of simultaneous but by no means uniform political/cultural trajectories and their effect on legacy informs Alisa Solomon's examination of the Living Theatre. At the most basic level, this understanding serves as the foundation for her discussion of legacy in the Living Theatre's recent productions of *Utopia*, which in New York played to "audiences [that] barely outnumbered the cast" but which in Mestre, Italy, played to enthusiastic young crowds in a working-class neighborhood. Explaining this stark contrast in reception, Solomon implicitly characterizes legacy as a site-specific phenomenon and argues that the "work of the Living Theatre resonates in places where people are looking for alternatives . . . and where the larger culture at least allows, if not supports, such exploration." Among the working-class youth in Italy that resonance marks a literal site where the work of the Living Theatre sustains a living legacy because it unfolds within a context that facilitates meaning and influence. Such contexts can hardly be dismissed as the mere product of naive youthful idealism, especially when one considers the Living Theatre's work in Beirut, Lebanon, where the hardships of international military conflict and internal civil war have left little room for either naïveté or idealism. There, the Living Theatre performed *Mysteries and Smaller Other Pieces,* only to discover that their Lebanese audience gave the work a painfully significant resonance and legacy that could not be foreseen in the original productions thirty years earlier. Is this not legacy: what we could not initially see but what theatrical work becomes as an active force in a future cultural discourse where it is shaped by the collective contributions of many?

Finally, any theory of legacy must ask, "When do we begin to speak of legacy?" For there must be a threshold and a crossing, beyond which a legacy no longer looms on the horizon but stands before us. Whatever one uses to mark that threshold, legacy oddly renders it an end that is not an end, and a conclusion that is not entirely a conclusion. Legacy renders that threshold the beginning of a new discourse and of a new way of thinking about a significant body of work, an important theater, or a departed artist. Even in the course of putting together this anthology, we have watched that threshold move ever closer with the deaths of Joseph Chaikin and Spalding Gray. What legacy do we make out of the work that they have so generously given to us? We hope that this collection marks a beginning.

NOTES

1. This is especially so when it is compared with the cursory readings of the history of group theaters found in works like Christopher Innes's *Avant Garde Theatre, 1892–1992* and Arnold Aronson's *American Avant-Garde Theatre*. At the opposite end of the spectrum are important works like Eileen Blumenthal's *Joseph Chaikin* (New York: Cambridge University Press, 1984), Stefan Brecht's *Peter Schumann's Bread and Puppet Theatre*, 2 vols. (London: Methuen; New York: Routledge, 1988), Yolanda Broyles-González's *El Teatro Campesino* (Austin: University of Texas Press, 1994), John Tytell's *The Living Theatre: Art, Exile, and Outrage* (New York: Grove, 1995), and Claudia Orenstein's *Festive Revolutions: The Politics of Popular Theatre and the San Francisco Mime Troupe* (Jackson: University Press of Mississippi, 1999). If the studies by Innes and Aronson are too superficial, the opposite is true of these latter works, which tend to appeal to a more specialized audience that, as in the case of Broyles-Gonzáles work, for example, is already familiar with a general history of the collective that the work challenges.

2. The term *deadly* plays upon Peter Brook's discussion of "deadly theatre" in his now classic manifesto *The Empty Space*, which was first published in 1968.

3. Karl Marx, "Theses on Feuerbach," in *The Marx-Engels Reader*, 2nd ed., ed. Robert C. Tucker (New York: Norton, 1978), 145.

4. Theodore Shank, *Beyond the Boundaries: American Alternative Theatre* (Ann Arbor: University of Michigan Press, 2002), 38.

5. Karen Malpede Taylor, *People's Theatre in Amerika* (New York: Drama Book Specialists, 1973), 239.

6. Margaret Croyden, *Lunatics, Lovers, and Poets* (New York: McGraw Hill, 1974), 171.

7. Malpede Taylor argued, for example, that the meticulous attention that the Open Theatre devoted to artistic explorations was "their greatest theatrical strength" even as it was "also the quality about them which is most infuriating to militant political instincts, their own included" (*People's Theatre in Amerika*, 240).

8. Harry Elam, *Taking It to the Streets* (Ann Arbor: University of Michigan Press, 1997), 104.

9. Roger Babb, e-mail, September 12, 2004.

10. Joseph Chaikin, *The Presence of the Actor* (New York: Theater Communications Group, 1972), 16.

11. Philip Auslander, *From Acting to Performance* (New York: Routledge, 1997), 62.

12. Ibid.

13. Ibid., 63.

14. Bell refers through his essay to the publication of Auslander's article "Toward a Concept of the Political in Postmodern Theatre," in *Theatre Journal* 39, no. 1 (1987). Since Auslander included that article as a chapter in his book *From Act-*

ing to Performance, our references here are to the latter text. The passage to which Bell refers can be found on page 59 of Auslander's book.

15. Auslander, *From Acting to Performance,* 59.

16. Judith Clavir Albert and Stewart Edward Albert, "Considering the 1960s," in *The Sixties Papers: Documents of a Rebellious Decade,* ed. Judith Clavir Albert and Stewart Edward Albert (Westport, Conn.: Praeger, 1984), 9.

17. Theodor Adorno, *Aesthetic Theory,* trans. C. Lenhardt (New York: Routledge and Kegan Paul, 1984), 60.

THE LIVING THEATRE
Historical Overview

Founded by Julian Beck and Judith Malina in 1947, the Living Theatre is the longest-extant radical theater collective in this anthology. Throughout its history, the Living Theatre has repeatedly redefined itself through the creation of aesthetic and political manifestos that address some of the most important contemporary social and cultural movements in the United States and elsewhere.

Malina and Beck met and married young in New York City and were part of the wave of post–World War II upper-middle-class white "bohemian" artists who were interested in "making something new" with their art, using European and American modernist texts as springboards for counteracting mainstream bourgeois theater. Malina studied acting and directing at Erwin Piscator's workshop at the New School for Social Research, and Beck mounted exhibitions of his abstract expressionist paintings at New York galleries. Beginning with the company's earliest "Theatre in the Room" performances in their Upper West Side apartment (1951), followed by two seasons of repertory at the Cherry Lane Theatre in Greenwich Village (1951–52), and at a loft on One Hundredth Street and Broadway (1954–55), Malina and Beck's goal was to challenge commercial theater by bringing "poetry back into the theater." Producing works by poets and playwrights like Gertrude Stein, especially *Dr. Faustus Lights the Lights,* with its examination of moral sensibility, was central to Malina and Beck's agenda. Malina describes *Dr. Faustus* as one of the company's earliest manifestos.

By the end of the 1950s, Beck and Malina began to conceptualize their theater through an aesthetic that combined the theories of Artaud and Brecht. Beck and Malina were among the first U.S. theater practitioners to read M. C. Richards' translation of Antonin Artaud's *The Theater and Its Double,* published in 1958. Inspired by Artaud's Theatre of Cruelty, they sought to evoke a transformative power through "cries and groans" and hoped to discover a "language that is active and anarchic, in which the habitual boundaries of feelings and words are abandoned."[1] At the same time, the company continued to utilize Piscator's techniques and Bertolt Brecht's texts. With these powerful, if somewhat contradictory influences, the Living Theatre embarked on a new epoch at the Living Theatre's Playhouse on 14th Street with productions of Jack Gelber's *The Connection* (1959), Brecht's *In the Jungle of Cities* (1960), *Mann ist Mann* (1962), and Kenneth Brown's *The Brig* (1963). Joseph Chaikin, soon to found the Open Theater, was prominently featured in these productions, as was actor Stephen Ben Israel, who remained a member of the Living Theatre through the early 1970s.

The Connection was one of the most noteworthy of these productions because its strategies of improvisation not only signaled the influence of John Cage but also foreshadowed the strategies of later Living Theatre productions. (Jackson Mac Low's *The Marrying Maiden,* part of an evening entitled "Theatre of Chance" in 1960, was the most extreme example of Cagean experimentation in the Living Theatre's oeuvre.) *The Connection* depicted the underside of jazz musicians' and junkies' worlds. Actors improvised with spectators in the audience space, panhandling for their next "fix." The division between art and life was blurred again, and the play-within-a-play format was deployed as well in Living Theatre productions of William Carlos Williams's *Many Loves* (1959) and Luigi Pirandello's *Tonight We Improvise* (1955 and 1959).

The 1963 production of *The Brig,* on the other hand, enforced and highlighted the separation between actors and audiences. Directed by Malina, *The Brig* was staged behind a proscenium-high barbed-wire fence. Rehearsals consisted of the arduous, exacting physical exercises and the rigid discipline of Marine Corps drills, which were based on Brown's own experiences as a marine brig prisoner and which, interpreted by the Living Theatre, became a paradigm of Artaud's theater of cruelty. At the center of the burgeoning off-Broadway movement, *The Connection* and *The Brig* in very different ways shocked, thrilled, and disturbed contemporary audiences. These productions transformed interactions between actors and spectators and brought widespread critical attention to the Living Theatre for the first time.

The Brig was an early highpoint in the Living Theatre's commitment to creating anarchist and pacifist art. Federal authorities closed down the production and the Living Theatre's Playhouse on 14th Street in October 1963, citing tax evasion; there is some speculation that the play's subversive views of the military provoked government action. Malina and Beck served jail terms; both had already served time for participation in anti-nuclear demonstrations in the mid-1950s. During the General Strike for Peace, which Malina and Beck organized in 1961, the Living Theatre produced pacifist street performances and demonstrations, which became a hallmark of their work from the late 1960s onward.

From 1964 to 1968 the Living Theatre toured Europe and evolved a working process they titled "collective creation," shifting the creative and authoritative power away from directors Beck and Malina, as the company sought a new level of creative equity and collaboration. The four new works the Living produced during this period were substantially more political than poetical: *Mysteries and Smaller Pieces* (1964), *Frankenstein* (1965), *Antigone* (1967), and *Paradise Now* (1968). These performances grew out of the company's anti–Vietnam War activism, belief in anarchism, and ongoing investigations of Brecht, Artaud, and Vsevolod Meyerhold. *Frankenstein* and *Antigone* reflected a critical attention to, and respect for, classical, canonical texts, while *Mysteries* and *Paradise Now* placed a greater emphasis on actor training (similar to Joe Chaikin's work with the Open Theatre), connected the company's political activism more directly to the content of the work, and focused on audience disruption, environmental staging, and textual deconstruction (as in Richard Schechner's work with the Performance Group).

In 1968–69 the Living Theatre returned to the United States for a much anticipated homecoming tour of their four-part repertory. Response to the tour was mixed; some audiences and critics found the group's message and methods out of sync with the political urgencies of the time. Commercial producers were interested in producing *Paradise Now* on Broadway, as had been the case with *The Connection* a decade earlier. Beck and Malina rejected these offers from the "capitalist, bourgeois money-system." This kind of decision making—ideology over practicality—became another hallmark of the Living Theatre, one that had an amazing impact on their self-fashioning as a collective. The company had evolved into a large and unruly tribe that lived and worked communally, experimented with drugs and sex, and just barely made ends meet. All of this fell within the company's vision of and call for a "peaceful, non-violent revolution." Although Beck, Malina, and company had been active participants in the revolutionary events of May 1968 in Paris and at the Avignon Festival, their lack of participation in demonstrations in New

Haven, Connecticut, and in Berkeley, California, were derided by antiwar and civil rights protesters during the U.S. tour.

Amid growing internal tensions, the group returned to Europe and in January 1970 split into four subgroups with different missions. Beck penned a new manifesto, declaring the work of the Living Theatre to be henceforth with the people and of the people, outside theater buildings and in the street. To this end Beck, Malina, and a core group of Living Theatre members went to Brazil in 1970. They created the *Legacy of Cain* plays, participating in street theater with people of the shanty towns, rejecting middle-class venues and values. Thirteen months later the company was arrested on drug charges, imprisoned, and freed after two months because of an international outcry.

Street performance was again the focus when the Living Theatre returned to the United States and reworked the *Legacy of Cain* in Pittsburgh (1975), performing in front of steel mills and police stations. In 1984, after extensive touring (and a return to theater buildings) in Europe, the Living Theatre presented a brief, critically unsuccessful run of four plays at the Joyce Theatre in New York City, including a remounted *Antigone* with Malina in the title role, and Beck playing Kreon, the same casting as in the production in the late 1960s.

After Beck's death from cancer in 1985, Hanon Reznikov (twenty-five years younger than Malina) became her husband and the codirector of the company. In 1989 the company opened the Third Street Theatre in New York City, where they produced poetic theater, street spectacles, and community-based performances, collaborating with homeless people, "squatters," and environmental activists from the East Village neighborhood. The theater closed in 1992 because of financial difficulties. Since 1994, a small group of Living Theatre stalwarts has presented Malina's anti–death penalty street play, *Not in My Name,* in Times Square whenever an execution takes place in the United States.

In 1995, with funding from the Italian government, the Living Theatre established a home in Rochetta, Italy. With local participants the Living Theatre created *Resistance* about the region's anti-Nazi activism during World War II. The Living Theatre continues to tour, co-creating "A Day in the Life of the City" with communities across the United States and internationally. At this writing, Malina, Reznikov, and a few company members spend half the year on the road. In 2006, Malina celebrated her 80th birthday.

—C. R.

NOTE

1. Antonin Artaud, *The Theater and Its Double,* trans. Mary Caroline Richards (New York: Grove Press, 1958), 245, 234.

ONLY CONNECT

The Living Theatre and Its Audiences

Erika Munk

I

Art itself is an externalization of the unspeakable cry. If I did this play I would try to make it unbearable for the audience. Only when the audience realizes its impotence will it rebel. If I could drive them to such extremes of exasperation in the theater that their restrained outcries began to materialize in their throats, then I might drive them to enact their needs when they hit the air outside the theater. The act of sitting in the theater is an agreement to tolerate the action as a demonstration and an enlightenment. The energy to change the unbearable situation mounts in the theater. Then we will go out and destroy the outer law and the inner chains: the state's yoke and the spirit's harness.

—Judith Malina, *The Diaries of Judith Malina,*
March 17, 1952

Judith Malina wrote the preceding remarks while considering Gide's stage version of *The Trial.* It was a good year for Kafka, what with McCarthyism, the Korean War, the Rosenbergs, and the first publication of *The Power of Positive Thinking,* and the Living Theatre had just begun its long experiment with staging the unbearable in the hope of changing its audience (and thus, with luck, the world). The spirit in which they perform still mirrors what Malina said then. But their work has gone through so many metamorphoses that the only way I can imagine saying anything useful about it in a short essay is to embrace a conventional idea, and then kick it a little off-center. The idea is that the essence of their project lies in the way they externalized—made theater of—their anarcho-pacifist politics through their interactions with the audience.

Malina, Julian Beck, Hanon Reznikov and their coworkers were constantly on the move, from continent to continent, peacetime to wartime, prosperity to poverty, decade to decade. Each new position meant rethinking the theater-spectator relationship. Facing new audiences in changing historical and cultural contexts, what unspeakable outcries did the theater articulate, what means did they use to drive the audience to feel these outcries as their own and then act on that feeling? What happened then? The Living Theatre wanted to shape, not just mirror, history. Yet it seems clear, looking back, that history shaped them instead, and their opposition to its repressive force mirrored other forms of opposition. But in what ways? Finally, as they chose to stake their art on its effectiveness, the question's inevitable: what effect did it have?

Of necessity, my discussion will be schematic, condensed, and subjective. I have been part of the Living Theatre's audience on and off since their production of *The Connection,* when I was an arty leftist kid straight out of college. In 1960 I already knew that theater could be more than *Our Town* from seeing New York productions of Genet and various angry young Brits, but was convinced that all exciting American work had to be apolitical, like Caffe Cino, or antitheater, like Happenings. *The Connection* was a revelation. When I later became a theater editor and then a critic, the Living Theatre was part of my radical-hip-experimental beat.

Naturally my perspective shifted from time to time along with my aesthetic and political convictions, as did ideas and work of the Living Theatre, though not always in the same direction. Like many who have watched the Living Theatre over the years, I shuttled between enthusiasm and hair-tearing irritation, always ambivalent, always hopeful. Now the memory of my original reactions is further bedeviled by hindsight, which never forgives because it knows too much, and by nostalgia, which always, fondly, understands. And both hindsight and nostalgia, the critique and the romance, are still in motion, as the present continues to reshape what seems valuable in their work, what seems wrongheaded, and why.

II

In the Golden Age, when artists were a community, it must have been like this.

Judith Malina, *Diaries*, March 3, 1953

For the Living Theatre's first ten years, the theater and its audience were part of the post–World War II New York avant-garde, vividly evoked by Malina's *Diaries, 1947–1957*. The opening entry, written on her birthday, June 4, 1947, begins, "Twenty-one already and I still haven't done a thing worth immortality." She rejoices at quitting a bookstore job; Beck brings her presents ("Cocteau, *Götterdämmerung*, Cesar Franck"); she visits her lover ("a tall red candle burns on a cake"); and rehearses a role in *Ethan Frome*, at the Cherry Lane. The day ends as she tells a classmate from the Piscator workshop about "the Living Theatre, the most important work of my life, for which I am now preparing."[1]

These few sentences reveal aspects of late-1940s bohemia in which the later Living Theatre remained rooted. Malina's embrace of European high art emphatically rejected patriotic, triumphalist, philistine middle- and upper-middle-class American culture. Everything she mentions went against its grain, even Beck's birthday gifts. Wagner? Our victory in World War II saved Europe from everything he represented. Cocteau—aesthete, homosexual—was suspect. Piscator connected Malina to left-wing theatrical experiment, the Jewish/"degenerate"/ "Bolshevik" art that he and other refugees from Nazism had brought to America, just when the House Un-American Activities Committee started to purge America of such ideas. She always had a day job and never went to college; in this milieu, professional or academic life seemed alien to creative thought. As for the red candle, nonconformist sexuality was dissent, especially for women (though men manipulated it). Finally, like Malina, most Greenwich Village artists conceived of their "important work" as a life, not a career.

Malina lived in a difficult freedom, earned by removing herself as much as possible from what was later called "the system" and made bearable by a community of the like-minded that was also the Living's audience. Most of this community simply wanted to find a space where they could live and work as they pleased, opposing American society but content to make a separate peace. The friends, lovers, collaborators, and supporters described in the *Diaries* and listed in the theater's early programs revolutionized their forms—music (John Cage), film (Maya Deren), painting (Robert Motherwell), dance (Pearl Primus); only the writer-intellectuals among them (for example, Joseph Campbell and Paul Goodman, to take great opposites) directly challenged conventional social thought. The Becks wanted a theater that subverted both accepted forms and acceptable content, and would be taken as seriously by these American experimentalists as other arts were, and as it was in Europe. Thus another diary entry: "January 14, 1952. The program is decided: Three plays to be called collectively *An Evening of Bohemian Theater:* Gertrude Stein's *Ladies Voices,* Picasso's *Desire Trapped by the Tail,* Eliot's *Sweeney Agonistes.* Julian says, 'If this won't save the theater, nothing will.'"[2]

Save it from what? The American commercial stage wasn't completely mindless in the 1940s; its most successful playwrights included Arthur Miller, Lillian Hellman, and Tennessee Williams. Writing later about the forties, Julian Beck said he and Malina

> believed that there was some kind of sociological lag in the development of the theatre. That is, we were reading Joyce and Pound, Breton, Lorca, Proust, Patchen . . . *und so weiter.* 1944: the painting of Pollock and DeKooning was implying a life which the theatre didn't know existed, a level of consciousness and unconsciousness that rarely found itself onto the stage.[3]

The Becks wanted to shake up their audience's perception of theater the way Jackson Pollock shifted the idea of painting. They didn't talk about the avant-garde or modernism; instead their motto was "poetic" theater, which their friend Harold Norse defined in a 1951 program note as "a performance of rites involving wonder and vision—the dramatization of dream and desire." He added, "It is incredible that the plays of the 'realists' constitute the theoretical norm in dramatic literature even today."[4]

In this period the Becks produced European antirealists—including Brecht, Lorca, Jarry, and Pirandello—and American poets and nonconformists, from John Ashbery to Paul Goodman. The repertoire alone was enlightening for spectators whose notions of theatrical daring had been limited to O'Neill's or Elmer Rice's semiexpressionist moments. But Malina and Beck wanted to go further, and started to think about their audience's ethics as well as aesthetics.

Malina's 1952 production of Paul Goodman's *Faustina* provides the first example of crossing the performance/audience line in order to challenge spectators. Goodman—a great influence as anarchist thinker, Malina's therapist, and gay-but-married exemplar to Beck—wanted theater that provoked: "either the audience is terribly offended . . . or in two hours the play affects a character-change in the audience, more than all the manifestos can accomplish."[5] At the end of *Faustina,* which concerned

Rome in the time of Marcus Aurelius, the actor playing the title character was supposed to address the spectators directly, telling them they were responsible for its murderous climax because they didn't leap onstage and stop the action. The actor playing Faustina refused to address the audience directly, and Malina took her place. They still didn't leap.

Faustina was a disaster. No surprise, when sophisticated playgoers were asked to feel real guilt for not taking steps to stop a purely fictive crime. This may be a "confusion of realms"[6] far greater than that which the theater was denounced for in the 1960s. Or simply a first, failed attempt to solve what Malina saw as the problem with the theater-audience relationship, and with the relationship between theater and society. In the *Faustina* program she wrote, "We are creators in an art where every night hundreds of people are ignored; a pretense is made that they do not exist; and then we wonder that the actor has grown apart from society; and then we wonder that the art itself staggers lamely behind its hope of being part of life."[7]

Yet the Becks' political and artistic radicalism usually coexisted as parallel rather than integrated forces in these first ten years. The Becks didn't care whether the writers they staged shared their convictions; they weren't what later was called politically correct. A Noh play translated by Ezra Pound was scheduled as the theater's first production back in 1948—only three years after the opening of the concentration camps, they felt no qualms about working with an anti-Semitic propagandist for Mussolini.[8] It was more important that their own government had imprisoned a great modern poet (Pound), whose expressive power and outsider status overshadowed any ideology. To them, T. S. Eliot and Picasso were more alike than different in the ways that counted. This weighting of values is worth noting because in many crucial ways it persisted.

In the later 1950s the context of bohemia changed. Organized dissent and the counterculture both blossomed: the peace and civil rights movements, the Beats, the folk revival, rock. The sixties were growing inside the fifties, fed by anticolonialism and the United States' blatantly reactionary world role, and given a final push in 1959 by the Cuban Revolution. The Becks' anarchism saved them from the disillusion felt by pro-Soviet leftists after Khrushchev's acknowledgment of Stalin's crimes and the Soviet invasion of Hungary—which go unremarked in Malina's 1956 diary entries, as she expected no better of any state—and they focused more and more of their energy on antinuclear resistance. The final pages of her diary record Malina's arrest and thirty-day imprisonment for refusing to take shelter during an air raid drill.[9] This observant, compassionate, and eloquent "I," writing about drug-addicted black prostitutes and the saintly pacifist Catholic Dorothy Day, is a far cry from the idealistic but self-involved twenty-one-year-old of 1947. Beck spent a hard month in the Tombs at the same time. Both were politicized in a new way. They and their audience weren't unified any more, and a repertoire of modernist classics no longer quite reflected their ideas.

III

> I was talking about the problem of naturalism. Did I say anything about that? Well, it is out of the question. Where could it lead? A sociologist's report on the pecking order of Bowery bums. No, out of the question. . . . What's happening backstage? Is everyone high before we start?
>
> —Jack Gelber, *The Connection*

From 1959, with the production of Jack Gelber's *The Connection,* to 1963, when the company went into exile during the run of Kenneth Brown's *The Brig,*[10] the Living Theatre seemed to be looking for a way to close the gap between their aesthetics and their politics without deploying the forms then accepted as political theater in America: agitprop, socialist realism, and social drama along the Odets line. They maintained their modernist stance in productions of Brecht, William Carlos Williams, and a rigorously avant-garde "chance" play by Jackson Mac Low. But with *The Connection* and *The Brig*—topical, contemporary plays by young Americans—they found ways to embody their politics using texts that were neither "poetic" nor "avant-garde." Instead, the scripts were as nearly documentary as any slice-of-life but staged as if naturalism were indeed out of the question, a contradiction that pulled the audience in deeper than could either theatricalism or realism alone. By 1959, this audience had expanded well beyond the friends and fellow artists of ten years earlier. Downtown New York's public was socially engaged and aesthetically literate, able to read many levels of meaning and question them from many points of view.

I remember how familiar yet new *The Connection* looked at the time, from the cockroach grunge of Beck's set to the actors' sexy hipness as they yearned for heroin, the least sexual of drugs. Now, Shirley Clarke's film of the production seems perfectly to preserve a certain moment right before cool slipped into hot, bop into rock, niche activism into mass protest, the depressive into the manic.[11] The subject itself wasn't new. Many 1950s novels and plays dealt with addiction, and like Gelber's, their characters often fell out of the middle class to drift along society's bottom, waiting for temporary relief from nothingness. Kenneth Tynan noted that *The Connection*'s atmosphere recalled Gorky's *The Lower Depths* and its theme resembled that of *Waiting for Godot*.[12] Its tone was, however, surprising in an American play. Gelber doesn't treat junkies either as "authentic" or as rebels—Tynan, right again, says "their relationship to society is not one of enmity, but one of truancy."[13] Nor does their situation directly symbolize or seek to explain the problems of society as a whole. After all, their one great desire is fulfilled: unlike Godot, the connection arrives. (He's called Cowboy and he's black.) A character overdoses himself, but doesn't die: the play doesn't fall into melodrama, and addiction doesn't bring retribution.

We, like they, lived in a society where human desire had been replaced by chemical addiction and happiness by a fix. You want life; you get dope (in one form or another). This "unbearable situation," never quite spelled out, was shown three ways. On one level the audience recognized the basic lifelikeness of the set, the action (or inaction), and the characters' stories. On another, a small jazz band, always on stage, improvised brilliantly around the actors' riffs, pleasing the audience in a way that conflicted with what we felt we should feel about this scene, willy-nilly making us share a high. (The musicians, all black, presented the question of race while leaving it mostly unspoken.)[14] Finally, a team of documentary filmmakers was constantly present, hovering, intruding, shooting events, shooting heroin. Thus we saw a play about the filming of a play interrupted by music, presented by characters who want nothing out of life except illusion. The overlapping devices created distance and dis-illusion; they also opened up interactions between the straight and hip worlds— the filmmakers with the junkies, the musicians with both, the spectators with everyone. The fourth wall grew blurry in a haze of jazz and cracked when performers didn't stay on stage. This formal slipperiness didn't confuse anyone. Instead, it drew on the audience's skepticism and alertness, and the effect was less to undermine conventional form than to create space for meaning. Though the play is far from Marxist, the audience was in an almost Brechtian position.

At intermission, spectators were faced with a version of Malina's *Faustina* gambit when cast members insisting they were "really" junkies came up to them. One asked me to give him money for a fix, and though I didn't give him anything, I felt put upon and somehow cheated, as if this was the wrong game: the lobby was "real," and he had confused the boundaries. Later I scolded myself for not asking him to roll up his sleeve and show me needle marks, to prove his authenticity. (We troubled ourselves considerably over authenticity in those preperformative days, as you'll see.) The art/life disorientations during the actual performance were thought-provoking; this smelled manipulative. Yet the play's final words are, "It's all yours now,"[15] and indeed all interpretation was left to the audience. We were infuriated or saddened by the characters' eloquent, "wasted" lives, but we hadn't been asked, "Which side are you on?" There were no sides, just situations. We left the theater with our thoughts and emotions unsettled, neither confirmed nor attacked.

The Living Theatre became famous with this production, so their audience expanded even further beyond their original community. They visited Paris in 1961, winning the Grand Prix of the Theatre des Nations as well as the Paris Theatre Critics Circle award for best acting. They toured all over Europe. On their return the Becks picketed the Soviet embassy because the Russians had resumed nuclear testing; by the time of the 1962 Cuban missile crisis Americans were deeply afraid, American militarism flourished, and nuclear war seemed not only possible—it was always possible—but likely. *The Brig* and the third General Strike for Peace were both produced in spring 1963.

Kenneth Brown had written an antiwar play without war—no battles, no gore, no patriotism, no foreign enemy. The script covers one day in a marine brig in Japan: A new prisoner is given his number, told the rules, forced into idiotic tasks, yelled at, punched; another prisoner is released; another has a breakdown. Dialogue and character barely exist. Marines who happen to be guards turn into persecutors, marines who happen to be prisoners turn into victims. The situation itself contained its moral. Camus's injunction to be "neither a victim nor an executioner" was engraved on my—and the audience's, and the Becks'—consciousness, images of Nazi concentration camps were recent and still shocking, and stories about the Gulag permeated the Cold War media, deployed to point up our own innocence. Brutality and a crazed lust for control weren't supposed to be part of American reality, and therefore our responsibility.

The audience couldn't avoid this brutality. Malina's direction turned the violence of the state into a hellish choreography and the language of the state into its dehumanizing score, without making them in any way seductive. The stage was crisscrossed by white lines, across which no soldier could step to obey his constant orders without being hit if he forgot to shout for permission in the exactly proper form. Frantic terror and furious authority marked every exchange between "sir" and "maggot." The noise, the speed, the repetition were pushed to an unbearable point, while we onlookers sat pinned to our seats, watching through a barbed wire fence. This fourth wall in *The* Brig was as absolute as *The Connection*'s had been permeable. It forced *The Brig*'s spectators to be aware of their distance from these ordinary young men and familiar representations of

The Living Theatre, *The Brig*, 1963. (Photo courtesy of Judith Malina and Hanon Reznikov, Living Theatre Archive.)

the military, while at *The Connection* they had been conscious of their surprising closeness to the illegal and asocial. Both modes of distancing fulfilled a similar didactic purpose. The audience at *The Brig*, however, was brought much closer to Malina's 1952 injunction.

Neither production lent itself directly to the activists' question: "What is to be done?" Instead both asked: "What is this society of ours? Can you look at it some new way?" In 1962, left-wing political groups were asking the same questions. The square, straight, sociologically minded leaders of Students for a Democratic Society didn't resemble the Becks in any way, but the SDS's Port Huron statement, the founding text of the New Left, reflects the same universe of critique and dismay from which *The Brig* and *The Connection* came. "We are the people of this generation, bred in at least modest comfort . . . looking uncomfortably to the world we inherit," it says before denouncing corporate lobbying, the growing gap between rich and poor, and the misuse of technology. "Our work is guided by the sense that we may be the last generation in the experiment with living." "The arts, too, are organized substantially according to their commercial appeal; aesthetic values are subordinated to exchange values." The concept of participatory democracy that SDS proposed as an alternative to both capitalist democracy and authoritarian socialism had much in common with the self-governing antihierarchy proposed by anarchism.

Reading the Port Huron statement more than forty years later can be unnerving. "A necessary part of the military effort is propaganda: to 'sell' the need for Congressional appropriations, to conceal various business scandals, and to convince the American people that the arms race is important enough to sacrifice civil liberties and social welfare." "Worldwide amusement, cynicism, and hatred towards the United States as a democracy is not simply a communist propaganda trick, but an objectively justifiable phenomenon."[16] The world of the Beats, the ideas of the New Left, and the goals of anarchy and pacifism are these two plays' contexts. In many ways those ideas and goals are again to the point, but the Living Theatre's recent work and its American audience are completely different. If they had stayed in America, would they have continued along the path set by *The Connection* and *The Brig*? Would, could, they still be as much a part of our time as they were then?

IV

Art has become a contained mental thing and it has a very detrimental effect on the way we look at the world. Now we have a need not for art but to revive ourselves, our own bodies, our own beings, our own lives. Therefore, yes, it's no longer a matter of being an artist, it's a matter of infiltrating into being, into the world, into the people.

—Beck, *Life of the Theatre*

A paradox: Almost everything that "typifies" the Living as the theater of the American 1960s youth movement developed in European exile, including *Paradise Now,* the anarchist collective that created it, and the political and spiritual ideas driving both. The intimate, "spontaneous," and sometimes hostile encounters with the audience that seem so peculiarly sixties and American were a profound change from the way the theater usually interacted with the audience in America. By leaving the United States in 1963, they were absent for the Kennedy assassination, "Freedom Summer" and the height of the civil rights movement, the Vietnam War and its opposition, the beginnings of Black Power and feminism: the country's great moments of passion, sorrow, and organization. Most of the work created from 1963 to 1968 was based on European sources—*Frankenstein, The Maids, Antigone*—and came from the experience of the European New Left, not the American New Left.

To Europeans, the Living's process and its productions seemed quintessentially "American"—spontaneous, emotional, nonverbal, untrained. But the Living's style sprang from the company's transformation after they left America into a wandering anarchist commune that had lost its outward community. The organizational principle was self-governing consensus (the Becks deplored their own guru-status); the practice was drugs, meditation, the occult, vegetarianism, anticonsumerism, and free love; the politics remained—with much debate—anarchism, pacifism, and civil disobedience. Life with the Living was a highly concentrated dose of themes prevalent throughout world hippiedom and the political counterculture. Thus after fifteen years of aesthetic oscillation between modernist unreason and an equally modernist rational distance, the Becks' version of Artaud finally trumped their version of Brecht, even when they produced Brecht. Group-created texts replaced or upended scripts by playwrights; the performer's body became a central source of meaning; interactions with the audience grew "cruel"; social and political themes were expressed as ritual. In rehearsal, rehearsal itself eclipsed results. Practical reasons again were at work here. Moving from country to country and language to language makes the spoken word ineffective as the primary means of communication, and turns subtlety or irony into impossible goals; in a company that lives as a commune, top-down directing—the insistence on "art," as per this section's epigraph—leads to resentment and squabbling.

The new work drew on *The Brig* more than *The Connection* in its physicality, *The Connection* more than *The Brig* in its direct interaction with spectators. But unlike either, it no longer set out from particular, familiar places and situations; abstractions—Society, the Future, Love—replaced the marine brig and the downtown pad. Malina's old idea of enraging the audience was increasingly attractive: the company faced an audience of strangers, and faced them as a group. European cultural radicals, many of whom joined the company, were even more furious than Americans at the class they came from. Slogans and manifestos were everywhere, and the theater's texts reflected them. After it had been in Europe for five years, it could demand of its audiences what had been only implicit in New York: Leave this theater and make revolution!

The nature of this revolution could not have been predicted from an experience of the New York Living Theatre. "There is something we need . . . It's the 12 Volume edition of THE ZOHAR. . . . And . . . if you can find it, my Mod. Lib. edition of DAS KAPITAL, that wd also be helpful. But the ZOHAR is what's important. . . . Am hoping that *Paradise Now* will be our really valuable contribution to the Revolution," Beck wrote to his

New York friend Saul Gottlieb when he and the company were devising *Paradise Now* in Sicily.[17] The Becks described the play as "a voyage from the many to the one and from the one to the many. It is a spiritual voyage and a political voyage. . . . [It] is a vertical ascent toward Permanent Revolution."[18] The conflict between the Zohar's and *Capital*'s voyages, the difficulties of setting out ballasted on the one side with the kabbalah and on the other with Marx, were apparently solved by throwing *Capital* overboard, if Gottlieb ever found it.

The program shows how far the theater had traveled. A drawing of two figures illustrated the evening's "plot." They face the reader, on the left a naked bearded man with Hebrew lettering on his body, on the right a naked, clean-shaven, slightly more androgynous figure marked with yogic circles. Between them three sequences of boxes and arrows lead upward through eight revolutions each, from cultural revolution through that of action and that of being. At the far sides of the figures are ladders, one with eight rungs from good-and-evil to god-and-man, another with eight patterns from the I Ching, another listing eight colors with black at the bottom and white on top, another rising from culture through hostility to stasis. The ladders are further subdivided by little boxes containing single nouns—peace, breakthrough, rigidity, prayer. The entire astounding proliferation of hierarchies is at once reminiscent of medieval magicians' charts, 1950s drawings of "evolution" or "progress" for children, and bad acid art.

The published play contains eight "Rites" almost all of which involve the audience. It opens with a "Rite of Guerrilla Theatre," then moves from "The Vision of the Discovery of the North Pole" through, among many scenes, "The Vision of the Magic Love Zap" on a path to "The Permanent Revolution." In "The Rite of the Mysterious Voyage," the voyager "flips out" and the audience "helps him take his trip"; throughout "The Rite of I and Thou" everyone chants "aum" until the life force overcomes the death force.[19] It's hard to reconcile either program or text with Beck's outline of the play's goals:

> it is not just revolutionary theatre. it is revolutionary action, direct revolutionary action. . . . if the play succeeds, it should stimulate the growth and development of newspapers, printing services, news services, green revolution cooperatives, handicraft cooperatives, industrial production and raw material production distribution geared for revolutionary services, to hasten the steps for the non-violent revolution.[20]

This sounds quite mad, and indeed never happened. To understand it, one must remember *Paradise Now*'s timing. The radicalism and militancy of the European student, antiwar, anticolonial, and labor movements peaked in 1968 when even sober analysts envisioned revolution right around the corner, the Left with hope, the Right with fear. The play was sketched out in March and April 1968, and first performed that June. In between came the events of May. In Paris, the Living Theatre took part in the French students' and workers' general strike by leading the student occupation of the Odéon, a theater picked, at the Becks' urging, precisely because it was what we'd now call "liberal"—directed by Jean Louis Barrault, it produced Genet, Ionesco, Beckett, and other playwrights considered experimental or avant-garde. To seize this theater as a stage for day-and-night revolutionizing was to declare how far beyond the limits of authorized dissent the students had moved, and how passionately they repudiated reform, in politics or art.

The Living Theatre and the students were in agreement. Yet a sermonizing voice resounds even in *Paradise Now*'s printed text; the Becks were in their forties, and though they clearly accepted the then-fashionable and intellectually respectable notion of students as a new revolutionary class, its tone is not that of people addressing their peers. Videos of *Paradise Now* in France show that the students did not respond passively. The theater had the charisma to lead their student audiences into the streets (and the arms of the police), but the same audiences often challenged its politics. The violent Left found the Becks' pacifism useless, and Marxists found them at best unanalytical. Unconscious fascism seemed to lurk in their commitment to unreason. Young audiences were quite aware that the avant-garde had a history of communism (which the student Left despised) among the surrealists and fascism among the Italian futurists. And after the defeat of May and its demonstration of the establishment's crushing power, many young rebels were moving away from spontaneous nonhierarchical action to better-organized resistance. The Living was much loved by European students, but also much questioned.

V

The same spring, Martin Luther King and Robert Kennedy were assassinated. The Chicago police savagely attacked protesters at the August Democratic Convention, igniting a division of the American New Left, with one part moving toward armed action. The Vietnam War continued. The Living Theatre came to America to tour four of its European productions.

Back in 1961, Malina and Beck had asked Martin Buber to support their efforts to organize a General Strike for Peace. He declined, though sympathetically, and ended his response with the sentence: "I dread the enormous despair that must be the consequence of the inevitable failure." By 1968 he sounded prophetic; Malina quoted the exchange in her diary of the tour, which she published as *The Enormous Despair.*[21] This was a period of great activism, but American student leaders were beset by gloom. "To be white and a radical in America this summer is to see horror and feel impotence," said one; another recalled later that "despair became a cliché among young white radicals."[22]

Paradise Now dropped into this dire landscape, its purpose to represent and inspire pacifist, mystical, revolutionary action. I still have a few notes from the first time I saw it, at Hunter College: "Chaos, fury, mindlessness. Damned if I'll be bullied into participating. Nothing to see anyway except crowds in a shapeless muddle occasionally punctuated by the actors' grossly rhetorical gestures or a couple of naked people groping or yelling at each other. Maybe it would have been OK 10 years ago? Would Beats have thought it was Artaudian? Right now, no joy. Something deadly here." I yearned for reason and humor. But what did I mean by "something deadly"? During the theatrical event, I felt enveloped in a miasma emitted by a false relation to spectators, an interchange that had taken a wrong turn, affection and respect gone sour. From a larger perspective, its source was the theater's contempt for the entire class, and world, from which the audience came.

Spectators were constantly involved in the action, in ways that deliberately frustrated them. Thus "The Rite of Universal Intercourse" was what it sounds like, but not quite; the actors' nakedness stopped at loincloths. Though this was meant to illustrate freedom's limits in contemporary society, not merely to acquiesce in them and avoid arrest, spectators saw only a cop-out. The opening "Rite of Guerrilla Theater," however, became every critic's paradigmatic, usually enraging, Living Theatre moment. The published text describes this event:

> Each actor approaches a spectator and, addressing him individually . . . speaks in a very quiet, urgent, but personal voice . . . "I am not allowed to travel without a passport." He goes from spectator to spectator and repeats this phrase. With each repetition, his voice and body express greater urgency and frustration. He speaks only this phrase. If the spectator addresses him, he listens to the spectator but repeats only this phrase. . . . He hears his fellow actors flipping out and is affected by the community of protest. He experi-

ences the spectators' growing frustration at the sense of a lack of communication. . . . At the end of two minutes the actors go beyond words into a collective scream. This scream is the pre-revolutionary outcry.[23]

Such an attempt to create an "audience at an extreme of exasperation" twenty years after Malina first wanted one reshapes the alienation-effect, replacing understanding with furious, or "cruel," emotion. Reading the description, one can easily imagine a true communication of the impossibility of communication. What occurred instead, not only the three times I saw it but from all reports at most performances, was a psychodrama of scorn and hostility. The actors screamed at the audience, and in turn the audience muttered, "You've got a passport, you traveled here, no one stopped you, get off it." An actor emptied a spectator's handbag, threw a fur coat in a corner. Actions that were intended to illuminate while infuriating us struck the viewer/object/victim as pure nihilist rage. As in: the *enragés* of Europe, the Days of Rage here.

The message was, as one actor said in New Haven, "Get those fucking liberals out of the house. I only want revolutionaries here."[24] What kind of political theater was this?

One great friend of the Living described it as "Forty people choosing to prophesy against the organized lucidity of political work. They don't need that continuous verifying that is the very basis of (conventional) political action. Their life is their action and their action is their spectacle."[25] Two things about this statement are striking. First, that clarity and reason in politics are what's prophesied *against*. Second, that change outside the theater is beside the point, an unnecessary verification. The political action is contained in the spectacle, which itself is indistinguishable from their collective life. The Becks might not have found such a description either agreeable or true. Yet it accurately reflects the effect their theater had on audiences. Despite Beck's expressed hope that *Paradise Now* would leave a trail of cooperatives and print shops in its wake, spectators were moved, at best, toward inchoate notions of freedom or possibility. As for prophesying to the audience, one of the actors typically said: "You have to psyche them out or be psyched out. There has to be psychic change. You or them has to go through a change. One of them has to be shattered. You cannot intellectually change anybody."[26] Upheaval, distress, destruction are the paths to regeneration. This path went through revolution, not reform, and the revolution itself was psychological, prepolitical.

The mainstream media—from the weeklies through the *Times* to the tabloids and network TV[27]—paid a now-unimaginable amount of attention to the Living Theatre. It could be viewed as a relatively acceptable face of the "revolution," because it kept its violence verbal and limited its actions to the emotional. (The police didn't necessarily see things this way, and the group was often harassed.) Jack Kroll at *Newsweek*, the most intelligent and sympathetic of the large-readership liberal critics, wrote that "exasperating, boring, outrageous and high-handed as they can be, their authenticity of spirit is beyond question as is their desire to settle for nothing but real change in the human beings who are the ultimate substance of both art and life."[28]

The Right, of course, hated the work and used it to exemplify many standard critiques of the 1960s movement—irrational, angry, all gesture and no program, nothing but sex and drugs, and so forth. So did most critics from the "old" Left of the 1930s, still wedded to realism, for example Harold Clurman in *The Nation:* "these folk are fanatics of amateurism . . . only marginally a theatrical organization . . . a cult [of] utopian anarchy."[29] But the Living wasn't addressing conservatives and philistines. Their difficulties came with the reactions of writers who had been supportive before they went into exile, who had been part of their audience.

Eric Bentley, known at that time as the man who brought Brecht to American attention and an eminent opponent of the Vietnam War as well as an incisive theater critic, is the most revealing example. He said about the "Rite of Guerrilla Theater": "They make a remark to you, and if you make a remark back, they repeat the first remark. To me that's unacceptable," and gave his reasons: "What the intelligence demands in the theater (and I believe outside it too) is dialectics—a sense of the interplay of opposites."[30] Bentley's reactions moved Malina to write: "I want him to raise his arms to heaven and cry out, and he doesn't want to raise his arms to heaven and cry out. And I know he doesn't want to, and I still want to get him to do it."[31] She wanted "to get him to," of course, because Bentley wasn't conservative like John Simon (who despised them), a philistine like the reviewers of the daily papers (even those who were admiring), or an establishment figure like Robert Brustein, who as dean of the Yale Drama School had invited them to perform but quickly grew disillusioned and hostile. By saying that Bentley simply refused to express his feelings, in effect that he was repressed, Malina ignored the politically crucial emotion he did express—anger at not being heard or responded to. Like the spectators at *Faustina,* Bentley refused the position in which Malina wished to place him. Richard Gilman, who had greatly admired *The Connection,* went further: "the terrifying righteousness of the Becks surely covered a radical hatred . . . the group had landed in another kind of artificiality after its flight from the artifices of theater."[32]

From the radical Left, the Living was criticized as not militant enough.[33] American student leftists saw that nonviolence hadn't stopped the Vietnam War, however much it had influenced public opinion. "Around SDS, it became chic to call the plodding marchers 'peace creeps,' turning around a taunt that American Nazis had thrown at SDS,"[34] despite the fact that by 1968 the peace movement had become the largest, most broadly based antiwar mobilization in American and perhaps any history (until the worldwide demonstrations against the Iraq War in 2003). Black nationalists similarly felt that the civil rights movement was fatally integrationist, and that King's murder showed the pointlessness of nonviolence. Malina called her American journal *The Enormous Despair* not just because the country seemed hopeless and desperate, but because at the very moment that many American audiences seemed to embrace them, the theater felt disconnected from the people whom they most deeply wanted to affect.

James Miller's history of the New Left quotes an SDS activist's analysis of its disintegration at the end of the sixties; he thought, in retrospect, that it came from the movement's delusions of revolutionary apocalypse, its inability to extend its middle-class base, and its failure to develop a durable organizational structure.[35] The Living Theatre in 1968–69 showed its own versions of these weaknesses. Not because it had forsaken the unspeakable cry, but because it offered nothing between that cry and the unattainable utopias of nonviolence and anarchy, addressed only students, and rejected professionalism. In 1968 Malina noted, "The American audience is more given to chanting and dancing and clapping than to discussion."[36] But the Living didn't offer any openings for discussion. They had returned to the belly of the beast, it was much more horrible than even they had imagined, and their work reflected frustration and dismay.

Bread and Puppet, the San Francisco Mime Troupe, El Teatro Campesino, and other political companies of the time had quite different relations with their audiences—more like the preexile Living Theatre even when, like the Living in exile, they became collectives, worked with company-created scripts, and performed agitprop in the streets. One reason was that they had never embraced the notion of frustrating or enraging the audience as a path to its enlightenment, another that they maintained a sense of community with those for whom they performed. Perhaps the smaller scale of their productions, the presence of humor and lightness, and the absence of the daunting mystique that enveloped the Living all helped too.

My own feelings about the Living's work were more vexed in 1969 than any time before or since, a disaffiliation that came from traits they again shared with the Movement. Feminism was undervalued as theory and absent as practice. The uneasy coexistence of gurulike leadership with anarchist egalitarian principles was never resolved. The conviction that their collective shaped dissent by demonstrating a future utopia in microcosm seemed delusional, while their dour rhetorical overkill made me suspicious of any revolution they had in mind. Yet . . . still . . . nevertheless . . . *Frankenstein* and *Mysteries* were better theater—better structured, breathtakingly designed, more complex—than *Paradise Now,* ultimate political statement though it might be, and *Paradise Now* at least failed at a task seriously conceived. No matter how alienating any particular production, how wrongheaded their politics, how maddening their mysticism, the constant surprises of the stage work and their underlying commitment to freedom remained worth respect. And their slightly loopy sincerity, warm in conversation if not on stage, would make an iceberg affectionate. Besides, they had already changed radically over the first twenty years, so they might well change again.

In exile the Becks had considered coming back for good, but now they felt disturbed and repelled by their country, happy to leave again. "America, Our parting word was: Zero."[37]

VI

> The Living Theatre, as institution (which was its fate, living life as it had lived it), the Living Theatre as projection of anarchist community (which it is only in process of becoming) has to transmute. 1969: the decision to dissolve and re-form, as cells, to meet our own needs and the needs of the time.
>
> —Beck, *Life of the Theatre*

Two months after leaving the United States, the company went to Morocco, where they worked on an activist play and were expelled three months later. The company broke up at the beginning of 1970. One part went to India "to emphasize the spiritual trip though at the same time they were interested in the social and economic trip." A second remained in Europe to work with the electronic media and perform in festivals, "keeping up a dialogue with the youthful bourgeoisie." But the ones who stayed with Beck and Malina felt their "primary concern was to take our small resources somewhere outside the oppressor world and reach a completely different audience from that we'd addressed before. Radical politics and radical aesthetics had not been a sufficient bridge of intellectual or emotional understanding between classes."[38] They decided to go to Brazil.

Paradise Now's missed connections, critiques like Bentley's, the unproductiveness of anger at their own audience, had all sunk in. As Malina said in 1971, "In *Paradise,* our approach to the audience was always aggressive and sometimes hostile. In Brazil we wanted to approach the audience in exactly the opposite way, and this changed our work more than any other single thing."[39] Again, the theater was reflecting the concerns of the New Left as a whole. The split between violence and nonviolence had been far from theoretical, and the Weathermen, the Red Army Faction in Germany, and the Italian Red Brigades sprang up. To no good effect: not only did they mobilize state power against them in a way that affected all opposition, but their actions, like *Paradise Now*'s rhetoric, showed a contradiction between ends and means that turned people off, creating considerable discussion and changes of policy.

Their move from Europe to Latin America was part of a strong current of "Third World–ism" rooted in angry identification with Vietnamese peasants, the hope that newly independent African and Asian countries would establish liberating societies, and a romantic need to create heroes out of victims. To shed one's own skin seemed the only way out of complicity with power. That taking art to a poor community suffering under a brutal military regime supported by one's own country rather than agitating at home against that support might smack of cultural imperialism and exotic adventure was something the Becks perceived later. Their stay ended in arrest, a two-month imprisonment, and expulsion.

I never saw the work they did in Brazil, though I published a section from their projected 150-play work *The Legacy of Cain,* which they performed in a favela. The organizing idea of the entire play is that the oppressed classes have been shaped into masochists who consent to their oppression; the only way they will be able to throw off their sadistic masters is by setting "in the place of the politics of Sadism and Masochism: eroticism, erotic politics."[40] I have found no report on audience reaction to the idea that they were getting pleasure from their impoverished lives or that they accepted their poverty. The theme of sadomasochism as a form of rebellion or liberation ran through intellectual-radical life at the time, and the Becks' response was ambivalently critical.

From Brazil, the company went to New York, joined the theater-workers branch of the Industrial Workers of the World (Wobblies)—once large and vigorous, the anarchist IWW was now tiny—and created *The Money Tower, Strike Support Oratorium,* and other activist works. They lived in a Brooklyn commune, then moved to Pittsburgh and divided into two cells, one more militant than the other, split again, ran out of money. Sketched like this, they seem to have moved in a theatrical parallel with SDS's hopeless drive to organize in working-class neighborhoods. I saw none of these productions: their intent, as in Brazil, was to engage the audience constructively.

VII

The Vietnam War ended; the Living went back to Europe. I didn't see any of their productions from 1969 until 1980, when they brought *Masse-Mensch, Yellow Methuselah, Archeology of Sleep,* and the 1967 *Antigone* to Manhattan. The three productions from the late 1970s returned to something like the modernism of the 1950s, using "difficult," culturally well known material (Toller's expressionist outcry, Shaw in *Yellow Methuselah*), with ambitious sets, big casts, an apparent commitment to amateur acting, and a new quality of occasional self-mockery and imaginative fun. They were completely remote from American political theater and activism, which were preoccupied with identity, and an American experimental stage that had turned to the theater of images. (If one looks now at photos of *Frankenstein* or *Mysteries,* with their astonishing and emotive stage architecture, they clearly lead to the work of, say, Robert Wilson, though every image expressed social meaning.) Nor did they speak to American political concerns as Reagan began what turned out to be more than twenty years of barely interrupted conservative rule. Though the Manhattan audience was once again Villagers and students, bohemia no longer existed, and the run was a failure.

Since then, the theater has several times tried, and failed, to find its bearing in New York, while keeping its subsidized base in Italy, and working around the world. Some of the plays have been imaginative and engrossing—I'm thinking particularly of *I & I* and *The Tablets*—but the acting remained mostly unskilled, and the spectators mostly acolytes, not young peers. A new generation of radical intellectuals interested in the avant-garde was neither to be found nor created. Yet at the same time, the group's audience-involvement agitprop, like the anti-capital-punishment performance *Not in My Name* done whenever there was an execution, truly involved both onlookers and performers.

VIII

Generally speaking, art is an expression of man's need for a harmonious and complete life, that is to say, his need for those major benefits of which a society of classes has deprived him. That is why a protest against reality, either conscious or unconscious, active or passive, optimistic or pessimistic, always forms part of a really creative piece of work. Every new tendency in art has begun with rebellion.

—Leon Trotsky, *Art and Revolution*

Trotsky detested both anarchy and pacifism. Yet there is nothing in this quotation Judith Malina or Julian Beck would have disagreed with, or that Judith Malina and Hanon Reznikov would disagree with now.[41] They too give first place to humanity's utopian desires, want theater to express these desires and prefigure utopia, and are convinced that social structures thwart or deform our needs. They have always coupled rebellion and creation, and are open to a multiplicity of means. But Trotsky doesn't mention rebellious art's effect on its audience; expression concerns him, not reception.

The Living Theatre tried to use expression to create a sense of frustrated desire within the spectator, and out of this awareness, action. At first the awareness was of a desire for a deepened aesthetic reality—poetic theater, antinaturalist theater, thumbing-its-nose-at-convention theater— the theater of bohemia. Then, with *The Connection* and *The Brig*, immediate American social content was added to antinaturalist stage work—a theater one could call that of analytical awareness. The collective works done in Europe in the 1960s were clearly deep in the fabric of student protest; the same pieces performed in America in 1968–69 changed in tone because America was not Europe and protest everywhere had entered a darker phase: the theater of rage became that of despair. Friendlier, more community-oriented attempts in the 1970s tried to overcome the pointless anger the theater hurled at its bourgeois audience by finding new audiences and approaching them as colleagues, though at least in the Third World there were new contradictions to trip over. Those productions I saw in the eighties and nineties failed to find an American audience, because that audience didn't exist—it had become primarily a theater of, and for, almost-vanished ideas and people.

Frederic Jameson talks about a horizon "in which what we formerly regarded as individual texts are grasped as utterances in an essentially collective or class discourse."[42] The Living Theatre has always tried to change the nature of these utterances, reshape them, and open up spaces in which the collective, indeed its own class, could question this discourse. They have also always, inevitably, staged utterances that are part of it. Given the discussion and organization and moral outrage we now have around Bush, war, terrorism, religion, and imperialism, won't the Living find itself once again before a community that wants it and that it wants to address? And what means will it then invent, what texts will it find, to speak to us?

NOTES

1. Judith Malina, *The Diaries of Judith Malina, 1947–1957* (New York: Grove Press, 1984), entry for March 17, 1952, 253.

2. Ibid., entry for January 14, 1952, 204.

3. Julian Beck, *The Life of the Theatre* (New York: Limelight Editions, 1986), 13.

4. The play was *Beyond the Mountain* by Kenneth Rexroth, poet, translator, and guru for the West Coast Beat poets. Program in the author's collection.

5. Note on Gertrude Stein's "Doctor Faustus Lights the Lights," 1952 . From program in author's collection.

6. Richard Gilman, *The Confusion of Realms* (New York: Random House, 1969), "The Living Theatre: Materials for a Portrait of the Professional as Amateur," passim.

7. Program in author's collection, 5.

8. For Pound, see accounts in Aldo Rostagno, *We, The Living Theatre* (New York: Ballantine, 1970), 11; and John Tytell, *The Living Theatre: Art, Exile, and Outrage* (New York: Grove Press, 1995), 47.

9. Malina, *Diaries,* 445–61.

10. Kenneth H. Brown, *The Brig* (New York: Hill and Wang, 1965).

11. The film is available on video, as is Jonas Meka's film of *The Brig*. Both suffer from the imposition of the camera's point of view, though in Clarke's film she makes witty use of superimposing her lens on the play's film crew.

12. Kenneth Tynan, in his introduction to the published play, Jack Gelber, *The Connection* (New York: Grove Press, 1970), 8.

13. Ibid., 10.

14. The published script has this stage direction on page 22: "The 1st Photographer is a Negro in a white suit, the 2nd Photographer white in a black suit. The 1st is swift and agile, the 2nd slow and clodlike. As the play unfolds they exchange, piece-by-piece, their clothing and personalities." The author adds, "However, there need not be any rigidity in casting."

15. Gelber, *The Connection,* 95.

16. The entire text of the June 1962 Port Huron statement is printed as an appendix to James Miller, *"Democracy Is in the Streets": From Port Huron to the Siege of Chicago* (New York: Simon and Schuster, 1987). These quotations are from pp. 329, 332, 330, 339, 345, and 360.

17. "Letters from the Becks" in *Yale/Theatre* 2, no. 1 (1969): 15.

18. Judith Malina and Julian Beck, *Paradise Now: Collective Creation of The Living Theatre* (New York: Random House, 1971), 5.

19. Ibid., 74, 89, 135.

20. Beck, *Life of the Theatre,* 16.

21. Judith Malina, *The Enormous Despair* (New York: Random House, 1972).

22. Todd Gitlin, *The Sixties: Years of Hope, Days of Rage* (New York: Bantam, 1987), 246.

23. Malina and Beck, *Paradise Now,* 15–16.

24. "Inside Paradise" in *Yale/Theater* 2, no. 1 (1969): 37.

25. Rostagno, *We, The Living Theatre,* 9.

26. Mel Howard quoted in "The Living Theatre Raps" in *Yale/Theater* 44.

27. For example, "October 27, 1968: We told CBS we didn't have time to do

an interview and also a filming of the Plague Scene and Brig Dollar [from *Mysteries*]. So they said they'd send a car." Malina, *Enormous Despair,* 102.

28. Rostagno, *We, The Living Theatre,* 231–32.

29. Ibid., 232.

30. Eric Bentley, *The Theater of War* (New York: Viking Press, 1972), 350 ff. Also "An Interview with Eric Bentley" by Michael Feingold in *Yale/Theater* 109–10.

31. Malina, *The Enormous Despair,* 231.

32. Gilman, *The Confusion of Realms,* 271.

33. See Tytell, *The Living Theatre;* the special issue of *Yale/Theater;* and Malina, *The Enormous Despair.*

34. Gitlin, *The Sixties,* 293.

35. Miller, *Democracy in the Streets,* quoting Richard Flacks, 293.

36. Malina, *The Enormous Despair,* 80.

37. Ibid., 235.

38. Erika Munk, "Paradise Later: An Interview with Judith Malina and Julian Beck," *Performance* 1 (1971): 91–92.

39. Ibid., 93.

40. Malina quoted by Beck in *Life of the Theatre,* 228.

41. "Art and Politics in Our Epoch," first published in *Partisan Review,* August 1938, reprinted in Leon Trotsky, *Art and Revolution: Writings on Literature, Politics, and Culture* (New York: Pathfinder Press, 1992), 104. In 1938 Stalin was killing Soviet artists wholesale, particularly those with experimental or nonrealist aims (for example, Meyerhold), sometimes on the pretext that they were Trotskyists.

42. Frederick Jameson, *The Political Unconscious* (Ithaca, N.Y.: Cornell University Press, 1982).

FOUR SCENES OF THEATRICAL ANARCHO-PACIFISM

A Living Legacy

Alisa Solomon

It's easy to blame the Living Theatre—and there's a lot of will to assign blame in these reactionary times for the myriad alleged sins that have collectively come to epitomize "the sixties" (though much of them took place in the seventies). With a triumphalist post–Cold War crow of victory, today's conservatives pronounce the moral defeat of all that druggy lassitude, sexual abandon, pious rebellion, romanticizing of the poor, and demonizing of the state with which they caricature the period. At the same time they warn that all those aberrant ideas wormed their way into America's universities, where "tenured radicals" now attempt to brainwash callow co-eds into supporting such thoroughly discredited notions as social welfare, disarmament, and racial and economic justice.[1] On the contrary, the Right's rise has been so absolute that such principles have been shoved decidedly out of mainstream discourse. To mention them is to be accused of harking back to those hippy-dippy times, those naive and destructive days of group-groping, fuck-the-system free-for-all that we're all supposed to have grown out of.

One of the quickest ways to call up that distorted picture has been to invoke images of the Living Theatre, widely regarded as the quintessential troupe of the period (even though the company was founded by Julian Beck and Judith Malina in 1947 and lived in voluntary exile from the United States during most of the 1960s). Still, for better or worse, the shorthand descriptor for the decade's theatrical experimentation—as well as for experiments with hallucinogens, communal living, and lefty attachments—is an image of nearly naked, long-haired men and women twined in a sweaty group embrace, groping at the audience, and leading them in Pied Piper procession through the streets.

For the cynical and dismissive—and even for the lazy—this is legacy enough for the Living Theatre. References to the troupe even decades after *Paradise Now* (the 1968 production that marked the Living Theatre's return to the United States after five years abroad and to which such images belong) cite those times. In calendar listings and reviews the *New York Times* has repeatedly drawn a condescending portrait of the Living Theatre as an unwashed relic of the 1960s, typically referring to the troupe with such quick-sketch phrases as "that shaggy old iconoclast" and "the bedraggled tribe of wandering anarchs."[2]

Less ideologically cranky critics might elaborate the troupe's significant (if not in every instance, unique) impact on dramatic form and theatrical process, noting their all-important introduction of such writers as Gertrude Stein and Alfred Jarry to the American theater; their decades-long efforts to dissolve the lines between actor and character, performance and reality; their development of the techniques of collective creation. What American theater artist of the last two generations was *not* affected by what Arthur Sainer called, in response to seeing *The Connection* in 1959, a "radical loosening of the fabric of drama [that] was taking place before our eyes"?[3]

But in the years that followed, the mainstream of the American avant-garde (a seeming contradiction resolved by the capaciousness of commodification) unraveled those threads of drama with a deconstructive drive that was never the Living Theatre's. Even when taking up Artaud's cry for "no more masterpieces," the Living Theatre sought coherence, unity, and transcendent meaning through their works. Their charge was never the postmodern dictum that Truth could not be claimed at all, but simply that bourgeois drama was not the best means for discovering and expressing it. While much of the American experimental theater—from Robert Wilson to the Wooster Group—declared the death of character and dismissed, or at least decentered, language in favor of postmodern nondiscursive and multiple meanings, modernist principles continued to pulse through the Living Theatre's work. That's part of the reason the plays the Living Theatre presented in its ballyhooed return to New York in 1984 after nearly ten years in Europe felt so static and out of synch: in the company's absence, experimental theater in the United States had developed a vastly different, abstract, visually precise—and sometimes precious—aesthetic.

More expressly radical theater, meanwhile, was following the Left's splin-
tering into identity politics, a tendency that simply had no traction in the
Living Theatre (though the company had long been multiethnic, multiracial, multinational, sexually diverse).

The Living Theatre, rather, has held fast to the Enlightenment principles affirming a universal human subject and the inevitability of progress; these ideals continue to fuel their convictions that a better world is
possible and that theater has a role to play in imagining such a world
and bringing it into being. The Living Theatre continues to tour the
world with workshops and productions, has maintained a studio, living
space, and theater in Rocchetta, Italy, and expects to open a permanent
theater in New York, this basic yet lofty idea is its living legacy.

What most interests me in tracing the power of this legacy is to highlight how and for whom the company continues to have meaning. Who
hears their voice today? Who responds to their call? This is very much a
question of context, and to get at it, I want to focus on several recent Living Theatre projects in several disparate places: comparing the reception
of *Utopia* in New York and in Italy; offering a critical reading of *Mysteries
and Smaller Pieces* as it was presented in Beirut, Lebanon; analyzing the
power of *Not in My Name* in two public squares; and providing an ethno-
graphic narrative of a workshop the Living Theatre conducted with
Lebanese college students in the summer of 2000.

Utopia is Nowhere, Baby (unless it's in Italy)

Calling the Living Theatre's—or any radical's—ideals "utopian" has long
been a means of dismissing their aims as naive and pie-in-the-sky and
therefore, presumably, not worth raising even for debate. This condescending slur has always bounced off the Living Theatre, which has typically embraced the intended insult as a badge of honor. In retort to the
accusation, frequently Malina or Reznikov will quote Paul Goodman:
"When they say 'utopian' they mean they don't want you to do it."[4]

In 1995, the troupe offered a more direct rejoinder, making a new
work boldly called *Utopia*. Fanciful, vaguely ritualistic, and surprisingly
witty, the piece offered an exploration of the concept of utopia more than
a vision of one. Rather than declaiming, say, a dream of world peace or
universal freedom from want, *Utopia* made the act of such dreaming itself
the subject. In notes as she was developing the play, Malina wrote:

> What stands between us at Utopia is our incredulity that what we
> want is what is possible. Our intention in working on a play about

Utopia is to overcome the spectator's disbelief in her own desires. Or is it, in a more Utopian sense, to augment the spectator's desires to the point where inaction becomes impossible?[5]

The production answered these questions by directly addressing theater as a space that can spur the imagination toward the inconceivable, indeed, as a place where one can exercise and stretch her imagination in order to keep it nimble and open enough to consider the world without squelching her highest hopes.

In a liquid series of scenes, an ensemble combines movement, chanting, singing, and spoken text to create images of wish fulfillment, sharing, limitation, and sensuality. For instance, in one sequence they dance sinuously with bolts of silk, as actors call out colors: "Blue! The cobalt rivers!" "Yellow! The lemons of Majorca!" The fabrics flap gloriously and the actors twist, bend and slither against the air. In another scene, they move among the audience, offering bread, cheese, and olives.[6]

Throughout, the company interjects droll ironic comments on its theme, reminding the audience that this play is not, in fact, invoking a naive idea of utopia. A running refrain, for instance, humorously suggests that utopia does not mean absence of conflict, obstacle, or loss by raising increasingly dire questions about that imagined realm. "What happens in Utopia when someone stubs his toe?" A performer asks. And the ensemble answers, "Ouch!" Later questions are left with no answers: "What happens in Utopia when a lover falls in love with someone else?" "What happens in Utopia when one's courage fails and meaning is lost?" "What happens in utopia when someone dies?" Periodically, the actors cite the etymology of Sir Thomas More's coinage to remind us that "Utopia is nowhere, baby."

In the center of the performance, the company invites spectators to "the lagoon"—a place where an audience volunteer "has nothing, needs nothing, has everything." The company adds, "At the lagoon, desire leads the way, and [the audience member] wishes for . . ." Here the audience member is asked to assert her or his desire. The ensemble enacts it, then asks what stands in the way of that desire, and then enacts the obstacle. Finally, as stage directions put it, "audience member is led through obstacle and unites with desire."

Audience members are recruited again at intermission to prepare a segment for late in the play: the final scene of Shakespeare's *The Winter's Tale,* that indestructible coup de théâtre in which Paulina brings the statue of Hermione to life. Some eight lines of Shakespeare's play are enacted, and the Living Theatre ensemble provides the music when Paulina bids "Music, awake her: strike!" They sing:

Hermione has been reborn
a thousand times and more
hope is given, courage taken
that's what theater's for
test the limit of your sight
lend your help, do what's right.

It's the most naked statement of the play's own function. Though it's delivered in a singsong language (and with several more stanzas) that rather
deflates the elegance of Shakespeare's, it is stirring nonetheless in the
context of the *Winter's Tale* scene—which itself is astonishing and exciting
even in this extremely abbreviated form, presented by rank amateurs with
only fifteen minutes of rehearsal.

Before calling on the music to strike, Paulina tells the onstage audience—and, of course, the public audience as well—"It is requir'd that you
do awake your faith." This need to awaken faith—in the imagination; in
one's capacity to break out of stultifying strictures, or at least out of the
status quo; in the possibility of a more just world—is really what the Living
Theatre's *Utopia* is driving at.

In the traditional context of New York theater, that's apparently too
much piety to demand. Presented in February 1996 at a second space
owned by the Vineyard Theater—which typically features new plays and
musical theater works in highly polished productions—*Utopia* could not
crack the hegemonic values and habits of mind of mainstream theatergoers. True, the production was not uniformly well acted, the text was not
always easy to hear, and much of the imagery is bald and downright
hokey; but *Utopia*'s failure to find—and reach—an audience in New York
had more to do with the ideological climate and the artistic expectations
an audience brings to a performance than with production values.

Though reviewed generously in the *New York Times,* houses for the New
York run were miniscule. When I saw it there, the audience barely outnumbered the cast, and the "volunteers" for the lagoon sequence—who
were selected by the performers and guided to the stage—seemed grudg-
ing and embarrassed. Expressing a desire publicly—and abandoning cynicism and self-consciousness—seemed difficult for them (for us, I should
say, as I slumped in my seat trying desperately to avoid being tapped).[7]
The two who participated the night I saw the play (the company didn't
even try for a third) grasped at ready clichés, both thoroughly individualistic: one sought inner peace, the other, success.

When I saw *Utopia* the following June in a starkly different context,
however, this sequence evoked a much more buoyant response. The the-

ater was an abandoned warehouse in Mestre, Italy, a depressed, working-class industrial city outside Venice—a town whose relationship to Venice resembles, say Gary, Indiana's to Chicago. This warehouse, like boarded-up factories, schools, churches, and other derelict large buildings around Italy, had been squatted by a local group of young countercultural activists, part of a loose network of self-run *centri sociale.*

Italy's social center movement began in the mid-1970s in Milan when some local communists took over a run-down building in a poor neighborhood and transformed it into a meeting hall and performance space, offering programs in vocational training, day care, and other services not otherwise provided to the community. (A couple decades later, this center—Centro Sociale Leoncavallo—has moved several times and developed; now it comprises a disco, concert hall, skateboard ramp, several bars, and an immigrant rights program.) Leoncavallo spurred others to create some 150 similar structures all over the country, many of them initiated and vaguely overseen by punks, anarchists, communists, and ravers. Though only loosely networked and lacking any officially ratified doctrine, the *centri* are nonprofit, generally anticapitalist, available to anyone who wants to crash in them, guided by a spirit of openness.

Mestre's *centro* stood on a large, dusty lawn in a run-down residential neighborhood. In some ways, the scene resembled Woodstock. Belt-makers, weavers, T-shirt tie-dyers, cheap jewelers, and others were peddling their wares on rows of tables set up across the grounds, and abundant vegetarian food—pasta, beans, salad—was for sale at a nominal price. Scores of young men and women in dirty jeans and T-shirts, some toting guitars, some toking joints—and a few middle-aged folks—milled around for well over an hour before the Living Theatre's 10:00 P.M. curtain time. Hard-edged rock music blared out of some gravelly speakers (the cause of the local residents' chief complaint about the *centro*) and some kids of both sexes had shed their shirts to dance in the thick summer breeze.

Inside the cavernous *centro,* the Living Theatre played on a large, raised stage at one end of the hall, while the audience sat in unranked rows of folding chairs set up on the cement floor. Despite the physical remoteness between spectators and performers, they forged a more energetic connection than had been achieved in New York, where Living Theatre played in an intimate, in-the-round space. In Mestre, the volunteers for the lagoon sequence offered visions that were just as clichéd as those called out in New York, but here, they were more communally oriented: "Da mangiare per tutti!" "L'anarchismo!" "Non facciamo la guerra!" More important, young people rushed to the stage every time volunteers were invited. They were eager to enter the optimistic action and merge themselves with the performance. The audience sang and clapped along at every opportunity and stomped and shouted in a long standing ovation at the end.

The comparison to Woodstock may be too easy—also a quick latching onto an available cliché—but the palpability of a countercultural movement seemed to provide the conditions in which the Living Theatre's *Utopia* could be not only legible but meaningful. It wasn't, however, the long hair, grungy jeans, and druggy glaze of many of the kids in attendance that made the difference. Rather, their rejection of consumerism along with an abiding, if inchoate, belief that there's got to be a better way are part of the atmosphere in which the Living Theatre can breathe. The work of the Living Theatre resonates in places where people are looking for alternatives, open to simple truths, and eager for affirmation—and where the larger culture at least allows, if not supports, such exploration. If in the twenty-first century, New York theatergoers are too resigned or jaded for such earnestness, in the *centri sociale* there's no shame in seeking an alternative, no embarrassment in hoping.

The Mysteries of *Mysteries and Smaller Pieces*

In Lebanon, where the Living Theatre traveled in the summer of 2000 to conduct a ten-day workshop with local theater students, the desire for new paradigms of expression and political organization were felt even more urgently, as reactions to a performance of *Mysteries and Smaller Pieces* in Beirut revealed.

Then thirty-seven years old, the ninety-minute piece is made up of nine sections built, once upon a time, of rehearsal games and company improvisations. In one, actors demonstrate the Sound and Movement exercise (the now common warm-up game, originally devised by Viola Spolin and used by Joseph Chaikin and the Open Theater) in which actors stand in a circle, one comes to the center making a noise and an action, passes them on to another actor, who imitates and then transforms them into new sounds and movements before passing them along in turn. They pursue these exchanges with a resoluteness that suggests the gravity of play. Later, Judith Malina sits center stage in front of a candle reciting what she announces as "Street Songs" by Jackson Mac Low: "Stop the war." "Open the jails." "Abolish money." Voices from the house—some company members sprinkled in the aisles, some audience members—chime in with their own slogans. Overall, much of the performance, virtually unchanged since 1963, comes off as a musty museum display, an exhibition of a once revelatory exploration of what comprises theatrical meaning, connection, and action. But like a laboratory experiment that long ago yielded information that has been put to common use, *Mysteries* has for the most part lost its power to surprise and ignite wonder, its utility.

An exception is the playful set of living-statue poses presented by four actors. Lights pop on to show each striking a position within a framed space—each is confined to one of four linked wooden rectangles. The lights go off, then blink on again to show a new configuration of bodies in the field as in the dark, the actors have struck, and frozen in, a new pose. In 1969, Gordon Rogoff noted how the scene offers "quick studies in human variety, sharp remembrances of animal reality."[8] What's more, this whimsical exercise allows one to recognize how theater at its most basic retains a powerful narrative undertow. As each new freeze-frame finds the actors in new random physical relationships, the spectator projects an instant ministory, takes a stab at significance. The Living Theatre invites audience participation at its most fundamental and fanciful in this sequence, showing how inescapably we seek to make meaning. This impulse is tested in other sections of *Mysteries* as well. In Beirut, it was the opening and closing scenes that functioned most forcefully as a screen for local projections.

Mysteries begins with a man—usually Tom Walker, as was the case in this instance—standing stiffly erect and absolutely still downstage center. He simply stands there at attention—chin up, chest out, hands at sides. Nothing more. He's a living Rorschach, provoking a range of responses. Over the years, some audiences have regarded his passivity as a generous invitation to take part in making the drama by entering the scene and initiating action; sometimes spectators have reacted with hostility to the apparent affront to their expectation to be entertained. One of the most enduring and challenging riddles of the way this stationary actor incites spectators is whether the antagonism that is frequently unleashed against him results from the desire to make drama by making conflict or from a kind of sadistic aggression—or whether, indeed, these two impulses are linked. Performing this piece on and off for more than three decades, Walker has been prodded, poked, pushed, and punched. More than once, his pants have been yanked down to his ankles; his face spat at. He's been tied up, gagged, covered with a trash can, and carried offstage. Sometimes other spectators come to his defense; more often they simply watch. In such encounters, it's not his limits being tested and put on display, but the audience's.

In Beirut, Walker stood for a long time before anyone transgressed the performer-audience divide. Five minutes, ten, even fifteen—an eternity on stage. Walker remained motionless. During that period, a couple of people clapped, others whistled, some whispered among themselves. All became silent when a pudgy middle-aged man with a thick black moustache ascended the stage and struck the same posture as Walker, standing shoulder-to-shoulder next to him. No shoving, no animosity, no violence: He simply joined the effort, standing there as motionlessly as Walker. The audience gasped audibly and after a few seconds, applauded this gesture of solidarity, this image of quiet commonality, as if amid Lebanon's current political anxiety, camaraderie is the action most called for.

This sequence in *Mysteries* seemed to speak to the stunned stasis that people I interviewed there said had gripped their country as it frantically tries to build a future on the rubble of its violent past. Once thick with the residue of bombed buildings, Beirut's air was now heavy with construction dust. But high-rises and luxury stores were going up with little effort to preserve or restore the Ottoman and Levantine architectural gems that once made the city famous—and contributed to its lucrative tourist draw.

Nobody directly mentioned it, but the dread of another war was as glaring as the Mediterranean. Every day the papers reported on the teetering tensions among government leaders—it's mandated by law that the prime minister be a Sunni Muslim, the president a Maronite Christian, and the speaker of parliament a Shiite Muslim. There were stories, too, of little eruptions—a brawl here, a shooting there—among young men of different religious or political allegiances whose quarrels escalate. With no war tribunal or truth and reconciliation process after the war, the trauma seemed to have become a taboo subject. *Mysteries* broached it, obliquely in the opening sequence, if only in the response it evoked, and bluntly in the closing one. In this last scene, actors spend a long time—more than fifteen minutes in the Beirut performance—moaning and writhing in the aisles, and in some cases, even on top of spectators. Eventually they all make their way to the stage, where they quiver or quake and then go limp and silent.

This miming of death by plague or violence seemed abhorrent to me in the context of Beirut, not so much because of the clichéd action as because of the context: how unseemly, I thought as actors twitched and drooled, to represent mass loss of life in such a hamfisted and indulgent way for an audience that lived through a brutal, fifteen-year civil war and Israeli siege, which claimed nearly two hundred thousand lives and displaced two-thirds of the population of four million. Some spectators grew uncomfortable during the prolonged die-in. They tittered, chatted with their neighbors, and one audience member even let out a loud, histrionic yawn. But when the thrashing and squirming stopped, the tone changed utterly. A hush came over the audience as three actors began to straighten and then stack the bodies of the others into a pyramid of corpses up-center, and to place their shoes in a row along the rim of the stage. This action, too, took a long time; but now, the audience remained silent and transfixed. When the three actors finished their solemn labor, they stood looking at the audience, a sense of bereavement and disgust shadowing their accomplishment. After a few moments, the crowd leapt to its feet to applaud.

Elias Khoury, the Lebanese critic and novelist—and also the editor of the cultural supplement of a leading Beirut paper, one of the only venues to have broached such subjects as Lebanon's abiding factions and the country's domination by Syria—told me the next day how for the current climate, what matters in the Living Theatre's work "is feelings more than slogans." He singled out the closing sequence, for example, from the "Street Songs" section, which he said was "very important in the sixties when we needed to name power and oppression, but this is done and things are more complex." (Even in the sixties, though, Richard Gilman dismissed the sloganeering as "fiercely adolescent and rhetorical insurrection.")[9] Crucial nowadays, Khoury suggested, was tapping into "experiences which are not dead," and showing the "interior forces that must come out." This was precisely why Khoury supported the Living Theatre's plans to perform with the workshop students in the streets and parks of Lebanon, and especially in Khiam, the site of the notorious prison where the South Lebanon Army, Israel's proxy militia, held and tortured thousands of those who resisted the Israeli occupation of southern Lebanon. Khoury explained that the audience that had attended the Beirut performances were secular intellectuals; the rest of the population could be reached only in public spaces.

From Times Square to Tripoli: *Not in My Name*

For fifty years the Living Theatre has frequently taken to the streets as part of its long-standing experiment in breaking down the performance-reality divide and to extend the scope of its audience and of its message. The troupe famously led spectators out of the hall into the public square at the end of *Paradise Now*, urging them to free the prisoners from local jails. This gesture has been deeply criticized—even ridiculed—as naive and downright absurd.[10] However, Beck and Malina asserted that they did not literally expect that the rush of spectators would, in fact, open the jails, but that they would experience the possibility—and limitations—of their collective power. In any case, the charge into the streets marked an important shift in the Living Theatre's political aesthetic that paved the way for some of the company's most significant work and, arguably, for its most successful projects at present.

Whatever the limitations of these efforts might have been, working in the *favelas* of Brazil and among the steelworkers in Pittsburgh in the 1970s, the Living Theatre acquired a street savvy and skill level that has made their outdoor performances the most effective, technically accomplished, and influential of their recent works. Built of blunt text, unambiguous messages, and simple-to-learn and easily executed choreography, the form, of course, not only forgives, but sometimes even requires, what Malina has acknowledged as the Living Theatre's "proclivity toward rhetoric."[11]

Not in My Name (1994) is one of the best examples. Speaking out clearly and emphatically against the death penalty, the play is meant to be performed at New York's Times Square whenever someone is executed in the United States. Made up of several short sequences—Malina has noted that most spectators will watch for only a few moments before continuing on their way—it asserts that violence breeds more violence and asks passersby to consider how morally indefensible such a practice is. Like any good street theater, the play is flexible, accommodating a cast ranging in size from a handful to dozens, and employs chanting, rhythmic choral speech and movement, and other surefire attention-grabbers. In the background the company pitches a couple of banners reading "Execution Tonight" and "Abolish the Death Penalty" so that the message is unmistakable.

Lasting about fifteen minutes, *Not in My Name* comprises several key sections: the condemned person is represented in a slow-motion chase and is named and described to the audience; the cycle of vengeance is decried in a chant as the actors enact it symbolically, moving around a circle with every other actor smiting the next, then the fallen actor arising and turning on the one in front of her or him; the actors pair off to represent and comment on the murder of Abel by Cain and then regroup and strike jagged poses as the Aeschylean Furies, transformed from enraged vengeance-seekers into the court of law (though, the play notes, the court of law is itself often unjust and unmerciful). Finally, in a vow to begin with themselves to end the cycle of violence, the actors engage audience members individually saying, "I give you my word that I will never kill you. Will you promise me the same?" They close by singing a text based on lines from Eugene Debs: "While there is a lower class, I am in it . . . While there is a criminal element, I am of it. When the government metes out vengeance, it devalues human life . . . While there is a prisoner on death row, life itself is at stake."

Not in My Name could reasonably be called agitprop as it seeks to mobilize its audience to take a particular action on or view of a pressing social issue. Malina has described it as adhering to "the demonstration form."[12] That distinguishes the play from the pieces the Living Theatre creates for more formal, indoor, theatrical settings (the best of which since the Living Theatre's return to New York in the mid-1980s being, like the Living Theatre's very earliest work, the most poetic and least rhetorical—*I and I, The Tablets, Poland/1931*). Malina's designation of *Not in My Name* refers also to the obvious ways in which such work functions *as* a political demonstration, and also to its use of techniques the Living Theatre has developed for works that are performed *within* political demonstrations—such as a forty-minute piece created for protests at the G8 summit in Genoa in June 2001, which included striking processions of actors in red clothing, parading through the crowd with unison, bio-mechanically inspired movements.

As agitprop, *Not in My Name* expects to make a difference. It intends not only to provide an opening to a discussion of violence in our culture more widely, but also to promote a cause that can actually be won.[13] (Indeed, days after Lebanese theater students performed the play in Tripoli and Beirut, in conjunction with the local Movement for People's Rights, which had been lobbying and protesting on the issue in a steady yearlong campaign, Lebanon did revoke its death penalty.)

But even as the "demonstration form" of agitprop, *Not in My Name* seeks to address its audiences on other levels too. It also belongs to other rubrics for political street performance, specifically to the theater of witness, and to the theater of integration. The former, Jan Cohen-Cruz writes, "uses heightened means to direct attention onto actions of social magnitude" and "supposes a connection between knowledge and responsibility."[14] Such work brings injustices into view, fulfilling theater's role as a place for seeing, even if it cannot act directly on righting those injustices. Specifying and representing the person slated for execution the day of the performance pushes the work into this category, as no one supposes that the play will help win any last-minute clemency. Indeed, in this respect *Not in My Name* critically inverts the state practice of allowing relatives of a murderer's victims and other select people to watch the execution itself—a witnessing claimed to help the viewers achieve "closure," a euphemism for retribution. In contrast, *Not in My Name* invites a random public to watch a critique played around the image of a condemned person as a means of opening up a debate.

In opening that conversation directly, *Not in My Name* also functions as theater of integration, which "abandon[s] formal separation of actors and spectators and insert[s] performance into everyday life."[15] Malina has said that the goal of the piece is "to diminish the difference between public and private utterance, between what I would say to you in our most private moment and what I would say in public. I say to diminish it, because of course this difference exists, but the goal is to overcome it."[16] That effort is greatest in the play's climax, when actors speak quietly to individual spectators and ask them to agree to the pact not to kill each other. When the actors return to the formal text of the play, they explain, "I will never be an executioner / Because I have vowed not to kill you. I will never fire into a crowd / Because I have vowed not to kill you. I will never bomb a city / Because I have vowed not to kill you." Each "because" phrase is stated quietly to the individual with whom the actor has made a pact; the alternating phrases are proclaimed chorally.

The exchange is a far cry from the infamous *Paradise Now* hectoring of audience members over the requirement that travelers carry passports, and from the actors' effort back then not to engage, but assiduously to avoid, any genuine dialogue with the spectators. In *Not in My Name* the company does not express hostility or impatience with the spectators, but invites the conversation to continue after the play. Amid the countless glittering distractions of Times Square, where I've seen the piece several times, responses range widely. Typically, passersby glance, maybe take in a bit of the action, but don't break their strides. Some stick around for a few minutes and then walk away. A few watch to the end. When approached by an actor for the one-on-one exchange, some grant the promise easily, some tell the actors to fuck off, some stay silent or titter in apparent embarrassment. Few linger for conversation afterward.

In the northern coastal city of Tripoli, Lebanon, however, where *Not in My Name* was, by all accounts, the first outdoor political theater ever presented, the public was enthralled. Some seven hundred people surrounded the playing area in Tripoli's downtown park, among the first row, police guards with automatic rifles. Though the municipality unplugged the sound system as soon as officials understood the play's message, the audience simply leaned in to listen more carefully. Spectators stayed to debate the death penalty with the performers for more than half an hour afterward.

The Road to Khiam:
A Narrative of the Living Theatre in Action

Many of the forty Lebanese university students who opted to take part in the Living Theatre workshops—learning, rehearsing, and performing *Not in My Name* and collectively creating and then presenting a piece for Khiam—have heard about the Living Theatre in their theater survey courses, but know little more about the troupe than that they are political and important.[17] Sophisticated, urbane, multilingual, they say they are drawn to the theater because its form offers a complex but direct, emotional way to break through the anxious factionalism and frozen feelings that, they fear, might hurl the country back into a violent free-for-all.

Working in the stone courtyard of Tripoli's arts center, the Beit el Fan, the students strike a quick affinity with the twelve Living Theatre members leading the workshop—Americans, Italians, Germans, and a Bulgarian. On the first day, Malina and codirector Hanon Reznikov offer rousing introductions about the power of theater, and soon the group is twisting, bending, stretching, crawling through a wordless physical warm-up. With their pierced noses and Nike T-shirts, they could pass for theater students from New York University.

The plan—concocted by Habibah Sheikh, a Lebanese-American singer currently living in Beirut who invited the Living Theatre and organized the project—is for the Living Theatre to teach the students a range of movement, voice, and play-development exercises through rehearsing *Not in My Name* for performance in Tripoli and Khiam.

Quickly, though, the easy sense of commonality begins to come unglued as the students mull over the itinerary, and their resemblance to NYU counterparts breaks down completely. They wonder: Can a Western—in fact, American—radical aesthetic practice be transferred whole to the Middle East? Does the Living Theatre really share the students' politics, and how could they since there are significant differences of opinion among the students themselves—who are Sunni, Shiite, Maronite, Druse, Palestinian, secular, leftist, not-quite Communist, vaguely liberal, environmentalist, apolitical. Why does the Living Theatre think they should do a play about the death penalty in Khiam? Do they even know what Khiam is? The students demand the first of what turn out to be daily group political discussions.

For ninety minutes, they explain the horror of Khiam, where fighters against Israeli occupation, as well as their relatives, neighbors, and many other innocent bystanders, were detained and tortured, mostly by troops in the South Lebanese Army, Israel's proxy militia. The Living Theatre doesn't argue, but suggests that they go ahead and prepare *Not in My Name* for Tripoli, and develop a separate piece for Khiam. And the students turn to debating the harder question: What, then, ought they say in Khiam?

"We shouldn't just say there was suffering there and then they were liberated. Everybody knows that. We have to say the *next* thing." "We should thank the people who fought and survived there. They did it so that we all could be liberated." "We should show how badly the prisoners are being treated now, a year after they have gotten out, and can't find jobs and don't have any support. They were celebrated as heroes and then forgotten." "Are we talking about a human cause or just a Lebanese cause? Shouldn't we object to all torture?" "No. Not a general humanistic message—but not the opposite, either. Our people have been treated like animals and we can't disconnect ourselves from what is happening in Palestine every day. We have to keep it specific." "We should imagine and express what the prisoners who died there never had a chance to say." "We should try to understand why the traitors tortured their own people." "We should give the people in the south some hope." "Yes. But let's not be sentimental." "It has to be poetry."

Reznikov takes notes, drawing out general themes around which small groups will develop short scenes. They'll rehearse *Not in My Name* in the first half of the day, and work on the new piece in the second.

The students are stunned—and fired up. "The Living Theatre was so open and willing to learn from us," says twenty-two-year-old Saseen Kawzally, in his perpetual posture—pitched forward to make a point. "This is so significant. The West is usually patronizing to the Arab world and trying to take us to our knees. Yet here was a famous theatrical group from America actually treating us as equals. This should be a model."

But Kawzally is one of the students who is strangely absent from rehearsal two days later—a day before the performance scheduled for Tripoli. Indeed, about a third of the group just hasn't shown up. It turns out they had spent the entire day—and the full night before—continuing to debate the project and its political significance. The next day they come to rehearsal with a prepared statement explaining why they can't carry on. The Living Theatre's commitment to pacifism has become more and more clear as their work has continued and the centrality of nonviolence to *Not in My Name* makes it impossible for them to perform it with conviction. They don't want to be misunderstood as not fully supporting the resistance in the south, which had, of course, used violence to drive Israel out.

So some lines are reassigned, some staging reblocked, and *Not in My Name* goes on in the park with a smaller cast. The Living Theatre bids farewell to the students who abandon the project with warm thanks and respect. They understand very well the problem of association. Indeed, they hold their own intense political meeting when they learn that the Khiam play will be subjected to censorship. It makes them squirm to think that they have to be declared kosher by Hizbullah.

"Why are we going there at all?" "Are we being hosted by murderers?" "Are we legitimating them?" "They don't need us to legitimate them. They've got a dozen seats in parliament and are totally accepted in the

The Living Theatre and Lebanese students performing in front of Khiam Prison, Beirut, Lebanon, 2000. (Photo by Alisa Solomon.)

Arab world." "We went to Milošević's Belgrade. And we went there to object to the violence, the same as here. I'll go and say 'peace' anywhere." "As a German I just don't want to be linked to a regime that wants to destroy the Jewish state." "But it's okay to be linked to a regime that destroys the Bosnian Muslims?" "You know, very few of the people who ever invited us anywhere were pacifist-anarchists."

The censorship turns out to be a good joke: Hizbullah insists on seeing a pre-performance run-through at Khiam—and two hundred spectators gather to watch. Hizbullah's skinny gray-suited apparatchik has one demand: when the group presents the piece again, one of the women needs to be careful when she lifts her hands over her head, because her shirt hikes up and her midriff shows.

There are some arresting images in the piece. A woman, stiff, carried overhead by a group of pallbearers, lists the ordinary things of life that pass through her mind: mother, poem, thirsty, kibbe. A man's hands are bound, then his legs, then his face, as he rhythmically vows, "I will resist." The truth is, though, that the piece doesn't really say much more than, they suffered and were liberated.

The students—including some who had left over the ideological difference, but came to see the performance—launch into a spirited critical debate on the ride back north. "It's too direct, too simple. Even naive." "No, it touches the heart. You shouldn't be so overintellectual. This is theater." "Those women from the village were crying. I think it really meant something to them." "I'm proud of it. But I think it could be deeper." "Right. It's too easy. It doesn't provoke questions. As the new generation we should be provoking questions." "As *artists* it's our job to provoke questions." The van turns onto Beirut's wide corniche along the sea and trundles north, carrying the Living Theater's legacy with it.

NOTES

1. See, for instance, Allan Bloom, *The Closing of the American Mind* (New York: Simon and Schuster, 1987); Dinesh D'Souza, *Illiberal Education: The Politics of Race and Sex on Campus* (New York: Vintage, 1992); and Roger Kimball, *Tenured Radicals: How Politics Has Corrupted Our Higher Education* (Chicago: Elephant Paperbacks, 1995). For a useful rejoinder, see, for example, *The 60s Without Apology*, ed. S. Sayres, A. Stephanson, S. Aronowitz, and F. Jameson (New York: Social Text, 1984).

2. Ben Brantley, Fall Listings, *New York Times*, September 19, 1994; Benedict Nightingale, review of *The Diaries of Judith Malina*, *New York Times*, August 12, 1984.

3. Arthur Sainer, *The Radical Theatre Notebook* (New York: Avon, 1975), 12.

4. Hanon Reznikov, "Sketches: Utopia," *Theatre* 26, nos. 1–2 (1995): 75.

5. Judith Malina, "Notes for the Utopia Play," *Theatre* 26, nos. 1–2 (1995): 72.

6. Living Theatre, *Utopia*, www.livingtheatre.org/utop/script.html (1995).

7. At the New York performance, my sympathy for the company's strained efforts to find volunteers in a small audience overcame my temperamental antipathy to audience participation, and I offered my services when spectators were invited to rehearse a scene during the intermission. I played Hermione in the enactment of the scene from *The Winter's Tale* and was surprised by how exhilarating the experience was.

8. Gordon Rogoff, *Theatre is not Safe* (Evanston, Ill.: Northwestern University Press, 1987), 122.

9. Richard Gilman, *The Confusion of Realms* (New York: Vintage, 1970), 262.

10. Robert Brustein, *Making Scenes: A Personal History of the Turbulent Years at Yale, 1966–1979* (New York: Limelight, 1984), 64–70; Gilman, *The Confusion of Realms*, 258–62.

11. Judith Malina, "What Do We Want to Achieve? A Conversation among Judith Malina, Hanon Reznikov, and Tameron Josbeck," *Theatre* 31, no. 3 (2001): 159.

12. Cindy Rosenthal, "Living on the Street: Conversations with Judith Malina and Hanon Reznikov, Co-Directors of the Living Theatre," in *Radical Street Performance: An International Anthology*, ed. Jan Cohen-Cruz (New York: Routledge, 1998), 154.

13. Rosenthal, "Living on the Street"; Malina, "What Do We Want to Achieve?"

14. Jan Cohen-Cruz, *Radical Street Performance*, 65.
15. Ibid., 119.
16. Rosenthal, "Living on the Street," 152.
17. This section originally appeared in the *Village Voice* on July 24, 2001, as "On the Road in Lebanon."

THE OPEN THEATRE
Historical Overview

More than any other group in this anthology, the Open Theatre was committed to investigating the acting process and to developing exercises and techniques that would generate performances characterized by vivid intensity and rapid transformations. This focus on the "behind the scenes" work of the actor in an environment of openness and receptivity to question and change was integral to the artistic vision of the group's central director, Joseph Chaikin, and it created a setting particularly conducive to collaboration between actors, directors, playwrights, and critics. Their collective efforts during the Open Theatre's ten-year existence (1963–73) led to four major productions.

When Chaikin helped to found the Open Theatre in 1963, he had already been a member of the Living Theatre for four years, having worked on their landmark production of Jack Gelber's *The Connection* (1953). He began as the understudy for the lead role, which he eventually played. An important transformation in Chaikin's own life in the theater occurred while he was playing Galy Gay in the Living Theatre's production of Bertolt Brecht's *Mann ist Mann* (1962). In this role Chaikin grappled with questions about the direct connections between actors and characters, and actors and audiences.[1] These questions combined with the genuine inspiration that Chaikin drew both from Brecht's political theater and from Julian Beck's and Judith Malina's commitment to activism, and led him to seek alternatives to mainstream, commercial theater. With actors from the Living Theatre and elsewhere, Chaikin took classes with teacher Nola Chilton on nonnaturalistic acting techniques. When Chilton left for

Israel, the workshops continued with Chaikin at the helm. These work-shops served as the foundation for what in 1963 became the Open The-atre. Initially, the Open consisted of seventeen actors and four writers, the latter being Megan Terry, Jean-Claude van Itallie, Irene Fornes, and Michael Smith. Richard Gilman, Gordon Rogoff, and Susan Sontag were critics connected to the workshop project during this period.

While the Open Theatre's basic commitments to collective creation and to ensemble-building invite comparisons with the Living Theatre, the differences between the two were significant. Unlike the Living Theatre, which, while touring Europe between 1964 and 1968, collectively created four new pieces without the participation of playwrights, Chaikin believed that playwrights played an essential role in the processes of collective cre-ation (he once described that role as a necessary "tyranny"). With regard to ensemble building, the differences were equally profound. Like the Liv-ing Theatre, the Open Theatre toured Europe extensively, but, unlike the Living, its members never lived communally. Instead, they came together to explore and transform a working process: "it was purely professional in a very good way," stated Open Theatre actor-director Peter Feldman.[2]

Chaikin encountered Viola Spolin's theater games (see her *Improvisation for the Theatre*, 1963), including the now ubiquitous Sound and Movement exercise when he worked with Second City in Chicago.[3] Spolin's work was the initial grounding for the kind of transformation-filled Open Theatre group "playing" that evolved into such productions at the Sheridan Square Playhouse as Terry's *Calm Down Mother* and *Keep Tightly Closed in Cool Dry Place*. Along with Fornes's *The Successful Life of Three* (Sheridan Square Play-house) and van Itallie's *America Hurrah* (at Café La Mama), these works were part of the group's first season of performances (1964–65).

During 1965–66 in workshops led by Megan Terry, the company ex-amined the Vietnam War, drawing on newspaper clippings, television, and eyewitness accounts. *Viet Rock*, the first full-length play developed out of transformation exercises, directed by Chaikin and assisted by Peter Feldman, was a commercial and critical success when it opened in May 1966 at Café La Mama. The company performed the work without sets and props and wore their own clothing. This was the only Open Theatre performance in which the company made direct contact with the audi-ence, engaging in what became known by the group as a "celebration of presence."[4] A second off-Broadway production of *Viet Rock* that opened in the fall of 1966 under Terry's direction was less critically successful.

In their workshops, the Open Theatre drew upon a wide variety of cul-tural and intellectual sources. Most significant perhaps was the work that the group did in late 1967 with the celebrated Polish director and theorist Jerzy Grotowski. Like Grotowski and his principal actor, Ryszard Cies-lak, Chaikin and the Open Theatre actors were dedicated to developing a regimen of exercises that strengthened the actor's physical and vocal instrument. At the same time that they focused on rigorous physical training, the workshops also sought inspiration in intellectual sources outside of the theater, most notably in the work of R. D. Laing, Herbert Marcuse, and Joseph Campbell. In fact, Campbell gave talks to the Open Theatre during fall 1967 when Chaikin began a workshop with the company on the Bible. In that workshop, the group experimented with a number of improvisations based upon the Book of Genesis. Jean-Claude van Itallie structured these explorative improvisations into the company's first major work, *The Serpent,* which premiered in Rome in May 1968.

Following *The Serpent,* the Open Theatre began exploring the subject of death and dying. These explorations were in part an extension of a concern with (his own) mortality that Chaikin had had since being seriously ill as a child, and they led to the second major performance work of the Open Theatre, *Terminal.* Susan Yankowitz was the playwright for this piece, and Roberta Sklar was Chaikin's codirector. *Terminal* opened in Bordeaux, France, in November 1969 at the beginning of the Open Theatre's second European tour. After returning to New York the group began to perform *Terminal* and other works in prisons, a practice that continued for the rest of the company's history.[5]

In fall 1970, Chaikin began streamlining the company, reducing it from the original group of eighteen that had created and performed *Terminal* to a core of six actors. He maintained this tightened and simplified structure until the end. Some of the departing actors formed a new company, the Medicine Show.[6] The remaining actors included Tina Shepherd, Paul Zimet, Tom Lillard, Shami Chaikin, Raymond Barry, and Jo Ann Schmidman. They first reworked *Terminal* with Chaikin and Sklar, and then were joined by the musician Ellen Maddow for the third major Open Theatre production, *The Mutation Show,* which premiered in 1971 in New York and was codirected by Sklar and Chaikin. This performance evolved out of workshops exploring the theme of social mutation—how and why do people adapt themselves to circumstances that ultimately transform them into mutants or freaks? The music in *Terminal* was created improvisationally; sounds and percussion were produced via the actors' bodies and voices, although the performers also played instruments, including flutes, accordions, and an assortment of homemade varieties.[7]

Chaikin's unusual and seminal acting text, *The Presence of the Actor,* was published in 1972 around the time that the company began work on its final major performance, *Nightwalk,* which investigated sleep, consciousness, presence and absence. The piece involved the collaboration of writers van Itallie, Terry, and Sam Shepard as well as dramaturg Mira Rafalowicz, and it premiered in March 1973 in New York. With the production of *Nightwalk,* Chaikin decided that the group had basically run its course, and he chose to disband the company before it shifted into an institution or a production company.[8] The beginning of the end was the Open Theatre's fifth and final tour outside the United States, during which the group performed *The Mutation Show* and *Nightwalk.* The Open Theatre disbanded at the beginning of December 1973 after a final performance of *Nightwalk* at the University of California, Santa Barbara.

—C. R.

NOTES

1. Robert Pasolli, *A Book on the Open Theatre* (New York: Avon, 1970), xiii–xv.

2. Roger Copeland, "Remembering the Real Open Theatre," *New York Times,* December 25, 1983, 11.

3. Pasolli, *Open Theatre,* 16.

4. Theodore Shank, *Beyond the Boundaries: American Alternative Theatre* (Ann Arbor: University of Michigan Press, 2002), 39.

5. Eileen Blumenthal, *Joseph Chaikin: Exploring at the Boundaries of Theatre* (New York: Cambridge University Press, 1984), 218.

6. Ibïd., 22.

7. Shank, *Beyond the Boundaries,* 44.

8. Blumenthal, *Joseph Chaikin,* 25.

AFTER PARADISE

The Open Theatre's The Serpent, Terminal, and The Mutation Show

Carol Martin

Joseph Chaikin (1935–2003) liked the name *Open Theatre* for the group he led "because it was an unconfining name, it implied a predilection for change. The name would serve to remind us of that early commitment to stay in process, and we called ourselves that."[1] "Open" meant open to theatrical discovery and the change that discovery might generate, even if it meant the dissolution of the company. "Open" also conferred on the group a radical 1960s identity. The name aligned the Open Theatre with its progenitor, the Living Theatre (which began performing in 1951), while departing from what began to seem like the Living Theatre's overly determined anarchistic perspectives. (It is often forgotten that the anarchism to which the Living Theatre was devoted was a political movement.) Like the Living Theatre, the Open Theatre was created around the idea of freedom: freedom from institutional governance, freedom from a fixed style and approach to theater, and freedom from critical determinations apart from the intentions of the company. Unlike the Living Theatre's more pointed political goals, the Open Theatre's radicalism was in their alignment with a nonnaturalistic approach to text, acting, staging, and costumes, in the relationship between actors and spectators, and in the way they created their work. The Open Theatre sought truth about human hierarchies, relationships, and power and new ways of theatrically expressing ideas, character, and narrative. The group's defining condition for existence, remaining receptive to change, was what it most celebrated and, ultimately, what led to dissolution. Although the Open was a group theater with a collective process, decision making was finally Chaikin's domain. This created problems about who owned the work and a sense of disappointment about inclusion and exclusion when a work was finally set.

As with other group theaters of this period, the Open Theatre existed within the context of the social and political watersheds of the times: the utopian ideals of the 1960s coupled with the dystopia of the Vietnam War—the first war to assail the idea of military heroism with televised images of what war really looks like—widespread student unrest, the ongoing fight for racial equality, feminism, and the assassinations of John F. Kennedy and Martin Luther King Jr., both of whom stood for, in very different ways, a new world order.

In this context what could the 1960s slogan "Make love, not war" mean? Some who used the slogan might have advocated the avoidance of political action in favor of sexual hedonism. For others it characterized a dramatic divide about the future of the country in the form of a rejection of the "death industry" of the Vietnam War and the military-industrial complex that sponsored that war. The slogan pitted celebratory life-sustaining youth culture against the death business of the older generations. The open call for lovemaking mocked an older generation that was perceived as impotently leading the nation down the wrong path. There was another way: sexual freedom could be imagined as a different kind of political potency. There were many who while protesting the war from the safe environment of home were also willing to put themselves on the line—for civil rights and for feminism: for race and gender equality. Many college students burned their draft cards or even gave up their citizenship in order to oppose the military draft. "Make love, not war" formulated an alternative social reality, a society founded on social welfare, pleasure, peace, and life-giving actions rather than on military force. As things worked out, the antiwar movement was able to stop the Vietnam War but not able to end the U.S. addiction to enormous military expenditures or interventionist military policies. "Make love, not war," signaled a utopian desire for a different reality, a different vision of humanity. Indeed, such a reality was a new paradise, a second Garden of Eden, even though many did not believe such a reality could exist. Much of the Open Theatre's works explore the fissure between a paradise lost and the reality of violence, both personal and social, that characterizes American life.

How did members of the Open Theatre collectively define political activism?—they didn't—at least not directly. Chaikin internalized some of the Living Theatre's deep political dissatisfaction with society. His response to this dissatisfaction was to develop ways in which the actor might "give testimony to other kinds of experiences and conditions."[2] These other kinds of experiences and conditions existed in the gap between what was officially socially and politically acknowledged and what was experientially understood as true. In *The Presence of the Actor* Chaikin described acting as "a way of making testimony to what we have witnessed—a declaration of what we know and what we can imagine."[3] Chaikin's goal was to create techniques for a physical and vocal theatrical expression capable of conveying a different realm of content; one that could speak to what people knew but were forbidden to say.

For members of the Open, theater was the means for both a critical vision of the world and a proposal for different possibilities. In this sense, the Open Theatre was America's first truly "alternative theater." Those who worked with the company were focused on a working process that enabled access to what was not yet known: not yet able to be spoken or enacted theatrically. The extreme difficulty, not to say incongruity, of creating a means of expression for what could not yet be expressed kept the Open Theatre inventing, trying on, and then discarding theatrical improvisations and prototypes for scenes. In their capacity as directors, actors, playwrights, and dramaturgs, they tried and threw away thousands of ideas over the ten years of the company's existence.[4]

The aim and process of the Open Theatre's work questioned progressive utopian sensibility, the institutionalization of life and death, and the possibility of individualism in a world where people are ripped from nature and imprisoned in social structures. *The Serpent* (1967), *Terminal* (1969), and *The Mutation Show* (1971) are especially compelling to consider in this regard.[5] *The Serpent* interrogates the ruling myths of our lives; *Terminal* interviews the dead to portray the institutionalization of life, and *The Mutation Show* cross-examines survival itself in order to show alternative possibilities for human behavior.

In *The Serpent* (1967), a work partly based on the Book of Genesis, there is no celebration of an imagined utopia. *The Serpent* proposes that Adam and Eve's fall from grace—if this is the appropriate description—gave humans the ability to contemplate the idea of God in their own image: an elaborate reflection on imperfection. Paradise was a world that preceded values, judgments, knowing. In the Open Theatre's Garden of Eden there was no loss, no sadness, no happiness—the consciousness necessary for recognizing these feelings did not yet exist. Not that consciousness was not important. "Consciousness" was a 1960s buzzword. Among many things, it meant knowing one's self, one's family and society; it meant knowing about one's sexuality, sexism, and racism; it meant knowing the truth about the American government; and it meant creating art that could speak new ideologies and enact new aesthetics.

The company explored the state of being before knowledge both by consulting experts and through their own research. Joseph Campbell visited and discussed myths as structures of the psyche and the world, and ritual as the vehicle enabling human participation in mythic stories.[6] Campbell proposed that the condition of paradise was one without binary distinctions. Paradise was "timeless, deathless, passionless, (desireless), egoless" until, of course, the serpent divided these unities into their opposites.[7] Finite and infinite, passionate and passionless, greedy and generous, good and evil, man and woman, and suffering and joy emerged to define one another.[8] When Susan Sontag spoke to the Open Theatre, she explained that the multiple creation stories in Genesis were the result of the Old Testament's different cultural sources. Sontag emphasized that because these stories were written in different time periods, they did not make a single seamless unity but a layered compilation of competing narratives.[9]

In November 1967 Jerzy Grotowski spoke to the Open Theatre, with Jean-Claude van Itallie translating.[10] Grotowski discussed physical exercises as a means for actors to connect action to deeper impulses and to the actor's intimate self. Grotowski worked with Paul Zimet on getting his voice to resonate from his back. The actor Ryszard Cieslak accompanied Grotowski to the Open Theatre loft and demonstrated Grotowski's psychophysical training.[11] Although Chaikin and his colleagues were very impressed, the "Grotowski method" did not much influence their course of research. By the time of Grotowski's visit, Chaikin had already set his course. He and Grotowski greatly admired each other; both were committed to acting that was not self-indulgent. But their methods and results were very different. Codirector Roberta Sklar describes the Open Theatre's working process as fluid, a condition that generated much dispute about the ownership of the work.[12] "You have a theme, an issue, an improvisational structure. Improvisational structures were open to everyone to enter and leave within the rules. Generally, these improvisational structures came from the directors. I might have participated sometimes and contributed something like a sound or an image. We moved toward making a work from all this data. The directors chose things, but so did the playwrights. Writing was a fluid process."[13]

The idea for *The Serpent* came from Chaikin's interest in imagery that conveyed the shaping of contemporary Western religious and social values, values he wanted to question.[14] His interest quickly migrated to the ways in which origin stories informed contemporary life—an apt subject for an ensemble creating the conditions for its own existence. In a series of exercises, the company explored the Garden of Eden, the first man, the first woman, the first discovery of sex, the first murder, and the path of these religious and mythical occurrences through the lives of actors and, by extension, through the lives of spectators.[15] "What is the Garden of Eden right now? What is our Garden of Eden?" members of the ensemble asked, without providing definitive answers. For some of the actors their Garden of Eden, for the duration of making the performance, was their workshop where they came together in a loft for four hours every day for many months.

In the group's workshops during this period, the personal self and the world were sutured to associate the biblical expulsion from the Garden of Eden with contemporary violence to humans and the environment.[16] Newly emerged after biting the apple were the watchman, the seer, the shaman, the protector: the new cops of a different world. Human beings were no longer innocent; they were responsible for their actions; they knew what they were doing; they were ashamed; they committed murder as graphically depicted by Cain's murder of Abel. The actor-generated exercises and improvisations were squarely situated within the idea that exploring the personal was integral to exploring the politics of theatrical and social worlds:

> The stage is totally empty. The action is to appreciate its emptiness . . . , then to project on it the image of your garden. One actor will get up and do his garden and if another actor is sensitive to it, he will join him so that they make a little world. A third actor may or may not join—depending on whether this garden does or does not signal anybody, give them something they can identify with and understand. Then it's over and someone else tries it. Soon somebody will start a world with its own logic, its own rules, and its own sense of things. Then we have the garden. Ah, but it's so delicate, the process.[17]

The company created their garden in the exhilaration of an exceptional physical and aural theatrical language; it was the answer to the problem of finding unique ways to say with theater what could not be said with words alone. The enclosure of the workshop-rehearsal space, even with the inevitable aesthetic and personal problems such a hermetic time-space created, was paradisically relative to ordinary life. The workshop was a place where risk-taking to express what was previously only imagined was encouraged.

The Serpent revealed a human condition that was not only flawed but

criminal. Paradise was transformed first by Adam's and Eve's shame and
lying, and then by the murder of Cain by Abel. As with orthodox Hebraeo-
Christian interpretations of the Eden story, an "original sin" stained all of
human life thereafter. In the Open Theatre's windowless black loft, they
created their garden and destroyed it over and over. Though their work critiqued the world around them, it was also an intensely personal experience. Making theater changed their lives without changing the world.[18]
The importance of the relationship between the personal and the political
would eventually alter Chaikin and Sklar's relationship. For all the forms of
oppression the Open Theatre explored, the condition of women as inher-
itors of a sexist world where their labor was not equally compensated and
their consciousness not equally valued was not to be among them.

The Serpent begins with an autopsy. A body has suffered a gunshot
wound. The Doctor explains:

> In gunshot wounds
> Infection ensues
> Unless an operation
> Is undertaken immediately . . .
> If the patient survives
> He may live for weeks
> Or months
> Or years . . .
> But there is no measure
> To what degree
> The mind imagines, receives, or dreams.[19]

The Doctor's account reverberates with God's curse after Adam and Eve
ate of the forbidden Tree of Knowledge:

> Now shall come a separation
> Between the dreams inside your head
> And those things which you believe
> To be outside your head
> And the two shall war within you.[20]

The garden will be eternally imagined and forever dying; each plant, each
creature in its own manner. The autopsy reveals that the death at hand
has been a violent one, and the Doctor's ritualized professional description of the corpse in front of him anticipates another past killing. The
staging of the murdered corpse before the Doctor on a table formed by

the backs of three actors on their knees is echoed later in *The Serpent* when Cain lays Abel's corpse on the backs of two actors playing Abel's sheep. Myth collapses time.

The stage time of *The Serpent* is *both* then and now—and more, a time suspended between then and now.

> I no longer live in the beginning.
> I've lost the beginning.
> I'm in the middle,
> Knowing.
> Neither the end,
> Nor the beginning.
> I'm in the middle.
> Coming from the beginning.
> And going toward the end.[21]

With the help of playwright Jean-Claude van Itallie, the expulsion from the garden was prefaced with the assassinations of John F. Kennedy and Martin Luther King.[22] In seeming time-lapse footage the actors physically imitated frames from the Abraham Zapruder film of the Kennedy assassination in all its details.[23] They reenact the crowds in Dallas, the assassin, and the presidential party in Kennedy's car in a precise twelve-count movement sequence. The actors performed the Kennedy assassination forward, backward, and then forward again, replicating the image-gone-mad ritual of the media replay of the shooting:

1: All four wave.
2: President is shot in the neck.
3: Governor is shot in the shoulder.
4: President is shot in the head. Governor's wife pulls her husband down and covers him with her body.
5: President falls against his wife.
6. President's wife begins to register something is wrong. She looks at her husband.
7. She puts her hands on his head.
8. She lifts her knee to put his head on it.
9. She looks into the front seat.
10: She begins to realize horror.
11: She starts to get up.
12: She begins to crawl out the back of the open car, and to reach out her hand.[24]

Seen through the lens of the Zapruder film, the Garden of Eden becomes its opposite, not only measuring our distance from perfection, but also repudiating the very idea of utopia. Yet paradise remains a myth important to our lives. But the Open Theatre's prescient piece warned that imagining Eden could be both compelling and dangerous. On April 14, 1968, less than a month before *The Serpent* premiered at Rome's Teatro delle Arti, Martin Luther King Jr. was murdered.

In *The Serpent* the stunning actor Paul Zimet paraphrases King's "I have a dream" speech:

Though we stand in life at midnight
I have a dream.
He's allowed me
To go to the mountain top
And I've looked over.
I've seen the promised land.
I have a dream
That we are, as always,
On the threshold of a new dawn,
And we shall see it together[25]

And then King too is shot. Both assassinations are then simultaneously replayed backwards and forwards, side by side, again and again as a chorus of actors repeats:

I mind my own affairs.
I am a little man.
I lead a private life.
I stay alive.

I'm no assassin.
I'm no president.
I don't know who did the killing.
I stay alive.

I keep out of big affairs.
I am not a violent man.
I am very sorry, still
I stay alive.[26]

Violence is endemic to daily life; sometimes it takes our attention, sometimes we ignore it as best we can. Mostly we protect only our private selves.

In *The Serpent,* the garden scene follows the loss of King's promised land. A sinuous five-actor tongue-flicking snake that is simultaneously Edenic apple tree and the Serpent who lives in it asks Eve, "Is it true you and Adam can do anything you want to do?" Eve replies, "We may do anything, Except one thing."[27] The flirtatious Serpent asks what that one thing might be, knowing all too well what it is. His question seduces Eve away from her resolution to obey God's command not to eat of the Tree of Knowledge, not even to touch it. (Nothing is mentioned concerning the Tree of Life, the other forbidden fruit in the Garden.) The Serpent tells Eve that all the things in the garden were once only imagined, proposing that if she eats, she too may well be able to imagine things into existence. Enticing Eve with the idea of imagination and knowledge, the Serpent gets Eve to equivocate, "I might. I might do it, I might do it if God didn't know."[28] Playing with Eve's logic, the Serpent asks her if a crime is only a crime when one is caught. Cleverly Eve momentarily outwits the Serpent by answering, "Shall I do what I want to then?"[29] The Serpent answers resoundingly, "Yes," but Eve outsmarts him by replying, "Even if what I want is to listen to God and not to you?" The Serpent consents, leaving Eve no choice but to choose the illusion of free will: "Then I will eat. Because I want to."[30]

The thirteen sections of the play—"The Doctor," "Kennedy-King Assassination," "The Garden," "Eve and the Serpent," "Eating the Apple," "The Curses," "Statements I," "Cain and Abel," "Blind Men's Hell," "Statements II," "Begatting," "Old People," "The Song"—add up to telling the audience that there are no new stories, that humanity repeats its own story again and again. This is what myth is—an archetypical repetition. The nine months of *The Serpent* workshops were guided by two questions: What are the myths that rule our lives? What are the myths that matter to us personally? "*Questions* was Chaikin's key word," recounts van Itallie. "We were engaged in refining and dramatizing questions."[31] To move from shared to personal myths, van Itallie and Sklar, who joined the work on *The Serpent* at about the same time, interviewed four actors about their personal experiences and then incorporated parts of these experiences into what would become the chorus of four women with their halting myths:

I went to a dinner.
The guests were pleasant.
We were poised,
Smiling over our plates,
Asking and answering the usual questions.
I wanted to throw the food,

Ax the table,
Scratch the women's faces,
And grab the men's balls.[32]

The same chorus of women narrates the story of Cain and Abel, "Statements," and "Begatting." They daven (a specific rhythmic movement while reciting prescribed prayers in the Jewish faith) throughout the second part of the performance as if their words were a prayer they needed to mark with a special ritual.

These narratives are remarkable for their nascent consciousness-raising impulse—an impulse that would finally not be fully embraced by the Open Theatre. As Sklar remembers,

> Members of the Open Theatre were against the Vietnam War and all sorts of domination. But they [the male members of the group] were not ready to see themselves in the category of dominators. The Serpent offers the apple to Eve; she takes it and poisons the world. We followed the Bible. Certain members of the group did not see Eve's gesture as a female action, but a human action. This is because there was no gender analysis. The Open Theatre was uncomfortable with the idea of gender and feminism. Frankly, there was a lack of understanding.[33]

In the final two sections of the play, "Old People" and "The Song," the actors transform from a line of old people facing the audience to a "slow kind of dying," to ghosts, and finally, to themselves as they walk through the theater while singing, not without a twinge of irony, "Moonlight Bay," a sentimental song about peacefully sailing across a moonlit water.[34]

The Serpent ends with a heap of broken images. The actors are neither living nor dead. Each has a small physical tremor as if shaking off the play and implicitly asserting that old forms, old rituals, old myths still preoccupy us in ways that need shedding. *The Serpent's* indictment of myth was also a critique of the 1960s counterculture. The myth of the Garden of Eden has helped create the dystopia of the present. "We were not thinking about critiquing utopia," remembers Zimet, "but about violence and the roots of where we are now."[35] Yet the Open Theatre was part of the very culture their work critiqued; they offered no other possibilities except for theater itself.[36] According to Zimet, "Utopia was gone, but the work itself was a kind of utopia. But we didn't believe we could sustain this outside the work."[37] Theater was seemingly the place where authenticity, independence, difference, and revolution had a home, and the idea of a utopia both was alive and murdered.[38] Zimet's view of the work was not shared by everyone. The Open Theatre would not be able to accommodate the tide of feminism as part of its political perspective. While some members did draft counseling when the Open performed on college campuses, the reaction to the abortion outreach that Sklar and Tina Shepard started doing generated a lot of tension. "Would it interfere with rehearsal time? Would it alienate the audience? etc. Unbelievable."[39]

With their next work, *Terminal* (1969), the Open Theatre explored the ways in which the institutionalization of death—the loss of physical functions, and the artificial preservation of the body through embalming—presses against and infects personal identity: society's literal and metaphorical attempts to ritualize the institutional governance of living, dying, and the dead. The actors wore black tape over an eye, a mouth, graphically portraying not only the loss of physical functions but also implying censorship of individual identity: the "real" relationship of the personal to the political is the suppression of the individual in favor of the secular rituals of institutions. *Terminal* is not a work about lament, about coming to terms with death, or about the cruel implacability of the living. *Terminal* is about the living dead, the terrain of conflict, of coming apart, the unraveling of a mechanical, uniform, and emotionally tepid culture best portrayed in its rituals of dying.[40]

Although a group project, the published text for the performance identifies the discrete roles of different participants. Playwright Susan Yankowitz is given credit for the text, and Chaikin and Sklar are credited for codirection. The participation of the six-member ensemble (Raymond Barry, Shami Chaikin, Tom Lillard, Jo Ann Schmidman, Tina Shepard, and Paul Zimet) is acknowledged, as well as the participation of many others. Yankowitz, who was new to the Open Theatre, quickly adapted to the collective ethos of the company.

> I came into the group as a stranger to everyone but Joe. Two writers were already working on *Terminal.* I quickly saw that we all shared a common vision and, like the actors, subordinated myself to the group's effort to create an outstanding piece. No one insisted upon being a star, having special billing, or being paid a higher salary.[41]

Terminal is in two sections: "The Calling up of the Dead" and "The State of the Dying." Each section is divided into subsections that, in their totality, create an incisive pastiche of the cultural construction of dying—a construction that forever severs us from heaven.

Terminal took place in the theater with presentational acting, and the props—a pallet, a clothing rack, and lights—were part of the theatrical world, where they stood for themselves. A pallet is a pallet but also used as a bed or a wall. Making theater is openly acknowledged as part of the play in progress. In white costumes, the actors generally evoke hospital wear and mummification. Roles are interchangeable: "The living are also the dying; the dying are potentially dead. And the dead will become living matter."[42] The actors make these distinctions with a style of acting that creates space, place, time, and characters with minimal reliance on props, set pieces, or costumes. The medically focused bright white lighting is seemingly unending. It reproduces the eternal daylight of hospitals, the intense white light of the operating theater, the clarity of death under the scalpel, the patient under examination, and the theater as an incisive instrument of social critique.

In *Terminal* being dramatic and being medical are analogous processes and occupations. Whether the dramatic theater or the medical theater, the constant scrutiny of a determinist gaze treats subjects as objects. Looking, examining, isolating, diagnosing, and staging are intermingled in ways that insinuate intimate relations between contemporary secular medical and theatrical rituals.[43] The Open Theatre's end of life was not only the end of human life in sterilized medical environments but also the end of theater in the soulless logic of commercialism.

Terminal begins with the most basic processes of life: eating and excreting. In theater, as in hospitals, the most private of acts becomes public. The dying are on view as they travel to the next place while appearing to go nowhere. An actor "runs" with only the top part of his body moving. In *Terminal* the last rights are "The Last Biological Rights," the last opportunity to use one's eyes, voice, and legs.[44] At the end, nothing can be seen, spoken, or gotten to. Death is privately experienced but publicly observed. The dying are alone on a public journey. In the second part of *Terminal*, the rituals of embalming are graphically described. Draining the blood, removing internal organs, repairing the skin, suturing the lips, cosmetic procedures, and finally dressing the corpse in a backless garment are all performed for the gaze of the living. The loss of the most primary human functions in the first part of *Terminal* is situated in the rituals of dying in an affluent mass corporate consumer society in the second part.

The eighteen subsections of *Terminal* reflect the collaborative process of creating a physical and vocal work from improvisations. *Terminal* partly emerged from Chaikin's lifelong experience with being near death, and this fact, of course, made the subject of living and dying an immediate and palpable one for a company in the flush of life. About a *Terminal* rehearsal, Chaikin wrote:

At a certain point last year I thought I was in the last days of my life and I carried on inside my skull where nobody else could hear. I wailed, I wept, I screamed, and I died very unwillingly. I bargained with the fates, and I lied to myself again and again. You'd think that at death's door the lying would stop. Not for me.

I said to myself that I felt things I didn't feel and I bribed people for pity. I've since learned that I'm not going to die so fast; I am functioning well, and when I no longer function this well, there's an operation which may revive me and keep me alive longer still. Chances are some of you will outlive me; chances are through accident or illness somebody in this room will take off before me. There's no way predicting any of this—but we're all here now. That's Number One. And we'll all leave this world one day. That's Number Two. We have a relationship to both of these facts about ourselves. The truth is they are as inter-related as day and night. To focus on one is to summon the other. "I see you. I don't see you dying. I see you. I don't see you living. I see you. I don't see you."[45]

Chaikin's talk to the actors emphasized the ways in which the condition of mortality is both painfully private and unforgivably public; life and death come to individuals in ways that can only be experienced in isolation but that always move through the public settings of hospitals, morgues, funeral homes, and finally a solitary grave in a public cemetery. The quote from *Terminal* about seeing and not seeing and living and dying that ends Chaikin's talk with the actors veers toward how the impending world of death makes living a "cold obstruction," more than an urgent existence. The overarching visual imagery of *Terminal* portrays the difficulty of living and dying in the cold-tiled institutional settings of corporate medicine.

The proximity of the living to the dead is at the theatrical heart of *Terminal.* It is here that the character of Marie Laveau makes her appearance.[46] Laveau was a mid-nineteenth-century New Orleans voodoo practitioner who cast gris-gris, black and white magic spells, and resurrected the dead. Laveau's magic appealed to the Open Theatre's investigation of transformation, of life in/after death. Yankowitz found an account of Laveau, and incorporated it into the text preserving the patois chant sung by Laveau and her followers:

Eh ye ye Mamzelle Marie, ye ye ye il konin tou, gris gris, li te
kouri, aver vieux kokodril, eh oui ye, Mamzelle Marie, Eh ye
ye. (My people come to me, they say).[47]

The dark-haired Zimet played Laveau speaking the patois as a dishar-mony of sound, not dialogue.[48]

Yankowitz culled from the actual and metaphysical lawlessness of voodoo—the social transgression of proposing that certain people can ac-tually control living and dying, negotiate between these spheres of exis-tence, and affect great actions at a distance by means of magic. This kind of power was analogous to what theater does: calling into bodily existence the absent, the dead, the distant; singing and dancing old and new stories; displaying great emotional power that moves both performers and spec-tators. At Laveau's voodoo rituals, black people secretly and illegally prac-ticed the rituals of their religion and in so doing challenged both the material and the spiritual worlds foisted on them by whites. In *Terminal,* the character of Laveau also knows well human avariciousness, betrayal, and treachery:

> my people come to me, they say:
> make that man poor so I grow rich
> make that man die so I can live
> kill my sister
> kill my brother
> and no one know the other
> and no one see the other
>
> Marie Laveau, she sees!
> See my people smile,
> and eat each other;
> wipe blood from mouth
> with dainty cloth.
>
> And my ocean stink with dead fish
> and my tress are hurt and broken
> and my fruit grows sick and rots
> and my air is black with poison
> that my birds cannot breathe
> and my people eat each other
> and my people live like slaves.
>
> Marie Laveau, she sees!
> See my people buying,
> see them selling,
> see them spending lives
> like slaves.[49]

What Laveau did with voodoo, *Terminal* also did with theater: both raised the specter of what was not visible to the realist eye. What Laveau did as a believed-in performance, *Terminal* did as art. Both summoned alien, dangerous, but deeply attractive worlds. This world of the "other" was brought close to the ordinary experience of theatergoers. The Open Theatre asked their spectators to see, to be free, and to live while insisting that seeing and not seeing, freedom and slavery, living and dying could swiftly and unpredictably morph into one another. If *The Serpent* told the story of the end of innocence, *Terminal* explored a certain aspect of the "guilt," of living.

Zimet notes the way in which Chaikin's lifelong illness made Chaikin see the proximity of life and death not only as a personal condition but as the basis for an aesthetic:

> For Joe, the breath was a more powerful tool than psychological analysis for discovering "the parts of yourself which have not lived yet." In all acting traditions the breath is important, but I think it loomed larger for Joe because his injured heart always made him aware of the immanence of death. He told us as actors to play each moment on stage as if it were the only chance we would get. Don't assume the present breath will be followed by countless more. This was not an abstract thought for Joe. It shaped the intensity of his work and the work of those who were fortunate enough to collaborate with him. It determined his aesthetic: Pare an event down to its essential emblem: an image, a phrase, a gesture. It governed the choices he made: Only work on what is important to you. Yet for someone so influenced by thoughts of mortality, Joe's theatrical work was anything but grim. He knew the darker the subject, the more important it was to find the humor in it. When we found it, he would break out in an infectious smile, an irresistible giggle. In 1996, when we were rehearsing the revival of the Open Theatre's *Terminal,* a piece about death and dying, Joe was afraid we were getting too gloomy and heavy. To make his point with the eloquent brevity of his aphasia he said, "Sarah Bernhardt. Slept in a coffin. Too much.[50]

Zimet is right. Even though *Terminal* is about mortality, the questions it asks, the scenes it presents, are not grim. This is not only because the research and the telling were, in and of themselves, life-affirming activities, but also because the performing had, at certain moments, room for lightness. The alternative ways of knowing at the heart of the theatrical mission of the Open Theatre proposed that there were radical ways of being in the world. According to Zimet, "We showed possibilities for human behavior that weren't shown elsewhere. A lot of the acting work we did tried to access these things."[51] Paradise revisited in the form of theater and theatrical knowledge.

Terminal also shows the inverse of unlimited possibilities. In tandem with Laveau but with alternating vocal and physical focus, Jo Ann Schmidman as the Soldier marches in place and obediently salutes, "Yessir, Yessir, Yessir, Yessir, Yessir."[52] The Soldier personifies the regimentation of ideas. "Yes when I wanted to say yes, Yes when I wanted to say no, Yes when I wanted to say yes, Yes when I wanted to say no."[53] As if she has no choice, the Soldier rhythmically recounts what was done to her, while Laveau mourns what was done to the world. The Soldier is Laveau's vision of seeing people spending their lives like slaves.[54]

Assessing the consciousness and culpability of individual lives was also part of *Terminal*. Mark Amitin pointedly explains Tina Shepard's scene, "The Dead Come Through: The Responsible One," in which she repeats the refrain, "What have I done?" as one in which the particular personal sense of responsibility that haunted so many in the 1960s was articulated. "I saw a child choking on air. What have I done? Oceans rising. What have I done? Buildings toppled. What have I done?"[55] Air pollution, the destruction of the environment, urban decay, violence, and war were problems a whole generation felt it inherited but did not have the tools to solve.[56] *Terminal* ends the story that *The Serpent* begins. A bite of the apple of knowledge enables human beings to do what they will with the world. The problem is that the knowledge gained is consciousness without positive generative consequence. "You shall use your mind, / Not to understand but to doubt. / And even if you understand, / Still shall you doubt," is one of God's curses in *The Serpent*.[57] The devastating reply to the rhetorical question, "What have I done?" hangs in the air as it summons the unrequited desires of the restless dead, and the struggling spirits of the living.

The fact of death, *Terminal* proposes, should make us assess life from curious, determined, and humorous vantage points. "The judgment of your life is your life. You will finally possess the thing you wanted most in life—and eternity will be that thing and that thing only," Shami Chaikin tells us in the "The Judgments," the final section of the performance.[58] The mourning in *Terminal* was only partly for life's passing. *Terminal*'s sorrow was also the grief of helplessness in the face of a world gone wrong. What's dramatically missing is the rage at the vacant garments of possibility, rage at the fading of the light, rage at life's lack of conclusion, rage at death's triumph, rage at the possibilities of paradise lost. The Open Theatre seems to have arrived at a new balance. Questions about authority, credit, and authorship were temporarily quiet. Yankowitz was energized by the aesthetic and intellectual environment of the Open Theatre.

> After rehearsal Joe and Roberta and I would go out and have something to eat together and discuss what had happened at the rehearsal and what needed to be done for the following day. I loved the whole process. Working with wonderfully creative people, especially actors, was tremendously educational for me. Fortunately I was pretty strong and rarely took rejection of what I wrote as a sign that I wasn't any good; I simply appeared the next day with a new speech or scene.[59]

The Mutation Show (1971) also elaborated a theme first touched upon in *The Serpent:* how socialization deforms individual lives. Chaikin described the workshop phase of the work:

> We're dealing with human mutation, with ourselves as mutations, contemplating the human form we haven't taken, on the experience of being torn away from ourselves. Working as part of this group is like having several sets of eyes, not just my own. I have felt the deepest and most sensitive collaboration during this period, and I hope we will be able to focus clearly enough and to move beyond the obstructions so as to be able to bring into this work some of what we are discovering together.
>
> It's exhilarating to work together through this confusion, toward some kind of clarity. As a group I'm never sure how long we will survive; endurance probably isn't the best criterion anyway. The more baffled and astonished we permit ourselves to be, the more we discover and learn. After Mutations I will be moving in a completely different direction, still looking into the theater event, and in the process continuing to change my relationship to it. Where that will take me I don't know.[60]

Chaikin wrote as if he were sensing a closure to the themes first encountered in *The Serpent* and to the ways of working the Open Theatre had developed thus far. Although not intended this way, *The Serpent, Terminal,* and *The Mutation Show* can be viewed as a trilogy about the beginning, formation, and end of life.[61]

It was as if the Open Theatre had to explore genesis and dying before it could delve directly into the unrelenting problems of living. *The Mutation Show,* like all the work of the group, went through a long workshop phase that kept shifting its subject matter. The themes of decorum, change, containment, exclusion, the complexity of individual identity, the fixity of naming, and the ways in which the conditions of living create inhibitions were all researched. The mutants of *The Mutation Show* were not so much freaks as incomplete and warped personalities.

The company explored outsiders—wild children who were raised outside of society. They researched Kamala, the girl raised by wolves in J. A. L. Singh and Robert M. Zingg's *Wolf-Children and Feral Man*. They also discovered what it meant to live in a high-security prison, and the "prisons" of racism and dysfunctional families by reading *Soledad Brother: The Prison Letters of George Jackson, Black Boy* by Richard Wright, and David Cooper's *The Death of the Family*.[62] The Open Theatre's account of mutation is about separation from wonder, from compassion, from our animal selves and our humane selves, about separation from "true" ways of knowing. This echoes what the crowd shouts after the assassination of King in *The Serpent:* "I mind my own affairs, / I am a little man. / I lead a private life. / I stay alive."[63] Living, *The Mutation Show* proposes, is contained and diminished in both self-imposed and societal restrictions.

The spare text for *The Mutation Show* is the result of the group working without a playwright. The ten sequences, "Rules for the Audience," "The Mutant Gallery," "The Boy in the Box," "The Animal Girl," "Ropes," "Breaking Out of the Box and Seeing," "Walking in Shoes," "Wedding Dance," "The Human Gallery," and "The Mutants Give Testimony," are discrete episodes.[64] One section follows another in the manner of association, pastiche, and interiority of logic—the nontextual material of theater. The performance begins with an admonition to the audience not to smoke, take photographs, crinkle paper, or have sexual fantasies about the performers or audience members—in short, setting limits on what one does and thinks, the very subject matter of the performance.[65] The contradiction between obeying and thinking for one's self is set upon the audience in Ellen Maddow's final imperative: "Try to think up a comment during the play so you can have an opinion later."[66]

Dressed as a master of ceremonies and speaking in the tone of "see-it-now-and-wonder," Shami Chaikin introduces "The Mutant Gallery" as the company enters, dressed in circuslike attire, dancing and prancing. They are the Bird Lady, the Man Who Smiles, the Man Who Hits Himself, the Thinker, and the Petrified Man. Wiggling, smiling, hitting oneself, thinking, and not moving eventually make up the repertory of this odd group. They are the stunted products of civilization, part-human and part-animal circus creatures: smiling, masochistic half-breeds, unmoved by the thoughts they don't know they're having.

The succeeding sections of the work show us how the mutants got that way. They have been torn from isolation and made to see the night sky, people, and light for the first time and then left alone on a hill.[67] An "animal girl" is lassoed from her closeness to nature by the noose of civilization; she is named, caressed, given words, dressed, and made to walk on two legs in shoes. What is natural is made into a freak show by society. The process of glimpsing what might be if one could regain the light, the wonder, color, moving, if one could break out of the box—the post-Edenic box of guilt and knowledge—was played by Raymond Barry's literally breaking out of a box and explaining his experience:

> Nothing with me in my box all the time closed I was still alone with only my fluids came out of here and here and here and here and here and then out of the box I saw for the first time only that one time saw light light light coming into my head from long time away moving and turning seeing long poles with green at the top hitting against my face and I saw another box the top was blue the bottom was many colors it had many colors moving and turning and then I saw and then I saw you and I saw you and I saw you seeing and then trying to stand falling saw stars moving across the light in front of the long time and many boxes with holes and people going in and out of the holes and when they moved it made a noise and the noise was in my head and the noise was in me and I saw the boxes and I saw the noise. I don't know if this happened to me or to someone else but I know it happened.[68]

He rejects confinement with his ecstatic account of a sensual of light, of color, of seeing, of an animal knowledge of the proximity of physical sensation and experience. The vertigo of this vision continues in "The Wedding Dance," where everyone whirls from expected to unexpected partners: the bride with the groom, the groom with the mother of the bride, the bride with the mother of the groom, the groom with the daughter of the bride, the mother of bride with the mayor, the father of the groom with the captain of police, the president with his assassin, the cow with the butcher, the king with the oilmen, and so on,[69] the special way in which the ritualized secular protocol of weddings makes something of an Oedipal dance drama. The dance culminates in "The Human Gallery" with the actors holding enlarged photographs of themselves as children while bits of autobiographical information are announced about each actor. The distance between the actors, their childhood photographs, and their autobiographical information proposes that the regulation of identity is anything but complete. The journey of life *The Mutation Show* suggests is one from near perfect solitude to deformation to finally constructing a semblance of self. And the results, the distance between the actors in the room and the photographs of themselves they hold, can be surprising.

"The Human Gallery" in *The Mutation Show* implied a complicated yet sympathetic relationship between individualism and collectivity in its juxtaposition of the distance between the two. This distance was, in fact, being enacted in the growing difference between those who saw feminism and gender as central to social critique. According to Sklar,

> I accepted the fact that the Open Theatre was creating work that stemmed from and resonated with our relationship with society. But then I went to a conference at Barnard College where the theater company It's All Right to Be Woman was performing. They didn't share my aesthetic—I liked surgically clean performance. It's All Right to Be Woman was amateur, but as I watched them I literally thought, "Oh my god I am not doing anything that is about my reality." I had actually never seen theater before that was about me, about my reality. I was not yet in a consciousness-raising group. I think I thought it might be important for other women, but I considered myself an exceptional woman, an independent director. Then I saw It's All Right to Be Woman and I came to understand that I am a woman like every other woman, not an exceptional woman.[70]

Eventually Chaikin and Sklar's relationship was challenged by feminism. Sklar realized that although they were "soul mates" ("There was never a moment when we didn't have something to say to one another"),[71] they were not equals. At the same time, "*The Mutation Show* was about domination and submission, and what did that have to do with gender? I remember having dinner with Grotowski and Joe and Joe said to Grotowski, 'Roberta is very caught up in women's liberation. What do you think of it?' Grotowski responded that he was too busy with men's liberation. Neither Joe nor I countered Grotowski's statement. There was so much ambivalence. This period was a boy's club."[72]

While the Open Theatre attacked uniformity in the content of their work, the change in American society resulting from the growth of a corporate economy served the most basic need of the company: collectivity. It wasn't that the final decisions for the work were made collectively, but that the primary creation of the work was a collective endeavor. The Open Theatre's embrace of the contradictory notion of collective anarchy guar-

Joseph Chaikin and Roberta Sklar, 1969. (Photo by Christen Johanson. Photo courtesy of Roberta Sklar.)

anteed that the company, like so many of the group theaters formed in the 1960s, would have limited longevity. Even after the Open Theatre disbanded after *Nightwalk* (1973), its final work, Chaikin continued working with several company members. The Open Theatre used collectivity to undermine conformity, even the conformity necessary to sustain their company. Casting a shadow on the Open Theatre's resistance to mainstream America was the planned obsolescence that was part of its radical genesis: a discarding of the old in favor of the new not unlike the planned product obsolescence of corporate America. At the same time, the Open Theatre, like other group theaters of the period, tried to enact a participatory democracy not unlike corporate America's revision of hierarchy as the determining principle of organization.[73] Ironically, both corporations and theaters called themselves "companies," but the word would eventually connote radically different meanings for business than for theater. And *new* was and still is a sanctioned word in both theater and advertising.

The theater companies formed in the 1960s envisioned themselves as limited in size, and closed, even monastic, for purposes of work, as opposed to the business model of continuous expansion and acquisition finally leading to the merger craze of the 1990s. To fuel their never-ending need for expansion to survive, businesses "outsourced," "diversified," and merged, while the group theaters looked inwardly to the core members and specialized in particular, highly individuated, performing styles. The Open Theatre was a costly, time-consuming, handcrafted artistic endeavor focused on the present. By the 1980s, this very particular kind of group theater in America was outmoded, vanished.[74]

In contrast, American regional theaters adapted the corporate business model. Regional theaters brought in the "right actors" for each production (equivalent to outsourcing), developed "outreach" programs diversifying and expanding their "client base," and cultivated boards of directors whose members were drawn from the business community. The "classic" group theaters such as the Open Theatre were organizationally archaic even as they were artistically avant-garde. Continuing to change, to stay in process, meant great artistic exploration without sustaining foundational security.

Like other radical group theaters, the contradictions at the core of the Open Theatre animated both the environment of its work and its existence: a leaderless company with a strong leader; an ensemble designed to create sensitivity and reception among its members while resisting communal collectivity in its decision-making process; a group formed to explore theatrical creation without the immediate goal of public performances of its investigations; a company that rejected the vested business interests of commercial theater and the political workings of the state but came to increasingly depend on state and federal grants for its existence; and a company with utopian ideals without a infrastructure to sustain those ideals. The contradictions of the company illustrate the complicated relationship between the aesthetic, political, and theatrical that were so much a part of the group theaters of the 1960s and early 1970s. As with other group theaters, the Open Theatre's specific notions of ideological *and* aesthetic significance produced the particular kind of ensemble theater they created: one bent on a paradisiacal vision of the world even as it proclaimed such a world could never exist.[75]

The Open Theatre's ten years of existence, from 1963 to 1973, remain a prophetic niggling in the consciousness of American experimental theater. Chaikin's devotion to socially and politically aware nonnaturalistic theater animated by an exploration of new types of expression is at the conceptual core of the radical American theater collectives formed in the 1960s and the 1970s.

NOTES

1. Eileen Blumenthal, *Joseph Chaikin: Exploring the Boundaries of Theatre* (New York: Cambridge University Press, 1984), 15.

2. Cited in Arthur Sainer, *The New Radical Theatre Notebook,* rev. ed. (New York: Applause, 1997), 1.

3. Ibid., 2.

4. The first Open Theatre members were Ron Faber, Sharon Gans, Gerome Ragni (the coauthor-creator-lyricist of *Hair*), Barbara Vann, and Lee Worley. The playwrights Arthur Sainer, Earl Scott, Michael Smith, Megan Terry, and Sharon Thie and the critic Gordon Rogoff were also there at the beginning of the company (Gene A. Plunka, *Jean-Claude van Itallie and the Off-Broadway Theater* [Newark: University of Delware Press, 1999], 64). Chaikin writes that the original group was "Lee Worley, Peter Feldman, and Meg Terry." After two or three months the group, according to Chaikin, expanded and Rogoff brought Jean-Claude van Itallie to a workshop. Joseph Chaikin, *The Presence of the Actor* (New York: Atheneum, 1972), 54.

5. For all three of these productions I both read the published texts and viewed videos of the productions. In the case of minor textual differences between the published text and the videos, I have quoted the published texts. Mark Amitin has been especially generous in loaning me his videos for an extended period of time. *The Mutation Show,* CBS Camera Three videotape, distributed by New York State Education Department (Albany, , 1973); *The Serpent,* Educational Broadcasting Corporation Film for Public Television, distributed by Arthur Cantor, Inc. (New York, 1969); *Terminal,* CBS Camera Three videotape, Distributed by New York State Education Department (Albany, 1970).

6. Blumenthal, *Joseph Chaikin,* 109.

7. Ibid.

8. Ibid.

9. Ibid.

10. Grotowski had been brought to New York by La Mama (Ellen Stewart), *TDR* (Richard Schechner), and New York University (Ted Hoffman and J. Michael Miller) to teach an acting workshop for NYU acting students, It was during Grotowski's workshop with NYU students that Richard Schechner invited NYU students and others interested in continuing this kind of work to join him in what became the Performance Group. It was also after this workshop that Andre Gregory formed the Manhattan Project with a number of students who were in the Grotowski NYU workshop. This began the close working and personal relationship between Grotowski and Andre and Mercedes (Chiquita) Gregory.

11. Robert Pasolli, *A Book on the Open Theatre* (New York: Bobbs-Merrill, 1970), 114. Van Itallie remembers a demonstrative Grotowski demanding van Itallie

translate with the same anger and emotional force that he was speaking (van Itallie, *Sex, War, and Dreams*. Unpublished memoir). Zimet remembers an autocratic and authoritarian Grotowski wearing black-rimmed glasses and a black suit. Paul Zimet, interview by the author, New York, May 11, 2004.

12. Sklar describes first being given codirector credit after expressing extreme disappointment at not being mentioned in an article in the *New York Times* by Margaret Croyden for which she was interviewed. Margaret Croyden, "Burning Bridges is Natural," *New York Times*, March 29, 1970, 77. "She interviewed me for two hours and also interviewed other female members of the company. None of the women Croyden interviewed were mentioned in the article. Joe was very uncomfortable about it. He told our publicist that I wasn't getting acknowledged for the work I was doing. The publicist said the solution was simple: we had to stop listing the entire Open Theatre in alphabetical order and Joe and I needed to share the directing credit line. After that, that is what we did." Roberta Sklar, interview by the author, New York, March 14, 2005.

13. Sklar, interview.

14. Van Itallie cautioned me against implying that *The Serpent* flowed from conceptual strategies. In a May 8, 2004, e-mail, he wrote: "Creating 'The Serpent,' we had no clear sense of the direction in which we were going—we were exploring emotional territory, asking questions. We did not proceed in a straight line. Of the scenes we attempted, Joe threw away many many more than he kept. I had no idea of the structure of the play (or the relation of one scene to another) until I was forced to create one because we were due to open. We worked always with questions that felt dangerous to us, never with answers. I think *The Serpent* succeeds because Joe and I and the actors went forward into unknown inner territory without knowing where we were going."

15. Blumenthal, *Joseph Chaikin*, 108.

16. Zimet recalls being aware of Carol Hanish's phrase "the personal is political" but not directly discussing it during the workshop (Zimet, interview). The phrase had great popular currency even for those who were not familiar with the essay in which Hanish coined the phrase. Carol Hanish, "The Personal is Political," in *Feminist Revolution*, Kathie Sarachild, ed. (New York: Random House, 1978), 204–5.

17. Blumenthal, *Joseph Chaikin*, 110.

18. In *American Avant-Garde Theatre: A History* Arnold Aronson writes: "In the 1960s, the festering dark underside of the American century—racial inequality, poverty in the midst of plenty, the threat of nuclear holocaust, and ultimately political assassinations and the disastrous involvement in Vietnam—bubbled to the surface as the nation faced civil rights demonstrations, race riots, anti-war marches, acts of anti-establishment violence, and the emergence of a so-called 'counterculture,' which was the product of the youthful rebelliousness and idealism of the demographically explosive 'baby-boom' generation" (New York: Routledge, 2000), 75.

19. Jean-Claude van Itallie, *The Serpent* (New York: Dramatists Play Service, 1969), 17–18.

20. Ibid., 33.

21. Ibid., 21. Various female members of the chorus say these lines.

22. During a 1966–67 workshop taught by Jacques Levy, Levy, van Itallie, and

Maria Irene Fornes created a sequence of the Kennedy assassination based on the Abraham Zapruder film. According to van Itallie's biographer, Gene A. Plunka (*Jean-Claude van Itallie*, 111) van Itallie suggested to Chaikin that this sequence be incorporated into *The Serpent* to connect Genesis to contemporary life. In a telephone interview on May 11, 2004, van Itallie recalled Chaikin's interest in contemporary myths as the link to trying the sequence from the Levy workshop in the context of working on *The Serpent*.

23. The silent Abraham Zapruder home movie shows the Kennedy motorcade just before, during, and immediately after the shooting. The Warren Commission in 1963–64 and House Select Committee on Assassinations in 1977–78 relied on it to answer questions about how the assassination happened.

24. van Itallie, *The Serpent*, 18–19.

25. Ibid., 20.

26. Ibid.

27. Ibid., 23.

28. Ibid., 28.

29. Ibid.

30. Ibid.

31. Jean-Claude van Itallie, telephone interview by the author, May 12, 2004.

32. van Itallie, *The Serpent*, 38.

33. Sklar, interview.

34. van Itallie, *The Serpent*, 55. "Moonlight Bay" was recorded by Doris Day, Bing Crosby, and Jerry and the Silverstones, among others.

35. Zimet, interview.

36. The Performance Group's *Dionysus in 69* (based on Euripides' *The Bacchae*), directed by Richard Schechner, which opened in June 1968, was also a cautionary tale about anarchy and utopian desires. Audience participation, performer (and sometimes spectator) nakedness, and the simulation of the bacchanal in the theater (the Performing Garage) ended not only dramatically with the killing and dismemberment of Pentheus but also theatrically with the actors marching out of the theater onto Wooster Street, Dionyus on their shoulders, with many of the spectators trailing behind. Those left in the theater had nothing and no one to applaud.

37. Zimet, interview.

38. The structure of *The Serpent* evolved with the staging. Van Itallie describes creating the work as a painful process in which he had to learn to abandon overall structure for a logic contingent upon the evolution of individual scenes. The final form of the *The Serpent* was decided on the way to its opening in Rome. Van Itallie writes: *The Serpent* company sailed on the S.S. United States to Europe. Many were seasick. Rehearsals were tense, and the play was long and shapeless. We were opening in two weeks in Rome. We wondered: are we sailing toward disaster? In a dramaturgical conference in stateroom, Joe, his assistant Roberta Sklar and I labeled each scene on a three by five card. We agreed on an 'A' pile of scenes we loved, a 'B' pile of scenes we weren't sure about and a 'C' pile of scenes to cut. After Joe and Roberta left, I laid out the 'A' and a few 'B' cards on the bed and played with them. I constructed the final shape of *The Serpent* to have a breathing alternation of tight and relaxed scenes. I gave this new order of scenes to Joe who announced it to the actors. On May 2 we arrived in Rome. To our relief, *The Serpent* was . . . 'an

important success,' as a Roman paper said. I put the play in verse form and entitled each section. *The Serpent* toured Europe, played in New York and received an Obie" (van Itallie, unpublished manuscript).

39. Cited in Charlotte Canning, *Feminist Theaters in the U.S.A.: Staging Women's Experience* (London: Routledge, 1996), 60.

40. For a discussion of the right-wing myths about the 1960s counter culture see Thomas Frank, *The Conquest of Cool: Business Culture, Counterculture, and the Rise of Hip Consumerism* (Chicago: University of Chicago Press, 1997).

41. Susan Yankowitz, interview by the author, New York, March 4, 2005.

42. *Terminal*, in *Three Works by the Open Theatre*, ed. Karen Malpede (New York: Drama Book Specialists Publishers, 1972), 43.

43. *Terminal* is perhaps Chaikin's most personal work. From early boyhood he suffered from a rheumatic heart and spent many months in and out of hospitals. Chaikin knew, throughout his life, what it meant to be in the process of dying. Van Itallie writes: "Perhaps the defining experience in Joe's life occurred in 1945 in Des Moines, Iowa when at the age of ten he had rheumatic fever which damaged his heart. Joe was taken by train by his eighteen-year-old sister Miriam a thousand miles away to a children's cardiac home in Florida and left there for two years. Feeling abandoned, Joe survived emotionally by organizing theater games among the children. Any one of them, including Joe, could be dead the next day. These terrible years left Joe distrustful of family and institutions while staking his life to the theater" (van Itallie, *Sex, War, and Dreams.* Unpublished memoir). It is certainly possible to read *Terminal* as a psychological portrayal of one aspect of Chaikin's life, but this would be a limited understanding of a work that had many contributors.

44. *Terminal,* 47.

45. Chaikin, *Presence of the Actor,* 112.

46. Marie Laveau's surname is typically spelled with the initial vowel *a*. However, in the published text of the play, it is spelled with an *e*. For this essay, I have chosen to spell Laveau with an *a* when referring to the personage and the character in the text for the sake of consistency.

47. *Terminal,* 54.

48. When I asked Zimet in April 2004 if he knew what the patois meant, he said he did not.

49. *Terminal,* 54.

50. Quoted in Michael Feingold, "He Made All That Happened to Him a Transcendent Experience: Joseph Chaikin (1935–2003)," *Village Voice,* July 9–15, 2003.

51. van Itallie, interview, May 11, 2004.

52. *Terminal,* 55.

53. Ibid.

54. Ibid., 54.

55. Mark Amitin, interview by the author, New York, May 5, 2004; *Terminal,* 58.

56. Amitin, interview.

57. van Itallie, *The Serpent,* 32.

58. *Terminal,* 64.

59. Yankowitz, interview.

60. Chaikin, *Presence of the Actor,* 160.

61. *Nightwalk* (1973) was the Open Theatre's final major work before disbanding.

62. Blumenthal, *Joseph Chaikin,* 150.

63. van Itallie, *The Serpent,* 20.

64. *The Mutation Show,* in Malpede, *Three Works.*

65. Ibid., 95.

66. Ibid.

67. Ibid., 97.

68. Ibid., 98.

69. Ibid., 98–99.

70. Sklar, interview.

71. Ibid.

72. Ibid.

73. See Frank, *The Conquest of Cool.*

74. Several groups still function: the Living Theatre, the San Francisco Mime Troupe, and Bread and Puppet. Mabou Mines continues, albeit very differently from its inception. The Performance Group spawned the Wooster Group, and the Talking Band is the progeny of the Open Theatre. The Manhattan Project, the Performance Group, the Free Southern Theater, and At the Foot of the Mountain no longer operate.

75. Sklar remembers: "During our second tour of Europe, when we were touring *Terminal* and *The Serpent,* Joe and I were watching a performance in Switzerland and he turned to me and said, "Wouldn't it be wonderful to work with a smaller ensemble?" I agreed, so right then and there we each made lists of who we wanted to work with and compared them. Our lists matched. Joe wrote everyone a letter. The letter was an invitation to those on the short list to work on our next project. It caused a very painful uproar, but by the fall season we were working with a considerably smaller ensemble. Some people who left eventually formed the Medicine Show; others went their separate ways." Sklar, interview.

WAYS OF WORKING

Post-Open Theatre Performance and Pedagogy

Roger Babb

In this chapter I will examine ensembles that emerged from the Open Theatre, most notably the Winter Project, which Joseph Chaikin initiated in 1976, and several other collectives, such as the Omaha Magic Theatre, the Talking Band, and the Woman's Experimental Theater, founded by former Open Theatre collaborators. I will also look at the pedagogical work of a number of master teachers like Lee Worley, Paul Zimet, and Nancy Gabor, who continue to extend the vocabulary and "ways of working" that the Open Theatre developed. These teachers, who also continue as working artists, have educated several generations of theater students using techniques and methodologies they helped generate within the Open Theatre. Chaikin suffered a debilitating stroke in 1983 that made it difficult for him to lead collectively created ensemble productions, but his work with Pig Iron Theatre and the Disabilities Project are two exceptions that deserve mention, as well as his more publicized collaborations with Sam Shepard and Jean-Claude van Itallie on work directly related to his aphasia.

The legacy of the Open Theatre is inextricably linked with Joseph Chaikin's later history. Although the ensemble was nominally a collective, by 1970 Chaikin was the undisputed leader and spokesman for the group. There were various resentments and legitimate complaints about this arrangement, but it is not unusual in the theater for the name of the artistic director to become synonymous with the name of the group. The history of the Open Theatre reflects the cultural changes that were occurring in the United States at the time. Loosely organized, politically progressive, even utopian artistic organizations, in the face of reactionary response to the antiwar, antiestablishment youth movement of the 1960s, shifted in the 1970s to more sober, centrally organized arrangements and, with the help of new sources of funding from foundations and the National Endowment for the Arts, incorporated themselves as not-for-profit entities with artistic directors, advisory boards, and business managers. Chaikin was not so reluctantly cast as the guru or genius of the Open Theatre. Without denying his incredible contribution to that company and to American theater, it is important to remember Lee Worley, Mira Rafalowicz, Peter Feldman, and many others who were important collaborators.

The Winter Project

The Winter Project, a group of theater artists and musicians who met for three or four months a year from 1976 until 1983, represents an attempt to continue the work of the Open Theatre. Most of the artists had worked with Chaikin before and were familiar with the processes that had been developed by him and his collaborators. Paul Zimet and Tina Shepard had been core members of the previous ensemble during its final five years. Ronnie Gilbert, who had been active in the company in the mid-1960s, was a central collaborator in all of the subsequent Winter Project productions. Mira Rafalowicz, the dramaturg for the final Open Theatre production *Nightwalk,* was an essential catalyst in the continuing extension of a particular process of creating theater. This process was not organized as a set of procedures and principles; in fact Chaikin actively discouraged promulgating a methodology. Yet there were areas of interest and "ways of working" that continued to stimulate Chaikin and his collaborators. Using improvisation to generate images, exploring the musical qualities of the spoken voice, examining the relationship between the actor and the spectator and employing a nonlinear, collage-like structure were some of the techniques and methods that recurred in the work of the project.

In the first two years of the project there were no public performances. The emphasis was on experimentation in a kind of theatrical laboratory, which had also been a focus of the early Open Theatre. Even when the main concern of the Winter Project was the generation of a performable product for a paying audience, a rehearsal process that emphasized non-restrictive and open-ended investigation was key to the collaborations. Participants were given leave, in fact were encouraged, to investigate a

Roger Babb, Ronnie Gilbert, and Harry Mann in *Lies and Secrets,* directed by Joseph Chaikin, 1983. (Photo by Jerry Vezzuso, courtesy of Ellen Stewart and La Mama E.T.C. Archive.)

topic as fully and as personally as possible. Chaikin and Rafalowicz, the "eyes" of the project, then subjected the material generated from this type of exploration to critical scrutiny. The company's freedom was tempered by Chaikin's demand for rigor and discipline and his uncontested position as the final arbiter on artistic questions. There was no pretense that decisions within the company would be arrived at democratically. Rafalowicz wrote: "Collaboration is not to be confused with equal input or democratic procedure. In reality some people's input is more inspired and inspiring."[1] Here is a clear difference between the Open Theatre and the Winter Project, reflecting a shift in the experimental artistic community in the 1970s away from the ideal of communal decision-making toward a more practical if less egalitarian process of central control.

Too often Chaikin and his collaborators are lumped together with Julian Beck and Judith Malina's Living Theatre or Richard Schechner's Performance Group as examples of artists who practiced a "politics of ecstasy." The term is Schechner's and refers to Artaudian performance practice of the 1960s that valorized communitarian process and antiestablishment, utopian politics. The stereotypical image conveyed is one of undisciplined excess and strident new age proselytizing. In fact, the late Open Theatre (1970–73) and subsequently the Winter Project had a more formalist orientation. Although Chaikin was interested in Artaud's notion of a theatrical language "halfway between gesture and thought," his principal preoccupation was to generate refined theatrical images and emblems that owed more to Brecht's notion of "geste" than to Artaud's vision of a "theater of cruelty." Chaikin's groups were clearly sympathetic to progressive political causes, performing benefits for leftist political events and in prisons, but the work itself was not polemic. In 1973, just after disbanding the Open Theatre, Chaikin wrote:

> It is not the responsibility of art to serve any politics or psychology or philosophy. The realm of art is inspiration, and inspiration cannot be policed even by noble motives.[2]

Rafalowicz's contribution to the Winter Project as dramaturg was important both in the way she helped structure material and in her friendship with Chaikin. One cannot consider the history of this ensemble without recognizing Rafalowicz's presence and her influence, particularly on the five productions that the Winter Project created from 1979 to 1983. After *Nightwalk* (1972) she worked on Chaikin's productions of *Electra*, *Fable*, and *Chile, Chile*. She translated S. Ansky's Yiddish classic *The Dybbuk*, for which she worked as dramaturg at both the Public Theater in New York and the Habima in Israel. All of the material rehearsed during the seven years of the Winter Project was presented to Chaikin and Rafalowicz, who sat side by side, usually on the floor, conferring and exchanging notes. Although the actors and musicians could change from project to project, Rafalowicz worked on all the Winter Project productions. The work reflects her concern with structure and flow. Allen Kuharski, in an essay in *Dramaturgy in American Theater*, has pointed out that despite her important contributions, critics and academics have consistently overlooked Rafalowicz.

> Out of the samplings of twenty reviews of the Winter Project productions . . . only one referred to the dramaturg by name or her function in the creation of the piece. Rafalowicz has expressed frustration that both the popular press and the few academic studies of the work of the Winter Project (including Blumenthal's) have created a false impression of the ensemble's work as "Auteur theater" with Chaikin as the single defining presence.[3]

Rafalowicz wrote a significant and enlightening essay on being a dramaturg, and what the title means in the fall 1978 issue of *Theater*. Written in free verse, this "poem," according to Kuharski, "can be taken as the dramaturgical credo of the Winter Project." In the unedited version, there are a number of specific references to the Winter Project. The essay provides an important perspective on the process of creating a theater piece collectively. Rafalowicz clearly describes a way of working that was forged by the Open Theatre, refined and developed by the Winter Project and used as a dramaturgical model by many theater companies that were subsequently influenced by them.

Rafalowicz listed many of the functions that she performed: an internal critic, an intimate participant, an extra eye, and most importantly an asker of questions.

> I try to help guard those basic questions as the work develops,
> Those questions become part of a vocabulary of work.
> I keep the whole in mind—an overall structure,
> which frees others in the process to lose themselves
> in details.[4]

Rafalowicz described four different stages of work. The first stage was to define the area of exploration by finding the questions the group wished to be concerned with. "Together with the questions, we start to establish a vocabulary, a code, a common work history. A crosscurrent of work is going on between writers, actors, director, dramaturg, through improvisation, devising of exercises and through dialog."[5] The next stage involved the development and shaping of the material and criteria for making choices. Some ideas are wonderful but have to be rejected because of limitations of the actors or the writers or because the original improvisations cannot be repeated or because the ideas eventually seem to belong to a different piece. In this stage, a lot of cutting, editing and choosing goes on and by trying out sequences of images, a structure begins to be formed. As mentioned earlier, Rafalowicz made it very clear that collaboration was not to be confused with "equal input or democratic procedure."

> The actor, whether or not s/he is working on material
> s/he has created, needs feedback.
> The differentiation between those who act
> and have to repeat the chosen action and those who shape the
>   material
> becomes clearer.[6]

In the third stage, the piece begins to emerge and take shape. Although changes are still being made and sequences rearranged, the nonactors or "participant onlookers" are losing control and power. They are no longer able to be objective and are too involved. Consequently, outsiders are asked in to look at the piece and give criticism.

> We have to figure out what is really there or not there,
> rather than wish it were there. We have to give up
> ideas that don't work, even if we still have some
> hope that they might work.
> But we also have to evaluate other people's comments,
> pick out the perceptions that are valuable to the
> intentions of the work, screen them and use them carefully.
> And especially, we have to try and stay open, not biased and
>   defensive.[7]

In the fourth and final stage, the piece is given over to the actors in performance. Details can be changed, but the main questions are questions of repetition "about how to keep a piece alive, about maintaining or deepening intentions." This is the end of the process and a time for distance and reevaluation.

The Winter Project followed a daily routine that was similar to the work schedule established in the last three years of the Open Theatre. In this extremely fruitful period from 1970 to 1973, the streamlined company produced a revised *Terminal* and two new pieces: *Mutation Show* and *Nightwalk*. The major difference between the ensembles, apart from historical context, was the severely reduced funding and consequent limited rehearsal time allotted for production. Whereas the Open Theatre rehearsed and developed a project for up to a year, the Winter Project had about two months to produce a fully mounted play. One result of this abbreviated rehearsal period was less time allotted to developing new exercises. The Winter Project relied on shared vocabulary and accumulated work experience to develop text and images, but, after the initial two-year period, there was not the luxury to experiment without a particular product in mind. The primary focus of the company became production and not process.

Collectives after the Open Theatre

Around the time the Open Theatre disbanded in 1973, a number of new theater companies and collectives were started by former ensemble members. Joseph Chaikin, with the help of Artservices (an arts management agency), set up the Other Theatre as a nonprofit umbrella organization, which would produce many of his future projects. Paul Zimet, Ellen Maddow, and Tina Shepard formed the Talking Band. JoAnn Schmidman and Megan Terry moved to Nebraska and started the Omaha Magic Theatre. Ray Barry started the Quena Company, and Roberta Sklar formed Women's Experimental Theater.[8] All of these companies used techniques and methodologies developed by Chaikin and his collaborators, and many of them created new ways of working in reaction to political and aesthetic differences that had arisen within the Open Theatre. Terry, Schmidman, and Sklar formed collectives with feminist orientations in reaction to sexism in the society at large but also within the Open Theatre itself. Sklar remembers *The Mutation Show,* which she codirected, as an important early example of a play with a feminist content that reflected the company's own latent sexism.

> For me it was the beginning of my feminist expression, and it was the piece about which there was the greatest struggle between Chaikin and me. During the earlier pieces, I worked much the way women did in the peace movement and the student movement. We did a lot of the work, got little of the credit, and didn't realize yet that there was a major section missing in the political analysis—the section that was about us.[9]

Sklar notes that although some concepts of the women's movement were problematic within the organization and difficult for some of the men, "they were difficult for the women as well."[10] Nevertheless, she credits the Open Theatre's investigative, laboratory approach to theater making as a strong influence on her work.

> That way of working, with the actor as a primary researcher, with acting exercises as a method through which you learn something and the actor as a cocreator alongside you—that was what the Open Theatre was about doing, and I certainly went about doing it in my work in the Open Theatre and in my work in general.[11]

Sklar, like Rafalowicz, emphasizes the asking of questions and the search for a technique to research the answers as a principle of developmental theater. What is a woman's voice? What are the names of the matrilineage? How do we retrieve our history? These were some of the questions that fueled her research in her work after the Open Theatre.

Paul Zimet, Ellen Maddow, and Tina Shepard formed the Talking Band very soon after the Open Theatre disbanded. The initial productions were based on "an exploration of the borderlines of language, image and music," according to Shepard. This work was similar to the investigations being done by the Winter Project at the time. The Talking Band became interested in working with poets as playwrights (they developed pieces with Mark Kaminski and Sidney Goldfarb), and their work became more text oriented than the work of either the Open Theatre or the Winter Project. Over the last ten years they have developed small operatic pieces written mostly by Zimet and Maddow. Zimet says that one of the attractions and inspirations of the Open Theatre was that it was actively engaged with the world and that it presented an alternative way of perceiving that world than did the commercial theater of the time. He points to Chaikin's beginnings in the radical Living Theatre and notes that Chaikin was frustrated by the limitations of craft within that group. A hard-won precept of the Open Theatre was, "If you want to be political, you have to find the right aesthetic."[12]

The Talking Band also runs the Talking Band Laboratory, which meets throughout the year with actors, musicians, and writers to explore particular areas of interest such as melodrama, Meyerholds's biomechanics, Greek tragedy, the presentation of time, and so forth. These workshops are modeled on the research done by the Open Theatre and the Winter Project and are designed to engage with younger artists. Zimet wants the workshops to reflect the eclectic perspective Chaikin preferred. "There shouldn't be a clutching for a method. Joe was antimethod and tried to find exercises that were useful in the moment. The idea is not to impose. There is not one way of working, psychological or physical. For some actors, that's upsetting. They like to be handed a recipe."[13]

Another theater company influenced by the Open Theatre, and consciously modeled on it, is the Pig Iron Theatre Company, based in Philadelphia. The ensemble was founded by former students of Allen Kuharski's at Swarthmore College. Kuharski uses the Open Theatre, Grotowski's Polish Laboratory, and the companies of Peter Brook and Ariane Mnouchkine as pedagogical examples of alternative, collective ways of making theater. Students at Swarthmore are encouraged to form companies and create ensemble-based work in opposition to the dominant model of "independent contract work" that pervades commercial and regional theaters in the United States. Chaikin collaborated with Pig Iron on *Shut-Eye* in 1999. Dan Rothenberg, who was the codirector of the piece, remembers that Chaikin encouraged the actors to be personal and emphasized internal conditions. Pig Iron, also influenced by Jacques Le Coq, admired the emblematic, physically refined later pieces of the Open Theatre, expected a more formalist approach. "Joe gave us the freedom to trust our feelings and provided the final step for an empirical approach-following intuitions."[14] Although the Open Theatre pioneered a somatic approach to acting concerned with discovering outward forms for internal conditions, Chaikin was adamant in his refusal to advocate a specific approach to acting: "Don't let anyone tell you to go from the inside out—or the outside in. It's a circle."[15]

After 1983, because of a debilitating stroke and more importantly the difficulty of funding experimental theater work, it became increasingly difficult for Chaikin to form an ensemble to do the kind of theatrical research for which he was famous. Chaikin defined his primary identity in relation to theater as one who does investigations: "Trying things out but following a strong intuition without knowing where I'm headed." With a few exceptions (a remounted *Terminal* in 1996, a brief reconvening of Winter Project members in 1995, the Disabilities Project, and a collaboration with Pig Iron Theatre in 2000), Chaikin restricted his work to directing preexisting work and solo performance in collaboration with Sam Shepard and Jean-Claude van Itallie on pieces related to his aphasia. *The War in Heaven* (Chaikin and Shepard) and *Struck Dumb* (Chaikin and van Itallie) were performed to critical acclaim in the United States and Europe. Mostly, Chaikin directed scripted pieces such as the New York premiere of Shepard's *The Late Henry Moss* at the Signature Theater in 2002. He also remounted and toured a collection of Beckett texts that included "What is the Word," a poem Beckett had written for Chaikin after his stroke.

In the early 1990s, Chaikin initiated the Disabilities Project at the Public Theater. This work, although sporadic and never adequately funded or produced, continued to occupy Chaikin's interest for more than ten years. He and dramaturg Bill Hart assembled a group of disabled people who were either missing limbs, used wheelchairs, or had physical birth defects. According to Hart, Chaikin didn't develop the work in the manner of the Open Theatre or Winter Project pieces but was more interested in a simple comedic approach using a review or cavalcade format. Because of his aphasia, Chaikin had difficulty keeping track of the interweaving and overlapping of images that had distinguished the collage structure he had developed with his two previous ensembles. He continued to work on the Disabilities Project at various venues throughout the 1990s and up until 2002. The Public Theater sponsored a number of the workshops, and another was rehearsed and presented at Westbeth, a large artists' community located in Greenwich Village. These events were minimally funded and never shown more than once to an invited audience of friends and colleagues. A number of playwrights, including Charles Mee, were involved at one time or another, and John Belluso, who went on to run the Other Voices Project at the Mark Taper Forum in Los Angeles, was the playwright for the final two years. Belluso saw the work with disabilities as ahead of its time and as part of Chaikin's lifelong commitment to examining "exiled emotions" such as mourning, loss, and suffering, emotions familiar and well understood by the disabled.[16] Hart emphasizes Chaikin's tenacity in continuing to return to the topic of disability despite little support and encouragement. The morale and enthusiasm of the ensemble, their willingness to explore difficult territory with humor and dignity, was an inspiration for Chaikin, who was fighting not to be defined by his own disability.[17]

Pedagogy

After 1983 Chaikin continued to work as a director and teacher but never again on long-term developmental theater pieces with a core company of trained actors who shared a common theatrical vocabulary. That vocabulary, initially formed out of exercises from Viola Spolin and Nola Chilton and developed by collaborators within the company, became a basis for a "way of working," one that continues to be taught and practiced by many theater artists and teachers who had been members of the Open Theatre and the Winter Project. Through their pedagogy and practice, these artists pass on the legacy of the Open Theatre. It is important to point out that although Chaikin and such collaborators as Peter Feldman and Lee Worley developed hundreds of exercises over the years, they discarded most of them as they became repetitive or locked into a sterile perspective. They pushed for subtler and more inventive ways to redefine basic exercises like Sound and Movement, which according to Robert Pasolli became "a basic unit of expression for the company." Eileen Blumenthal has pointed out both Chaikin's great facility at developing exercises and his ambivalence concerning their general use for other theater artists:

> The record of his investigations, he says, must not be taken as a collection of recipes. Exercises should be developed ad hoc to grapple with specific problems and then thrown away. Though he still believes one can get clues from other people and, in fact, sees lasting value in some lines he has developed, he has come to believe that every work for the theatre, every company about to do the same work, even different actors within the same company require different approaches.[18]

Despite these reservations, I believe it is possible to discuss a "way of working" that was common to both the Open Theatre and the Winter Project and to trace its development over the years. In interviews and conversations with former Open Theatre members who have become recognized as master teachers, three areas of interest emerge as crucial to their pedagogy.

1. The use of exercises and improvisations
2. The method of arranging developmental work into a collage-like structure of images
3. The focus on the actor's presence in relation to the audience

The Use of Exercises

Most of the members of the Open Theatre had studied the American version of the Stanislavski system, the Method, under such master teachers as Stella Adler, Sanford Meisner, and Herbert Berghof. These teachers imparted a strict methodology with a concise vocabulary. Actors Rhea Gaisner and Nancy Gabor remember the sense of freedom and discovery they felt in Open Theatre workshops, a result of "another way of working which was the asking of questions." Gabor relates this to a "new and hopeful" politics of the sixties and to the budding influence of feminism, which encouraged women to reevaluate, question and transform their lives.[19]

Gaisner at Emerson College, Paul Zimet at Smith College, Tina Shepard at Williams College, and Gabor at Princeton University, as well as Lee Worley at the Naropa Institute, have educated several generations of theater students. The use of exercises is reflected variously in their approach to teaching. Peter Feldman, who taught at Columbia University and for many years at St. Catherine's College in Ontario, Canada, believed that Open Theatre exercises were "advanced work" and not appropriate for undergraduates. Lee Worley, on the other hand, starts new students right away with Sound and Movement, because it sensitizes participants to basic concepts about physical approaches to theater, ensemble playing, and nonverbal communication.

Worley led an important series of Open Theatre workshops in 1967 based on Sound and Movement, and she believes "that communication happens with the whole being and that words are what happens on top of that."[20] Sound and Movement has an interesting and particular history. Inspired by Viola Spolin's work with improvisations for children, it was developed by Chaikin and Worley as a principal tool for investigating physical and vocal conditions and behavior. This exercise reflects an interest of the time in the body and in physical as opposed to psychological approaches to acting. Jerzy Grotowski of the Polish Laboratory Theater and Peter Brook at the Royal Shakespeare Company, who were doing similar work, exchanged their exercises and a focus on physical rigor and discipline with Chaikin and the Open Theatre. A simplified version of Sound and Movement has become a ubiquitous warm-up exercise in many college theater departments

"Transformations" are part of the dramaturgical structure of most Open Theatre and Winter Project productions and can be considered a foundation in their way of working. The exercises involved enacting radical and rapid changes of the given circumstances in an improvisation. An actor could suddenly transform from a character into an animal or the embodiment of his or her desires. One important aspect of this exercise was the speed of the transition between conditions. The shift could be instantaneous with no apparent justification, the actor revealing numerous "ways of being" and problematizing the notion of a fixed and stable self. Megan Terry incorporated the transformation device as part of the action of *Calm Down Mother* and *Keep Tightly Closed in a Cool Place,* both performed by the Open Theatre in 1965. She continued to use it in her work with the Magic Theatre of Omaha. Transformations has been widely used by many of the playwrights associated with the Open Theatre, including Maria Irene Fornes and Jean-Claude van Itallie. Rhea Gaisner argues that "if you don't understand Transformations you can't do Sam Shepard." Teachers like Gaisner and Gabor continue to use the exercise in acting classes and as a device to generate material for developmental pieces.[21] Helene Keyssar in *Feminist Theatre,* noted the importance of the exercise:

> What was always true of the theatre—that the human being could in this arena transcend her or himself—now became not just an unquestioned aesthetic principle but a manifestation of political and aesthetic struggle.[22]

Paul Zimet and Tina Shepard use early exercises like Sound and Movement and modified Transformations exercises in their work with students but are especially influenced by work on "Conditions." These are improvisations that were created in the later period of the Open Theatre and further developed in the Winter Project. This work focuses on the breath, sound, and gesture of particular conditions, such as those of a refugee during forced relocation, to use an example from *Tourists and Refugees* (1980). Chaikin was interested in what he called "exiled emotions," expressions of feelings that had been abandoned by commercial theater, like grief and certain expressions of ecstasy. To find a form for these conditions, the actor concentrates on finding the breath and the voice produced by a way of breathing, expanding this information into gestural phrases and ways of moving. Exploring the sound of a moment, talking into a particular moment and "jamming" on the words of a particular phrase are techniques that can be used in this work. In the My House Is Burning exercise, the actor uses the sound of the words, emphasizing their textural and nonverbal qualities to motivate and affect the listener. Zimet says, "You are using sound as a tactile and active force not to convey information to the listeners but to get them to help you put the fire out. The emphasis is on the expressive intention rather than the content of the words."[23] Chaikin in *The Presence of the Actor* wrote, "The question is how to use the voice, not to refer to a condition, but to enter it."[24]

Collage Structure

Making theater pieces without a preexisting script based on the research of dramaturgs and actors within the ensemble has become such an accepted practice in American theater that it is difficult to recall a time when it was considered revolutionary. The form, as we have seen from the remarks of Mira Rafalowicz, owes more to the visual arts and music than to the logic of dramatic literature. Improvisation and "jamming" are techniques that experimental theater of the 1960s shared with other contemporary forms, such as jazz and Happenings. Piecing together fragments of behavior and images of imagined conditions, linked by musical bridges and nonverbal modes, became prevalent in the work of Robert Wilson, Meredith Monk, Ping Chong, Anne Bogart, and many other experimental theater artists. The Open Theatre was a pioneer in assembling performance events in a nonlinear, fragmented, imagistic manner. The work was called dreamlike or hallucinatory at the time but in retrospect could be considered postmodern. Most of the former members of the Open Theatre and Winter Project who continue to make theater and teach have constructed pieces in professional and educational venues that use the improvisation-driven collage format as a structural device. Bill Coco, a dramaturg and close friend of Chaikin's, points to *Struck Dumb,* the postaphasic collaboration of Chaikin and Jean-Claude van Itallie "as a recapitulation of methods used by the Open Theatre."[25] Other examples are the Talking Band / Otrabanda Company's production of *No Plays . . . No Poetry* directed by Anne Bogart and based on the theoretical writings of Bertold Brecht, which won an Obie in 1988 and Otrabanda's Bessie Award–winning *Brain Café* in 1987. In universities and colleges, courses in developmental theater are based on assembling student-generated material using collage-like structures and logic.

The Persistence of Presence

Part of the legacy of the Open Theatre—along with the soft focus pictures by Max Waldman of *Terminal* and the grainy videotapes of *The Serpent*—involves the often fierce debate about the nature of presence, a quality of performance that the Open Theatre rigorously explored throughout its ten-year existence.

The title of Chaikin's 1973 book was *The Presence of the Actor,* and many of the people who teach and perform in the tradition of the Open Theatre continue to negotiate the meaning of this highly contested term. For Rhea Gaisner, presence is "being there—not acting being there, but actually being in the room."[26] For Zimet, presence relates to

> how aware you should be of the audience—the actor as a "double agent," fully in the part and at the same time aware and in dialog with the audience. The aim is not to be in a trance but to have both things going on at once.[27]

Chaikin's use of the word *presence* was problematic for many theorists who wished to make a distinction between classical and more postmodern notions of the term. Chantal Pontbriand, in an often quoted 1982 essay in *Modern Drama* titled "The Eye Finds No Fixed Point on Which to Rest," wrote that to even speak of presence "can indeed seem retrograde." She was more comfortable with terms such as "neo-presence" or "renegotiated presence" and finally "reactualized presence."[28] Pontbriand and other early theorists of postmodern performance saw an attack on presence as a way to critique the structures of authority embodied in theater.[29] Through the use of presence, representation, and the presentation of the actor as an exemplary figure, theater invested itself with an authority to make "truth claims" that was unsupportable. Performance, on the other hand, according to Josette Feral, "rejects all illusion" and "is the absence of meaning."[30] Pontbriand claimed that performance "presents; it does not represent." Of course, in retrospect it is clear that performance did not "escape" presence. It sometimes questioned it or interrogated it, but no more so than did the Open Theatre with their experiments. As Marvin Carlson has pointed out,

> The post-structuralist rejection of the "pure" presence of modernism (and of early performance art) did not, however, inspire a

postmodern rejection in toto of either presence or performance, but rather a reinterpretation of both concepts.[31]

What Chaikin means by "performing in the present" has to do with the actor recognizing the audience and being aware of his own somatic changes, as well as the character's given circumstances. All of this happens "in the moment" or simultaneously. As John Cage would have it, we do not perceive nor accomplish only one thing at a time; rather, "everything happens at once."[32] Roland Barthes described the theater as informational polyphony or a "density of signs."[33] He was referring to the simultaneous messages and items of information proceeding from the set, costumes, speech, lighting, acting, and so on. The actor can also be seen as involved in "an extremely dense semantic act" in that his breath, focus, gestures, tone, sexuality, and many other factors are being generated and manipulated simultaneously. Rather than submerging one's self (or selves) in the portrayal of character, the actor's task, according to Chaikin, was to maintain an open focus that included the spectator, the space of performance, the other actors, the fiction of character, and the visceral reality of the actor's body.

The work that the Open Theatre produced from 1967 to 1973 was actor oriented. It valorized acting as well as the communion between actor and spectator in a way that came to seem old-fashioned by the 1980s. Groups such as the Wooster Group, Richard Foreman's Ontological Hysteric Theatre, and Mabou Mines, which called forth a more favorable critical response and came to be dubbed postmodern, had a different relationship to the actor. These companies still employed highly skilled and charismatic performers like Richard Foreman's partner Kate Manheim, the Wooster Group's Ron Vawter, and Ruth Maleczech from Mabou Mines,[34] but the acting had become highly mediated. Through the use of microphones, video, and almost continual sound environments, the presence of the actor came to be renegotiated and problematized. Whereas Chaikin had been interested in emphasizing presence and communion, absence and distance became the conceptual concerns of the 1980s.

Although it is difficult to trace Chaikin's ideas about acting and composition in the work of contemporary artists who did not directly collaborate with him, his influence continues to resonate. Theater directors such as JoAnne Akalatis, Julie Taymor, and David Leveaux, who were peripherally associated with Chaikin or with members of the Open Theatre, would freely acknowledge being strongly affected by the work. Anne Bogart, who studied with Roberta Sklar at Bard College, cites Chaikin as a "huge influence" on her work.

Roberta introduced me to the philosophical and technical way of approaching the stage. The stage, she and Joe taught, is a place to ask questions. And you should choose questions that are vital to your life and can reverberate beyond your wildest expectations. This is big. Also the notion of the ensemble coming up with the material, from their lives and dreams is central and continues to affect the way I work and with whom I work.[35]

Bogart also notes that commercial shows like *A Chorus Line* could not have happened without Chaikin's innovations, and here the question how one traces the legacy of radical theater companies becomes both interesting and problematic. *A Chorus Line* (like *Hair* or any of the other Broadway shows that borrowed techniques from the sixties theatrical avant-garde) could certainly be termed innovative but hardly radical (although one can imagine the appellation "revolutionary" was freely used by the show's producers and publicists). Clearly, part of the legacy of such legitimately radical theater companies as the Living Theatre and the Open Theatre is to have their techniques and methodologies expropriated and assimilated into the omnivorous mainstream culture that they were rebelling against in the first place. This has happened before. It is an integral part of "showbiz" or what Chaikin referred to as "the set-up." It seems natural, but it is useful to remember that Bertolt Brecht insisted that "when something seems 'the most obvious thing in the world' it means that any attempt to understand the world has been given up."[36] What seems "natural" must be examined and explicated; what is taken for granted must be questioned. This is a legacy that Chaikin inherited from Brecht and passed down to his collaborators and to his audience.

In the twenty-first century, the Open Theatre and its contribution to theater practice are being reevaluated. Open Theatre–inspired acting techniques—along with the "Viewpoints" work of Anne Bogart (via Mary Overlie) and LeCoq's physical approach to acting—can be seen as important alternatives to Stanislavski-based systems in the United States. In an influential book, *Twentieth Century Actor Training*, Alison Hodge includes Chaikin along with Grotowski, Brook, and Mnouchkine as seminal forces in the development of nontraditional, nonrealistic acting practice over the last thirty years. Peter Thomson, a noted Brecht scholar, acknowledges Chaikin as a practitioner who has further developed Brecht's theories.[37] Chaikin's recent death has instigated symposiums at Columbia University and New York University. Allen Kuharski, who has written extensively about Chaikin and the Open Theatre, particularly concerning their influence in Poland and Europe, sees the group as "a fundamental revision and contribution to the American canon of theatrical practice."

Bert States in *Great Reckonings in Little Rooms* discusses the ways in which innovations in the theater become conventions and eventually are reduced to the merely conventional. Innovations are interesting because they are new; then because they help to initiate a new order; finally they disappear into the order and become the building blocks out of which new paradigms are made.[38] "Above all in the theater, as in any art, there is always the need to defamiliarize all the old defamiliarizations."[39] Many of the innovations that Chaikin and the Open Theatre developed to escape the conventions of American realist acting in the 1960s, such as an emphasis on improvisation, transformations, sound and movement, non-verbal modes, and a collage-like, nonlinear structure of images, became part of the normative vocabulary of experimental theater in the United States in the following years. Now, looking back over thirty years, it is possible to see, with the help of historical distance, how strange and estranging these techniques were. Through the work of former members of the company and the practice of a second generation of performers influenced by it and by videotapes, images, and books, the task of "defamiliarizing all the old defamiliarizations" seems possible. The work of the Open Theatre and the "ways of working" continue to have an existence in the memory and practice of many theater artists, ever mindful of Chaikin's warning to resist conventionalization and to remain open:

> I believe that any work for the theater, any different company about to do the same work, and even different actors within the same company require a different approach. There is no path laid out beforehand. The exercises, discussions, and relationships within the group and toward the material must be newly assessed at the beginning of each new adventure of work.[40]

NOTES

1. Mira Rafalowicz, draft of article for *Theater* (Yale University), February 3, 1978. Chaikin Papers, Kent State University Library, Box 6, Folder 10.

2. Chaikin, "Notes on Acting Time and Repetition," in *Three Works by the Open Theatre*, ed. Karen Malpede (New York: Drama Book Specialists, 1974).

3. Allen Kuharski, "Joseph Chaikin and the Presence of the Dramaturg," in *Dramaturgy in American Theater*, ed. Susan Jonas and Geoffrey S. Proehl (New York: Harcourt and Brace, 1997), 156.

4. Mira Rafalowicz, unedited manuscript, Chaikin Papers 2, Box 6, Folder 10.

5. Ibid.

6. Ibid.

7. Ibid.

8. Other theaters started by Open Theatre alumni were Jim Barbossa and Barbara Vann's Medicine Show and Ralph Lee's Mettawee Theater Company. In addition, Joyce Aaron, Peter Feldman, Rhea Gaisner, and Jenn Ben Yakov worked in the Netherlands on several projects.

9. "Roberta Sklar: Toward Creating a Woman's Theatre," interview by Cornelia Brunner, *TDR* 24, no. 2 (1980): 30.

10. Roberta Sklar, interview by the author, tape-recorded, September 11, 2003.

11. Ibid.

12. Paul Zimet, interview by the author, tape-recorded, September 20, 2003.

13. Ibid.

14. Dan Rothenberg, interview by the author, tape-recorded, August 29, 2003.

15. Eileen Blumenthal, *Joseph Chaikin: Exploring at the Boundaries of Theatre* (Cambridge: Cambridge University Press, 1984), 56.

16. John Belluso, telephone interview by the author, April 14, 2004.

17. Bill Hart, telephone interview, February 14, 2004.

18. Blumenthal, *Joseph Chaikin*, 70. Chaikin, although initially suspicious of Pasolli's book, came to regard it as an important contribution to the legacy of the Open Theatre and was concerned that it was no longer in print.

19. Nancy Gabor, interview by the author, tape-recorded. September 7, 2003.

20. Lee Worley, telephone interview by the author, August 23, 2003.

21. Rhea Gaisner, interview, tape-recorded. August 21, 2003; Gabor, interview.

22. Helene Keyssar, *Feminist Theatre* (London: Macmillan, 1984), 59.

23. Zimet, interview.

24. Joseph Chaikin, *The Presence of the Actor* (New York: The Communications Group, 1991) 132.

25. Bill Coco, interview by the author, tape-recorded, September 25, 2003.

26. Gaisner, interview.

27. Zimet, interview.

28. Chantal Pontbriand, "The Eye Finds No Fixed Point on Which to Rest," *Modern Drama* 25, no. 1 (1982): 155.

29. See the special issue of *Modern Drama* cited in the preceding note, which, in addition to Pontbriand's article, contains Jossete Feral's "Performance and Theatricality." 170–81 Philip Auslander helps explicate the issues in the third chapter of his *Presence and Resistance* (Ann Arbor: University of Michigan Press, 1992).

30. Feral, "Performance and Theatricality," 171, 173.

31. Marvin Carlson, *Performance: A Critical Introduction* (New York: Routledge, 1996), 136.

32. Cage quoted in Schmitt, *Actors and Onlookers* (Evanston, Ill.: Northwestern University Press, 1990), 16.

33. Roland Barthes, "Literature and Signification," in *Critical Essays*, trans. Richard Howard (Evanston, Ill.: Northwestern University Press, 1972), 262.

34. In fact, it is difficult to contemplate Foreman's success without acknowledging the extraordinary contribution of Kate Manheim. Similarly, one can point

to the significance of Spalding Gray to Liz LeCompte's work or David Warrilow to Lee Breuer's.

35. Anne Bogart, e-mail to author, March 30, 2005.

36. Bertold Brecht, "Theatre for Pleasure or Theatre for Instruction," in *Brecht on Theatre,* ed. John Willett (New York: Hill and Wang, 1992), 71.

37. Peter Thomson, "Brecht and Actor Training," in *Twentieth Century Actor Training,* ed. Alison Hodge (London: Routledge, 2000), 106.

38. States acknowledges the influence of Thomas Kuhn's *Structure of Scientific Revolutions* as an influence on his thinking.

39. Bert States, *Great Reckonings in Little Rooms* (Berkeley and Los Angeles: University of California Press, 1985), 43.

40. Chaikin, *Presence of the Actor,* 134.

AT THE FOOT OF THE MOUNTAIN
Historical Overview

At the Foot of the Mountain was a Minneapolis company whose trajectory and challenges paralleled many other cultural feminist theater collectives of the 1970s and 1980s and was one of the first of its kind. The group was launched as an experimental theater in 1974 by Paul and Martha Boesing, Jan Magrane, and three others who consulted the I Ching for a name and inspiration. As was often the case with radical theaters, At the Foot of the Mountain had creative roots in preexisting collectives. Paul had been an actor with the Open Theater in New York; he and Martha met when he was hired as a director for the Firehouse Theater in Minneapolis, where she was a member. The Boesings had first considered Atlanta as a starting place for their theater; it was there they met Magrane, an actor, when they toured through.

Collectivity, community, and political commitment were essential elements of the theater company from the beginning, but by the end of the company's first summer season (1974), which consisted of two one-act plays about sexuality and gender relations written by Martha Boesing, *The Gelding* and *The Pimp*, the group had shifted toward a focus on women's experience. In 1975 Paul Boesing left the group, as did the other men in the company, and At the Foot of the Mountain began to identify as a feminist theater. The Boesings' marriage split apart as well; Martha's new partner was Phyllis Jane Rose (then Wagner), who resigned as chairperson of Southern Illinois State University's directing program in order to form a collective with Martha Boesing and Magrane.[1]

These three were the central figures in the group's evolution over the next ten years. Under Boesing's artistic directorship (1974–84) the company produced more than twenty of her plays. The first to be called "feminist" was *River Journal* (1975), a controversial work among audiences, as among spectators throughout the group's history. *Moon Tree*, in 1976, was the first piece produced by the revisioned, separatist women's theater company. It was a collaborative work by Boesing and At the Foot actors, much in the manner of the collective creations of the Open Theater and playwrights Megan Terry and Jean-Claude van Itallie. Boesing's scripts were frequently based on actors' improvisations in rehearsals and were often drawn from the Feeling Circle, a practice in feminist theater-making at the time, where actors used improvisations to explore issues or ideas that emerged out of women's shared experiences—rape, motherhood, insanity, and so on. A statement of purpose in a company brochure (1976) declared that At the Foot of the Mountain was a theater of questions, not answers, composed of female/matriarchal values, spirit, and qualities: "circular, intuitive, personal, involving. We are a theatre of protest . . . and a theatre of celebration."[2]

River Journal and *Raped,* which premiered in 1976, were influenced by Boesing's and the group's interest in Brechtian theater. *Raped,* an adaptation of Brecht's *The Exception and the Rule,* was developed from a Marxist-feminist perspective, with rape seen as a violent metaphor for women's oppression in a patriarchal, capitalist society. *Raped* marked a pivotal moment in the company's political theater work, for the play was restructured to allow for and encourage audience participation in the form of interruptions by women in the audience who would tell their own rape stories. This personal storytelling element was an integral part of the consciousness-raising strategy of feminist theaters at the time and a central contribution of this phase of the feminist movement.

Critical reception to the company's first decade of work was extremely positive, which was unusual among feminist theaters. Unlike the members of many other feminist collectives, At the Foot of the Mountain participants were well trained in academic or professional theater and the level of ensemble acting was high. During the first decade of its history, At the Foot participants were white women twenty to forty years of age, and the theater's audiences were predominately of the same racial, gender, and age group.[3]

Although the work was process-oriented and nonlinear in structure, performances were always in small theaters and not in the street or other alternative spaces.[4] In 1977 with a production of *The Story of a Mother,* the collaboration with the audience began at an earlier point in the process and was expanded into what has been described as "open-ended rituals."[5]

For Boesing and other feminist theater workers, ritual in the theater had healing power.[6] *The Story of a Mother* was developed not just from actors' stories in rehearsal (At the Foot of the Mountain also collaborated with Boston's Caravan Theatre on the mother/daughter material), but in workshops with women in communities outside the theater, including senior citizens' groups.[7]

Other plays Boesing cocreated with the company include *Junkie* (1981), *Ashes, Ashes, We All Fall Down* (1982), and *Las Gringas* (1984). A well-known "collage" work created by Boesing was *Antigone Too: Rites of Love and Defiance* (1983). *Love Song to an Amazon* (1976), written by Boesing "as a gift for Phyllis," was the only Boesing play specifically about lesbian lovers.[8]

The Story of a Mother II, produced under Phyllis Jane Rose's directorship after the company had overhauled its staff, its board of directors, and its acting ensemble in an effort to become multicultural (1987), caused one of the greatest controversies associated with the group when the play was presented at the Women and Theatre Program Conference in Chicago in 1987.

According to some spectators, the piece was coercive, reflecting a kind of oppressive representational framework women had experienced in traditional, patriarchal theater and society. Spectators' names were randomly selected from a tambourine and those chosen were expected to join the telling of "mother stories" onstage. There was (purportedly) no space or opportunity to reject or resist the ritual, which seemed based on the prescribed centrality of the mother/daughter relationship and the nuclear family. Some spectators (the audience was mostly white academics) also objected to the (purportedly racist and outmoded) cultural feminist perspective of the ritual, which had not been revisioned since its original presentation in 1977 and, in some spectators' views, did not take into account the presence or experiences of the women of color on stage. Conversely, At the Foot felt that the audience's negative critique was racist in its rejection of the performance by women of color.[9]

While under Rose's leadership the company collaborated with Spiderwoman Theater on *Neurotic Erotic Exotics* (1985), and produced plays by well-known Latina and African-American writers including Maria Irene Fornes (*Fefu and Her Friends*) and Adrienne Kennedy (*Funnyhouse of a Negro*). African-American poet and playwright Nayo-Barbara Watkins, who also worked with Junebug Productions (an offshoot of the Free Southern Theater), became managing director of At the Foot of the Mountain in 1987.

At the Foot of the Mountain ceased to exist in 1991. During the theater's final two years, the company de-emphasized theater production altogether and focused on process, community outreach, and on work-shops with social action as the goal, rather than art or aesthetics. Critical response, not surprisingly, was negative in this final phase.

—C. R.

NOTES

1. Linda Walsh Jenkins, "At the Foot of the Mountain," in *Women in American Theatre,* ed. Helen Krich Chinoy and Linda Walsh Jenkins (New York: Theatre Communications Group, 1987), 302.

2. Dinah Leavitt, *Feminist Theatre Groups* (Jefferson, N.C.: McFarland, 1980), 67–68.

3. Ibid., 66–70.

4. Ibid., 69.

5. Charlotte Canning, *Feminist Theaters in the U.S.A.: Staging Women's Experience* (New York: Routledge, 1991), 131.

6. Ibid., 127.

7. Ibid., 184.

8. See Lynne Greeley's essay in this volume.

9. Jill Dolan, *The Feminist Spectator as Critic* (Ann Arbor: University of Michigan Press, 1988), 92–95; Canning, *Feminist Theaters,* 200–201.

CUT BY THE CUTTING EDGE

Martha Boesing and At the Foot of the Mountain

Lynne Greeley

Initially an experimental theater, At the Foot of the Mountain became explicitly feminist after its first summer of productions in 1974, when for various reasons, the men dropped out of the company and issues of importance to the women dominated. The company thereafter produced over twenty plays by Martha Boesing during her tenure as artistic director (1974–84), five of which were written collaboratively, and the rest authored by Boesing alone. In the early to middle 1980s, At the Foot of the Mountain was featured in the critical literature and at theater conferences for its original application of consciously articulated feminist politics to the creation of their plays. Then, in 1987, after a workshop performance of the multicultural collaborative piece, *The Story of a Mother II,* at the Women and Theatre Program in Chicago, heated discussion ensued between women of different feminisms; subsequently labeled cultural feminists, Boesing and At the Foot of the Mountain lost momentum as subjects for study in critical scholarship.

Three connections, first, between a collaborative theater and its artistic director and writer, second, between the theater and its audience of critics, and third, between criticism and the construction of history, illustrate the complex dynamics by which a performance and critical response to it serve to historicize the group performing, eventually standing as evidence not only for the corpus of work of the group, but also for the social or political group they are seen to represent. By briefly reviewing the origins of

At the Foot of the Mountain, the wider scope of the plays produced with Boesing beyond the several collaborative pieces most often discussed, and the events that shaped the theater's critical and scholarly reception, we can consider the ways in which the shift in feminist criticism from the celebratory, embracing women's experience, to the critique, evaluating without necessarily celebrating,[1] not only influenced the writing of feminist theatrical history, but reflected a theoretical hegemony emerging in the critical literature.

Critical Beginnings

The immediate context for the beginnings of At the Foot of the Mountain was Minneapolis, a city in which feminist theatrical activity was varied and intense. In November 1975, Linda Picone of the *Minneapolis Tribune* noted while reviewing several productions that those that "take the title 'feminist theatre' vary as widely as do the definitions of feminist."[2] At the time of Picone's writing, At the Foot of the Mountain was just beginning, and by 1980, two previously dynamic companies, the Alive and Trucking Theatre and the Lavender Cellar Theatre, had stopped producing while At the Foot of the Mountain was prospering.

At the Foot of the Mountain really began in Cambridge, Massachusetts, in 1970, when Martha and Paul Boesing became interested in establishing a theater, transiting through Atlanta, where they felt "the soul of the city was really black"[3] and their theater wasn't a match, and arriving in Minneapolis in 1974. The company turned to the I Ching in search of a name, responding to the hexagram "The Spring at the Foot of the Mountain," which suggested their own search for roots both personal and theatrical.[4] In its original form, At the Foot of the Mountain was an experimental theater, an offspring of the Open Theater and the Firehouse Theater, with which both Boesings had been associated,[5] opening in the summer of 1974 with two one-act plays by Martha: *Pimp*, in which women sell out each other and themselves for men, and *The Gelding*, in which men struggle to make contact with each other in spite of frozen emotion.[6] Both plays were inspired by newspaper articles dealing with parent-child relationships, the first about a woman indicted "for selling her daughter for $40,000.00, the second about a father accused of castrating his son."[7] The two plays exemplified the daring with which Boesing presented her ideas before At the Foot of the Mountain declared itself feminist.

During the six months that followed, the company went through changes, partially because of individual work on primal therapy, partially because the Boesings were experiencing marital difficulties, and partially because Phyllis Jane Rose, who had joined the group, became Martha's partner, both professionally and personally. Jan Magrane, an actor who had come with the Boesings from Atlanta, described those early years:

> We were so ambitious. We just decided on a season of plays that we were going to do. . . . We were doing all the beginning things of an institution. We were getting nonprofit status. We were writing grants. I built sets in my basement. I did the costumes. After that season, we toured in Phyllis's van. We worked really hard, and I look back on that as one of the richest and most exciting times of my life.[8]

While the company was developing, Martha continued to write, and, together, they produced *River Journal* (1975), which she dubbed a "feminist morality play," thereby, for the first time, identifying her work as feminist.[9] Though in 1987 Boesing admitted embarrassment at the dated subject matter of the play, an exploration of the masks women are trained to wear in their relationships with men,[10] *River Journal* was significant for the company for two reasons. First, the play provoked controversy in the press because, as Boesing had hoped, it effectively aroused audiences, both positively and negatively, a tendency in her writing that worked to her detriment when she later antagonized feminist audiences. Second, around the time the play opened, "the men, through lack of interest and energy merely dropped out of the company,"[11] so that the opening of Boesing's "feminist morality play" marked the company's beginnings as a feminist/woman's theater. At no point did they see themselves as separatists, but it was their common experience as women around which their performances coalesced. Unlike other grassroots theaters, about which Patti Gillespie noted that the "artistic quality of the productions is often quite mediocre when judged by traditional criteria,"[12] the company of At the Foot of the Mountain included both professionally and academically trained members[13] whose vision of the art of theater was polished and specific.

Collaborations

The cornerstone of At the Foot of the Mountain's work was collaborative play production in which, like most experimental theaters, they undid hierarchical arrangements "to maximize individual participation and equalize power."[14] Unlike the Firehouse Theatre,[15] which both Boesings found to be undercut by sexism,[16] At the Foot of the Mountain attained a successful collaboration between actors and playwright, by maintaining that directors were facilitators who built ensembles from cooperation, not competition. Boesing scripted the projects as they evolved from the actors not only in the collaboratively produced scripts but also in the plays created by her alone, moving ahead of some of their radical predecessors in which the "atmosphere was competitive . . . and the writer was clearly the outsider . . . [in a] position that was a priori tenuous."[17] Even though at this point in the women's movement, oppression was a point of unification for performers,[18] other feminist theaters resisted a single author as voice of the many, focusing on the process of subsequently unrecorded and unpublished plays.[19]

Each collaboratively produced piece grew out of an idea from which improvisations were explored until the play itself started to take form. Boesing took the material of the improvisations away from rehearsal to craft the piece into a repeatable structure on which the performers could build in subsequent rehearsals, a technique Megan Terry described as "not easy to do."[20] In the end a play would emerge that reflected the input of all performers, often containing personal stories in which the actor and the character would become one in a theatricalized blend that was not merely the actor playing herself. The repeatability of the pieces, however, depended on the work Boesing brought to bear on the writing, for without it, the improvisations would have disappeared with the experience of their performance, as have works from other feminist theaters producing during the same period. Rose, who became the producing director of At the Foot of the Mountain, considers the collaborative pieces Boesing's best work because her architectural skills were brought to the experiences of others so that some movement she wanted to play out was made visible;[21] hence, the messages that are filtered through the performers paradoxically serve as windows for the ideas Boesing inspired. Nonetheless, the characters in the collaborative plays reflect a collective view because, as Boesing explained, the actors really bring female energy to bear on an issue while contributing to the movement of the plot through constantly transforming characters,[22] so that no one role is central and no actor stars, another obvious expression of collectivity. The concern among feminist critics in the late 1980s and 1990s for the "mutable feminist subject in a theatrical context"[23] telling stories without participating in the inquiry about the constructiveness of those stories[24] was irrelevant to women for whom theatrical performance was the expression and healing of their life experiences. Developing what they called the Feeling Circle, a practice adopted by other feminist theaters of the period,[25] improvisational work centered on the feelings evoked in the actresses in response to an idea, such as rape, motherhood, or insanity, around which the play was organized. Evocative of artistic traditions derivative of Antonin Artaud and Jerzy Grotowski, without the emotional violence, the techniques called for a penetration[26] into the psychic experience of the individual actors that in turn penetrated the psychic experience of the audience.

The result of both the Feeling Circle and collaborative script creation is what Boesing describes as drama that is ritual. More than a final ceremony such as chants, candle lighting, or invitations for audience participation, Boesing's rituals are actually built into the texture of the plays as part of the dramatic structure for the sole purpose of affecting the emotions of the cast and the audience.[27] As with other theater ensembles of the period, the ritual was a "tool for allowing the community of performers [and] spectator . . . to succumb to something larger and nobler than itself."[28] By means of "repetitive motions or through a litany . . . or music, or finding the emotional presence that is so profound under that—the love expressed, or the hate expressed, or whatever is expressed—embellishing it by taking the gesture and the feeling, crystallizing the ceremony of that—then you have lifted it into something . . . [it becomes] ritual."[29]

The group discovered that "larger something" through political directives that both shocked and attracted the audiences of Minneapolis. When the adaptation *Raped: A Woman's Look at Bertolt Brecht's "Exception and the Rule"* was produced in 1976, audiences stood in line for hours waiting to get into the cramped basement space where ice cubes in rags were distributed to offset the unusual and unbearable summer heat[30] for a performance that used rape as a metaphor for women's oppression.[31] The ritual of storytelling from audience members, who had the right to yell "Stop!" at any point in the performance to do their sharing, kept the performers constantly on an edge that could cut both ways. As Jan Magrane described, "They could stop us in the middle of a song, and the songs were a capella. Then we'd have to keep the note in our heads so we could start again a capella,"[32] so the play could keep moving. Boesing summarized their work, saying, "I am finally convinced that what we are dealing with culturally is the question, 'What are we?' . . . we are looking for *more,* and MORE is not flesh and bones. We need to look into the center. We need to all meet somewhere in a real way to heal."[33]

At the Foot of the Mountain expanded techniques of collaboration inherited from the experimental theater of the 1960s, interpreted politically through the experience of their womanhood. From Paul Boesing's work with the Open Theater and their joint work at the Firehouse, the Boesings had internalized the processes of creating from collaboration and valuing collective interpretation, positions that became fundamental to the

At the Foot of the Mountain, *Raped,* 1976. Performers include Miriam Monasch, Jan Magrane, Robyn Samuels, Anne Bowman and Martha Boesing. (At the Foot of the Mountain Theatre Records, Performing Arts Archives, University of Minnesota Libraries, Minneapolis.)

group's work. Feelings, however, were not part of their experimental inheritance, primarily because the focus of predecessors was on either politics or art, without the personal connection to both sought by the women in the company. The impact on the audience, however, was double pronged: first, in the tradition of Brecht, the group created distance by making the art of theater visible through the nonrealistic use of the stage space and the episodic structuring of the plots; second, in the tradition of Artaud, they closed that distance through the self-disclosure of actor as character or audience member as participant for the purpose of invoking emotional response. Probing for thought while exorcizing feelings provoked complex and sometimes conflictive responses in spectators, which Boesing considered to be positive and essential to the evocation of action.

The Plays

The plays between 1974 and 1984 can be divided into two major groups, the collaboratively created pieces and the single-authored pieces. In the collaborative works, Boesing wrote a skeleton and then the dialogues and characters were created out of improvisations with the company.[34] *Journey to Canaan* (1974), *The Story of a Mother* (1977), *Junkie!* (1981), *Ashes, Ashes We All Fall Down* (1982), and *Las Gringas* (1984) are examples of this process. *The Moon Tree* (1976) is a mixed-collaborative piece because it was first written by Boesing and then rewritten with the company. Of those plays written by Boesing alone, there are two subgroups: the historical collages and the original pieces. The collages were created out of texts not original to Boesing, either classical materials or public statements of historical figures. *Antigone Too: Rites of Love and Defiance* (1983) was written predominantly in collage style, whereas *Dora Du Fran's Wild West Extravaganza or The Real Low Down on Calamity Jane* (1979) and *The Mothers of Ludlow* (1983) contain actual words only of the main characters, while the rest of the cast is fictionalized. The single-authored plays include two of full length, *The Web*[35] and *River Journal*,[36] and eleven one-acts.[37]

With the exception of *Journey to Canaan,* the collaborative and collage plays were created after At the Foot of the Mountain had declared itself a feminist theater. Exemplary of collaboration between playwright and actors, the plays also illustrate experimentation with all the elements of performance. The use of the stage space, for example, expands outward and upward physically as the plays become more complex textually, ranging from total "emptiness to complex sets of several levels with multiple scenes occurring simultaneously" in womblike images, in which "stark lights focus on two or three actors moving against dark emptiness," to those in which a central point is the pivot, as higher and wider levels of action unfold on expanded sets.[38] Similarly, in the collaborative pieces, the plots build momentum with an increase in the formality of the rituals; mundane objective reality is "translated into a more abstract subjectivity as the characters reveal their private thoughts and feelings, through words, themes, or images that may repeat." The plots move forward in spirals, not circles, because with each return they expand wider and ultimately draw the audience in,[39] a constantly moving structure held only momentarily by a single point of view. The modus operandi of the collaboration is to capture multiple perceptions around a central idea, which in turn refract multiple reactions in the audience. To what extent the momentary single point of view universalized women's experience, suggesting that all women could relate to it, and thus implied an expected reaction from the audience, is the question the company later confronted with their feminist spectators.

Of the collaborative plays, the most controversial are *The Story of a Mother* and its multicultural revision, *The Story of a Mother II.*[40] Of the collage pieces,

Antigone, Too: Rites of Love and Defiance has repeatedly appealed to colleges and universities for production.[41] Neither play, however, represents the intimacy between actor and playwright in the collaborative process as well as *Junkie!,*[42] a full-length piece created out of the "testimonies of addicts from both within and outside the company." The play explores the addictions of the performers, whose characters came from themselves, shaped by Boesing and scripted as a play. In addition to the addicted characters, a seventh cast member plays a clown, a dramatic device to both lighten the dialogue and integrate the stories as she interacts with the other characters, who are disconnected because of their addictions. The play concludes with the sharing of recovery stories by actors and audience in an attempt to create "a spontaneous and immediate communal renewal, as the first step to spiritual surrender and recovery."[43]

One of the actors, Kay Bolstad, expressing her own life experience as a mother of six deserted by her husband after twenty years of marriage, created a character who translated her need for love into a need for food. She exposed her addictions as well as their hidden manifestations, such as beatings of her daughter.

> The work started when we got together with Martha and started doing improvisations. . . . The process was one of revealing one's innermost secrets, [a] process . . . very dependent on being an ensemble. We were working off one another and being thoroughly connected to one another. It's that pushing the edge of telling our thing that's just shocking about *Junkie!* . . . I beat the shit out of one actress at one point in a mother/daughter scene. There were some real cathartic kinds of experiences for people. . . . *Junkie!* changed my life.[44]

The play ends with a ritual in which all of the addicts place their bags, symbolizing their addictions, in the center of the stage. Urging audience participation,[45] a process sometimes resisted by the unconverted, the actors come into the audience, offering gifts, incense, water, grain, a poem, a candle, dabs of red and white paint that represent both their addictions and their healing. They say a blessing invoking earth, water, air, and fire, for example, "I give you the sweet air, source of my wounds, source of my power."[46] Finally they introduce themselves by name: "I am Anne, recovering alcoholic."[47] Paradoxically stripping away artifice in the artificial setting of the performance space, *Junkie!* crosses boundaries between personal and public, safe and unsafe. Conflictive for some audience members, others found freedom to express what was taboo outside of that space, such as the police officer who entered the stage after the last ritual, threw down his badge, and announced he was addicted to power.[48]

Junkie! illustrates the process by which At the Foot of the Mountain developed a play collaboratively around a single idea. Using the material of their addictions, the actors improvised scenes that Boesing crafted into a theatrical piece. It spiraled internally in its textual use of language and music, and externally in the choreography of the actors on the stage, who reached in widening circles to the audience, which was in turn provoked to spiral into a place of vulnerability. Repeated words and images, juxtaposed against sung refrains that also repeated words and images, were matched by movements on the stage that started small, two actors moving around each other, and then expanded until the actors were circling the edge of the performance area, often drawing audience members into it. The process rendered visible the concept of "actor becom[ing]. . . audience."[49] Simultaneously, audience members were confronted with sometimes painful personal responses to the issues raised by the plays.

The collage pieces, three in total, represent another kind of collaboration, a playwright in cooperation with living communities, both past and present. *Antigone Too: Rites of Love and Defiance,* the most complex of the collage pieces, includes the speeches of seventeen to twenty historical and living women (the text is flexible in this regard) woven into the Antigone myth. Through a chorus of misfits and single-gender casting, Boesing reminds her viewers how women have been "cast out" both of theater and society, the play an act of historical recovery that celebrates "a community of women whose names have been forgotten by many but who have played a vital role in social change."[50] A sampling of the contrasts include Mary Dyer, an eighteenth-century Quaker, hanged in Boston for preaching the individual's right to a personal inner light; Fannie Lou Hamer, a twentieth-century black southerner, jailed for trying to vote; Jessie Lopez de la Cruz, a migrant worker from the San Joaquin Valley, arrested for her work with the United Farm Workers; and Starhawk, a witch originally from New York, arrested for antinuclear demonstrations against the Diablo Canyon plant.[51] Each of the characters committed an act of civil disobedience that is dramatized in the play.

One of the ways in which Boesing tied her characters to their audiences was through the emotional resonance of music. Songs such as the first-wave feminists' "Bread and Roses," the South African "Freedom Song," the civil rights movement's "We Shall Overcome," and the American folk song "Oh, Mary, Don't You Weep, Don't You Moan" occur as emotional climaxes are reached in the episodic plot. In one of the college productions of *Antigone Too* at the University of Maryland in 1986, Bobbi

Ausubel,[52] who consulted with Boesing on the production, directed each of the individual stories as a choreography between actors and audience in which music served as a bridge. For example, after the scene that concludes with "Bread and Roses," Starhawk and the cast enacted the weaving of a web across Diablo Canyon, crisscrossing pieces of thick orange yarn from one side of the stage to the other, the ends of which were given to audience members, thus, literally tying them to the events on stage. Alternately humming and singing as they dashed across the "canyon" closing off a nuclear power plant, the actors continued to sing as Starhawk spoke above them, saying, "We fear for the life of this planet, our Earth, and the life the children who are our human future."[53] Creon entered and cut the strands of yarn, and Barbara Demming, civil rights activist,[54] shouted above the choral swells, "We cannot live without our lives!" and Marjorie Melville, one of the Catonsville 9,[55] concluded, "We know there is a healthy, sensible, loving way to live, and we intend to live that way."[56] As Creon stepped to his platform, the song ended abruptly—silenced.

The collaborative and collage plays express the workings of multiple viewpoints. By contrast, the solo-authored works rely on Boesing's artistic vision alone. Two of these plays, *The Web* and *River Journal,* have received significant response in the critical literature. The lead character in *The Web*, Abigail Sater, has been interpreted as a *raissoneur* whose "orgasmic theory" of feminist aesthetics expressed in the text of the play is assumed to be Boesing's own.[57] Boesing maintains that the character and she have separate opinions, that multiorgasmic writing is interesting conceptually only, but isn't necessarily a basis to her own writing structures.[58] She did admit, however, that the story of Abigail, playwright and mother, is partially autobiographical.[59]

The stage directions in *The Web* are unusually explicit: a chair downstage center that faces upstage, a pivotal point where Abigail begins and ends the play, reinforces the impression that she is watching her own life on the multileveled set containing rooms to different moments in the past. Viewing not only herself as a child, but also her mother, aunt, cousins, uncle, and brother, while rushing repeatedly to answer the phone from her unseen daughters and give lectures to unseen students (or the audience), Abigail compresses her life into two acts that conclude with the Child, Abby, and the Adult, Abigail, facing a collage of scenes as all of the other characters appear in different parts of the set simultaneously. Looking at her past captured on one stage, she comments, "I'd like to hoard you all up, save you— the way you are right now; the way you fit."[60] The most polished of her pieces, *The Web* contains sophisticated theatrical crafting but gets bogged down in discussions centering on the content of Abigail's lectures.

River Journal, on the other hand, is the morality play that launched At the Foot of the Mountain as a feminist theater. Again, sophisticated in its theatricality, the play incorporates masks, mythical characters, found costumes and objects, and dolls of "every kind imaginable,"[61] in a text that crosses from convention into madness through the journaling of a young bride as she confronts the roles imposed on her. Declared dated in content by Boesing herself,[62] the play's manipulation of objects and bizarre characters places it decidedly in the tradition of the avant-garde. Other plays that illustrate the breadth of the company's experiments include *Love Song to an Amazon* (1976), *Labia Wings* (1979), and *The Last Fire* (1981). The radio play *A Song for Johanna* (1981) presages Boesing's later concern with ecology.[63] I mention these plays, two of which have been clustered with the "hag plays,"[64] because they wonderfully illustrate the radical theater's facility as "a midwife to dreams."[65]

In the preface of *Love Song to an Amazon,* Boesing writes, "This is a play for two women. It is a celebration and ritual enactment of their friendship,"[66] revealed through a "prism like series of images created through sudden and frequent transformations [in which] they are seen as school chums, career women, mothers, daughters, teachers, students, lovers, Amazon warriors, visionaries."[67] Written as a gift for Phyllis Jane Rose, *Love Song to an Amazon* is Boesing's only play that deals specifically with lesbian lovers, evoking sensuality rare in her writing. The play begins, "Once upon a time, there was a little girl,"[68] and Aisha becomes the child whom Rose joins in a spoken song with images and memories of childhood. As the rhythms increase, the poetry turns from that of a lullaby to a love song: "She leaned over and kissed me. She kissed me on the mouth. I held my breath."[69] Aisha asks Rose, "Is this a play?" Rose answers, "This is a song," spoken, not sung, as stones rolled from one side of the playing space to the other provide the rhythm that builds as the lovers discover their child selves, their adult selves, their mutual love, and their love for all women. Bonding first to each other, they extend their bond in rising rhythms to "thousands":

The space was open.
There was an open space
for each of us
to walk in.
The love for one
was also the love
for another.
There was no difference.[70]

As a song, *Love Song to an Amazon* crosses boundaries the collaborative pieces do not: in language that is sensual and mildly erotic, verbal love-making is extended first to performance and then to all women. Much in the mode of Adrienne Rich,[71] it is the lesbian in Boesing that gravitated from one strong woman to find strength in all women, opening the intimate to the political with assumptions about "no difference" that, though misunderstood later, ultimately undercut her outreach.

Labia Wings, a mockery of Christian mythology, takes place before a backdrop of a "huge, single flower, a lily, perhaps, or an iris," evoking Judy Chicago's *Dinner Party,*[72] which faces front and looks as if it could be entered.[73] The play, a "zinger at the Christmas pageant shot with a blunderbuss,"[74] is a "mad, surrealistic romp into a world in which three old crones predict the end of any era . . . [and] the world's change-over into a matriarchy. . . . the Three Headed Goddess comes for a visit,"[75] arriving from the audience as three characters: a bird with a woman's head, a fat whore on stilts, and a woman with four arms and huge feet. Before the lily, the goddess enacts the birth of the new age in which a burst balloon represents the death of the patriarch as Mary is recast without a son. Joseph enters followed by a donkey, and in the course of the play commits suicide several times while Mary mourns for him: "My husband! My lover! My father! My paramour! My son! My sweetheart! My swain! My flame! My cock-a-too! My cunt tickler! My meatgrinder!"[76] Henriette, the third in the trinity of Father, Mother, and Daughter, represents woman, transforming from a six-year-old to a governess, a wife, and back to a child, who greets the three goddesses and rides off on the donkey led by Mary, carrying a balloon wrapped in a blanket, which she pops "with a great explosion as church bells ring."[77] Resolving into generalized meanings, Joseph ends the age of violence with his own shooting, and the new age is greeted by a woman, a female child, and a trio of crones.[78] With absurd exaggeration, *Labia Wings* casts doubt on the meanings of any religious ideology.

The Last Fire: An Illumination is a one-act that predicts the future in the surrealistic style of *Labia Wings.* However, instead of ushering in a new age, the world after a nuclear holocaust is portrayed; here: "the frightened opportunist, Babaganoose, seeks redemption by burning a witch and a faggot; and Karushka, the old hag, cries out for repentance from all."[79] Karushka is situated on a raised platform, the only set piece on the stage, and the props (an apple, stakes, coins, Bibles) symbolize some aspect of the mythology of the dying planet. The play integrates political themes with emblematic characters and staging in a style that lines humor with horror.

A Song for Johanna, Boesing's only radio play written during this period, relies on language, and best represents the haunting way in which she can cycle through the material and into the listener. The play has a cast of three: Johanna, a woman in her late forties, Gerry, her husband, and Matthew, her son. The stage directions indicate that "all of the words . . . spoken by Johanna . . . take place in her mind, are not heard by the others, and are always accompanied by the recorded songs of the humpback whale."[80]

In the narrative, Johanna has shut herself up in the bathroom, and Matthew discovers that "Mom's sitting in the bathtub. But she's not taking a bath. She's . . . she's just sitting there with all her clothes on."[81] Johanna stays in the bathtub with the water running for ten days while her husband and son are in torment until she departs for "Anchorage to study the songs of the Humpback Whales,"[82] with only a note as her farewell. Looping its listener in cycles of repetitions, the play moves from Johanna to her husband and son with repeating images, the men referring to the same mundane items as Johanna literally spans the horizon looking for the whale, eventually zooming in as she hugs its rounded mass with her legs:

> I will lay my head against your huge
>   humped back
> and straddling my legs across your
>   heaving sides
> I will travel down the grey-green-by-
>   way of the ocean's sphere . . .
> and I will wind my arms around
>   your massive flesh
> and you, Goliath, you will breathe
>   me back
> to the origins of time and sing
>   long-voweled songs
> about the meeting of the heavens
>   and the earth,
> 'til Naiad-born again from you fat
>   maw, great grampus,
> I will sail unfettered, free at
>   last, into the light
> from which I first emerged.[83]

Johanna seeks origins that go beyond her lifetime. As the largest, longest-surviving mammal, the whale symbolizes the wild, and through language that juxtaposes the freedom of the deep with the controlled familiarity of hot dogs, Boesing interrogates a social order that permits its members to be the larvae of the natural environment rather than the protectors. In "Song to Johanna" the plot moves because the cyclic repetition of poetic and mundane language occurs in harmony with the call of the whale, which increases in volume as Johanna speaks in poetry and decreases in volume as the men speak in prose. The effect is that the sounds and the words create a spiraling narrative in which civilization and its rules are secondary to the need to protect a prehistoric mammal.

The plays produced by At the Foot of the Mountain during Boesing's tenure range in size of cast from thirty-two to two; from sets containing a precarious balance of detail and symbol to an empty stage with only lights and actors; from a cacophony of voices to the song of a single singer. The dramatic texts produced by the company in combination with the reviews and criticism available in print archives form a rich composite of evidence for feminist theater.

The Criticism

In the final ritual of *The Story of a Mother II,* enacted at the Women and Performance Program in Chicago in 1987, audience members were asked to reenter the body of their mothers. The performance of provoked considerable debate, as Sue-Ellen Case recalls.

> The thing was that going into the body of your mother would be a positive experience. And so I remember raising the issue that my mother had some really horrible social attitudes, and I thought that the generalized technique of going into the mother's body overlooked differences between mothers, social class differences, and other differences that might not be positive images. . . . And that didn't seem to be an acceptable reaction . . . because there was an idealization going on about the relationship [between mothers and daughters].[84]

Case's observations were echoed by other materialist feminists present at the performance who reacted vehemently to the final ritual. Jill Dolan described the play as an "outmoded 1960s artifact dusted off in the 1980s context . . . reminiscent of an earlier historical moment [before] a decade of theorizing, practicing, and refining [feminist] politics."[85] Dolan suggested that Boesing's absence at a conference where her own play and company were performing reflected her unwillingness to face criticism. However, her presence was dynamically felt through asking the audience for participation in a ritual that Dolan and others present found coercive. Boesing herself has described the difficulty of inviting audience participation without coercion,[86] suggesting her critical awareness of defects in the process. Dolan, however, also objected to the reverential stance taken in the play toward women, identifying that stance as a conservative cultural feminist position.[87] In 1987, when feminists in theater were expanding the implications of critical theory, Boesing was already seen as irrelevant to the discussion.

The nature of this discussion was not unlike the discussion led by Joan Holden three years earlier in which she responded to a speech made by Abigail in *The Web:* "women's plays should be multi-orgasmic in form, small mini-scenes . . . coming in waves of emotions, crests and valleys, like the ebb and flow of changing tides, and finally consummating in a sense of nourishment and plentitude, the creating of new life, birth."[88] What if a feminist playwright, Holden argued, doesn't write in miniscenes? How could this particular structure be situated as a defining element in a feminist aesthetic?[89] While Boesing denied that the character was expressing Boesing's own opinions, considerable discussion occurred after performances of At the Foot of the Mountain concerning the differences between masculinist and feminist views of art and politics.[90] These discussions were the prelude to the Chicago event, which clearly demarcated the widening gap between the theater and its audience of feminist critics.

Specifically, in the mode of their earliest days of discovery, At the Foot of the Mountain was seeking to uncover what women shared. Overlooking differences was essential for group empowerment, and yet these differences ultimately caused the collapse of the group. The company was accused of universalizing a white, middle-class perspective, though the production featured multicultural actors,[91] because "the interweaving of the narratives . . . under the rubric of *the* story of *a* mother . . . works to collapse the differences between them."[92] When the company carried over its artistic efforts at multiculturalism to the management of the theater, they discovered that they were still serving white audiences, without a body of works to draw on that was truly multicultural.[93] As a consequence, the theater gave up the attempt, stopped producing original plays at all, and by 1991, no longer existed.[94]

The peak years for At the Foot of the Mountain were 1974–84, when Boesing was artistic director and resident playwright. Her body of works, both collaborative and solo authored, encompassed political ideas that were jarring, experimental techniques that cut deeply into the fabric of women's experience while sustaining firm ties with the craft and the art of theater, and an idealism through which she created archetypes that became interpreted as universals. Boesing has been classified one of the first feminist playwrights in the United States, with a corpus of plays that remain on the margins and, for the most part, are forgotten. Case remembered another performance of one of Boesing's plays:

> It was at a performance of *Love Song to an Amazon,* and Jane Chambers and I were standing there with beer bottles, and [Rose and Boesing] were wearing long skirts, and it was really hard to get into because it takes all kinds . . . but we laughed and said, "It's not my idea of a love song to an Amazon." But at the same time they were there and made it happen. And I admire that. And the seventies was like that. . . . I remember having that reaction: "Oh, okay." It just wasn't me.[95]

The unfortunate result of their delayed understanding of difference is that At the Foot of the Mountain not only closed its doors, but the debate occurring in Chicago tipped the critical balance against them. Women defining themselves in opposition to the male cultural norm were still personalizing what theorists were seeking to depersonalize, so as critiques of the apparatus of representation overtook the analyses of performance, the work of these cultural feminists fell through the cracks, even as critics argued for the desirability of a positioning "in the cracks,"[96] between labels that are unable to contain the work of an artist or a theater. "To dismiss the work of women playwrights because their ideology is faulty seems dangerous . . . no matter how subjectively the analysis is worded. The power of scholars and theorists to affect the careers of drama practitioners should not be underestimated."[97]

With hindsight, we can see that At the Foot of the Mountain and Martha Boesing were strenuously—if not tragically—affected by the discovery that sisterhood does not mean sameness. Differentiating women's experience, defining what is "me and not me," shattered the mirror At the Foot of the Mountain was holding up to their audiences. In 1996, Boesing wrote a play to celebrate her sixtieth birthday entitled *These Are My Sisters*, which relives the woman's movement in a one-woman show. One of the play's five characters, Martha, "is still looking for her story. She thinks if she can find the truth about her own story that it might illuminate something for others."[98] In the end, it's an entire movement her works illuminate. The "femme" for whom emotions provide access to an understanding that is ultimately spiritual, beyond stereotypes or universals, a communal vision that "we are one,"[99] Boesing led At the Foot of the Mountain through ten years of vital artistic output that foreshadows the new experiments in American theater into matters of the spirit,[100] with the renewal of Hindu, Buddhist and Old Testament themes in festivals to the Next Wave.[101] Even with the fulsome quantity of print evidence available, the contributions of At the Foot of the Mountain and Martha Boesing to feminist and radical theater are, as yet, largely unrecognized. For Boesing, now a Buddhist, perhaps impermanence will prove to be her strongest ally.

NOTES

1. Charlotte Canning, *Feminist Theaters in the U.S.A: Staging Women's Experience* (New York: Routledge, 1996), 2.

2. Linda Picone, "Feminist Theatre Covers Wide Range in Twin Cities," *Minneapolis Tribune,* November 16, 1975, 80. Picone reviewed several feminist productions: Martha Boesing's *River Journal,* produced by At the Foot of the Mountain; *Lady in a Cage,* written collectively by the feminist theater Circle of the Witch; Pat Sun Circle's *Cory,* produced by Lavender Cellar Theatre; and the Women's Patrol, the guerilla theater whose main effort was to "pass out roses and smiles, plant flowers in unexpected places and perform a periodic show of song, dance and comedy."

3. Jan Magrane, interview by the author, March 1987, Minneapolis, reported in Lynne Greeley, "Spirals from the Matrix: The Feminist Plays of Martha Boesing, An Analysis," Ph.D diss., University of Maryland, 1987, available from UMI Dissertation Services, 1997, 67.

4. Meredith Flynn, "The Feeling Circle, Company Collaboration, and Ritual Drama: Three Conventions Developed by the Women's Theatre, At the Foot of the Mountain" Ann Arbor, Michigan: University Microfilms International, 1984, 24.

5. Paul Boesing had worked in New York throughout the 1960s as an actor; a member of the original Open Theater, he performed with Joe Chaikin and Megan Terry, as well as Sam Shepard, Maria Irene Fornes, Jean-Claude van Italie, and Ellen Stewart. He moved to Minneapolis with Sydney Walter when he was hired as a director at the Firehouse Theater, where Paul met Martha, a member of the Firehouse Company. They were married a year later. He was invited by Peter Brook to participate in the Parisian experiment of the intercultural reinventions of Shakespeare and was in Paris during the 1968 student riots. See also Arthur Sainer, *The New Radical Theatre Notebook* (1975; New York: Applause, 1997), 14, 337. Sainer mentions that At the Foot of the Mountain is an offspring of the Open Theater linked to Walter and Paul Boesing without any mention of Martha Boesing, who was not invited to Paris.

6. Martha Boesing, *Plays by Martha Boesing,* pamphlet (1981), 2, available from At the Foot of the Mountain Archives in the Special Collections at the University of Minnesota.

7. Pat Monaghan, "Reports at Random: Foot of the Mountain: A New Theater Names Itself," *Preview,* December 1974.

8. Magrane, interview.

9. Flynn, "Feeling Circle," 25.

10. Martha Boesing, interview by the author, March 1987, Minneapolis.

11. Flynn, "Feeling Circle," 24.

12. Patti P. Gillespie, "Feminist Theatre: A Rhetorical Phenomenon," *Quarterly Journal of Speech* 64 (1978): 285.

13. Jan Magrane was a professional actress when she met the Boesings in Atlanta. Paul, as indicated above, was professionally established as an actor in New York and directly influenced Martha's artistic development. Rose wrote on Megan Terry for her Ph.D. dissertation from the University of Denver, and Martha, herself, completed her masters in English at the University of Wisconsin in Madison. She also enrolled in the Ph.D. program in theater at the University of Minnesota but was more interested in doing theater than writing about it.

14. Alice Echols, *Daring to Be Bad: Radical Feminism in America, 1967–1975* (Minneapolis: University of Minnesota Press, 1989), 16.

15. Martha and Paul Boesing described the Firehouse as "the most extreme of all the groups creating experimental theater in the sixties, the closest to Artaud's [artistic] vision." Interview by the author, March 1987, Minneapolis.

16. Boesing's play *Free Rain* (1986) documents the experience of the women of the Firehouse Theater during the 1960s who discovered after years with the company that it was, though radical in its politics, conservative in its assignment of social roles. The women maintained the internal workings of the company, whereas the men chose the plays, directed them, and associated with any external directors and artists from New York. Boesing noted that the women's "experiences include the admission that they were powerful insofar as they were lovers or wives of the men" (interview, March 1987).

17. Sainer, *New Radical Theatre Notebook,* 112.

18. Echols, *Daring to Be Bad,* 90.

19. Canning, *Feminist Theaters,* 228.

20. Megan Terry, "Two Pages a Day," *Drama Review* 21, no. 4 (1977): 61; Phyllis Jane Wagner alias Rose, "Megan Terry: Political Playwright," Ph.D. diss., University of Denver, 1972, 101.

21. Phyllis Jane Rose, interview by the author, March 20, 1987, Minneapolis.

22. Boesing, interview, March 1987.

23. Patricia Schroeder, "American Drama, Feminist Discourse, and Dramatic Form: In Defense of Critical Pluralism," *Journal of Dramatic Theory and Criticism* 7, no. 2 (1993): 110.

24. Juli Burk, "In the *I* of the Storm," *Journal of Dramatic Theory and Criticism* 7, no. 2 (1993): 123.

25. Harriet Schiffer, *Lilith Letter* (Lilith: A Women's Theatre), Spring 1984, 1.

26. While the word has obvious sexual implications, Boesing has consistently expressed the intention of breaking down the defenses of her audience members through a real penetration of their psyches that both ruptures and heals. The sexual implications are, I think, unconscious and intentional.

27. See Lynne Greeley, "Making Familiar: Martha Boesing and Feminist Dramatic Structure," in *Theatre and Feminist Aesthetics,* ed. Karen Laughlin and Catherine Schuler (Teaneck, N.J.: Fairleigh Dickinson University Press, 1995), 160–81.

28. Sainer, *New Radical Theatre Notebook,* 39.

29. Boesing, from her personal notes, undated, given to the author April 1985.

30. Boesing, interview, March 1987.

31. Canning, *Feminist Theaters,* 164.

32. Magrane, interview.

33. Boesing, interview by the author, April 1986, College Park, Maryland.

34. Boesing, telephone interview by the author, December 1986.

35. Boesing, *The Web,* in *Plays in Process,* vol. 4, no. 1 (New York: Theatre Communications Group, 1981).

36. Boesing, *Journey Along the Matrix: Three Plays by Martha Boesing* (Minneapolis: Vanilla Press, 1981).

37. They include, in chronological order, *Pimp* (1973) in *A Century of Plays by American Women,* ed. by Rachel France (New York: Richards-Rosen Press, 1979), *The Gelding* (1974), *Journey to Canaan* (1974), and *Love Song to an Amazon* (1976), in Boesing, *Journey Along the Matrix; Mad Emma* (1976), *Trespasso* (1976), *The Moon Tree* (1977), *Labia Wings* (1979), *Song for Johanna* (1979), *The Last Fire* (1981).

38. Lynne Greeley, "Martha Boesing: Playwright of Performance," *Text and Performance Quarterly* 9 (1989): 208.

39. Greeley, "Making Familiar," 178.

40. See Dinah Leavitt, *Feminist Theatre Groups* (Jefferson, N.C.: McFarland, 1980); Elizabeth Natalle, *Feminist Theatre: A Study in Persuasion* (Metuchen, N J.: Scarecrow Press, 1985); Jill Dolan, *The Feminist Critic as Spectator* (Ann Arbor, Mich.: UMI Research Press, 1988); and Canning, *Feminist Theaters.*

41. The play was produced at the University of Maryland, directed by Bobbi Ausubel, in 1986. It was part of the retirement celebration of Helen Kirch Chinoy at Smith College, also in 1986, and was adapted by Celia Rocca in 1996 for a production at Baltimore City College with a mix of high school and college performers, among others.

42. Boesing, *Junkie!* (Minneapolis: At the Foot of the Mountain, 1981), preface.

43. Ibid.

44. Kay Bolstad, interview by the author, March 19, 1987, Minneapolis.

45. This technique of reaching out to audience members provoked angry response in 1966, when the ending of Megan Terry's production of *Viet Rock* at Yale University, which included the actors moving into the audience, was criticized by Joe Chaikin and Robert Brustein, who objected to its sentimentality. See Rose, "Megan Terry," 105–7.

46. Boesing, *Junkie!* 28.

47. Ibid..

48. Boesing, interview, March 1987.

49. Karen Malpede, ed., *Three Plays by the Open Theater* (New York: Drama Book Specialists, 1974), 11.

50. Boesing, *Plays by Martha Boesing* (pamphlet), insert.

51. Other characters include Anna Mae Aquash, Dorothy Day, Barbara Demming, Emma Goldman, Mother Jones, Marjorie Melville, Rosa Parks, Lucy Parson, Alice Paul, Margaret Sanger, Agnes Smedley, and Rose Winslow.

52. Bobbi Ausubel is considered by some to be the among the first feminist playwrights in the United States with her play written with Stan Edelson, *How to Make a Woman,* produced by the Caravan Theatre in Cambridge, Massachusetts, in 1967. Ausubel was a major influence on Martha Boesing, who claims that before

she met Bobbi, she didn't think feminism applied to her. See also Natalle, *Feminist Theatre.*

53. Boesing, *Antigone, Too: Rites of Love and Defiance* (Minneapolis: At the Foot of the Mountain, 1983), 15.

54. Barbara Demming participated in the Canada to Cuba civil rights walk of the 1960s.

55. Marjorie Melville was expelled from Guatemala, where she worked as a teacher for revolutionary activities. Upon returning to the United States, she and her husband worked in the peace movement against the Vietnam War, culminating in the napalming of draft files in Catonsville, Maryland, which led to her two-year imprisonment.

56. Boesing, *Antigone, Too,* 15.

57. In her keynote address in 1984 at the American Theatre Association's Women and Performance Pre-conference in San Francisco, Joan Holden argued against Boesing's definitions of masculinist and feminist methods of creation, a discussion to be considered in the conclusion of this chapter.

58. Boesing, interview by the author, April 1986, Silver Spring, Maryland.

59. Boesing, interview by the author, April 1998, College Park, Maryland.

60. Boesing, *The Web,* 36.

61. Boesing, *River Journal,* in *Journey Along the Matrix.*

62. Flynn, "Feeling Circle," 25.

63. *Love Song to an Amazon,* cited above, is available in Boesing, *Journey Along the Matrix. Labia Wings, The Last Fire,* and *A Song for Joanna* are available from the playwright.

64. Review of *Prehistoric Visions of Revolting Hags,* by Martha Boesing, *GLC Voice,* December 1979. "Hag plays" refer to Boesing's invention of *hagology,* a play on the word "hagiology: the history of sacred writings or of sacred persons." Hence, she implies that women called "hags," or older women, are, in fact, sacred.

65. Geraldine Lust, quoted by Sainer, *New Radical Theatre Notebook,* 15.

66. Boesing, "Love Song to an Amazon," unpublished version, preface.

67. Boesing, *Plays by Martha Boesing* (pamphlet), 3.

68. Boesing, *Love Song to an Amazon* in *Journey Along the Matrix,* 2.

69. Ibid., 3.

70. Ibid., 8.

71. Adrienne Rich, "It's the Lesbian in Us," in *On Lies, Secrets, and Silence: Selected Prose, 1966–1978* (New York: Norton, 1976), 199–202.

72. Review of *Prehistoric Visions of Revolting Hags* in *GLC Voice.* Judy Chicago's *The Dinner Party* consisted of thirty-nine place settings on a triangular table based on a white tile floor inscribed with 999 women's names. The plates suggestive of labia represent historic or legendary women and were the collaborative work of over four hundred people. See Judith E. Stein, "Collaboration," in *The Power of Feminist Art: The American Movement of the 1970s, History and Impact,* ed. Norma Broude and Mary D. Garrard (New York: Harry N. Abrams, 1994), 226.

73. Boesing, *Labia Wings* (Minneapolis: At the Foot of the Mountain, 1979), 1.

74. David Hawley, review of "*Visions for Hags,*" by Martha Boesing, *St. Paul Dispatch,* November 30, 1979. Hawley wrote a letter to Martha Boesing, also dated November 30, apologizing for the editing of his piece "in a manner that distorted the entire tone of the review," deleting almost entirely references to *Labia Wings*

in a "reflection of the personal prejudices of the copy editors." Archives of At the Foot of the Mountain, University of Minnesota.

75. Boesing, *Plays by Martha Boesing* (pamphlet), 2.

76. Boesing, *Labia Wings,* 5.

77. Ibid., 3.

78. Greeley, "Spirals from the Matrix," 154.

79. Boesing, *Plays by Martha Boesing* (pamphlet), 2.

80. Boesing, *Song for Johanna* (Minneapolis: At the Foot of the Mountain, 1981) 1.

81. Ibid., 4.

82. Ibid., 14.

83. Ibid., 13–14.

84. Sue-Ellen Case, interview by the author, November 17, 2001, San Diego.

85. Dolan, *Feminist Spectator as Critic,* 92, 94.

86. Martha Boesing, talk at Smith College, April 18, 1986, as part of the festivities in honor of the retirement of Helen Krich Chinoy.

87. Dolan, *Feminist Critic as Spectator,* 94.

88. Boesing, *The Web,* 6.

89. Holden, keynote address, 1984.

90. Boesing's theories are defined quite eloquently in handouts distributed at the University of Maryland in 1986. Handouts in possession of the author and also available from Martha Boesing.

91. Boesing and Rose auditioned actors in New York for this production, in search of multicultural actors. The irony of the criticism the production provoked is that the directors had striven to work against their white, middle-class positioning; hence, the revision of the play in the first place.

92. Dolan, *Feminist Critic as Spectator,* 93.

93. At the Foot of the Mountain, "Annual Report," unpublished, 1990, At the Foot of the Mountain Archives, University of Minnesota.

94. Canning, *Feminist Theaters,* 87.

95. Case, interview.

96. Gayle Austin, *Feminist Theories for Dramatic Criticism* (Ann Arbor: University of Michigan Press, 1990), 4.

97. Schroeder, "American Drama, Feminist Discourse," 113.

98. Boesing, in collaboration with Carolyn Goelzer, *These Are My Sisters,* July 1996 and May 1997, 25. Available from the playwright.

99. Magrane, interview.

100. Elinor Fuchs, "Year of the Spirit," *American Theatre,* February 2001, 53.

101. Fuchs reported an upsurge in the Brooklyn Music Academy's offerings in 2000, which "were spiritual in ways unthinkable" in previous years of the festival. "Anything can be 'next,'" she concludes, "including the oldest things there are" (ibid., 59).

THE BEAUTIFUL LEGS OF FEMINIST THEATER

At the Foot of the Mountain and Its Legacy

Charlotte Canning

At the end of March 2005, Peggy Shaw and Lois Weaver arrived in Austin, Texas, for a residency in the Department of Theatre and Dance at the University of Texas at Austin. Ultimately, the product of the residency was to be the revival of *Dress Suits to Hire* (1987), a play written expressly for Shaw and Weaver by Holly Hughes. This piece won Obies for Shaw, for her performance of Deeluxe, and Hughes. This production was the much-anticipated culmination of "Throws Like A Girl," a performance series jointly sponsored every other year by the department and the Rude Mechanicals, an Austin-based experimental theater collective.[1]

Shaw and Weaver's first activity was an informal question-and-answer session for the M.A. and Ph.D. students in the department. Not advertised to the public, the discussion was relaxed and social. Both Shaw and Weaver had been guests in the department before and knew many of those present. The students had not yet seen the current work, so there was no real agenda for the session, and Shaw and Weaver ran it as they run the start of their workshops. There are two ground rules: everyone must ask a question, any question he or she wants, and Weaver and Shaw must answer any question put to them. The questions that afternoon ranged from the serious, about their process, current projects, and a variety of political issues, to the more humorous, one student asking Weaver where she got her shirt. I asked the last question: "What might you say is the legacy of feminist theater?" It was late, and there was a party that night to welcome Weaver, Shaw, and their director, so everyone was ready to get going. Perhaps had I asked it earlier, I might have gotten a different response. Shaw and Weaver laughed wryly, and Shaw hooted, "Don't talk about the legacy of feminist theater, talk about the beautiful legs of feminist theater."[2] This got a huge laugh and we adjourned.

I never followed up on the meaning of their initial reaction to my question. But what I read in their response was an ambivalence about the question that matched my own feelings about exploring the legacy of feminist theater groups. On the one hand, these groups have made a rich and valuable contribution to feminism and performance, which deserves to be recognized, studied, and discussed. The mere suggestion that they have a legacy is a positive one, since it suggests that the groups have had an impact. The idea, however, raises questions of its own. What was the impact of the groups? Who or what experienced it? How did it happen? It is impossible to imagine a notion of legacy without focusing on its beneficiaries. This in turn throws methodological approaches into relief—it is not just a focus on beneficiaries that is crucial, but, more importantly, on how one identifies someone or something as a beneficiary. What criteria would one use to recognize and explore such a legacy? How has the larger field of feminism grappled with the idea of a legacy? Feminism and theater have intersected in very specific ways with a conscious focus. An attempt to establish a legacy for this intersection would have to work within the goals and motivations of the feminist theater groups themselves.

On the other hand, an obvious implication of studying the legacy of any kind of political performance or movement is that you are looking at the surviving effects of something that has ended, of something that is no longer an active contributing presence. While the term *legacy* can imply an ongoing effect and importance, it can just as strongly suggest that the thing itself is no longer relevant. In order for something to have a legacy, it must itself be over, completed. This sense of the term has very grave political implications in this context. The very idea that feminist theater groups have a legacy makes it possible to historicize them, in the least productive sense of the word: consigning them to the past. A search for the legacy of feminist theater, whether of a specific group like At the Foot of the Mountain, or for feminist theater groups as an entire category, could safely relegate them and their concerns to an archive as something of great historical interest and value, but without daily presence or impact. The sense might licence everything from paucity of women represented in theater departments' seasons to mainstream media assumptions that feminism is over, that we are now "postfeminist." This wariness about the dangers of legacy may have been what Shaw was trying to convey in her response to me.

Legacy's most common usage is in the sense of something bequeathed in a will or handed down by an ancestor or predecessor. This encapsulates the concerns I expressed above because embedded in the definition is the necessary death of that which creates the legacy. It also implies that legacy is a fixed and known quantity. This understanding works well when applied to a legal document quantifying possessions. It is less helpful when applied to the relationship of past ideas and practices to a future moment. Here the idea of legacy becomes more complicated because of the processes of history. Understandings are not fixed. How a theater movement or politics of a particular moment is viewed by those who come later has everything to do with how the theater movement or politics is remembered in the contemporary context. How something is remembered has to do with the ways in which the needs and positions of the current moment construct and represent that past idea or practice. The question of legacy is the question of historiography—how is history to be written, by whom, and why. The legacy of groups such as At the Foot of the Mountain is less about the necessary waning of feminist theater groups than about how the ideas, approaches, and work such groups created have been remembered and used. The circulation of that memory is evidence, transitory and mutable though it is, of the legacy of At the Foot of the Mountain. The focus of a discussion of that legacy, in other words, is a discussion of how feminist theater groups have legs.

My argument will work within this set of assumptions: that legacy is a historiographical question, and that to answer it one must look at the challenges facing the writing of feminist history. Within such a context, one can understand why At the Foot of the Mountain continues to be an important feminist theater group. To achieve this understanding, I will focus, first, on some of the challenges facing historians as they have written the history of the larger feminist movement. Concomitantly, this focus will be connected to similar challenges centering on the history of feminist theater groups. In this context I will read two examples from At the Foot of the Mountain's history. The first is from near the end of the group's existence. In 1987 At the Foot of the Mountain presented a revised, multicultural version of their germinal 1978 work *Story of a Mother* to the Women and Theatre Program at their annual conference. The ensuing debate had huge implications for both groups, but it also had an important effect on how feminist theater has been subsequently represented. The second example comes several years after the group ceased to exist. In 1997 Martha Boesing opened the final version of her one-

At the Foot of the Mountain, *Story of a Mother,* 1978. Performers include Phyllis Wagner, Jan Magrane, Cecilia Lee, Jennifer Boesing. (At the Foot of the Mountain Theatre Records, Performing Arts Archives, University of Minnesota Libraries, Minneapolis.)

woman show *These Are My Sisters* in Minneapolis. This show was her attempt to make sense of feminist history and to figure out what her experiences could mean to herself and others. A close reading of this production will also demonstrate that At the Foot of the Mountain continues to have a changing feminist presence, participating in how feminist theater groups are remembered and influence current theatrical practices.

Feminism as it emerged in the late 1960s and early 1970s has always had a keen interest in its own history, while espousing a distrust in the larger project of history. Women urged each other not to be in thrall to the past. The past was what, in the view of second-wave feminists, had licenced the oppression of women. Tradition and history were oft-cited reasons for the paucity of opportunities available to women for self-expression or definition. This suspicion of the past helped create the feminist investment in the idea that the personal is political. Rather than relying on established emphases and perspectives, that is, official histories, as guides to political action, women would rely on themselves and their own experiences as a way to orient their actions.

At the same time that women were celebrating their liberation from what they understood as the oppressive constraints of history, they were writing histories of women and feminism as sources of encouragement. One of the earliest writings to emerge from the newly invigorated feminist movement was the 1968 collection of mimeographed essays *Notes From the First Year*, edited by Shulamith Firestone. Her essay, the first, begins,

> Indeed, the few historians of the women's rights movement in the U.S. complain that the records have been lost, damaged, or scattered due to the little value placed on them. Anyone who as ever researched the subject knows how little is available, and how superficial, slanted, or downright false is the existing information. I would like to suggest a reason for this. It is the thesis of this article that women's rights (liberation, if you prefer) has dynamite revolutionary potential; that the Nineteenth Century WRM [Women's Rights Movement] was indeed a radical movement from the start, that it was tied up with the most radical movements and ideas of its day, and that even to the bitter end, in 1920, there was a strong radical strain which has been purposely ignored and buried. To show this, we will have to dig out and completely review the whole history of the WRM in the U.S., to weigh just what it meant in political terms, and to understand the political and economic interests causing these distortions.[3]

Firestone was one of the earliest to articulate feminism's contradictory relationship with history, and her essay was intended to recuperate nineteenth-century feminism as a radical forebear of the contemporary moment. The idea that women had fought these battles before was a legacy that feminists struggled with in all its complexity. Just as Peggy Shaw and Lois Weaver expressed ambivalence about the question of feminist theater's legacy, so Firestone questions the legacy she inherited. She calls for a new legacy, one crafted by the women who will use it and uses history to legitimate current work by constructing a history crafted in the image of that current work.

But those actions did not completely solve the problem of how history gets written, whom it empowers, and how it licences present and future action. In 1975, Kathie Sarachild in "The Power of History," the opening essay in a collection of writings from the Redstockings collective, ends on precisely that note. "The 19th century women's liberation movement faced the problem of no history unless they wrote their own. And the present moment faces the problem of false history unless it writes its own. It is a somewhat different problem because already with the movement less than a decade old there has been no dearth of books about it. The problem has been that the actors themselves have not been writing about it—and have not been using history, of either the past or the present."[4] Sarachild echoes Firestone and other feminist writers as she suspiciously embraces history. She acknowledges its importance in bringing about radical change, but simultaneously emphasizes the ways in which that power can work against women just as easily as for them. The history Sarachild calls for is created from the practices and lessons of feminism, relying less on documents than on lived experiences.

The books that Sarachild referenced from the early 1970s were written about a flourishing movement. In the late 1990s books began to appear by the women Sarachild called upon twenty years before. Ruth Rosen describes the moment that inspired her to write *The World Split Open: How the Modern Women's Movement Changed America* (2000). She asked her students at the University of California, Davis, what they knew about the world before second-wave feminism and found that they knew nothing. "I could have been depressed by how little they knew. Instead, I felt a strange sense of elation. It wasn't just the enormity of all that women had challenged that still seemed breathtaking. What stunned me was the changes in women's lives had been so deep, so wide-ranging, so transformative. I realized that the women's movement could not be erased, that it had brought about changes that these young people now took for granted."[5] For Rosen the students' ignorance was generative; she describes her reaction as "elation." The act of explaining second-wave feminism to undergraduates in the early 1980s coalesced for her how feminism's legacy was effective but invisible. Like Firestone, Rosen sees the problem as how to tell feminism's story effectively so that people can understand its connection to the current moment.

Two years before Rosen's book, Rachel Blau DuPlessis and Ann Snitow commissioned over thirty women activists from the 1970s to write autobiographical reflections of their experiences. Their motivation for the project was similar to Rosen's, although they did not share her elation. "We two editors, old friends, looked at our lives and saw that feminism had been decisive. For us, there was a before the women's movement and after. But when the histories of the sixties began to appear with the women's movement relegated to the footnotes and the margins, we realized how urgently we wanted to read women's own accounts of their diverse historical participation and agency. So we began this memoir project."[6] For these two editors the project is less about explaining the source of the benefits currently enjoyed than about erased labor and marginalized accomplishments.

While they do not dispute that some of the changes feminism wrought were permanent, they do know that the ability to inspire continuing change rests on the ways in which feminism is historicized.

When I began interviews for what would become my book, *Feminist Theaters in the U.S.A.* (1996), I witnessed a similar feeling of erasure and marginalization among the women I interviewed. Many of them were surprised I found them and surprised that anyone remembered their work. For some, the fact that I was a child when they were doing their work made it difficult to believe in my interest. "What do you care?" they would ask, but not unkindly. "You weren't even there." Their position was a contradictory one because, despite their astonishment that anyone else still cared, they still believed in the work they had done. They did believe that they had reinvented theater—altered its processes, practices, and performances in ways that fostered new knowledge and political action. It was their belief in their work that inspired me. In the late 1980s and early 1990s, 1970s feminism was viewed with great suspicion as naive, simplistic, and limited. I approached my project with great trepidation, fearing that the work I was going to record would be of little interest to anyone. What I found was quite different. The work I researched was sophisticated, thoughtful, and engaging. Women had used theater to reflect on the world they lived in and on the one they were creating. In their work was a complete picture of why and how feminism mattered.

Sue-Ellen Case observes that the primary legacy of feminist theaters of the 1970s is the requirement that feminist theater "address the issues of the moment."[7] Feminist performance scholars and practitioners learned from feminist theater groups that "that is what a feminist does."[8] Certainly the groups of the 1970s did just that. They created works about the political issues women had to negotiate in their daily lives. No topic was too quotidian or too immense. Nor was any topic taboo. They openly discussed issues that had been absent from public discourse. Lesbians created performances that explored their experiences as they had lived them and in resistance to mainstream homophobia. Women of color put racism of both the larger culture and feminism into their performances unapologetically. These kinds of performances challenged feminism's attempts to see itself as white and heterosexual. Feminist theater group practitioners explored the way they created works, pioneering collaborative and collective techniques, and they emphasized the relevance of their performances to the everyday lives of women.

Two subjects were ubiquitous among feminist theater groups—violence against women and the mother-daughter relationship. In 1976 At the Foot of the Mountain used Bertolt Brecht's one-act play *The Exception and the Rule* as the basis for a work on rape. They adapted Brecht because his Marxist analysis of capitalism allowed them to draw parallels to the violent patriarchal oppression of women. *Raped: A Woman's Look at Bertolt Brecht's "The Exception and the Rule"* had an electric effect on audiences. For many women it was the first time that they saw a public exploration of rape that matched their own experiences. This vital connection with their audience around articulating a common women's experience, taught At the Foot of the Mountain to look to ubiquitous experience for inspiration. This led them to their next work, *Story of a Mother* in 1978.

In their mission statement At the Foot of the Mountain embraced fostering "new rituals for our time" in order "to renew hope and celebrate the healing power of women by re-creating life giving cultural myths."9 *Story of a Mother* would be the strongest articulation of this mission. The play was in five parts, each part containing a ritual requiring audience participation. For Boesing this was crucial because it transformed audiences: they were "no longer . . . witness, they literally participate in the event."10 These rituals asked the women in the audience to name their mothers, to identify with their mothers, even to become their mothers. This show would become At the Foot of the Mountain's signature piece, the one for which they were best known. When reorganized themselves during 1986–87 as a multicultural company in response to the growing sense that they did not speak, as they had formerly believed, to all women, they returned to *Story of A Mother* to inaugurate their new identity. It was this revised play, performed by the newly multiracial group, that arrived in Chicago in August 1987 to perform for the Women and Theatre Program (WTP).

Most accounts of the clash over At the Foot of the Mountain's performance attribute it to the controversial use of critical theory within feminism, racism of each feminist theater group, or tensions between theory and practice. I myself have argued all of these positions, and it is not my intention here to contradict them. What I do want to do, however, is point to the ways in which this crucial moment was also about how feminism would historicize itself, and, by extension, its legacy. The postshow discussion quickly turned rancorous. The focus was on the rituals in the performance, which many women found coercive. Some WTP members felt that the return to a previous production undermined the investment in the new ensemble because of that show's roots in the group's all-white past. Additionally, the choice of that particular piece did not speak as acutely to feminism in 1987 as it had in 1978. Others felt that some members of WTP were not sufficiently open to what At the Foot of the Mountain was doing, and were being racist themselves by not taking into account what the performers of color were saying about their sense of their involvement. The performers felt attacked, and that they were being denied agency. The charges that they were being manipulated by the white women of the theater group was offensive to them. In her interview with Anna Deavere Smith, Rebecca Rice noted how familiar were the racial politics, indeed typical of white women's groups.

> By performing "Story of A Mother" I was rewarded with a negative response and it said to me once again you're making a mistake you know better than this when "Story of a Mother" was done before it was done by a predominately white group for a white group we're moving into something more personal but we're moving into the language and language forms of our different mothers.[11]

Rice's diagnosis was perceptive. *Story of a Mother* was about language. The mother of the title was not just a biological or physical one, but also a genealogical one. Both WTP and At the Foot of the Mountain were being asked to struggle with their pasts—of each group and of feminism—and with how those pasts were going to direct the future of feminism. As Jill Dolan observed in 1989: "The factions and contentions currently dividing feminist critics, theorists, and practitioners in theater and performance seem to reflect the social movement's historical progress and the tensions caused by changing perspectives so rapidly."[12] Feminism was changing, and in front of everyone at the conference, performers and scholars alike, was a moment from feminism's past. Everyone in the room was confronted with what that past meant to them.

At the Foot of the Mountain's performance is not the only evidence that the past was on the agenda at the conference. Sue-Ellen Case had given the keynote, an early version of what would become her influential and widely reprinted "Toward a Butch-Femme Aesthetic." This essay argued that the butch-femme bar culture had been erased by 1970s feminists who mistakenly understood the butch-femme relationship as the product of patriarchal identification. Case neatly turned the tables on the feminist view and demonstrated that feminists were themselves homophobic, and this led them to try to transform lesbians, particularly butches, into feminist versions of middle-class straight women. As Case remarked caustically about these historical circumstances: "The contemporary lesbian-identified reader can only marvel at the conflation of gender identification in the terms of dominant, heterosexual culture with the adopted gender role-playing within the lesbian subculture."[13] Rather than seeing this lesbian past as a shameful product of the closet experience, Case recuperated it as a model for a feminist subject position. Instead of basing her argument in biology and traditional psychoanalytic theory, Case relied on performance practices that resist the fixed, essentialist notions usually associated with subject positions.

No accounts of the conference that I am familiar with have framed the clash between WTP and At the Foot of the Mountain, between theorists and antitheorists, between scholars and practitioners, in the context of Case's keynote. Jill Dolan does discuss the address, but to indicate the ways in which homophobia circulated at the conference, as well as in WTP. Dolan noted that the address "textualized lesbian issues for the WTP and implicitly charged the group with a kind of tacit homophobia. Her lecture was applauded, but largely ignored."[14] Had it not been ignored by those at the conference, observers might have seen how the two events—Case's address and At the Foot of the Mountain's performance—together took up the pressing question of feminism's future by looking at its past.

It is easy to dismiss what At the Foot of the Mountain contributed to the discussion because, as most who have written about the event agree, *Story of a Mother* in 1987 no longer had the power it did in 1978. This became clear to the group itself, and this was its last production. At the Foot of the Mountain folded in 1991. But the event at WTP and the group itself made a spectacularly important contribution to the discourse of feminism and theater. If, as Case emphasized, the hallmark of 1970s feminist theater was to "address the issues of the moment," then there is no better example than the 1987 WTP conference. *Story of a Mother* brought all the women in the room to confront crucial issues facing feminism—racism, homophobia, and intellectual development, to name just three—and required they identify their different feminist positions. While these positions conflicted with one another, they all agreed on one point: how feminism is performed is crucial to how it develops.

This event is evidence of how closely academics and practitioners attend to one another. Most feminist scholarship in performance is inspired and challenged by actual performances and feminist performance practitioners. Practitioners, too, attend to what scholars say about them. Playwright Joan Schenkar publically declared at the 1989 WTP conference in New York that scholar and theorist Vivian Patraka's "critical study of her plays had strongly influenced her subsequent work."[15] Feminist performance theory and criticism is not developed in isolation. It is created through interactions—some cordial, others tense—with feminist performance practitioners. History plays an important role in that relationship. What feminism has meant and how it will mean is something

performance can demonstrate productively. In 1987 the confluence of
Case's recuperation of the historical performance of the butch and
femme and At the Foot of the Mountain's revised version of *Story of a
Mother* allowed feminists to make choices about where they wanted to take
feminism, what precedents they would embrace in that process, and
which ones they would reject. But those choices are not permanent. History's meanings will always change as the historical moment itself shifts,
and performance will always be a productive place to make decisions
about those meanings.

In 1997 Martha Boesing joined the very distinguished ranks of alum-
nae from feminist theater groups who have crafted one-woman shows for
themselves. *These Are My Sisters* emerged out of a scrapbook Boesing had
been compiling over the years. She had the sense that its material could be
the basis for a performance piece for herself. She was overwhelmed, however, by the amount of material she had collected and the many things she
wanted to say. Boesing approached Carolyn Goelzer, an actor, playwright,
and director based in the Twin Cities, and asked her to collaborate. The
two women discussed the piece, Boesing kept writing, and an early version
emerged. Boesing and Goelzer knew it was too large and sprawling for performance. "Then a period of fact-finding, book-reading. She [Boesing] interviewed many of the women she knew in the '70s whose lives were irrev-
ocably altered by the politics of the times. We watched videos together. We
listened to music. We even attended a Chris Williamson concert the night
of a horrible snow-storm in early December. 'I want it to be funny,' she
said. 'I want it to honor the lives of these women.'"[16] These joint experiences sharpened the collaborators' focus. After several drafts, in which
some characters were added, others dropped, and production values were
debated, the final version emerged. In it Boesing and Goelzer found a balance between the polyvocality of feminism and the monologic nature of
solo performance.

There are six characters in the cast of *These Are My Sisters,* and their
monologues make up the first half of the piece. Jane is a former hippie
who reminisces wryly about her life in various communes and political
movements. She ends her monologue, the first of the five, with a tri-
umphant story of her coming out. "I'd . . . yell: 'Hey! I just made love to a
woman—it's great! You should try it! Everybody should try it!'"[17] Char is a
housewife whose boredom with her life leads her to have affairs and eventually an illegal abortion. For her feminism addressed her deep sense that
"This is not enough."[18] The least radical of all the characters, Char is the
one for whom feminism is the most daring choice. Rhea is an academic
who writes on goddess worship and for whom feminism is primarily a spir-

itual practice. With a twist, this character is the only one who found material wealth through feminism. Rhea's books are best sellers, and she is a
frequent guest on television talk shows. A red diaper baby, Naomi unites a
materialist politic with her academic work. "But in spite of these obstacles,
we invented Women's Studies. And it was incredibly exciting!"[19] Interestingly, Boesing does not describe Naomi as a scholar, like Rhea, but as a
"revolutionary." This choice foregrounds the activist work that went on in
the academy when women began bringing feminism into universities and
colleges. Perry is the last of the five women, and the only one who never
really discusses the women's movement. For her, it was the emergence of
lesbian politics that was empowering. "And I'm asking myself why does
every dyke in America have to off herself? And suddenly I realize no one
is ever going to force me to kill myself. In fact no one is ever going to mess
with me again."[20] She charts her path from a closeted butch bar dyke to
the communal celebration for the opening of a lesbian resource center.
Throughout this journey Perry keeps her experience as someone with
"something different" about her in the forefront of her consciousness.[21]

There is a sixth character in the play, one whose name does not appear
in the character list. The first voice in the play is named Martha. It is this
voice that begins and ends both halves of the play. The first section, "The
Interviews," with the five characters' monologues, opens with Martha
singing the Chris Williamson song "Waterfall." Martha frames the section
by juxtaposing the past the performance invokes, "the 'second Wave' of
the women's liberation movement," with an image from the 1995 Beijing
women's conference: "These are my sisters."[22] This dramaturgical choice
leaves nothing to chance, and ensures that the audience understands that
the pasts these women discuss are directly relevant to current and future
moments. Martha closes with a poem that gestures toward the different
but connected stories we have just heard, as well as the tensions they indicate. "No one remembers / They do. / They don't. / Does she? / Sometimes. . . . Not always. / It doesn't matter. / It does. / It doesn't. / It
does."[23] The sense that despite doubts and uncertainties, feminism matters, is carried into the second half, "The Gathering."

Martha moves the chairs that each character occupied for her monologue into a semicircle, and the characters talk to one another about the
issues they raised in their monologues. The dialogue may be polyvocal,
but it is not voices raised in harmony. Char is demoralized about what has
happened to the feminist movement, and she cries in despair: "There are
days when it's like the women's movement never happened."[24] Naomi, in
contrast, is furious. "We women, we erase our history. We should stop
doing that."[25] Naomi's call for action shapes the second section, and

Boesing's characters argue over some of the differences that have riven feminism. Perry and Jane, in particular, clash over the unresolved tensions from the past that Sue-Ellen Case so eloquently critiqued in "Toward a Butch-Femme Aesthetic." Jane remembers dreamily the women's farm she lived on, where women did all the labor collectively and stripped to the waist to work. Perry disrupts her reverie. "Your idea of a lesbian nation, Jane . . . not mine."[26] In the ensuing argument Boesing neatly captures the historical and continuing challenges facing feminism.

Much of the meaning the piece creates is through Boesing's physical presence. The humor, for example, often comes from Boesing's acting choices rather than the words themselves. Rhea's hesitancy and lack of self-assurance is expressed through a hesitant near-stutter and rapid delivery, so that when she responds to the other characters her words are often unintentionally (from Rhea's point of view) funny. The audience's voice is also important. When Naomi declared triumphantly, "We invented Women's Studies," the audience whooped in celebratory recognition. Boesing paused to acknowledge the spectators' delight and add a shout of her own. The place where the history of At the Foot of the Mountain, Boesing, feminism, and live performance intersect most demonstrably in a Brechtian-like gestus happens in a small aside in one of Jane's longer monologues. She is lamenting the differences between older and younger feminists, particularly as evidenced in her own daughter. Jane remembers how close feminism once made them: "We used to do everything together. We'd go to see plays together over at that women's theatre—At the Foot of the Mountain."[27] What the written text does not indicate is how Boesing milked the moment for all she could. In searching for the name Jane snaps her fingers impatiently and her face creases with the strain of recalling it. When she finally comes up with it, the audience laughs loudly. The joke is not that Jane cannot recall one of the country's most important feminist theater groups, but that Boesing is signaling her offstage identity through the character. The audience knows that Boesing knows the group—she founded it. The humor comes from a recognition of who she is and the history she brings to the theater. Throughout Boesing intertwines audience knowledge of her identity with the questions the performance poses. Near the end Martha asks: "Will things every clarify themselves? / Will the questions stop repeating themselves?"[28] Boesing's task, however, despite Martha's questions, is not to resolve these tensions, but to perform them. As one astute reviewer noted: "By leaving questions open, . . . she puts the ball in our court. The movement is unfinished."[29] Not only does the performance signal the ways in which the struggles are ongoing, but also the ways in which history is always formulated in response to current needs. The audience is implicated—ultimately it is they who must answer the questions Martha poses.

Feminism in the 1960s and 1970s always envisioned itself as a collective movement. It resisted, sometimes savagely, any attempt to establish a party line, a monolithic approach, or the identification of a spokesperson or leader. This is a critical defining element of feminism, and no methodological approach can ignore the understandings that created the work under examination. Feminist theater in the 1970s and early 1980s was less about a specific group than it was about the expression of politics through performance. A focus on one group distorts the picture, and creates a false sense of the historical import of the movement itself. Any legacy that At the Foot of the Mountain has, it has because it was part of a larger effort to understand the world, empower women, and call for change through live performance. If legacy is a historiographical question, as I have argued here, then any one group's larger legacy will be found in its relationship to other groups.

Based on this argument, does feminist theater indeed have legs, beautiful or not? Can one definitively identify a legacy for the work that At the Foot of the Mountain and its contemporary groups did so compellingly in the 1970s? In *Feminist Theaters in the U.S.A.* I argued that the most important legacy of feminist theater is the fact that feminism and theater are seen as mutually compatible and informative.

> The theater groups left their mark on theater and feminism in a variety of ways. The most obvious is the phrase "feminist theater." Earlier than some other artistic activities feminist theater groups demonstrated that there was and could be a political aesthetic enterprise that could exist within the second wave feminist movement and still maintain its autonomy. This seemingly obvious fact should not be underestimated. The fact that people assume that feminism and theater can intersect profitably was originated by the theater groups. . . . Theaters toured to small towns, community centers, churches, synagogues, colleges, universities, women's centers, schools, and conferences across the U.S.A. Many of the practitioners are still active in theater and brought their politics and discoveries with them to their later careers and activities.[30]

Boesing's *These Are My Sisters* is an excellent example of the women of the theater groups continuing to create theater and build on the knowledge and experience they gained in the 1970s. Both subsequent work by feminist theater group practitioners and the intersection of feminism and theater document how the memories of the labor and effects of feminist theater groups continue to circulate culturally.

In the summer of 2005, scarcely two months after Peggy Shaw expressed her opinion about the legacy of feminist theaters, I saw a show in New York that demonstrated all that Shaw had implied in her response to my question. *Big Times,* written and performed by three members of the Women's Expressive Theatre (WET), took up many of the same questions that theater groups in the 1970s asked. WET was founded in 1999 by Sasha Eden and Victoria Pettibone. These thirty-something women, born as feminist theater groups were proliferating, were motivated to found their group because, as they told the *New York Times,* "We decided we should just produce the kind of work we're not seeing out there. . . . It's not about teaching the world a lesson. It's about producing media that we love."[31] Like the feminist theater groups of the 1970s whose primary motivation was to create the performances they were not seeing, WET responded to a dearth of theater that spoke to them by founding their own. In their mission statement they proudly embrace a feminist politics. "WET [was] founded on the desire to empower women to surpass limited expectations of self and to achieve their extraordinary goals. WET's mission is to produce media which transcends female stereotypes; to celebrate women's diversity and strengths; to mentor emerging artists and to create opportunities for new and celebrated talent to thrive within a woman-centric environment. . . . WET is committed to creating an artistic haven for sisterhood; we create an empowering community of women who recognize and respect one another's individual and diverse perspectives and choices. We define this as the new era of feminism."[32] Much of their mission echoes the work of the 1970s—the focus on providing women with opportunities not available elsewhere, the emphasis on supporting notions of community, and the enthusiastic sense that something new is being created are all hallmarks of groups founded thirty years ago.

No matter how much WET echoes past feminist performances, it has to be discussed differently than the groups that preceded it. It is not happening in the midst of a larger feminist movement or an explosion of feminist theater groups across the country. Despite their obvious connections, however, it is not even clear how much the founding women knew about previous feminist theater groups, and how much they intend their work to be a recognition of their predecessors. Their mission statement may sound very much like the 1970s with its emphasis on women's community and sisterhood, but they also may be distinguishing themselves from that historical moment. The mission statement reflects the feminist ambivalence with its own past. "The new era of feminism" implicitly critiques what happened before, suggesting that "a new era" is needed, and that this era will be successful where previous ones failed. It is not clear if WET is referencing the feminist movement of the 1970s as a whole, feminist theater groups in particular, or both, but it is clear that they see themselves as doing something new. To return to one of the methodological questions I posed in the introduction to this essay, can WET be identified as a beneficiary of the work of feminist theater groups, either as a whole or individually? Certainly their name gestures toward one the leading groups of the 1970s, the Women's Experimental Theatre, which also called itself WET. Founded in New York in 1977 by Roberta Sklar, Sondra Segal, and Clare Coss, WET and At the Foot of the Mountain were the two most widely discussed and reviewed feminist theater groups of the time.[33] But nowhere—on their website, in their programs, or in the 2005 *New York Times* article on the group—does the Women's *Expressive* Theatre ever directly or obliquely reference the Women's *Experimental* Theatre. Ultimately, I think that whether or not they know their debt to the first WET, the debt is still there. More importantly, it illustrates the ambiguity of discussing legacy. Can one benefit from a legacy of which one is ignorant? Perhaps. It is really through the second WET's work that their connection to feminist theater groups taken as a collective whole can be understood.

The show itself, *Big Times,* employed a metatheatrical device. The three women are brought back together to perform the vaudeville act of their youth. The show within the show is about how the three women tried to get into show business, and at every turn—failed auditions, attempts to sneak into shows for free, evictions for not paying their bills—kept running into each other. The audience is given plenty of opportunities to see what poor performers the women are, and much of the humor and suspense centers on how they will become the stars to be. Finally at the end they unite and perform together. The "big time" producer whom each has been desperately trying to see declares, when he sees their new, collaborative act: "Individually you're awful, together you're awful good."[34] This is the triumphal moment of the play. The three women discover their power lies in working together, rather than individually. This understanding, an emphasis on collective strength, is clearly a legacy of the intellectual and practical work of the feminism and the feminist theater groups of the 1970s.

As these historical and current examples demonstrate, feminist theater's legacy—whether of an individual group like At the Foot of the Mountain or of the movement as a whole—is not something tangible and immutable. Rather, it is something that is reinvented and reimagined each time feminism and theater intersect. Feminist theater certainly has legs, and judging by the success of various theater projects, beautiful ones, in part, because of the work of groups like At the Foot of the Mountain. At the end of *These Are My Sisters,* Martha returns to the Chris Williamson song with which she began the performance. When she reaches the line "The changer and the changed," she points first at the audience, "the changer," and then at herself, "the changed." She then smiles broadly. A lot is implied in this gesture. The dynamic and essential relationship between the performer and the audience is underscored. How a one-woman show can demonstrate the feminist focus on communities of women, rather than individuals, is evoked. Most importantly, however, is the emphasis on change. Presence, memory, and legacy are not fixed quantities. They are forever shifting and changing; they are in part created through the needs of the present moment, rather than solely through the events of the past. If feminist theater groups and At the Foot of the Mountain are to have (beautiful) legs, theater practitioners, scholars, and audiences will have to keep in front of them a legacy, the idea that performance and feminism together can address and imagine a better world—not a world where legacies are sought, but one where legs are the goal, and in this case legs mean addressing the current moment to bring about compelling change.

NOTES

1. The series is primarily funded by the Z. T. Scott Family Chair in Drama held by Jill Dolan. The 2005 series also included *Single Wet Female,* created and performed by Carmelita Tropicana and Marga Gomez, and *Index to Idioms,* written and performed by Deborah Margolin.

2. Peggy Shaw, question-and-answer session, Department of Theatre and Dance, University of Texas at Austin, March 25, 2005.

3. Shulamith Firestone, "The Women's Rights Movement in the US: A New View," in *Notes from the First Year,* ed. Shulamith Firestone (New York: New York Radical Women, 1968), http://scriptorium.lib.duke.edu/wlm/notes/#newview (visited September 20, 2005).

4. Kathie Sarachild, "The Power of History," in *Feminist Revolution: An Abridged Edition with Additional Writings,* ed. Redstockings of the Women's Liberation Movement (New York: Random House, 1975), 41.

5. Ruth Rosen, *The World Split Open: How the Modern Women's Movement Changed America* (New York: Viking, 2000), xiii.

6. Rachel Blau DuPlessis and Ann Snitow, "A Feminist Memoir Project," in *The Feminist Memoir Project: Voices from Women's Liberation,* ed. Rachel Blau DuPlessis and Ann Snitow (New York: Three Rivers Press, 1998), 3.

7. Sue-Ellen Case, "Playing in the Lesbian Workshop: Migrant Performance

Labor," presented to Department of Theatre and Dance, University of Texas at Austin, April 15, 2005.

8. Ibid.

9. At the Foot of the Mountain, "Mission Statement," n.p, n.d. From the author's collection.

10. Meredith Flynn, "The Feeling Circle, Company Collaboration, and Ritual Drama: Three Conventions Developed by the Women's Theatre, At the Foot of the Mountain," Ph.D. diss., Bowling Green State University, 1984, 189.

11. Anna Deavere Smith, *Chlorophyll Postmodernism and the Mother Goddess/A Conversation,* in *Women and Performance* 4, no. 8 (1989): 33. Smith was commissioned by the Women and Theatre Program to create a performance about At the Foot of the Mountain. This was done in the style of her better-known *Fires in the Mirror* and *Twilight: Los Angeles.* It was then performed at the 1988 WTP conference in San Diego at the Hahn Cosmopolitan Theatre on Monday, August 1.

12. Jill Dolan, "Staking Claims and Positions: The Women and Theatre Program, San Diego, and the Danger Zone," *Women and Performance* 4, no. 8 (1989): 46.

13. Sue-Ellen Case, "Toward a Butch-Femme Aesthetic," in *Making a Spectacle: Feminist Essays on Contemporary Women's Theatre,* ed. Lynda Hart (Ann Arbor: University of Michigan Press, 1989), 285. This landmark essay was first published in *Discourse* 11, no. 1 (1988) and widely reprinted since then, most notably in *The Lesbian and Gay Studies Reader,* ed. Henry Abelove, Michele Aina Barale, and David M. Halperin (New York: Routledge, 1993), 294–306.

14. Dolan, "Staking Claims and Positions," 49.

15. Patricia Schroeder, "American Drama, Feminist Discourse, and Dramatic Form: In Defense of Critical Pluralism," *Journal of Dramatic Theory and Criticism* 7, no. 2 (1993): 114.

16. Carolyn Goelzer, "Director's Notes," *These Are My Sisters,* Martha Boesing, unpub. playscript (1997), n.p. I would like to thank Martha Boesing for generously sharing her work with me.

17. Boesing, *These Are My Sisters,* 5. Also *These Are My Sisters,* 1997, video.

18. Boesing, *These Are My Sisters,* 7.

19. Ibid., 10.

20. Ibid., 13.

21. Ibid., 12.

22. Ibid., 1.

23. Ibid., 14.

24. Ibid., part 2, 1.

25. Ibid., part 2, 2.

26. Ibid., part 2, 4.

27. Ibid., part 2, 11.

28. Ibid., part 2, 13.

29. Kate Sullivan, "Past Lives," *City Pages,* July 17, 1996, http://www.citipages.com/databank/17/815/article2826.asp (visited October 4, 2005).

30. Charlotte Canning, *Feminist Theaters in the U.S.A.: Staging Women's Experience* (London: Routledge, 1996), 210.

31. Ada Calhoun, "From Very Private Schools to Very Public Stages," *New York Times,* June 19, 2005, sec. 2, p. 5.

32. Mission statement, Women's Expressive Theatre, http://www.wetweb .org/, October 4, 2005.

33. For a complete history of the Women's Experimental Theatre, see Canning, *Feminist Theaters,* 88–93.

34. Mia Barron, Maggie Lacey, and Danielle Skraastad, *Big Times,* performance at WalkerSpace, New York, July 8, 2005.

THE SAN FRANCISCO MIME TROUPE
Historical Overview

Rivaled only by the Living Theatre in terms of its longevity, the San Francisco Mime Troupe is quickly approaching its fiftieth year as an ensemble dedicated to progressive social change. The Mime Troupe was founded in 1959 by R. G. Davis, who remained its artistic director until leaving the troupe in 1970. Prior to founding the Mime Troupe, Davis had trained "with Paul Curtis of the American Mime Theatre and [with] Étienne Decroux in Paris," and, at the time of the troupe's founding, he was an assistant director in the San Francisco Actor's Workshop.[1] While at the Actor's Workshop, he organized a small group of private students and other acting colleagues into what initially began as the R. G. Davis Mime Studio and Troupe and then in 1963 was renamed the San Francisco Mime Troupe.[2] Although the San Francisco Mime Troupe would ultimately gain renown for its politically oriented use of commedia dell'arte and other popular theatrical forms in outdoor public venues like San Francisco's Lafayette Park, this early manifestation of the Mime Troupe experimented with innovative trends in mime—experiments that provided the Mime Troupe with physical training and bodily discipline that would later prove immensely valuable once it began to develop the outdoor theater for which it is now famous. Their first public performances, however, had a more conventional setting. In October 1959, the Mime Troupe performed at the San Francisco Art Institute, where they presented "'Games—3 Sets' and two other numbers" created by Davis.[3] By 1960, the company of eight performers had begun a weekly Sunday evening series at San Francisco's Encore Theatre that was called *The 11th Hour Mime*

Show. The Performers included Norma Leistriko, Robert Doyle, Susan Darby, William Raymond, Ruth Bruer, David O'Neill, Barbara Melandry, and Davis. During the following year, they also performed short pieces by Samuel Beckett, and, by this time, they had begun to cultivate a following among middle-class intellectuals.

In 1962, the Mime Troupe inaugurated two changes in their performance format that would have a defining impact on the course of their theater both aesthetically and politically. First, they began to vie for a much broader audience than the loyal but limited circle of intellectuals who had frequented their early performances. Although still doing some performances in theaters, they deliberately stepped beyond the theater itself. Moving outdoors and into the local parks, the Mime Troupe attempted to bring their performances to the working classes and to an emerging counterculture. Second, this shift from indoor to outdoor theater coincided with an embrace of commedia dell'arte, echoing the political overtones of the Mime Troupe move outdoors. The "intrinsic nature" of commedia, at least according to Davis, was "its working-class point of view."[4] The Mime Troupe's first outdoor production was entitled *The Dowry* (1962), which they had constructed out of traditional "commedia scenarios," songs and improvisational exchanges with the audience.[5] *The Dowry* was followed over the next eight years by a series of adaptions of works "by Molière, Goldoni, Machiavelli, Beolco, Bruno and Lope de Rueda," all of which were performed outdoors and "in the manner of *commedia dell'arte*."[6]

While the Mime Troupe's change to an outdoor venue had political implications in its conscious appeal to the working classes and in its calculated departure from the strictures of bourgeois theater, the front line of the Mime Troupe's politics turned out to be with the San Francisco Park and Recreation Commission, which decided to issue park use permits to them on a conditional basis. The permits were contingent upon the commission's approval of the content of the Mime Troupe's often bawdy and politically outspoken work.[7] Not surprisingly, the Mime Troupe interpreted this policy as an infringement on their right to free speech. Protesting the commission's decisions, the Mime Troupe quickly won widespread public support and attracted the attention and advice of the American Civil Liberties Union. On August 7, 1965, the Mime Troupe deliberately provoked the commission by performing after it had just revoked the troupe's permit. As the Mime Troupe had expected, Davis was immediately arrested. The event galvanized the public behind the group, and ultimately, it successfully challenged the Park Commission's decisions on the grounds that they had violated the Mime Troupe's Fifth Amendment rights.

Against the backdrop of these events, the San Francisco Mime Troupe, which had also begun to perform on college campuses, positioned itself ideologically not only in line with the Free Speech Movement in neighboring Berkeley and hence with the student movements of the 1960s but also with the civil rights movement and the growing opposition to the Vietnam War. Of particular importance in this regard were productions of *The Minstrel Show, or Civil Rights in a Cracker Barrel* (1965, 1967) and *L'Amant Militaire* (1967). The former piece toured widely and, while maintaining "the spirit of commedia," also adopted long-standing avantgarde strategies of provocation, shock, and offensiveness in its critical use of the grotesque racist stereotypes embedded in the traditions of American minstrelsy. The latter piece, which Joan Holden adapted from Goldoni's eighteenth-century drama, began to take shape as Davis cut the Mime Troupe from fifty-nine members to a core of fourteen committed and experienced performers. Although the Mime Troupe had previously done a number of antiwar skits, the production of *L'Amant Militaire* was their first full-length dramatic expression of opposition to the Vietnam War. Drawing parallels between U.S. soldiers waging war in Vietnam and Spanish soldiers waging war in Italy, Holden's adaptation of Goldoni's drama decried the waste of war and implicitly called for revolutionary action to end U.S. involvement in Southeast Asia. The production was phenomenally successful with park audiences, and the troupe performed it almost fifty times.

The success of Holden's adaptation of *L'Amant Militaire* foreshadowed the increasingly dominant role that she would assume as the principle playwright for the San Francisco Mime Troupe after Davis left in 1970. Davis's departure was in part the product of resistance to his desire to remain "the company's sole director" and in part the product of ideological differences that had surfaced within the group toward the end of the 1960s, differences that also led to the departure of the more militant Marxists.[8] As Davis departed, the Mime Troupe reorganized as a collective, and the women members, who had become critical of their own subordinate position in the decision-making process, successfully challenged not only their previously subordinate roles but also the troupe's "lack of concern" with women's issues.[9] Although these changes would have longterm effects on the trajectory of the Mime Troupe, they were most immediately evident in the production of Holden's drama *The Independent Female, Or A Man Has His Pride* (1970), which not only put feminist issues center stage in Mime Troupe productions but which also marked a shift from commedia to melodrama.

Throughout the 1970s, the Mime Troupe experimented with a range of styles, extending their repertoire to include techniques drawn from eclectic sources like vaudeville, cartoon strips, and a wide variety of movie genres. Despite the fact that their performances continued to focus on working-class issues like fair wages in *Frozen Wages* (1972) and *Electro-Bucks* (1978), their performances tended primarily to attract progressive middle-class audiences, and when the Mime Troupe took their theater to ethnically and racially diverse working-class communities, they were acutely conscious of their own lack of diversity. Ruby Cohn has noted that "the San Francisco Mime Troupe was formed by white middle-class actors," and it was well into the seventies before the company's composition began to change.[10] By the mid-1970s, the troupe began recruiting an ethnically diverse collection of performers and returned to questions of race in works like *The Great Air Robbery* (1974), *Frijoles or Beans to You* (1975), and *False Promises / Nos Engañaron* (1976).

As the political landscape began to shift in the 1980s, the Mime Troupe began to take on a host of new issues, not the least of which was countering the neoconservative backlash and right-wing fundamentalism that ushered Reagan into office in 1980. Perhaps the most memorable of these efforts was the series of performances that the Mime Troupe constructed around an invented comic book character whom they named "Factwino." In *Factwino Meets the Moral Majority* (1981), *Factwino and Armageddonman* (1982), and *Factwino: The Opera* (1985), the Mime Troupe created a nonviolent superhero whose superior power of knowledge and humor repeatedly debunked neoconservative political rhetoric. The shift in political landscape in the 1980s also initiated a period of introspection in the work of the Mime Troupe, an introspection that, among other things, involved a recognition that costs of operating necessitated accepting federal funding, which might compromise their politics. On the stage itself, the introspective turn was played out in works like *Spain/36* (1986), *Ripped Van Winkle* (1988), and *Back to Normal* (1991), where the Mime Troupe reassessed its long-standing political ideals within the context of social and political changes that did not coincide with early hopes and expectations.

Perhaps the most difficult transition for the San Francisco Mime Troupe has been the inadvertent consequence of its own stamina as an activist theater. After four decades of perseverance, it has had to come to terms with its own gradual evolution from an antiestablishment troupe into a Tony Award–winning theatrical institution that advertises itself as "America's Finest Theater of Political Comedy" and has been described by Holden as America's "most established antiestablishment theatre."

—J. M. H.

NOTES

1. Claudia Orenstein, *Festive Revolutions: The Politics of Popular Theater and the San Francisco Mime Troupe* (Jackson: University Press of Mississippi, 1998), 126.

2. R. G. Davis, *The San Francisco Mime Troupe: The First Ten Years* (Palo Alto, Calif.: Ramparts Press, 1975), 18.

3. Ibid.

4. Ibid., 31.

5. Orenstein, *Festive Revolutions,* 128.

6. Theodore Shank, *Beyond the Boundaries: American Alternative Theatre* (Ann Arbor: University of Michigan Press, 2002), 60.

7. Orenstein, *Festive Revolutions,* 129.

8. Shank, *Beyond the Boundaries,* 62.

9. Orenstein, *Festive Revolutions,* 132.

10. Ruby Cohn, "Joan Holden and the San Francisco Mime Troupe," *Drama Review* 24, no. 2 (1980): 45.

REVOLUTION SHOULD BE FUN

*A Critical Perspective on
The San Francisco Mime Troupe*

Claudia Orenstein

During the warm summer months, in public parks and plazas throughout the San Francisco Bay area, the San Francisco Mime Troupe's outdoor shows attract passersby with their colorful backdrops, their lively music, their outlandish, caricatured costuming, and their performance style of exaggerated gesture. The festive atmosphere surrounding these events—families sprawled on blankets with their picnic lunches, hawkers selling food or handing out leaflets—belies the image of an occasion devoted to serious engagement with the crucial political issues of the day.

For the Mime Troupe, however, an exuberant theatrical encounter is not only compatible with a consideration of fundamental social and economic questions, but essentially linked to it. The troupe's chosen theatrical aesthetic, which encompasses not only their popular artistic mode of presentation, but also their selection of community performance venues and their collective company structure, challenges dominant theatrical models in order to empower the company's artists and audiences in working for social and political change. The Mime Troupe's project of taking theater out to the people, in the shared, open spaces where they congregate, and presenting lively, entertaining performances that reveal, with clarity and humor, the big picture of political events and how ordinary individuals can affect them, is all consonant with the grassroots political practices of the 1960s. For social and political activists of that turbulent period, instigating change in cultural models and habits went hand in hand with working for social and political reform, since they saw these spheres as fundamentally linked. The Mime Troupe grew up in the sixties, and the activist ideologies of the day shaped the company's cultural perspective and artistic aesthetic. The ebullient, carnivalesque spirit that infuses a Mime Troupe production mirrors the volatile energy that invigorated that era, and indeed all periods of social and political transformation. The Mime Troupe's marriage of popular entertainment and politics is not one of expedience, but is, at its best, a harmonious union in which theatrical form manifests the company's revolutionary ideals.

This essay will explore the connections between the Mime Troupe's overall artistic aesthetic and the company's political agenda. I hope to provide a broad framework for understanding how the Mime Troupe's shows and setup for artistic production communicate their political vision. Sometimes this correlation occurs in the inspired match of a particular popular tradition with a certain topical issue. For example, in their 1972 production *Frozen Wages* they used a decreasing line of jugglers with an increasing number of juggling pins to illustrate the effect of the Nixon administration's wage freeze on factory workers. More generally, the affinity between politics and popular forms goes above and beyond the unique content and staging of any particular piece to encompass the entirety of the troupe's theatrical style and means of production.

The first section of the essay concerns the nature of the popular traditions the Mime Troupe draws from in their work, and how their use of these forms provides them with performance strategies that aim to empower their audiences. The second section examines the Mime Troupe's theatrical exploitation of familiar social and cultural material, including the use of recognizable, even stereotypical social masks. The final section shows how the company's offstage actions reflect their political commitments.

The Legacy of Popular Entertainment

The Mime Troupe's unique performance style has evolved during the group's forty-year history, but its roots are found in a long lineage of popular performance traditions that go back centuries. Over the years the Mime Troupe has mined the rich inheritance of European and American (and more recently, Asian) popular performance forms and adapted them for its own use. The essence of the traditions they use, their historical origins, and the social and political legacies they bring with them, all contribute significantly to the Mime Troupe's aesthetic and political vision. They have used commedia dell'arte, vaudeville, puppetry, mime, minstrel shows, and circus clowning, among others, in creating their productions. These traditions have a quality in common that I call "festive revolutionary."[1] This brand of rousing entertainment embodies a spirit of chaotic renewal and enacts disruptions in the status quo to invigorate the imagining of a new future. The Mime Troupe has also borrowed characters, plots, and dramatic tropes from the nontheatrical forms of comic books, film noir, television sitcoms, and B movies, generally subjecting them to parodic treatment within their own festive-revolutionary style.

The theatrical tradition that underlies all the Mime Troupe's work is the commedia dell'arte. Originating in sixteenth-century Italy, this form has been reincarnated in every era since its inception, and its broad characterization of cunning servants and ridiculous masters can be found likewise in the comedies of the seventeenth-century French playwright Molière and the antics of Bugs Bunny cartoons. When the Mime Troupe first used commedia in their 1962 production, *The Dowry,* they discovered that the form's broad physical stylization, easily recognizable stock characters, and use of *lazzi,* or standard bits of stage business, were perfectly suited to their own outdoor venues. Over the years they have taken commedia characters, such as the resourceful servant Arlecchino and the miserly merchant Pantalone, and come up with their own, updated American versions. The commedia's division between servants and masters offers a useful template on which to graft the political power divisions the Mime Troupe represents in its plays. One of the Troupe's own stock creations is a slick, ruthless capitalist, generally a businessman or political figure, reminiscent of Pantalone, but much more powerful and dangerous. These days he is usually played by company member Ed Holmes; like his commedia predecessors who performed only one stock figure throughout their entire careers, Holmes has honed the character to perfection. In the Mime Troupe's 2002 production *Mr. Smith Goes to Obscuristan,* Holmes's archetype becomes Dick Cheney.

It was in using commedia dell'arte conventions that the company first recognized the deep connections that were already being forged between their choice of theatrical techniques and their growing political interests. Getting permission from the San Francisco Park and Recreation Commission for outdoor shows brought the Mime Troupe up against limitations on their right to free speech in public venues, especially as their plays began to address topical issues ever more fervently. In 1965 the Troupe's conflict with the commission broke out into a full police confrontation when actors were arrested during the fourth performance of *Il Candelaio,* an adaptation of a play by the sixteenth-century Italian heretic Giordano

Mime Troupe, foreseeing the police action, played the mo-
.p, filling the park with a large crowd of supporters and introduc-
the arrests as part of the Troupe's theatrical presentation that day.

The *Candelaio* imbroglio brought home the fact that outdoor, public venues were vital sites for political discourse, and that using them in this way was in itself a subversive act. Furthermore, employing comic, bawdy plays for this purpose had the double advantage of engaging a large, mixed audience with laughter, and simultaneously making the authorities who tried to regulate the practice of free speech look ridiculous. The sight of a line of policemen stopping a play and arresting actors in clown costumes is bound to strike viewers as a case of absurd and excessive vigilance.

The Mime Troupe's predecessors had discovered this same fact. During the period of the Interregnum in England in the seventeenth century, when theater was banned by religious Puritans, Punch and Judy puppet shows were still allowed, being considered "too lowly for legal interdiction."[2] Italian puppeteers reaped a similar advantage in their work. On one occasion in Italy, officials were caught in the trap of self-ridicule when they actually arrested a Pulchinello puppet to upbraid a politically outspoken puppeteer.[3]

Like the commedia dell'arte, many of the forms the Mime Troupe has employed arose as marketplace and fairground entertainments in the public squares and common areas of Europe during the Middle Ages and the Renaissance. These entertainments appealed to a popular audience and provided not only raucous amusement, but also an opportunity to voice the common people's dissent regarding political and social conditions over which they had little legitimate control. The theatrical conventions these traditions yielded provided tactics that facilitated both objectives.

For example, most of those forms were easily portable, with simple stages and few props. This setup allowed itinerant performers to move easily from one venue to another, giving them access to a wide audience. Mime Troupe founder Ron Davis eloquently extolled the political value of portable stages in his "Guerilla Theatre Manifesto, 1965." He compared mobile theater companies to troupes of guerilla fighters who, traveling light, traverse the local terrain incognito, making friends with the populace and supporting them in their struggles. They come into a town to strike (or in the case of the Mime Troupe, perform) and then pack up and leave before the authorities can catch them. Historical records testify to performers like the nineteenth-century Italian puppeteer Ghetanaccio, who took advantage of the portability of his puppet stage to set it up under the windows of people, such as the mayor, whom he satirized in his shows.[4]

Traveling shows are generally free, supported by an audience that demonstrates its appreciation after the show by dropping money into a hat. Popular performers must be continually speaking to a common cause if they are to keep an audience watching and paying. Like their popular predecessors, the Mime Troupe wants its plays to reflect the interests of the ordinary people they speak to, rather than those who can afford to pay a fixed price in advance. The model of the itinerant performer as entertainment is the opposite of that of the permanent theater building, which often becomes a kind of museum promoting a theatrical heritage that speaks only to the wealthy and well educated. The impermanence of the popular player's theater embodies the flexibility they envision for the social world at large. Continually on the move, they are not financially invested in maintaining the status quo. Today the Mime Troupe's stages may take a few hours to set up, but the model of the mobile production that goes out in search of its audience, wherever it may be, and then moves on before it can be regulated by official supervision, is still at work in the Mime Troupe's shows.

Portability engenders other performance strategies that are also conducive to politically subversive performance. Traveling shows are actor-centered. Being forced to travel light, their sense of the spectacular flows primarily from the skills of the performers themselves, rather than from lavish production values. Individual players become masters of their art in all areas of production, allowing them more leeway to express their point of view freely. Although popular forms rely on replaying well-known character types, plot devices, and other stylistic features, they are porous structures that always leave ample room for improvisation. Practically speaking, popular forms need an accordion-like ability to contract and expand through improvisation. If players are having a good day and see a growing crowd, they can lengthen their performances with new material. Likewise, on a bad day, they can cut things short and move on to more potentially lucrative venues. Improvisation also allows them to be continually responsive to new audiences. On a political level, these open spaces for individual invention offer expressive freedom, beyond the fixity of a theatrical text or the control of anyone but the performer in the moment of performance. They provide important opportunities for subversive utterances that might be tempered in other contexts.

Since itinerant performers travel, they often reach audiences who speak different languages. The performers must therefore rely on physical expressivity as much as verbal. Popular players include acrobats, jugglers, tightrope walkers, and others exhibiting physical dexterity and virtuosity. Even the commedia's Arlecchino is known for his acrobatic agility.

In all of these instances the popular entertainer takes what is ordinary and shared by all, the human form, and demonstrates its extraordinary possibilities, its potential for transformation. Again, these techniques, developed out of necessity, lend themselves to political theatrical work. The metamorphosis of the mundane and ordinary into something unexpected and marvelous can inspire a vision of radical social transformation. It is empowering in revealing the ability of individuals to take the common substance of everyday life and refashion it in amazing ways. In a Mime Troupe piece the flexibility of the daily world is also demonstrated in simple sets that, with little effort, accommodate themselves to innumerable situations. In the 1977 production *Hotel Universe,* a single, sheer, black cloth placed over a backdrop immediately transformed the painted image of a hotel into that of a charred building after a fire. Simplicity of means allowing maximum flexibility is a rule of thumb in all aspects of a portable production, one that continually suggests the inherent mutability of the material world.

Popular performers also use humor to attract and entertain their crowds. Even jugglers, whose major skills lie elsewhere, need a continuous and engaging comic banter to keep audiences watching. The clown figure could be said to be the representative of the popular *par excellence* and appears in some form or other in popular traditions throughout the world. For political purposes, clowning is not just an entertaining ploy to keep spectators listening, but a formula that can reveal the strength of the lowly and the weaknesses of the rich and powerful. Clowns are blasphemous, defiant, and obscene. In all cultures they trespass social norms. By virtue of their foolish, debased characters, they are given license to say things that would otherwise be inappropriate or ill-advised, no matter how astute. Political players exploit the ability of the clown to say the inadmissible and use it as an opportunity to shatter the decorum that generally governs public discourse, obscuring possibilities for political action and social change.

For instance, in *L'Amant Militaire* the Mime Troupe borrowed the puppet figure Punch, a low-status character of wild abandon, a carefree anarchist who defies social norms. The English Punch beat his wife, dropped his child out a window, beat a policeman, and even outwitted the devil himself, laughing all the while. In *L'Amant Militaire,* the Mime Troupe's Punch the Red gave the audience outrageous, anarchic advice on ways to foil the military-industrial complex. One of his suggestions was to throw a mortar into a napalm depot. For the Mime Troupe, such an act is extreme and unacceptable; indeed, the Troupe used the production to question the effectiveness of its own pacifism. For a character like Punch, however,

Factwino Meets the Moral Majority, 1981. (Photo by Robert Miller. Http://www.sfmt
.org/company/archives/factwino/factw2y.shtml.)

being "over the top" is the only reasonable choice. By being excessive and
outrageous, clowns like Punch explode the boundaries of acceptable discourse, opening up new imaginative possibilities.

Through their use of comic conventions the Mime Troupe also lam-
poons the politically powerful and shows the wisdom of ordinary individuals. They often do this through a plot that moves, in a traditional comic
manner, from confusion to clarification. What is generally regarded as
normal in our everyday world appears as absurd or out of whack on the
Mime Troupe stage. The plays offer a central character with whom the audience can identify. These figures, in trying to make sense of the clownish
world around them, reveal the political machinations taking place behind
the masks of "normalcy."

In the 1980s the Mime Troupe created a comic-book-style hero called
"Factwino" who appeared in a number of different plays, including *Factwino
Meets the Moral Majority* (1981) and *Factwino vs. Armageddonman* (1982).
Factwino is a drunken bum who is given magic powers that allow him, when
he is sober, to zap people into seeing the facts of a situation clearly. This superhero allows reason to prevail in a world of folly. In several different productions he uses his abilities to shake people awake from the conservative
rhetoric of the Reagan era. Significantly, his alleged "superpower"—to see
the facts—is something within the grasp ordinary individuals.

Similarly, in *The Mozamgola Caper* (1986), the central figure is "Regretta," a washed-up African-American spy known as the "Mahogany Mata Hari." She is brought back to spy work by a U.S. government official who intends to use her as an unwitting assassin. Instead, through the course of the play, she reveals the U.S. government's secret work in destabilizing the African countries it professes to be helping. Mime Troupe plots use the popular comic trope of farcical confusion to shed light on the political landscape.[5]

As significant as any of these particular strategies are in opening up theatrical possibilities for political scrutiny, equally important is the overall spirit that popular forms embody. In order to work for social change, it is crucial to believe on some level that change is possible, that the status quo is contingent and ultimately transformable; and moreover, for the Mime Troupe, to believe that transformation can be effected through grassroots initiatives. The popular forms the troupe uses have inherited an optimistic outlook from their connection with European folk culture and the theme of cyclical change and renewal they embody. It is uncertain whether European theatrical traditions actually grew out of seasonal rituals celebrating the end of winter and the coming of spring, but this natural cycle of death and rebirth certainly impressed itself on the commoners who lived by the agricultural calendar, and the entertainments they enjoyed echo this essentially hopeful pattern. In using traditional forms, Mime Troupe plays draw on this positive perspective and give their audiences a feeling of empowerment in the face of seemingly insurmountable odds.

Mikhail Bakhtin's critical analysis of folk motifs in the literary works of Rabelais reveals the way in which the structures and images of folk performance express a positive—and potentially subversive—view of the power of the people against the political establishment. For Bakhtin, folk humor, or what he calls "the carnivalesque," works by reversing the social hierarchy so that what is ordinarily base is elevated and what is normally exalted is brought down, usually in close association with the lower bodily functions. The lower body represents sexuality and procreation, and so connotes rebirth and regeneration. All elements of folk performance—language, characterization, dramatic action—work to elevate what lies at the lower end of the social hierarchy and to debase what stands at the top in order to bring about a renewal of the entire social order. Moreover, this transformation is firmly grounded in the materiality of the world, relying on human bodies to reproduce a new, self-regenerating world. In folk performance, the life cycle of death and rebirth is significantly played out on the level of the community rather than the individual. It is a celebration of the community's political power to overturn hierarchies and create a new world.[6]

The carnivalesque also presents a double world where old and new exist side by side, the old on its way out and the new waiting to take the lead. This moment of transformation is what lends these traditions their sense of hope. But while these forms celebrate the natural cycle of death and rebirth, they are not just cyclical, but also progressive, since they envision a new future.

The overall festive atmosphere of popular performance helps to build what anthropologist Victor Turner has called "communitas," a kind of community cohesion.[7] Audiences laughing together at such performances experience a feeling of harmony and coming together. If Bakhtin is right, then at least in the past this sense of unity solidified and affirmed a communal viewpoint that sanctioned radical social change. Historical evidence also shows that European communities did use occasions of festive celebration to express, sometimes violently, a popular political point of view. For instance, as Emmanuel Le Roy Ladurie shows in *Le Carnavale de Romans,* in the sixteenth century the people of the French town of Romans turned the annual carnival celebration into a masked revolt.[8]

The festive spirit of fairground performances is closely linked to the volatile atmosphere of revolutionary action. The essential nature of both is one of disruption and disturbance of the status quo. Both provide freedom in their release from social norms. Each gathers unruly crowds who act en masse in unregulated ways. The merriment of festive celebration can erupt into violent action, and the explosion of repressed desires in aggressive revolt can release revelry.

Historical instances in which festive celebration and revolution have come together, one providing the opportunity for the other, are numerous. The Russian Revolution provides an interesting example. In 1917, the people's storming of the Czar's Winter Palace brought festive outbursts in the streets. In 1920, theater director Nikolai Evreinov restaged the event for an anniversary celebration. Performers and spectators mingled together in the culminating action. The reenactment of the revolution became a festival that reflected the celebratory nature of the original event. When the Mime Troupe performed their anti–Vietnam War commedia piece, *L'Amant Militaire,* during the student protests of the sixties, the ebullient spirit of the production and the student marches of which they were a part fed off of and mirrored each other.

Mime Troupe productions similarly capture and emulate the explosive force of festival and revolution. In periods of political action their shows work in concord with the activities around them. In times of political rest, they serve as a reminder of the promise of freedom available in social transformation. Some critics regard art that allows audiences to experience a release from oppressive social norms as a mere safety valve affording a carefully bounded, licensed experience of freedom without truly committing anyone to social reform—just an opportunity to blow off steam. But on a different view, this vicarious engagement with social disruption as the initial taste of freedom that leaves one craving more—a kind of dress rehearsal for revolution. By speaking to the audience's desire for real social transformation, the Mime Troupe aspires to the cultivation of future activists.

Transforming the Familiar

In searching for fresh cultural and political models, some of the Troupe's contemporaries, like the Living Theatre, sought to construct alternative communities outside the existing social spheres, and to strip all familiar elements and habits of daily life and theatrical tradition from their artistic endeavors. They made a conscious effort to move away from anything that even hinted at stereotypical action or theatricalization in the hope of rediscovering more authentic, preconventionalized human relationships. The Mime Troupe, by contrast, has always plunged into our shared social world and used this common reality as the basis for envisioning a new one, both on and off stage. This is one reason for their interest in traditional theatrical forms. Their exploitation of the familiar occurs in the topical cultural references sprinkled throughout their shows, the introduction in the plays of well-known figures from the worlds of politics and entertainment, and the use of common dramatic tropes in their plots, as well as stereotypical characters.

Yet this familiar world is anything but the reproduction of our daily social, psychological, and physical reality one finds in the theater of realism. Instead it underlines its own theatricality in order to point up the artificial and highly transformable nature of those elements that underlie our ordinary thoughts and actions. The Mime Troupe's productions enact a remodeling of the immediate social and political world, and to this end they are steeped in the common cultural icons and artifacts of our times. The Mime Troupe's theater makes use of our shared cultural connections and revels in theatricality itself.

Even without considering the Mime Troupe's socialist, anticapitalist orientation, or their creation of a theatrical model to rival the entertainment industry, troupe members are surprisingly well versed in the continually changing icons and images of today's popular culture. They are always up on the latest MTV rock stars and recent personality profiles in *People* magazine. The shows are up-to-date in topical references so as to make less culturally *au courant* spectators aware of recent fads in clothing, television shows, technological gadgetry, and self-help trends. The Mime Troupe makes it their business to stay abreast of these trends and saturates shows with references to the common media-driven cultural world we all share. Unlike the mainstream magazines that simply promote the fads, the Mime Troupe satirizes and deconstructs them.

In the 1991 production *Back to Normal,* produced the summer after the Gulf War, a welcome-home celebration for a military hero served as an opportunity for a jab at a variety of celebrities and the entertainment industry's insipid response to political issues. A group of actors portraying Mike Tyson, Tony Orlando, Joan Rivers, Arnold Schwarzenegger, Arsenio Hall, Brooke Shields, and Kenny G—who contributes his talents with a single, endless note on his soprano saxophone—join together in a musical tribute to the soldiers. They sing the following indicting lyrics:

> We're voices in the air
> We're over here
> You're over there
>
> Don't know who is right or who is wrong
> You go fight
> We'll sing this song
> . . . .
> War's a fluffy cuddly thing
> Can't hear the bombs
> Over our singing[9]

The Mime Troupe's dim view of the limited political awareness of Hollywood stars speaks for itself.

Of course, political figures have an even larger role to play and often get rougher treatment. At the end of *Back to Normal,* President George Bush (the elder) becomes the object of bitter satire. While watching Bush make a statement about the Gulf War on TV, Hetty, the main character, unwittingly uses the last of three wishes a genie has granted her when she accidentally says, "I wish you'd can the jive." Bush suddenly stops making his familiar, reserved, and inane proclamations, such as "Operation Desert Storm: dawn of a New World Order of justice and liberty, where might no longer makes right." Instead, he reveals his true view of the situation and exposes himself as a vulgar opportunist:

> All you hicks, micks, and spicks, I mean fellow Americans: think you're winners now, right? . . . The New Hitler. You *buy* that; we buy

the U.N.! Congress rolls over like a dead dog. Nobody hears Saddam say Uncle. Bomb his sadass country back to the Stone age! Poor towelhead still don't know what hit him—he thought he was part of the club! . . . Best club in the world. We ain't Republican or Democrat or American or Jap or German! We're bidnissmen. We got brains, bucks, and balls. Take a look at this (Mimes Unzipping fly).[10]

The accepted, controlled image of George Bush, as orchestrated by his handlers and disseminated in the media, is superseded by this glimpse of an unchecked, politically ruthless president.

But even Mime Troupe characters who don't reference specific figures have a ring of familiarity about them. Whether they are drawn from a known theatrical or cinematic genre or not, they are usually recognizable social types, if not stereotypes. The Troupe uses habitual social masks and stereotypes as the cornerstone of their theatrical constructions. In early shows like *L'Amant Militaire,* based on the plays of the commedia dell'arte, the Troupe donned the leather half-masks used by commedia actors, which allowed them to draw on the traditional characterizations of commedia figures.

Similarly, in their 1967 production, *The Minstrel Show or Civil Rights in a Cracker Barrel,* the Troupe used blackface as a kind of social mask. This production continually contrasted the blackface stereotype of the happy, comical, singing and dancing slave—an image promoted by minstrel entertainment and prominent in the culture at large—with more realistic portraits of black men in American society and their daily struggles. At the end of one sketch called "Negro History Week," the minstrels, played by both black and white actors in blackface and fright wigs, explode the reactionary minstrel stereotype by standing on their chairs shouting for "Black Power!" and "Blood in the streets!"[11] By using rather than avoiding the minstrel stereotype, then tearing it apart on stage, the Mime Troupe forced the audience to confront the deep racial prejudice in American society, in the process illuminating the issues of the civil rights movement of the period.

In subsequent shows, the Mime Troupe has relied less on traditional theatrical forms of masking and created its own new characterizations. Portraits are drawn directly from the current social scene and portray character types by means of all the elements available: costume, accessories, physical vocabulary, and verbal idiom. As with the characters drawn from traditional forms, the strategy is to inflate the type, and to this end the Troupe uses large wigs, glasses, exaggerated costumes, and extravagant physical and verbal styles. The characters are not only clearly discernible outdoors, but immediately recognizable as types. The artificiality of character construction stands out, making spectators aware of possibilities of transformation inherent in them and the social conditions they embody. Moreover, the Mime Troupe blows up these stereotypes so that they are unmistakable. As with *The Minstrel Show,* political views we might otherwise take for granted are made to stand out in larger-than-life characterizations. This technique is particularly effective when the types are placed against a backdrop that exposes misinformation disseminated by political machines and the media. Whereas our daily experience impresses on us a viewpoint of events as sanctioned by the dominant culture, at a Mime Troupe show, even the most near-sighted spectator will see the political landscape, as the Mime Troupe understands it, in high relief.

While Grotowski and his followers aimed for a "poor theater" that eschewed the artifices of wigs, makeup, and costuming, the Mime Troupe indulges in these theatrical devices. The overt theatricality and quotation of popular types in the troupe's characterizations carries over into other aspects of their productions, such as sets and music. In all these areas the Troupe follows a Brechtian idea of presentation, consciously showing the creation of artifice within the theatrical environment in order to point up the constructed nature of the status quo. The Troupe consciously adopted Brechtian ideas in 1969 with the production of Brecht's *Turandot or Congress of the Whitewashers.* The buoyant spirit and comic nature of their work today is not what we usually associate with Brecht. To be sure, during the Mime Troupe breakup in 1970 some of the members did leave in order to explore Brechtian theater more fully. Nonetheless, the way the Troupe highlights the social construction of roles and the artifice of theatrical illusion is true to Brecht and continues to play an important part in their aesthetic orientation. The same can be said of the cartoon-like scenery and the introduction of songs in popular musical styles, which disrupt and comment on the action.

The Mime Troupe's deceptively simple style of presentation echoes that of the political cartoon. Both shoot for clear images that sum up the contemporary situation in a way that is pithy and illuminating. The best Mime Troupe shows accomplish this in their dramatic premises. The troupe's 1989 piece, *Seeing Double,* described the Israeli-Palestinian conflict in a plot involving a Palestinian-American man and a Jewish-American man who look identical. Both go to Israel, and in the confusion after their plane crashes, are mistaken for one another. At the end of the piece they end up in a Palestinian house that is accidentally bombed by the Israelis. One is killed, the other wounded, but we are not told which. The highlight of the piece is a chase scene in which Michael Sullivan, who played both main characters, pulls off a feat of virtuosity as he changes from one character to the other each time he runs behind the set. The plot device of mixed-up twins goes back to Plautus' *Brothers Menachmus,* if not earlier. The Mime Troupe pulls out this age-old trope and places it in a context in which it is not just a comic setup, but an apt metaphor for the intertwined fates of the Israeli and Palestinian peoples, both seeking a secure homeland.

Mime Troupe shows are not addressed to a few brave, privileged souls who have the means and will to challenge cultural norms, but to ordinary people who, working in concert with others like themselves, can collectively give birth to a new future. This agenda leads the Troupe to enact theatrical transformation through the substance of the everyday and to be overtly theatrical in the process, pointing up contingent social constructions around us. Instead of removing themselves from the shared social context, the members of the group reflect this reality and use the stage world to illustrate the possibilities that exist for refashioning it.

The Politics of Production Offstage

Using fictional plots and imagined characters, it is relatively easy to construct a dramatic world that lives up to one's highest ideals—a world of perfect equality and justice where those in positions of authority are answerable, in the end, to ordinary people. In one way or another, all Mime Troupe plays project this moral utopia as a desired and sometimes even attainable goal. It is important for the Troupe's shows to keep holding up this ideal as a way for troupe members to remind themselves and their followers of the political ends for which they are fighting. This vision, which the Mime Troupe tries to actualize in the festive nature of its theatrical events, provides the inspiration needed to keep fueling political engagement. Indeed, one of the important roles the performing arts play in social and political movements is that of making an organization's theoretical goals concrete and imaginable by embodying them in performance.

Of course, it is much more difficult to live out these ideals in daily practice. However, the Mime Troupe tries to support its dramatic credibility with an offstage work ethic consistent with its principles. Political philosophy necessarily informs the organizational structure and artistic process and is as much a part of the troupe's creative contribution as the stage work. The Troupe tries to model in its own social, economic, and political relationships those it would like to foster in the world at large. But realizing a utopian vision in daily life is not easy, especially when the dominant economic and social forces conspire against it. Some of the most significant moments in the Mime Troupe's long history have been those in which it had to confront and negotiate the rupture between ideals and everyday reality.

Ron Davis founded the Mime Troupe in 1959 and until 1970 served as the group's artistic head, making all directorial and business decisions. His departure in 1970 was fueled in part by the desire of other company members, especially the women in the group, to have more say in the artistic work—to own the artistic views of the productions by contributing to them during the creative process. They were particularly disturbed by the gap they perceived between the power inequities they were fighting against in their shows and out on the streets, and the unfair power distribution within the group itself. This conflict within the company emerged at the same time as the rise of the women's movement on the greater political scene. Women activists throughout the country were making the same discovery, that although they devoted themselves to fighting against the Vietnam War and for civil rights as much as their brethren, they were continually oppressed in the male-dominated, hierarchical structures of their own families and institutions. In the Mime Troupe this situation led to a breakup within the group. In 1970 Ron Davis and others left the company, and those who remained behind restructured it as a collective.

The company continues to run on that egalitarian model. Today artistic and business decisions are reached through group discussions of the organizing collective. While this can be a slow and cumbersome process, it guarantees Mime Troupe members a say in their creative life and the company's progress. (Members are invited to join the governing collective when they have demonstrated their dedication to the work, and they must be willing to commit to staying with the Troupe for at least three years.) Since all workers contribute to the success of the company in different and essential ways, members of the collective receive equal financial rewards for their work— the director or writer's job is not financially gauged at a higher or lower level than that of the actors or the technical director. When a financial crisis occurs, as it often does, the company comes together to decide where the budget cuts will come from, and they have in the past agreed to across-the-board salary cuts to save the group. While longtime members of the company tend to hold more sway in discussion, this engagement of everyone, from actors, to office workers, to stagehands in shaping the artistic and financial aspects of the Troupe and sharing power over the means of production, is rare in the theater world. The group's collective structure sets it apart from the greater theater community with which it interacts, and favorably rivals that of most theatrical organizations in which artistic directors and business managers exclusively make major decisions that affect the life and work of all the theater's personnel.

The collective structure has other artistic advantages. Members of the collective, who today often take outside jobs to supplement their income, are given the first chance to participate in upcoming projects. These artists have a say in when and how they take part in production, sometimes even taking on new artistic roles; for example, an actor may write, design, or direct. Mime Troupe members work continually with others who know their strengths and can help them build new skills. Unlike most theater artists in the United States today, who live as freelancers at the whim of the entertainment industry, uncertain of their next opportunity and hoping for a "big break," the members of the Mime Troupe have an artistic home with an investment in nurturing their talents.

The differences between the Mime Troupe's collective structure and the operational model of other American theatrical organizations is reflected in the Troupe's need for a special contract to allow members of Equity to participate in the company. In 1985 the Troupe ironically found itself on the AFL-CIO boycott list because the actors' wages fell below Equity requirements.[12] Equity's usual role is to protect and represent artists in relationship to management. In the Mime Troupe, however, the artists are the managers. Salaries are set through group discussion and are based on the overall needs of the company. The Troupe eventually negotiated a contract with Equity that takes this situation into account. The contract also allows for the fact that all Mime Troupe actors also work as technicians, taking part in every aspect of production including stage setup and strike.

The group's collective ideal carries over to the creative process itself. Joan Holden served as the company's main playwright for many years, until her retirement in 2000. During her tenure, however, she always shared the job of constructing the plays with other members of the group, and this practice continues. The collective as a whole decides on the political topic that will be the focus of each piece, and all members of the company take part in researching the subject and in suggesting dramatic angles for approaching it. Research and discussion of the issues at hand force all the artists to educate themselves about the political realities confronted in the show. They are not "just actors" or "just designers," but people with a political stake in the views the plays advance. Having an understanding of and commitment to the play's political agenda necessarily informs their artistic work. This is especially evident in performances by longtime troupe members like Ed Holmes, Arthur Holden, and Sharon Lockwood. (Arthur Holden and Sharon Lockwood are regrettably no longer with the company.) Their work captures the elusive Brechtian technique of commenting on the situation within their acting of a character, thereby illuminating the political context framing the events.

Joan Holden has often had others collaborate on the actual writing of the plays as well. Holden wrote *Ripped Van Winkle* (1988) with the help of company members Ellen Callas and Bruce Barthol, and *Mozamgola Caper* with nonmembers Robert Alexander and John O'Neal. Holden might also ask an actor to write his own speech for a particular scene that was closer to his personal experience and voice than her own. Furthermore, every script is subject to extensive transformation and rewriting during the rehearsal process, depending on how well it works on stage, and on whether the company feels that it tells the dramatic and political story successfully. This model of collective composition dismantles the view of the playwright as a lone artistic genius, and of the text as a finished, immutable masterpiece. In the Mime Troupe, the playwright is one member of a collaborative group working toward communal artistic and political ends. The text is more or less a group creation subject to change in accordance with the needs of the company and the continually shifting political scene.

Over the years, changes in the company's personnel and their choice of performance venues have also reflected their changing political perspective. When Ron Davis ran the group, he felt strongly that as a young, white man from a middle-class background, his plays should speak to others like himself about the role they could play in effecting social and political change. As such, the company generally directed their shows to white, middle-class kids and often played on college campuses. Little attention was paid to creating diversity within the company itself. After Davis left, the Troupe more and more saw the need to address a diverse community. They sought a more mixed racial balance within the group and varied their performance venues to include more inner-city areas. In 1984 they took *Steeltown*, a piece that dealt with the closing and downsizing of factories, directly to steelworkers in the Midwest.

Funding has always been an issue for the Mime Troupe, as it is for all artistic organizations. But the Troupe necessarily worries not only about staying afloat, but also about the political implications of their funding sources. From the beginning, the ideal was for the Troupe to survive only on what they took in from passing the hat at the end of their shows and from individual donations. They feared that accepting money from foundations or government agencies, as almost all arts organizations do, might compromise their political values. Their ideal became less and less workable as the cost of living rose and Mime Troupe members began having

families and assuming other financial responsibilities. The Troupe's first ac-
ceptance of public funding came when they fought to receive money from
San Francisco City's Hotel Tax allocation for the arts in 1965. They reasoned that, since this money was collected to assist organizations that contributed to making San Francisco an attractive town for tourists, they
should benefit from it. In this case, their fighting for funds usually reserved
for more traditional art institutions was a political statement in itself. In
1984, in the face of ever rising costs, the Troupe finally accepted their first
grant from the National Endowment for the Arts. In recent years their NEA
funding has been drastically cut. Nonetheless, accepting government funding went against the Troupe's scruples. Some see the decision as a confir-
mation of the Troupe's increasingly innocuous political stance. The Troupe
sees a necessary compromise that allows it to continue offering audiences
free outdoor performances.

The Mime Troupe also puts its political values into practice offstage in
its educational programs, in its support of and connections with other activist organizations, and in its direct theatrical actions. Since the 1990s the
Troupe has conducted a Youth Theatre Project in which Troupe members help at-risk teens write and stage Mime Troupe–style plays about
their own issues and concerns. In their ongoing connections with other
like-minded activists, they do benefit performances for various organizations and split the take with them at the door. They also often appear at
marches and political rallies for a variety of leftist causes.

Occasionally, the Mime Troupe performs theatrical actions outside of
their usual performance venues, and in contexts that place them close to
the heart of the political issues they are addressing. It is in these instances that their theatrical projects and their political advocacy come
closest together. In 1973 the San Francisco city government considered
using tax money to create a San Francisco performing arts center. The
Mime Troupe and others saw this apparently laudable enterprise as a plan
that would use taxpayer dollars to remove poor people from their communities in order to build arts organizations that the former residents
would probably not be able to afford to attend and that did not represent
their cultural interests. The Troupe captured the situation in their *San
Francisco Scandals of 1973,* a play about a displaced group of vaudeville
performers. The Troupe did a version of this piece before the San Francisco commission considering the issue, then headed by Diane Feinstein.
At the end of the piece one performer, in classic vaudeville style, got a
cream pie in the face. The cream ended up all over the room. Feinstein
memorably stated that the Troupe was way too talented for these antics,
and the Troupe used her words in publicity for years to come. The San

Francisco Performing Art Center was built in the end with revenue-sharing funds and large private donations.

In 1995 the Troupe created a short piece that showed up the cruelty and absurdity of laws that forbade people from feeding San Francisco's homeless population. These laws were part of the mayor's attempt to clear the homeless off the streets in order to promote business and hide hunger and poverty in the city. The Troupe's Valentine's Day show of *Captain Bob's Hungry Heart; or a Bagel in the Hand is Worth Two in the Bush,* performed on the San Francisco courthouse steps, highlighted the case of Keith McHenry from the organization Food Not Bombs. McHenry had been arrested numerous times for the soup and bagels he gave to the homeless on a regular basis. McHenry introduced the piece, announcing the verdict on his recently reduced sentence. In the Troupe's comic melodrama, the McHenry character is a shady figure in a trenchcoat who opens it to reveal the contraband he carries hanging inside: bagels, apples, cheese. In the end the police, out to save society from this criminal, arrest him when he offers a homeless woman a bagel and cheese. After the Troupe's playlet was over, a Food Not Bombs member came to the steps with real soup to hand out and was arrested by the real San Francisco police. As Joel Schechter reports on the crowd, "The same people who laughed at the Mime Troupe's police force shouted 'Shame, Shame!' at the second act's officers; and a few spectators became actors as they resisted the arrest of the bagel server and tried to pull him away from the police."[13]

The Mime Troupe provides a comic theatrical perspective on situations that heightens the public's understanding of political circumstances and their implications. In pieces like these, where the Troupe's work is placed within the context of real-life events, the significance of their presentations is further enriched. In contributing its art to these activist causes the Troupe reaffirms its commitment to a political agenda outside of the theater.

Conclusion

In 1987 the San Francisco Mime Troupe received a special Tony Award for its artistic work and found itself in the awkward position of being applauded by the very theatrical establishment it had so long resisted. This award and the NEA grant seem to confirm the troupe's ironic claim to be "the most established antiestablishment theatre in the country." A turnaround from their original position as counterculture revolutionaries—getting arrested rather than awarded—the situation necessarily raises questions about the continuing political efficacy of the group's work. Precisely because the company received its political and cultural education in the sixties, many critics wonder whether the its vision for the future and the artistic means of presenting it remain effective in today's cultural climate. Some also point to the Troupe's tendency to "preach to the converted" as evidence of ineffectiveness, especially when the "converted" look like so many aging lefties.

But in fact preaching to the choir has always been part of the Mime Troupe agenda. Even in the sixties the group provided both moral support to, and critique from within, the Left. In these more politically complacent times, when those who still believe that social and political institutions can be changed from below to serve the greater good are few and far between, the Troupe's work is perhaps more valuable than ever.

Its chosen aesthetic may also be an important asset in helping to keep activism alive today. The Troupe enacts a living memory of the revolutionary values and spirit of the movements of the 1960s. In the offices and rehearsal spaces on Treat Street in San Francisco, and at the productions in parks and community centers, the very presence of the Mime Troupe process takes us back to a moment when faith in the power of the people to transform the world for the better seemed unhampered, fueled not just by optimism but by commitment and conviction. In spite of its members' all-too-conscious awareness of the new social, economic, and political realities of the day, the Mime Troupe offers a dose of idealism in a world of shabby compromise, but an idealism that is connected to models of action.

The Mime Troupe's greatest service lies in offering concrete images of change at a time when a fractured postmodernist perspective on the world combined with information overload leaves many feeling politically inconsequential, ineffectual, and apathetic. The Mime Troupe gives us a way to reassess the goals of the past in light of contemporary realities, as well as an opportunity to build new bridges between the two. In the space between the idealism of the past and the compromises of the present the seeds of new activism can take root and grow.

In their 1988 piece, *Ripped Van Winkle,* the Troupe captured this ideal onstage. The play tells the story of Rip, an activist from the sixties, who falls asleep when a strange woman in the park gives him two tabs of purple LSD. He wakes up twenty years later, in 1988, only to discover that the world has completely transformed: the political causes he fought for have dissolved, his activist girlfriend is working for then San Francisco Mayor Diane Feinstein, his hip pad has become a chic yuppie restaurant, and public telephone calls cost twenty cents. Through the course of the play he uses his

1960s, supposedly outmoded subversive tactics to make the people around him reconsider their actions and the values of the new world in which they live. In the end the revolutionary spirit of the sixties that Rip preserves proves not only politically effective, but desperately necessary for re-kindling a sense of empowerment and optimism in the other characters. This production may reflect a kind of wishful thinking on their part, but with each new production the Mime Troupe and their followers find opportunities to test the strength of the bonds that tie their aesthetic sensibility to their political ideals, and to reassess that agenda for contemporary times.

NOTES

1. Claudia Orenstein, *Festive Revolutions: The Politics of Popular Theater and the San Francsico Mime Troupe* (Jackson: University Press of Mississippi, 1998).

2. George Speaight, *Punch and Judy: A History* (Boston: Boston Plays, 1995), 37.

3. Michael Byrom, *Punch and Judy in the Italian Puppet Theatre* (London: Centaur, 1983), 95.

4. Ibid., 35.

5. Joan Holden et. al. "The San Francisco Mime Troupe's *Mozamgola Caper,*" *Theatre* 20, no. 1 (1988): 55–71.

6. Mikhail Bakhtin, *Rabelais and His World*, trans. Hélène Iswolsky (Bloomington: Indiana University Press, 1984).

7. Victor Turner, *From Ritual to Theatre: The Human Seriousness of Play* (New York: PAJ, 1982).

8. Emmanuel le Roy Ladurie, *Le Carnavale de Romans: De la chandeleur au Merredi des Cendres, 1579–1580* (Poitiers: Gallimard, 1979).

9. San Francisco Mime Troupe, *Back to Normal*, nnpublished manuscript, 1991, 19–20.

10. Ibid., 32–33.

11. R. G. Davis, *The San Francisco Mime Troupe: The First Ten Years* (Palo Alto, Calif.: Ramparts, 1975), 57.

12. Janelle Reinelt, "Approaching the Sixties: Between Nostalgia and Critique," *Theatre Survey* 43 (2002): 43.

13. Joel Schecter, review of "the Arrest of the Anarchist Keith Henry" by the San Francisco Mime Troupe and the San Francisco Police Department, *Theatre Journal* 47 (1995): 541.

SAN FRANCISCO MIME TROUPE LEGACY

Guerrilla Theater

Susan Vaneta Mason

On August 7, 1965, R. G. Davis, creator and artistic director of the San Francisco Mime Troupe, was arrested while performing the opening line of a play, *Il Candelaio,* in a San Francisco park without a permit. The event was staged. The police were real and the arrest was real, but the Troupe had publicized its planned civil disobedience, and spectators had come from all over the Bay Area to witness it. Davis even stepped into the role of Brighella, usually played by Luis Valdez, in order to perform the apprehended actor. According to Peter Berg, then a member of the Mime Troupe, that merging of life and theater defined for him what he would call "guerrilla theater."[1]

This chapter examines the San Francisco Mime Troupe as guerrilla theater by tracing the evolution, descendants, and ramifications of the concept, primarily in the 1960s when the company coined and adopted the term to describe the kind of theater they were doing. In addition, two developments in the Troupe's organization in the 1970s, collectivity and multiculturalism, outgrowths of their guerrilla ideology and important elements of their legacy, will also be discussed.

Davis began challenging the boundaries of theater in 1959 when he first created his company. The R. G. Davis Mime Troupe was a subsidiary of the San Francisco Actors' Workshop, famous for the production of *Waiting for Godot* at San Quentin in 1957. Davis had become an assistant director at the Workshop shortly after he arrived in San Francisco in 1958. He

R. G. Davis arrest in Lafayette Park, 1965. *Left to right:* Bill Graham, R. G. Davis, Luis Valdez, Paul Jacobs. (Photo by Erik Weber.)

had just completed a Fulbright in Paris, studying with mime artist Etienne Decroux. By pursuing mime, Davis rebelled against the narrow bourgeois concept of legitimate theater in the United States in the 1950s. His vision was to "free the stage from its constipated décor and reaffirm the essence of theatre—a vital human performing for a live audience."[2] However, his emphasis was on economy rather than silence, and in 1962 he wrote that the ancient tradition of mime included "improvised dialogue."[3]

Because Davis was trained in dance as well as mime, he regarded the actor's body as the primary tool for communication. However, at the time he created his company, San Francisco was experiencing a literary renaissance, with writers and poets such as Allen Ginsberg, Michael McClure, Jack Kerouac, and Gary Snyder. Language evoking the improvised quality of jazz was a prominent feature of this artistic milieu, along with a Zen simplicity. Davis's minimalist concept of theater complemented this beat, avant-garde aesthetic.

With the *11th Hour* (then *Midnight*) *Mime Show* from 1960 to 1962, his small troupe first produced performance art—improvised "events" with music, utilizing the entire theater, lobby and staircases, and replacing narrative with visual images and sound. Artist William Wiley, composer Steve

Reich, actors Ruth Maleczech and Bill Raymond, and director Lee Breuer were among the creators of these outrageous happenings. Breuer has described them as "thirty years ahead of their time and unchanged they could open at The Kitchen or P.S. 122 today."[4] They used the Actors' Workshop's Encore Theatre rent free by performing at the only time the space was available: late Sunday nights. They solicited contributions instead of charging admission.

Meanwhile the Workshop was the recipient of Ford Foundation money. Production costs and advertising increased; actors were brought in from Los Angeles and New York. They became a full-time professional company embodying all the values Davis was challenging. So, in January 1963, Davis left the Workshop and moved performances to his small studio on Capp Street in the Mission District, a working-class Latino neighborhood away from the Beat center in North Beach. By then, he had begun experimenting with commedia dell'arte, drawn to its improvised style, bold physical expression, and working-class perspective.[5] In May 1962 he returned theater to the open air by performing in Golden Gate Park. Two park performances of *The Dowry* (adapted from scripts by Molière and Goldoni with improvised contemporary references) that summer started the Troupe on a course it has followed ever since: making theater accessible to the public by taking it outside. The commedia acting style also coalesced during that first park performance when an actress raced off stage announcing: "The reason for the large movements and gestures is because they performed outside." Davis describes the effect: "Once outside, theory and reality crashed together into a screaming joyous perception."[6]

In 1963 the Troupe gave five park performances and in 1964 eight. Thus, by the summer of Davis's arrest while performing another commedia in a San Francisco park, the Troupe's signature style that would epitomize guerrilla theater, was essentially defined: free performances in public parks employing music and a broad, improvisational, physical acting style, in anachronistic productions updated with topical references. The major change in the work from its inception until 1965 was the development of a radical political ideology that, coupled with bawdy irreverence, ultimately led to the arrest.

When the Troupe first moved out into the parks in 1962, they applied for and were given a permit from the Park and Recreation Commission. The following year they were granted permission to perform in the parks on five occasions with the proviso that the commission approve the content of the shows. They ignored this attempt at censorship and performed *The Root* (based on Machiavelli's *Mandragola*) without incident. The same stipulation, also ignored, followed their request for even more park appearances of an original play, *Chorizos*, in 1964. However, political tension in the Bay Area was rising. At the Republican convention in San Francisco that July, Barry Goldwater accepted the nomination with the pronouncement, "Extremism in defense of liberty is no vice." As if in response, the Free Speech Movement erupted in Berkeley that fall.

By 1965 the Troupe was gaining a reputation as a radical theater company, and many members were participating in the protest movements that were spilling into the streets of San Francisco. That spring their production of Brecht's *The Exception and the Rule* toured with journalist Robert Scheer speaking against the escalating war in Vietnam. In June, Davis opened what became the most notorious show in Mime Troupe history: *A Minstrel Show, or Civil Rights in a Cracker Barrel*. It was immediately controversial ostensibly because of two simulated sex scenes but also because of its unsettling exposé of white liberal hypocrisy.

Consequently the commission granted forty-eight park performances of *Il Candelaio* with a proviso that the production not use obscene words or gestures. Civil liberties lawyers found nothing offensive in the production, and performances commenced. However, after the third performance, the commissioners deemed the performance "indecent, obscene and offensive" and revoked the troupe's permit.[7] Ironically, the play was an adaptation of a satire by Giordano Bruno, who was burned at the stake in 1600 for challenging authority.

A fourth performance was scheduled for 2:00 P.M. in Lafayette Park on August 7. Troupe publicity and word of mouth drew a crowd of at least a thousand. Davis explained the permit situation to the crowd, then he moved into the playing space and announced: "Ladieeeeees and Gentlemen, Il Troupo di Mimo di San Francisco presents for your enjoyment this afternoon . . . AN ARREST!"[8] As a trained dancer, Davis executed a perfect leap into the air, was grabbed by a police officer, and arrested for performing without a permit. *Ramparts'* writer David Kolodney, in sympathy with the Troupe's opposition to bourgeois theater, later suggested Davis had been arrested for performing free entertainment in a public park without a Ford Foundation grant.[9] Davis's arrest brought to a head the increasingly confrontational relationship between the establishment and the counterculture over censorship brewing in San Francisco since the obscenity trial of Ginsberg's *Howl* in 1957, and it galvanized the Bay Area's New Left.[10]

The Troupe continued performances without incident that summer, but on November 1 Davis was tried and convicted of performing without a permit. The following summer, when the increasingly hostile commission demanded approval of play summaries as a precondition for issuing a park permit to perform *The Miser,* the ACLU filed a suit on behalf of the Mime Troupe arguing that the commission's rules were unconstitutional. They won this suit and then two others granting them the right to perform uncensored in parks in and around the San Francisco Bay Area.

The *San Francisco Examiner's* Kenneth Rexroth recalled the function of theater in ancient Greece and Renaissance Italy while praising the troupe's park appearances in 1963: "Audiences in the parks in the Western Addition or the Mission turn out to be no different than those 300 years ago in Italy or 2,000 years ago in Greece or Alexandria. They loved it. Let's hope this is an entering wedge, and that eventually we will have all sorts of musical and dramatic activity in the parks. I can think of few better ways to raise the muscle tone of a flabby community."[11] The Troupe later noted that "the 'liberation' of the parks set a precedent for theatres in other cities to go outdoors without fear of arrest, and this test case opened the door for most of the free activities that burst upon the San Francisco scene in the next few years."[12]

As a result of legal fees incurred in liberating the parks, Mime Troupe promoter Bill Graham held a series of appeals to raise money for the Troupe's legal defense. The first appeal, held in the Mime Troupe's studio in November 1965, initiated the phenomenon of rock concerts as fund-raisers. Charles Perry describes the event: "The censorship issue rallied the art world and Graham was showered with names of people who wanted to be involved. Some were big names, like the Committee, the folksinger Sandy Bull, Allen Ginsberg. . . , a jug band composed of poets known as the Fugs. Jefferson Airplane would play, of course—the Airplane had used the Mime Troupe loft for rehearsals."[13] The line of people waiting to get in stretched around the block, and the event raised two thousand dollars.

Because of the scale of this unexpected success, Graham followed it a month later with a second appeal for the Troupe, this time in a rented auditorium, the Fillmore, and featuring Jefferson Airplane, the Grateful Dead, Big Brother and the Holding Company, Quicksilver Messenger Service, and the Great Society. Over thirty-five hundred people paid $1.50 each to attend. With Graham's third fund-raiser in January 1966, he paid the bands to perform, launching what would become Bill Graham Enterprises. Graham left the Troupe a month later when he couldn't convince the membership to become rock promoters, but he continued to contribute to their yearly appeals (as his foundation continued to do even after his death in 1991).

In spite of the funds raised by these bands for the Mime Troupe's legal fees, by the end of the decade its members were outspoken in their hostility to the commercial venture most big bands had become and the radical chic they represented. In contrast, the troupe defined its own mission as working for social change, not money. In an unpublished company document from about 1969, the Troupe denounced the change in rock music since the mid-1960s: "What is now the hottest of commercial properties was still a communal art form." The Troupe defined their own mission as convincing artists "to stop working for art's or money's sake and to start working for the people and social change . . . distinguishing the true cultural revolution, which aims to change the institutions, from the fashion 'revolution' as represented by hip capitalism and *Hair*."[14]

Because of the anticapitalist ideology in both the content of the shows and the group's practices, it performed free theater. However, Davis was adamant that they were professionals. Among other things, this meant the artists had to be paid, even if only a dollar a show. Consequently they had to devise nontraditional ways of generating income. Three of Davis's solutions are still practiced: pass the hat after the show, in what the Troupe calls "the pitch"; solicit contributions through appeals to potential contributors (frequently in the form of a letter, although some, like Bill Graham's, were advertised events); and acquire paid bookings on college and university campuses and with activist organizations.

"How does one keep alive doing independent, radical, chaotic, anarchic theatre?" wrote Davis in 1964. "By finagling, which is a variation on thievery, cunning, conning and opportunism. And by not boring the audience."[15] The system worked so well that by the end of the decade the Troupe was able to pay a small office staff and twenty-five dollars a week to company members.

The Mime Troupe was in the vanguard of the free movement in the San Francisco Bay Area. Two members, Emmett Grogan and Peter Berg, began an organization called The Diggers, named after the seventeenth-century English Diggers, whose vision included a society devoid of private property, buying, and selling. The San Francisco Diggers "combined street theatre, anarcho-direct action, and art happenings in their social agenda of creating a Free City."[16] They distributed free food and created a free medical clinic and free stores (an intentional oxymoron). They coined the phrase "Today is the first day of the rest of your life" and popularized tie-dyd clothes.

Peter Coyote, who along with several other Mime Troupe members eventually left the Troupe for the Diggers, describes many of their free activities in his book *Sleeping Where I Fall*. They created several street events such as the Human Be-In in January 1967 in Golden Gate Park, where over fifty thousand people danced, sang, and dropped acid. The Mime

Troupe hung animal parts on a fence to represent the slaughter in Viet Nam. Attendees included a vast panorama of countercultures from Hells Angels to Zen poets. The event received national attention, and the hippie phenomenon centered in the Diggers' neighborhood of Haight-Ashbury was born.

Since some of the Diggers came out of the Mime Troupe, theater remained a central metaphor for a while and the life/theater concept Berg had named "guerrilla theater" after Davis's arrest evolved into Digger happenings: the street as theater. Some Digger members in the Troupe wore orange frames on a string around their necks to hold up and frame whatever they looked at through an orange proscenium.[17] Berg also called this blurring of the boundaries between theater and life "breaking the glass," and the participants were "life-actors."[18]

Another organization to emerge from the Mime Troupe's activism was the Artist Liberation Front (ALF), a grassroots arts coalition. In 1966 when San Francisco mayor Jack Shelley created an Art Research Development Committee comprised of twenty-six prominent businesspeople and civic leaders, he neglected to include representation by artists. Lawrence Ferlinghetti learned about their first meeting and alerted the Troupe. Members, dressed in commedia and minstrel costumes, crashed the luncheon meeting on May 2 at the Crown Zellerbach Building. Davis recalls reading a manifesto that opposed the downtown event and called for neighborhood art. Harold Zellerbach, chairman of the committee, tried to push the Troupe out, but Davis pushed back and insisted on finishing.[19]

Two days later, the Publicity and Advertising Fund, the primary source of arts grants in San Francisco, also under the mayor's office, announced the year's awards. The Troupe had received one thousand dollars in 1964 and 1965, although the latter was rescinded after Davis's arrest. They had applied again but received nothing in 1966 or any of the following years up to 1977 when Thomas Mellon, the chief administrative officer of the fund, appointed by Mayor Shelley in 1964, was replaced. The Troupe had won a lawsuit against Mellon's office in 1974, but funding was still denied.

In order to unite local artists in resistance to the increasing collusion between business and bourgeois art institutions, one week following the Crown Zellerbach luncheon the Troupe created a guerrilla arts council, the Artist Liberation Front (ALF), taking their name from the National Liberation Front, the Communist rebels in South Vietnam. The membership of about forty-five, one-third of them Troupe members, included Bill Graham, Lawrence Ferlinghetti, Kenneth Rexroth, Ralph Gleason, and Hunter Thompson. Coyote, still a member of the Mime Troupe at that time, writes that the ALF was "intended to bypass 'official' city-sponsored art and bring recognition to the work of community-based artists and people of color who were being ignored."[20] A benefit for the ALF at the Fillmore on July 17, 1966, was so successful that the line stretched around the block. The event, a Mardi Gras masked ball, included Allen Ginsberg wearing an Uncle Sam hat, reading his new poem "Wichita Vortex Sutra," and the Mime Troupe's Gorilla Band performing "I Got Fucked in Vietnam," sung to the tune of "The Ballad of the Green Berets."[21]

That fall the ALF held a series of free fairs in low-income neighborhoods, with music, puppets, painting, and assorted forms of entertainment. The following February the ALF and the Diggers created what was intended to be a seventy-two-hour happening known by various titles: "It's Yours," "It's Here," or "The Invisible Circus: The Right of Spring." Glide Memorial Church welcomed the event, believing it would be like the street fairs, but it wasn't: and after eight hours and at least five thousand participants, one performing cunnilingus in a light show on the altar, the church called it off.[22]

According to Davis, around this time a lawyer whose wife was a filmmaker tried to turn the ALF into a nonprofit so he could apply for grants. Peter Berg retaliated by leading the Troupe in a vote to rename it "Acme Cement."[23] Soon after that, the organization disappeared.

The Mime Troupe continued some of the ALF activities, primarily opposition to what it considered cultural mausoleums, such as performing arts centers (PACs). Davis had scorned the rising popularity of repertory companies in 1964, suggesting they were "extensions of large corporations."[24] He was equally disdainful of the structures, like Lincoln Center, that housed them, accusing their promoters of having an "Edifice Complex."[25] From 1972 to 1981 the Troupe joined with other local activists in opposing the proposed PAC at the Civic Center. The Troupe attacked the structure and its primary supporter, Harold Zellerbach, in *High Rises* in 1972, revised as *San Fran Scandals '73* later that year. In the latter a toilet paper tycoon, Smellybucks, is building a shrine in his honor.

The Troupe also opposed building the George Moscone Convention Center and staged their play *Ghosts* (1981) by invitation at its opening. *Ghosts* borrowed from Dickens in looking at the community of Yerba Buena—where the convention center was built—in the past (a working-class neighborhood), present (the Convention Center), and future (all condominiums and office buildings). Troupe opposition stemmed from the use of public money for shrines to elitism and commerce, but also for working-class housing razed in urban redevelopment.

Although guerrilla theater as defined by Berg referred to a merging of theater and life, for Davis it also implied a merging of theater and politics.

He wrote three essays developing the concept. In the first guerrilla theater essay, which was published in the *Tulane Drama Review* in 1966, Davis defined it as a theater of social commitment dedicated to "teach, direct toward change, and be an example of change."[26] The term was immediately co-opted by scholars and practitioners, and guerrilla theaters sprang up on both coasts.

In the "Handbook" in this first essay, Davis describes the physical aspects of the kind of theater he is proposing: low-rent rehearsal spaces, open-air performance in spaces where people congregate, popular theater forms, eclectic performance style adapted by performers, music, no money on advertising, free shows supported by donations, and paid actors.[27] Guerrilla theater also often included an element of stealth. Because of the minimal physical elements, this theater can be set up and struck quickly. Furthermore, by being staged in open public places, where life can and does intrude at any moment, it embodies a revolt against structure.

Luis Valdez, who spent a year with the Mime Troupe in 1964–65 before creating El Teatro Campesino, said he was drawn to the Troupe because "there was obviously something happening, a fantastic difference from all that bullshit in the academic theatre about scenery and lighting. . . . The Mime Troupe is outside, in the park. They're out, they're alive."[28] Davis sometimes used *radical theater* as an equivalent of guerrilla theater, and in 1968 he created a Radical Theatre Festival in San Francisco with the Mime Troupe, Bread and Puppet, and El Teatro Campesino. The companies traded techniques and held performances and a symposium.

In Davis's succeeding guerrilla theater essays, self-published by the Mime Troupe in 1970, his rhetoric becomes more revolutionary. He focuses less on the physical attributes of guerrilla theater than on its underlying theories. In his 1967 essay, Davis defines his theatrical premise: "Western society is rotten in general, capitalist society in the main, and U.S. society in the particular." Private property, he suggests, is the source of the disease. Later in this essay he explains that guerrilla theater needs to live by imitating "the Latin American guerrilla who is a low-class socialist"; dropping out of middle-class America is necessary.[29] In the 1960s the term *dropping out* meant walking away from bourgeois society. In the third guerrilla essay, in 1968, Davis writes: "The middle-class mind with its bourgeois desires and goals of profit, efficiency, specialization, and materialism, must be subverted, destroyed and replaced."[30]

Davis's target audience was the middle class, and he firmly believed that the personnel in a guerrilla theater company "must come from the class they want to change." He opposed cultural colonialism, arguing, "Social work theatre is out; play for your own kind—you understand them, and they identify with you."³¹ At that time the Troupe was essentially white and middle class, although Latino and black actors had participated in several plays in the 1960s. Former member Steve Friedman described the membership in 1971 as "white, middle class college dropouts or disgruntled college graduates."³²

In *Theatre for Working-Class Audiences in the United States, 1830–1980,* Daniel Friedman describes the Mime Troupe in the 1960s as "*the* theatre of America's left-wing community." "However," he continues, "the leftist community at that time was made up primarily of white students and counter-culturists, not workers, and it was essentially this audience that they played for throughout the decade."³³ In 1970 when the Troupe became a collective, one of the first changes was the demographics of the audience, which meant changing the demographics of the company.

Davis left the Mime Troupe in 1970 after the membership voted to reorganize as a collective. He believed collectivity was an ineffective way to organize and would compromise the art. Although the company structure went through a radical change at that time, they retained many practical and creative features from the 1960s that continued to define the company for years: weekly meetings, a weekly schedule, reading in political theory, the park setup procedure, passing the hat, and college tours to generate income, the broad physical performance style, training in specific acting skills, and the mission of social change. Furthermore, the company's reputation as theater of the movement (both civil rights and antiwar), gained during two national tours in the 1960s, defined them well into the 1980s, when the movement essentially died.

Also, although commedia dominated the Troupe's shows in the 1960s, Davis experimented with style, finding the appropriate approach to each production. In the 1960s the Troupe experimented with minstrel show and epic as well as commedia and mime. This practice has, to an extent, continued into the present although by the mid-1980s there was an identifiable Mime Troupe style, heavily influenced by melodrama and comics.

Davis's greatest contribution to the American theater was, as Antonin Artaud writes in "No More Masterpieces," to take theater away from "the self-styled elite" and give it back to the general public.³⁴ He should also be credited with infusing it with a radical political ideology. Arthur Holden, who joined the San Francisco Mime Troupe in 1963 and retired in 1996, described the debt the company owed Davis: "We've been overly meticulous in giving Davis the credit—and he deserves it—for starting the Troupe, and starting it with the right idea, which is that theatre had achieved a level of sacred temple art. . . . So, in taking it away from the hall and bringing it to the park, that was a very important fundamental basis on which we have worked ever since."[35]

Although theater collectives existed in the United States prior to 1970, the Mime Troupe was the first with a national audience, and numerous articles were written about its collective methods, especially during the 1970s when it invented and refined its structure. The group had arrived at the concept of collectivity by reading the political theories of Marx and Mao while preparing a production of Brecht's *Congress of Whitewashers* in 1969, but the reality of running the company without a leader both terrified and energized them.

At first everyone tried everything. Each member had an office job, a household job, and a creative job. They stopped identifying actors in roles on programs. They tried rotating leading roles and other artistic assignments. They experimented with collective play creation. In describing their collective processes, Joan Holden, the Troupe's principal playwright for thirty-three years, noted: "We have not made team work a hard and fast rule, but it is harder when you work alone to remember that your work is not your property."[36]

Some plays, such as *The Dragon Lady's Revenge* (1971), were written by several writers working together. *The Independent Female* (1970) was scripted by one writer, Holden. *Frozen Wages* (1972) and *Hotel Universe* (1976) began with improvisation, and the scripts came later. More recently, scripts such as *Seeing Double* (1989) and *Offshore* (1995) have been created by an international team of writers.

The Troupe's collective script creation practices differ from show to show, but some stages can be summarized. The process begins with group consensus about a topic, usually arrived at in January. Once agreed on, a period of research follows. At some point early in the process, the style is determined. The actual scripting is done in a variety of ways depending on the proximity and practice of the playwriting team. For example, *City for Sale* (1999) was developed by Holden, her daughter Kate, and lyricist Bruce Barthol, by e-mail. This process takes anywhere from one to three months. Rehearsals are fairly conventional and generally have just one director. Even in the early 1970s, when some shows had more than one director, they usually worked separately, and in 1975 Holden cautioned: "Don't have two directors for one rehearsal."[37]

The protagonists of Mime Troupe plays are almost always oppressed people in conflict with a capitalist economic system indifferent to their needs and rights. Frequently the plays end with a political awakening when the people take collective action against their oppressors. This conflict and the call to collective action mirror the company's history both in the struggle to survive as a small political theater collective in a society where noncommercial art is not valued, and in its participation in collective action with numerous organizations from grassroots housing coalitions to international movements for nuclear disarmament.

The Troupe process has often included input from outside activists as part of research or as respondents at previews. This collective practice predates 1970, beginning when Davis directed *A Minstrel Show, or Civil Rights in a Cracker Barrel* (1965) and invited members of two civil rights organizations, CORE (Congress on Racial Equality) and SNCC (Student Nonviolent Coordinating Committee) to previews for feedback. The troupe has continued this practice up to the present.

Because the company has survived against all odds and continues to create at least one new musical theater production every year, reaching sometimes as many as three thousand spectators at a single performance, their collective practices have been an area of ongoing fascination for scholars and practitioners.

Besides collectivity, another major change in the company after 1970 was the choice to become multiracial. In 1970 the Troupe created a three-point program to define its mission: (1) All art is political; (2) serve the people, and (3) smash individualism.[38] In the 1960s the Troupe had already determined that all art is political, and in early collective practices the group attempted to do away with individualism. Serving the people was a more complex issue, beginning with defining "the people." In the 1960s it had been the middle class. However, their political reading suggested social change needed to come from the working class. Consequently, in order to expand the class and cultural base of their audience, without creating what Davis called "social work theatre," they had to change the demographics of their own organization. To accomplish this, in 1974 they put a hiring freeze on white actors, and by the end of the decade they were multiracial.

While their collective organization attracted much critical commentary, especially in the 1970s, little has been written about the Troupe's struggles and victories with ethnicity in spite of their role as pioneers in multicultural theater. Race is a loaded issue in American society, and race relations have, on occasion, become volatile in the Mime Troupe. When this has occurred, the members have usually held long meetings to work out problems.

One source of ethnic tension in the company has been casting. The Troupe is primarily committed to nontraditional casting, both cross-gender and cross-ethnic. They have also had a commitment to rotating responsibilities (more in the 1970s than at present). Furthermore, in spite of collective practices, the director of a Troupe production wields the same kind of authority as in traditionally structured theater companies, including making casting decisions. Consequently, these commitments can be and have been, on occasion, at odds.

For example, in 1991 the Troupe produced *I Ain't Yo' Uncle,* a revisionist *Uncle Tom's Cabin* where Harriet Beecher Stowe's characters accuse her of creating stereotypes. The black characters were all played by black actors. The director, Dan Chumley, wanted to cast an Asian actress, and collective member, as Little Eva. Lonnie Ford, the company's first black actor in the 1970s, who returned to play Uncle Tom, objected. He felt strongly that Little Eva should be white and went so far as to threaten to leave the production. Ford prevailed. Chumley, who is white, later explained that the rehearsal period was fraught with arguments and that "as a white male in a position of authority at the company, he had an unconscious expectation that performers would defer to his judgment. They didn't."[39] In a play where black characters confront their white oppressor, this conflict was inevitable.

In some other productions, nontraditional casting has proved to be an inspired choice. In *Seeing Double,* the troupe's mistaken-identity Middle East play, for example, Michael Sullivan, an African-American actor and collective member, played both the Jewish and Palestinian look-alike characters. This casting choice, as well as the ensemble playing both Jewish and Palestinian characters, was especially effective in reminding spectators that ethnic roles are social constructs. Stacy Wolf describes the results: "By casting a black man as the David/Salim character, the Troupe not only de-authorizes realism—it is visually clear that this actor is probably not Jewish or Palestinian—they also suggest the similarities between the Palestinians and Jews."[40]

Many Troupe shows include mixed-race families, with sometimes humorous backgrounds. In *Back to Normal* (1991), Hetty, played by a white actress, Sharon Lockwood, is a radical leftist radio talk-show host and the mother of a black son, Jamal, played by Michael Sullivan, who has sneaked off to join the marines and becomes a hero in the Persian Gulf War. All Hetty can tell Jamal about his father is, "It was a hot weekend at Monterey Jazz." When he criticizes her for the lack of black cultural education in his upbringing, she responds, "I played jazz, I read you African stories, I sent away for dashikis." Jamal counters, "You never took me to Oakland!" However, ultimately he is more frustrated by his ignorance about popular culture since his mother wouldn't own a television.[41]

The Troupe is probably less committed to nontraditional ethnic casting than to multiracial casting. Because all the plays are written by and for the multicultural collective, the characters as written come from various cultures. However, in 1971, before the Troupe became multicultural, *The Dragon Lady's Revenge*, set in Southeast Asia, with several Asian characters, had an entirely white cast. When it was revived in 1987, nontraditional casting included some white actors playing Asians and Asians playing whites.

Because Mime Troupe shows usually involve actors playing multiple roles, cross-gender casting is a common practice. Most of the Troupe's work in the 1960s was gender specific, although in the "Chick and Stud" scene in *A Minstrel Show* (1965), one of the actors playing a blackface minstrel plays a white woman, and Sandra Archer played the pope in *L'Amant Militaire*. The practice of cross-gender casting has been employed regularly since 1970 and, as an epic technique, serves to remind spectators they are watching actors performing gender roles.

Most of the techniques and practices in the Troupe's work today can be traced to their groundbreaking achievements in guerrilla theater in the 1960s and 1970s. In the twenty-first century it might be hard to imagine that only half a century ago theater was considered so powerful a force in society that city officials in San Francisco were threatened by commedia dell'arte. But Peter Brook reminds us of the socially liberating role of rough theater: "anti-authoritarian, anti-traditional, anti-pomp, anti-pretense."[42] The Troupe's guerrilla tactics, especially their free and sometimes unannounced public appearances, reminded officials of their lack of official control over artists and artistic expression. Furthermore, the Troupe quickly became a daunting force, able to draw a crowd and provide a hub for leftist activists in and around the San Francisco Bay Area.

The San Francisco Mime Troupe's success in breaking class and race barriers and persisting in the right to use public property, to bring theater outside and back to the public, has had a profound influence on the role of theater in society in the United States. The liberation of the parks opened the door for other groups, and the free movement mushroomed, challenging basic assumptions of our capitalist economy. The Troupe's free performances in San Francisco parks, like their ancient counterparts in classical Greece, have become a yearly summer ritual drawing thousands of people together to celebrate the possibility of social change.

NOTES

1. Peter Berg, telephone interview by the author, May 18, 2002.
2. R. G. Davis, "Method in Mime," *Tulane Drama Review* 6 (June 1962): 61.
3. Ibid.

4. Lee Breuer, letter to author, May 14, 2000.

5. R. G. Davis, *The San Francisco Mime Troupe: The First Ten Years* (Palo Alto, Calif.: Ramparts, 1975), 31.

6. Ibid., 35.

7. Harry Johanessen, "Park Show Cancelled; 'Offensive,'" *San Francisco Examiner*, August 5, 1965; Lloyd Zimpel, "Surprise in the Wings," *The Nation*, March 7, 1966, 276.

8. Davis, *San Francisco Mime Troupe*, 67.

9. David Kolodney, "Ripping Off Ma Bell," *Ramparts*, August 1970, 26.

10. Lenny Bruce's obscenity trial in New York City during the previous June exacerbated this already tense situation. In addition, the House Committee on Un-American Activities hearings in San Francisco in 1960 played a crucial role in uniting the Bay Area's Left. See Eric Noble, "The Artists Liberation Front and the Formation of the Sixties Counterculture," Diggers website, December 16, 2001, http://www.diggers.org/alf_version_1996.htm.

11. "Performing in City Parks," *San Francisco Examiner*, July 21, 1963.

12. "San Francisco Mime Troupe," n.d., n.p. This is an unpublished four-page document generated by the Troupe on Troupe stationery (San Francisco Mime Troupe Archives 1959–1999, University of California, Davis, General Library, Special Collections). Various internal references suggest it was written in late 1969 or early 1970. There is no mention of the collective, but there are descriptions of planned 1970s productions, suggesting it was probably written late in 1969, before the collective vote.

13. Charles Perry, *The Haight-Ashbury: A History* (New York: Random House, 1984), 31–32.

14. "San Francisco Mime Troupe."

15. R. G. Davis, "Radical, Independent, Chaotic, Anarchic Theatre vs. Institutional, University, Little, Commercial, Ford and Stock Theatres," *Guerrilla Theatre Essays 1* (San Francisco: San Francisco Mime Troupe, 1970), n.p.

16. "Overview: Who Are the Diggers?" March 26, 2002, http://www.diggers .org/overview.htm.

17. R. G. Davis, interview by the author, May 8, 2002.

18. Peter Coyote, *Sleeping Where I Fall* (Washington D.C.: Counterpoint, 1998), 33; Peter Berg, telephone interview by the author, May 18, 2002; and "Trip without a Ticket" in *The Digger Papers (Aug 1968)*, http://diggers.org/digpaps68/twatdp .html.

19. R. G. Davis, e-mail to the author, July 28, 2002.

20. Coyote, *Sleeping Where I Fall*, 77.

21. From the San Francisco Mime Troupe Songbook (unpublished) (San Francisco Mime Troupe Archives, University of California, Davis).

"I GOT FUCKED IN VIET NAM"
(*To be sung to the tune of "The Ballad of the Green Berets."*)
(*Author unknown*)

Fighting men who jump and die
For God knows what and God knows why—
A hundred more will die today
All for the sake of LBJ.

I was just an ordinary man,
Getting along was all I planned
Comes a letter from Uncle Sam,
Says, "We need you boy in Viet Nam."

(Chorus)
I got fucked in Viet Nam
I got fucked in Viet Nam
I got fucked in Viet Nam
Now I don't know where I am

High cheekbones and slanty eyes,
Yellow skin on them viet cong guys,
But when a body's burned and maimed,
Everybody looks just the same.

To Negro boys this war ain't fair—
Ol' LBJ wants 'em all over there.
Why should they go; it doesn't figger—
No viet cong ever called them Nigger.
(Chorus: add your own verses)

22. Perry, *The Haight-Ashbury,* 145–47; Coyote, *Sleeping Where I Fall,* 77–78.

23. Davis, e-mail.

24. Davis, "Radical, Independent."

25. Noble, "The Artists Liberation Front."

26. R. G. Davis, "Guerrilla Theatre," *Tulane Drama Review* 10 (Summer 1966): 13.

27. Ibid., 133.

28. Radical Theatre Festival program, San Francisco, San Francisco Mime Troupe, n.d., 19.

29. R. G. Davis, "Guerrilla Theatre: 11 Nov 1967," in *Guerrilla Theatre Essays 1,* n.p.

30. R. G. Davis, "Cultural Revolution U.S.A.: 'One step forward,'" in *Guerrilla Theatre Essays 1,* n.p.

31. Davis, "Guerrilla Theatre: 11 Nov 1967."

32. J. Dennis Rich, "An Interview with the San Francisco Mime Troupe," *Players* 46 (December–January 1971): 58–59.

33. Bruce McConachie and Daniel Friedman, eds. *Theatre for Working-Class Audiences in the United States, 1830–1980* (Westport, Conn.: Greenwood Press, 1985), 201.

34. Antonin Artaud, *The Theater and Its Double,* trans. Mary Caroline Richards (New York: Grove Press, 1958), 74.

35. "Celebrating the Presence of Mime," *San Francisco Examiner,* July 5, 1992.

36. Joan Holden, "Collective Playmaking: The Why and the How," *Theatre Quarterly* 5 (June–August 1975): 32.

37. Ibid., 33.

38. Rich, "Interview with Mime Troupe," 55.

39. "A Renovated Cabin," *Los Angeles Times,* October 16, 1991.

40. Stacy Wolf, "Politics, Polyphony, and Pleasure: The San Francisco Mime

Troupe's *Seeing Double,*" *Journal of Dramatic Theory and Criticism* 8, no. 1 (1993): 107.

41. San Francisco Mime Troupe, *Back to Normal,* Susan Vaneta Mason, ed., *The San Francisco Mime Troupe Reader* (Ann Arbor: University of Michigan Press, 2005).

42. Peter Brook. *The Empty Space* (New York: Atheneum, 1978), 68.

EL TEATRO CAMPESINO
Historical Overview

Although most of the collectives that came to prominence during the 1960s and 1970s had strong political commitments, El Teatro Campesino (Farmworkers' Theater) was, with Free Southern Theater, one of only two collectives to emerge from specific political organizations. Founded in 1965, El Teatro Campesino began under the auspices of the United Farm Workers, which, aided by the charismatic leadership of César Chávez, had proven to be surprisingly successful at organizing farm laborers against long-standing exploitation by agricultural businesses in the western United States. At the time of El Teatro Campesino's founding, Chávez had helped to organize a major strike against California grape growers, a strike that would lead to one of the UFW's more significant victories. Since the overwhelming majority of the farmworkers were Chicano/as and Mexicans, the successful labor movement spearheaded by the UFW became a major source of inspiration for a larger, burgeoning Chicano/a movement. It was against this political and cultural backdrop that El Teatro Campesino came to prominence. Originally conceptualized as a tool for organizing workers and for fund-raising, El Teatro Campesino was in good part the brainchild of Luis Valdez, an aspiring playwright and member of the San Francisco Mime Troupe who recognized in the labor movement an opportunity to combine his Chicano/a activism with his theatrical training.

As the son of migrant laborers and a former farmworker himself, Valdez had deep sympathies with the plight of those exploited in the fields of agribusiness, and when he approached the United Farm Workers union about the value of doing a farmworkers' theater, his proposal was greeted with enthusiasm. To some extent this was because Chávez had already envisioned a troupe that, drawing upon the Mexican comedic *carpa* (tent theater) traditions—which were to become a hallmark of early El Teatro Campesino performances—would help to politicize workers and raise funds for the cause.[1] Founding El Teatro Campesino with Agustín Lira and others, Valdez became its artistic director and playwright, collaborating extensively with the members of the ensemble whose creativity, as Yolanda Broyles-González has noted, did as much to direct Valdez as Valdez did to direct the ensemble.[2]

El Teatro Campesino's affiliation with the UFW lasted for a little over two years, during which time the performances took the form of short, humorous skits that addressed the plight of the farmworkers. These *actos,* as they were called, were initially worked out in improvisations by ensemble members and were then refined and written into a general skit. The *actos* drew heavily upon Mexican oral and popular cultural traditions. Ensemble members like Felipe Cantú were masters of the performative aspects of these traditions, and within the context of El Teatro Campesino's work with the UFW, the Teatro was able to translate those traditions into a highly effective tool of political theater. Other ensemble members who, over the course of the Teatro's first decade, contributed to its rich grounding in Mexican popular performance traditions, included Olivia Chumacero, Roberta Delgado, Lupe Valdez, Rogelio Rojas, Philip Esparza, Diane Rodríguez, and José Delgado.[3] Of particular importance during this period was the performance of *Las dos caras del Patroncito* (The Two Faces of the Boss) (1965), in which a rich grower, wearing a pig mask, "is ridiculed and exposed as just an ordinary man."[4]

By 1967, the Teatro began exploring issues relevant to Chicano/as more generally, and after a national tour to raise funds for the union, they became independent from the United Farm Workers and ventured out on their own. Though still supporting the union in various performances, El Teatro Campesino began to focus on itself as a theater committed to a variety of artistic styles and to a variety of political causes pertinent to urban and working-class Chicano/as. In short works like *Los Vendidos* (The Sellouts) (1967), which was first performed for a Brown Beret gathering in East Los Angeles, the Teatro moved away from the *huelga* (strike) *actos* and shifted to *actos* addressing issues like discrimination and Chicano/a identity. In works like *Dark Root of a Scream* (1967) and similar subsequent pieces like *Soldado Razo* (1970), the Teatro began to develop a new stylistic form called *mitos* (myths). In general, these works relied on allegorical figures, many of whom were nonhuman characters like *calaveras* (skeletons) from Mexican folklore or embodiments of the Seasons and Elements, or forces like the Sun, Moon and Terra [Earth] that were modeled after deities in Aztecan mythology. But in the particular instance of *Dark Root* and *Soldado* and also the *acto* titled *Vietnam Campesino* (1970), the Teatro drew upon its growing stylistic repertoire in order to dramatize the effect of the Vietnam War on the Chicano/a community. It was during this period that El Teatro Campesino won an Obie (1968) and gained international attention at the Théâtre des Nations in Nancy, France.

Moving from Delano to Del Ray and then in 1969 to Fresno, the Teatro focused its attention more and more on urban Chicano/as and the Chicano/a movement. In this regard, the production of *The Militants* (1969) is a milestone in the Teatro's evolving sense of direction. The piece offered a critique of the self-destructive undercurrents of the Chicano/a movement and in particular of those who had embraced a militant discourse but had never committed themselves to a course of action that would actually change society. Ending with two militants shooting one other, the piece attempts to set the internal conflicts of the movement in vivid critical relief. Combined with an interest in Native American (specifically Mayan and Aztecan) philosophies and culture, the Teatro's concern with such internal conflicts would have an increasingly profound effect on its work and on a growing conviction that only a cultural/spiritual renewal of the Chicano/a community at large would keep "hostility against an unjust system . . . [from being] vented on each other."[5]

The depth of this conviction was evident when, for the final time, the ensemble in 1971 used a Mayan model to set up its own community on the land purchased just outside of San Juan Bautista. In six years, El Teatro Campesino had grown from "a core performing troupe of five" at its founding to thirty members who "similar to avant-garde groups of the period . . . lived and worked communally."[6]

The move to San Juan Bautista coincided with "an intense collective human and aesthetic exploration" that was called the "Theater of the Sphere."[7] The *mitos* were certainly a part of this exploration, but the Theater of the Sphere was far more encompassing in scope, not only affecting the mission of the ensemble's theater but also the organization of daily lives. Seeking to dislodge a Western cultural/mythological matrix with a reassertion of the indigenous mythologies of the Americas, the explorations of the Theater of the Sphere blurred the boundaries between art and life, affirmed indigenous Native American heritage in contemporary Chicano/a culture, and linked spiritual renewal with political transformation. As Broyles-González has noted, "The Teatro Campesino clearly regarded the Theater of the Sphere as a model of human liberation indispensable to the larger social struggle."[8]

The most visible product of the explorations associated with the Theater of the Sphere was *El Baile de los Gigantes* (The Dance of the Giants), which re-created a ceremony of the Chorti Indians and which El Teatro Campesino performed in 1974 at the Quinto Festival in Mexico. The intense spiritual focus of this work met with strong criticism, especially from those who interpreted its spirituality as a subtle reaffirmation of the status quo and a distraction from the political theater that more directly addressed social issues and that had characterized El Teatro Campesino's earliest work.[9] The impact of this criticism is difficult to calculate since the ensemble always relied on a variety of theatrical styles, but performances after *El Baile de los Gigantes* were marked by a distinct shift in emphasis and by the prominent emergence of the *corrido* style, which drew upon the popular tradition of narrative folk ballads and employed musicians whose singing narrated the action on stage.

The content of the *corridos* combined elements from the *actos* and *mitos* and became the dominant mode of artistic expression for El Teatro during its final years. Beginning with *La Carpa de los Rasquachis* (Tent of the Underdogs) (1972) and progressing through the four variations of *El Fin Del Mundo* (End of the World) (1975–80), the *corridos* represent in many respects a successful balance between the political and spiritual concerns that shaped El Teatro Campesino's earlier work. But even as this balance was achieved, new priorities emerged when Valdez toward the end of the 1970s began to explore the opportunity of negotiating a place for Chicano theater in the mainstream.

While *La Carpa de los Rasquachis* was on tour, Valdez wrote *Zoot Suit* (1978) and agreed to co-produce it with the Center Theatre Group of Los Angeles at the Mark Taper Forum. The phenomenal success of this production, which ran for eleven months, led to a Broadway production where *Zoot Suit,* the first Chicano play to make it to Broadway, opened in 1979. This was followed by a film adaptation that Valdez wrote and directed in 1981. Even though the Broadway production closed after a short run of four weeks, the overall success of the piece marked the beginning of the end of El Teatro Campesino as an ensemble. Valdez "began to write for actors outside the group" and "to move seriously into filmmaking."[10] Despite these external successes, Valdez remained committed to El Teatro Campesino, investing his profits from *Zoot Suit,* for example, into the purchase of a packing house in San Juan Bautista that he and the other members of El Teatro Campesino transformed into a permanent theater for the company. But it was a very different theater, shaped in part by a new generation of El Teatro members: more commercial and certainly less focused on politicizing the farmworkers who served as the original audience for El Teatro Campesino.

—J. M. H.

NOTES

1. Yolanda Broyles-González, *El Teatro Campesino: Theater in the Chicano Movement* (Austin: University of Texas Press, 1994), 11.

2. Ibid., 151.

3. Ibid., 132.

4. Jorge Huerta, "When Sleeping Giants Awaken: Chicano Theatre in the 1960s," *Theatre Survey* 43, no. 1 (2002): 27.

5. Theodore Shank, *Beyond the Boundaries: American Alternative Theatre* (Ann Arbor: University of Michigan Press, 2002), 78.

6. Harry J. Elam Jr., *Taking It to the Streets* (Ann Arbor: University of Michigan Press, 1997), 100, 159.

7. Broyles-González, *El Teatro Campesino*, 82.

8. Ibid., 123.

9. Shank, *Beyond the Boundaries*, 82–83; Broyles-González, *El Teatro Campesino*, 119.

10. Jorge Huerta, "From Flatbed Trucks," Introduction to Luis Valdez, *Zoot Suit and Other Plays* (Houston: Arte Publico Press, 1992), 11.

RE-CONSTRUCTING COLLECTIVE DYNAMICS

*El Teatro Campesino from a
Twenty-First-Century Perspective*

Yolanda Broyles-González

Viewed from a twenty-first century perspective, long after the heyday of El Teatro Campesino, this famed Chicana/o theatrical ensemble's collective functioning, which included both collective/cooperative living and the aesthetic process of collective performative creation, invites further analysis. At the dawn of this millennium our efforts to understand collectives, cooperatives, community-building, and group social dynamics of empowerment have a new resonance and urgency. We live in an era characterized by a breakdown of stable communities and of collective functioning, of social cohesiveness. Ties among people and between people and their environments are said to be deteriorating at an unimaginable pace. The deterioration of the relational web of life is due to many factors, such as economic and political dislocations triggered by global capital, growing job stresses, social or state violence, and media. Luis J. Rodríguez in *Hearts and Hands* provides us with insight into contemporary youth efforts at community-building even in the face of violence. The author describes today's malaise: "The disconnection today is deeper than it has ever been."[1]

Today's disconnection observable between people is an outcome of many historical forces. The period from World War II to the present has seen a historically unprecedented global human dislocation and relocation. Dramatic postwar increases in immigration, intranational movement,

exile, and migration have effected the disintegration of stable rural institutions, the family, and neighborhood connections. One can add in the
dissemination of disconnective media, ranging from television to electronic computer games, as key elements of contemporary social reality.
Metal bars on windows and doors have replaced the old neighborly ways.
Social disintegration is exacerbated by the increased globalizing reach of
capital and its violent displacement of local networks and local autonomy.
A heightened philosophy of individual profit-seeking and competition—
not community and collaboration for the common good—also underlie
today's public and private educational systems.

In its performance work, as well as in its form of self-organization, the
Teatro Campesino envisioned and realized expressive collective structures
of freedom within a larger social structure whose thrust was (and is) to
limit, control, and even destroy the human agency of low-income peoples
of color. Since its inception as an organizing tool for the United Farm
Workers, the Teatro Campesino (Farmworkers' Theater) was propelled by
a vision of social justice and by native philosophical values concerning humanness and the place of humans in the society and the cosmos. Gustavo
Esteva and Madhu Suri Prakash in *Grassroots Post-Modernism* cogently examine the ways in which what they call the "world's social majorities" at the
grass roots manage to escape the monoculture of a single global society
while weaving the fabric of human community. El Teatro Campesino provides us with an important example of a program of autonomy from what
Esteva and Prakash call "the Empire of the Law." That Empire of the Law
seeks to control through the multiple institutions of the nation-state and
its corporate interests. Indeed, El Teatro can be revisited as an important
collective institution, which did not conform to the needs of capitalist economic accumulation. That famed collective struggled to affirm an alternative vision of the world while it contested, for example, the established exploitative power of agribusiness, the Vietnam War, the racist educational
system, and other social injustices. At the same time, El Teatro Campesino
affirmed an alternative social vision based in the humanistic and social
governance structures of precolonial American antiquity. As such the
Farm Workers' theater built its own powerful alternative base as a moral/
political/cultural/critical voice and radical collective institution at the
margins of this society. It was from that vantage point during the civil rights
movement (1960–80) that El Teatro Campesino powerfully affirmed and
engaged indigenous culture as one path to freedom.

In this era of capital's globalization and continued disruption of so
many stable communities, we are inspired by the success of any grassroots
collectivizing project such as that modeled by Teatro Campesino. We have

much to learn from any collective organization or movement that fosters local control and autonomy, a vision of shared resources, and the liberation of human creative force. That foundational collective and cooperative spirit and power informed the creative dynamic of the Teatro Campesino. I only began to explore that collective legacy in my book *El Teatro Campesino: Theater in the Chicano Movement.*[2] It now deserves a closer look. In this inquiry I examine how the Teatro's collective functioning was culturally and aesthetically rooted in the indigenous Mesoamerican (i.e., Native American) cultural/social matrix and its knowledge system known as the oral tradition. My analysis of the Teatro's utopian potential leads directly through a discussion of the native social matrix—the indigenous conception of human work and human society—and of that civilization's knowledge base: the oral tradition. The four questions I address in my analysis of the Teatro's indigenous-based utopian collective potential are *(a)* What is the nature of the native social matrix and its oral tradition? *(b)* How did the native social matrix and orality play out within El Teatro Campesino performances? *(c)* How did the Teatro Campesino develop these two into the Theater of the Sphere performance project? *(d)* What internal contradictions and external pressures led to that famed collective's demise?

The Mesoamerican Social Matrix: Foundation of Collective Creation

To uncover the deepest social roots of El Teatro Campesino's collective functioning involves focusing on the indigenous-based origins of its collective work. Within the ancient indigenous cultural matrix human work is understood as a collective agreement bearing reciprocal benefit. Work is not merely an individual undertaking for private benefit. From the perspective of today's widespread individualism, a form of social organization and governance whose highest priority is the harmonious collective based on shared resources seems unthinkable. Yet a social economy of collectively shared resources remains central to Native American tribal cultures; it certainly was central to the Teatro Campesino. The Native American social matrix involving collective governance has many regional names: Ikatz (Mayan), Siliyik (Chumash), Altepetl or Calpulli (Nahuatl), Allyu (Inca), Haudenausaunee (Six Nations). Since time immemorial Native American (Mesoamerican) tribal societies have valued and cultivated collective values and functioning based on communally held and shared resources and on natural law: take only what you need and never take without giving back. Within these collective social systems based on reciprocity (equal exchange, not exploitation) knowledge is transmitted not by written means (individually authored books) but by means of the inherently collective memory and knowledge system of oral tradition. The oral tradition or memory arts in fact have traditionally been central to indigenous collective ethos and functioning, including its decolonial social struggles.

El Teatro Campesino was established in 1965 as an organizing collective for the United Farm Workers unionizing struggles. In all their early plays the Teatro Campesino thematized farmworker struggles and collective solutions to a host of farmworker problems. Working within the oral tradition meant working without scripts, using a collective improvisational process (discussed below). The most immediate solution proposed in many of those early one-act performances called *actos* was worker unionization aimed toward securing labor contacts (collective bargaining). Just as significant as those themes was the behind-the-scenes reality of the rural collaborative ethics, which informed the work of the Teatro Campesino. *Campo* is the Mexican word for the land; it resonates with a millenarian connection between the land and people of this continent. Among the connotations of the word *campo* is the ancient cultural knowledge of how humans interact with each other and with that land. (The word *human* is rooted in *humus*, or "land.") The Teatro Campesino ensemble marked its indigenous land-based connection in its very title. *Campesino* (land worker) also connotes multiple historical periods of the (now) landless farmworker and the struggles for economic justice they waged throughout the twentieth century. More profoundly, the ensemble's ruralness embraced an ancient mode of reciprocal work ethic observable in Mexican rural enclaves in Mexico and the United States. Where Mesoamerican (i.e., Native American) lifeways persist, work has entirely different meanings and outcomes than in the industrialized urban world or the world of industrialized large-scale agribusiness. "Work" involves a sophisticated system of shared collective labor and mutual help. Crops and fields are held, tended to, and harvested in a rotational system where the entire collective shares in each individual's labor. What is important is the system of cooperative relationships, which create and strengthen community ties. These reciprocal relationships are played out both in times of work and at times of celebration.[3] Rites of reciprocity establish social networks and the life of the collective. Individuals who consistently show themselves most responsible toward the collective (often through self-sacrifice) acquire prestige and authority. In a continuous cycle of reciprocal work activity, individuals become linked to each other. The social fabric is thus tightly knit and continually mended: the welfare of the collective is safeguarded through an economy of reciprocity. Work is a collective reciprocal relationship and not simply an individualistic activity.

The reality of existing in an alternative and contestatory relationship with the dominant powers was not without considerable hardship for members of the Teatro Campesino collective. Here the collective self-help dynamics of Mesoamerican civilization come into play. Economically speaking, the performance spectacles of the Teatro Campesino were for the most part frugal undertakings and not particularly lucrative. When the ensemble made a good amount of money through the Public Broadcasting System filming of *Corridos* (aka *La gran carpa de Jesús Pelado Rasquachi*) in 1978, they purchased forty acres of land in San Juan Bautista. That collectively purchased land was acquired in the hopes of establishing a farm commune and alternative performance school. At the very least, property ownership facilitated the elaboration of the Veinte Pasos (Twenty Steps, treated below). How did the Teatro Campesino otherwise make ends meet, survive, and thrive? The ensemble lived at bare subsistence level or below during much of its fifteen-year existence. Each member was paid ten dollars per week and housing. Being a Teatrista meant much personal sacrifice as well as organized efforts to secure collective survival. Guillermo Bonfil Batalla describes this contemporary indigenous dynamic of what he calls *Mexico profundo:* "Such sacrifices indicate an orientation toward life that is difficult to comprehend from the individualistic, acquisitive perspective of modern capitalist society. . . . Full individual development is realized through community service, and the reward is prestige and authority."[4]

The power of Teatro Campesino's community service imbued its members with prestige and authority. Through the course of the civil rights movement El Teatro Campesino enjoyed a leadership role as standard bearers of that movement. Yet its commitment to service entailed personal and collective sacrifice. Survival was always hard. In lean times the company survived through a collective dynamic of mutual support, which included shared economic resources. Indeed, the Teatro, as well as the United Farm Workers, was only able to *survive* by virtue of that age-old indigenous dynamic of reciprocity. The company lived together frugally and relied on a collective support system coupled with individual hustling. Individual and collective survival was only safeguarded through the rotational system described by Olivia Chumacero: "we lived on the stage. Up to twenty persons ended up living on that stage . . . with regard to food, since nobody was paying you, each one of us was in charge of a different month, to see who could hustle some food stamps (laughter). And if that was not enough we would hit on Felix's mom, for example, because she had a restaurant. If not then we would go round up some government food. Those horrible eggs, that ugly Spam."[5] For the duration of its first fifteen years, the Teatro Campesino embodied a collective functioning at many levels. All resources (and the frequent lack of resources) were a shared responsibility. The ensemble's daily and long-term survival was only possible by virtue of a deep sense of mutuality and reciprocity.

Collective Performance Process and Oral Tradition

The cooperative system also had multiple artistic implications. There was virtually no artistic division of labor into playwright, director, set designer, stage designer, and so on. And although Luis Valdez held the title of "director," he was more typically taking direction from the others than giving it. In shaping its performances, the Teatro drew artistic resources from the rich storehouse of the oral tradition of performance. Long-standing oral performance conventions included the use of stock characters (especially the raggle-taggle *pelado/a* figure ensnared by injustice); exaggerated acting techniques that physicalized ideas; Spanish-English bilinguality; traditional song repertoire elements including *corridos* and *rancheras;* multiple comedic techniques of satire and humorous reversals; and the enactment of performance pageants handed down orally across many generations. Prime examples of the pageants included the Shepherd's Play entitled *Pastorela* and the performed story of the Indian Madonna Guadalupe *(La virgen del Tepeyac)*. The work of creating performance pieces was carried out orally (without writing) and in collective fashion, not by individual playwrights. A rigorous process of collective improvisational creation harnessed the collectivized energy and vision of the ensemble. It deserves closer scrutiny.

Improvisation was, in essence, a collective and reciprocal decision-making process involving group research, discussion, exploration, consensus, and full consultation from all members of the ensemble. Improvisational creation typically began with extensive discussion of the meanings to be conveyed to audiences, which included searching the depths of the members' historical experience and historical memory. At all times there was a confluence of collective political, physical, and spiritual meanings. Sometimes the discussion involved preparation through teachings from Native American elders such as Andrés Segura Granados and Domingo Martinez Paredes, through participation in native ceremonial activity such as the *danza de los Concheros,* or doing exercises connected with the Teatro's Theater of the Sphere training (see below). Sometimes print materials were also consulted. The shaping of ideas then naturally flowed to and from body movements until a conceptual scenario was created. Through the living improvisation process all phases of creation were tenuous and subject to continual change. Exploratory movement continued throughout the elaboration and into the production of any piece. Experimentation with dialogue emerged from experimentation with body movement—and vice versa—in an extended process of trial and error. Performance pieces continued to metamorphose throughout any particular run.

The living intensity of the Teatro Campesino's collective work meant that members reached a high level of proficiency or mastery in working off of each other as a collective. No performance piece was ever in stasis or what we might call "finished." Improvisation was always ongoing. In oral tradition there was never a verbatim memorization of a fixed script—or any script at all for that matter! Dialogue was never rigidly fixed (as in print culture) but always subject to change and improvisation according to the breathing/living creativity of each individual at any given moment. The nature and direction of such improvisation could depend on numerous factors, such as changes in political events. Another factor in the improvisation process was the ethnic and class composition of the audience and its response and participation.

Assuming a "role" entailed a high degree of creative responsibility for performers, very unlike that of dramatic traditions within print culture, whose more or less fixed "part" rests with written scripts. For the Teatro Campesino to perform a play was to collectively generate a play. Even the *Actos*—which were published in 1971 for the benefit of other groups and adopted by many other groups (and used in college classrooms)—were never rehearsed using scripts. Nor were the *Actos* ever performed the same twice. Even the Teatro Campesino's epic performances did not readily translate into written "scripts." Ensemble member Diane Rodríguez recalled: "When you take something like *Fin del mundo* and script it, it doesn't make sense. Because the piece that we performed in 1980 was a visual piece, and to explain that in a script and to have another theater company do it, well they just couldn't."[6] During the 1960s the Teatro's creativity evolved from the one-act *actos* advocating for farm labor unionization and worker's rights (such as *La Quinta temporada, El grito de la union, Las dos caras del Patroncito, Tres uvas, Schenley contract,* and more) to the inclusion of broader themes created as multiact pieces. Plots centered on topics such as educational injustice (*No saco nada de la escuela, Acto on Education, Los ABCs,* etc.), race relations *(Los Vendidos),* the colonization process *(La conquista de México),* the Chicano civil rights movement *(The Militants),* and opposition to the Vietnam War *(Soldado razo, Vietnam campesino, Los vatos locos de Vietnam).* Whatever the plot, it almost invariably revolved around one chief male protagonist.

The memory arts of the Teatro Campesino are a product of the indigenous oral tradition in multiple ways. Orality is by no means simply a matter of not using scripts. The oral tradition in the Americas runs as deep as
culture itself. For tens of thousands of years native peoples have transmitted scientific, spiritual, medicinal, philosophical, and artistic knowledge
by memory. And although those systems entered into collision and exchange with colonial systems of knowledge, the indigenous oral tradition
in its reliance on memory remained foundational. Memory has always
been a cultural storehouse for oppressed peoples. Together with the
human body, memory constitutes the central vehicle of cultural transmission within Mexicano/a oral culture. Memory should not be understood
here only as a cerebral, individualistic, psychological process, but in its
collective and *physical* manifestation: as remembrance and transmission of
the community's knowledge through that community's performance
forms, be they storytelling, corridos (narrative ballads) and other forms
of traditional music, *dichos* (proverbs), oral historical discourse, prayer
and ritual, mythology, dance, jokes, cuisine, and more. The Teatro Campesino drew from this storehouse of oral tradition as needed in order to
create its spectacles from combinations and reappropriations of those elements. Corridos, for example—one of the oldest song genres from the
oral tradition—were used to carry entire plot lines. The corrido formed
the backbone for performance pieces such as the epic *La gran carpa de la
familia Rasquachi* (1972–82), *Fin del mundo* (1980), or *Corridos* (1983–
87).[7] Within the storehouse of oral tradition the Teatro Campesino also
found the raggle-taggle comedic working-class protagonist of the pelado
figure (the impoverished survivor), which formed the axis of virtually all
of their performance creations. That figure was directly inherited from
the great twentieth-century *carpa* (itinerant tent theater) and film actor
Cantinflas (Mario Moreno). It was the down-and-out (always male) person ensnared by authority, yet capable of inverting power relations
through verbal acrobatics and cunning. The pelada/pelado underdog
figure precursor also dates back to precolonial times.[8]

A sung corrido or narrative ballad provided the narrative continuity in
what could be considered the Teatro Campesino's most ambitious performance piece: *La gran carpa de la familia Rasquachi* (The great tent show of
the Rasquachi family). *La gran carpa* is an epic story (a corrido) told simultaneously through song or other music, and stage performance. The constant presence of sung corrido lyrics (narrative ballad from the oral tradition) gives this performance its beat, rhythm, and sustaining drive. The
corrido epic centers on the oppressive life experiences of one poor Mexican man (named Jesus Pelado Rasquachi) who immigrates to the United

States. As a farm laborer he suffers lifelong exploitation, and establishes a family, which includes his children: today's Chicanas and Chicanos. Oppressive social conditions of Mexican immigrants are thus tracked across generations. *Fin del mundo* (meaning both "The End of the World" and "Mundo's End") also centers on a male protagonist (named Mundo), yet has a broader political and philosophical focus. Mundo moves easily between life and death in this musical allegory. His journey (which involves a marginalized wife figure named Vera) creates parallel worlds in which a satire and critique of political and economic life unfolds.

The improvisational physicality of the Teatro Campesino performances also involved various kinds of verbal dexterity inherited from the oral tradition of the itinerant tent show tradition known as the carpa (tent). These included double entendres, *albures* (sexual combative dialogue), *cábula* (work-play competition), deliberate misunderstanding, eloquent use of profanity, mockery in the form of praise, praise resembling mockery, and other comedic conventions from everyday speech. The reality of improvisation also gave performance spectacles very long lives. Performed pieces kept evolving, changing according to the times and according to the ensemble's own growth process. In working-class style the old and well-worn was never thrown out; it was reused and recycled. Each of the Teatro's epic plays, such *La gran carpa de la familia Rasquachi* or *Fin del mundo,* went through various reincarnations over a ten-year period. *La gran carpa* was staged in five wholly different ways, each time with a different outcome for the main protagonist. Each time the philosophical and political meanings changed while the play's rough skeleton remained. *Fin del mundo* went through four major reworkings. The first version of this life-and-death musical allegory in 1975 featured an almost complete focus on indigenous philosophy and ceremony, whereas the thematics of the second *Fin del mundo* in 1976 featured the United Farm Workers of America (AFL-CIO). In 1978 *Fin del mundo* was done with all actors in calavera (skeleton) outfits. It toured the Southwest, and later that year a new version of *La gran carpa* toured six European countries. In a separate enterprise during that time Luis Valdez premiered *Zoot Suit* at the Los Angeles Mark Taper Forum, and in 1979 it went to Broadway. A major turning point for the collective happened in 1980: the group finished the European tour of *Fin del mundo #4,* again in skeleton mode but this time featuring political critique of the oil embargo, of drug use, of the Jim Jones suicide cult, the Cold War, and more. That was to be the last collective performance of the ensemble known as El Teatro Campesino.[9]

Throughout its fifteen-year trajectory as a collective the Teatro Campesino's creative aesthetic did not manifest the kinds of actor professional training found in today's commercial theater houses, yet it lacked nothing in sophistication and power. On the surface the Teatro Campesino cultivated simplicity. Things always looked worn and torn. Yet the ensemble invariably created vibrant human spectacles. Teatro Campesino performances required a huge mental, physical, spiritual sensitivity and speed from actors. Improvisational theater honed actors' capacity to anticipate and react physically and mentally to the unexpected. This instantaneous mobility—thinking on your feet—is a working-class survival technique elevated within the improvisational performative to an art form. Bodily fluidity and expressivity in improvisational performance requires from performers the ability to instantly read and respond to each other's body movement, gaze, voice (pitch, volume, speed, tone, words), gestures, while also gauging and anticipating and moving to the rhythm, speed, and beat of the performance. Total body involvement was a performance "language" to which Chicana/o and Mexicana/o audiences were accustomed. Unlike the bulk of Western proscenium theater, the Teatro Campesino's improvisational performance aesthetic was for the most part carried by highly articulate bodies in motion. Words only refined the substantial meanings conveyed by physical action. Luis Valdez affirmed the primacy of the body in motion: "It's not primarily language-based theater. Okay? It's theater of rhythms, beats, of rituals, of visual imagery, you know, it's *something else*. It's theater of *action*. It's either social action or we're doing sacred theater, but it's *action*. Action."[10]

The Theater of the Sphere as Performance Project

Many members of the Teatro Campesino carried the living memory of indigenous tribal knowledge and functioning. For example, Olivia Chumacero had grown up among her Raramuri (Tarahumara) kin in Chihuahua; elder Felipe Cantú remembered his tribal legacy; Luis Valdez frequently acknowledged Yoeme (Yaqui) tribal roots. Ensemble member and musician Daniel Valdez proclaimed Indian presence in multiple song titles such as "America De Los Indios." On the cover to his first recording he proclaims:

El Indio de Hueso Y Sangre [the Indian of bone and blood]
Is Far From Vanished
The Flesh Has Merely Been Torn
From the Skeleton
Of the American Indigena
But the Indio lives On.[11]

What is more, the indigenous presence—however colonized—is at the heart of the multitudes of Mexican/Chicana/o campesinos (farmworkers) where the Teatro lived, struggled, worked, performed. It is not surprising, then, that the Teatro's work and creation ethos was uniquely collective and indigenous-based in multiple ways.

Since the earliest days of the Teatro Campesino, its members self-consciously and systematically cultivated indigenous knowledge systems. The early Teatro Campesino affirms the indigenous heritage in an essay entitled "Notes on Chicano Theater."[12] In that essay the Teatro proclaims the creation of "a theater that is particularly our own, not another imitation of the gabacho [Anglo]. If we consider our origins, say the theater of the Mayans or the Aztecs, we are talking about something totally unlike the realistic play." Later in that same essay the Teatro affirms "the indio fountains of Chicano culture." Beyond those rhetorical affirmations the Teatro Campesino actively cultivated the ancestral indigenous heritage in various ways: participation in ceremony (as Conchero ceremonial dancers); communication and exchange with indigenous tribal groups; actual ritual performance such as the Mayan summer solstice dance ceremony known as *El Baile de los Gigantes;* the cultivation of long-term learning from traditional indigenous elders such as Andrés Segura Granados and Domingo Martinez Paredes; and through frequent visits to Mexico and Native reservations in the United States.

A renewed recourse to indigenous ancestral knowledge became paramount around the world during the global, anticolonial, Third World liberation struggles that gained so much momentum in the mid–twentieth century, whether in Algeria, Cuba, Vietnam, Zimbabwe, El Salvador, or anyplace else. Liberation from colonialism necessarily required liberation from Eurocentrism in all its forms and a renewed commitment to ancestral cultures denied and denigrated by colonialism. For the Teatro Campesino—a participant in those global decolonial struggles—the ancestral native cultures were constituted as the performance bedrock. The Teatro Campesino's political involvement and performative vision for liberation was at all times linked to a spiritual evolution and collective elaboration of a performance discipline called Theater of the Sphere. The Theater of the Sphere was nothing less than a native-based program and life performance discipline (on and off stage) for human liberation involving the reappropriation of Mesoamerican knowledge (primarily Mexica "Aztec" and Mayan) and its reshaping into a reeducation program. The Teatro collectively elaborated and deepened that indigenous vision and discipline throughout the ensemble's collective history, and it found expression in all performance work I have mentioned. In many ways, the

Theater of the Sphere is the life-performance discipline behind the magical quality of Teatro performances.

Among the goals of the Theater of the Sphere was the attainment of human wholeness, of learning of moving in harmony with life, with the people in one's environment, with the whole of the environment, and with the cosmic movement: in short, to attain the condition of the Spherical Actor. That process was enabled by various means, most notably through what was known as the program of Los Veinte Pasos (The Twenty Steps). The Veinte Pasos constitute a holistic training that engages and synchronizes the entire field of mutually determining human faculties designated as the mind, the body, the heart, and the soul. Each of these human faculties corresponds to a progression of five of the Twenty Steps, each step named for one of the twenty Mayan days of the month used in the sacred year. The Twenty Steps can be described as a program of reflection and exercise leading through various psychophysiological stages of transformation. Each of the Twenty Steps has a number, a name, and a bundle of meanings ("energies") associated with that name. Those associated meanings are related to particular human states achieved through a specific movement program. The steps are also associated with different geometric figures illustrative of that concept and human state. These connections affirm the inextricable linkages between mathematics, philosophy, human movement, and the sacred.

Former ensemble member Olivia Chumacero described this complex pedagogy of human transformation: "What we would do was spend the whole day on just one of the Veinte Pasos in order to be able to capture and understand everything that evolved around that particular symbol, number, and the part of your body to which it corresponded. We then took it from there to very specific theater games and exercises that would reflect and focus on that particular theme."[13] The goal was to cultivate a consciousness of a particular human state and to internalize it while ultimately seeking to achieve a mastery of the entire system of interlocking signs. Training toward Sphericality was at once an individual, group, social, ecological, and political undertaking, given that the individual capacity for action and response only exists in relationship to group, social, environmental, and cosmic forces. There is a steady progression toward the highest and final series of five steps associated with a holistic awakening of the body, heart, and mind to an inherent spirituality (a kind of movement that manifests the divine). With regard to performing in front of audiences, the thinking was that the more highly evolved the performers, the more powerful the transference of energy and spirit to audience members.

Unfortunately, a fleshed-out description or analysis of the entire Twenty Steps is not possible within the confines of this short essay. Yet its significance for performance needs to be discussed. The Teatro described one performance outcome of the Theater of the Sphere training as follows: "It is the unity of the elements that we covered before—the body, heart, and mind all working together. This leads us to improvisations with creative focus, where people are communicating and interacting as different characters on a more spherical level, as true human beings."[14] The immensely sharpened sensitivity of the Spherical Actor allows for immediate and appropriate response to, or even an anticipation of, changing situations—both on and off the stage. That immediate response is an ideal within improvisational acting. In this regard the geometrical image of the Sphere is a metaphor of human action: because it is round it readily moves and responds to outside forces. At the same time the Sphere brings its own field of energy to the response. The concept of energy is key to a discussion of the Theater of the Sphere and to an understanding of how Sphericality (the realization of an actor's infinite potential) functions and how it is that actors affect audiences and others.

El Teatro Campesino's view of energy as the sustaining force of life corresponds to Mesoamerican culture, spirituality, philosophy, and science. Indigenous cultures view energy not only as the first cause and basis of human life, but also as the basis of all transformation or movement. This concept of energy is synonymous with spirit or power. All human interaction—and most certainly action before an audience—is an exchange of energy (vibration). Theater is regarded, above all, as an inspiring/inspiriting process. Audiences are to be inspired/inspirited by performances. A Teatro Campesino document from 1976 defines the purpose of theater in terms of a "transference of energy":

It is the purpose of teatro to infuse the people with *energy,* with *spirit.* The actor must find his internal source of ENERGY. ENERGY-VIBRATION—we must communicate ENERGY. The individual must "vibrate" and feel his energy. He must communicate this energy to his fellow actors. A company of actors must set up a flow of energy between them—a vibration—and then communicate this vibration to the audience. COARSE TO FINE VIBRATIONS determine the quality of the communication—*the transference of energy.* Energy must be fluid (light) in order to flow from one place to another, from one person to another. The aim is to discover BEING in people. The idea is to illuminate a person's life by uncovering the presence of the CREATOR.[15]

In this view of creative movement, energy is differentiated into physical (bodily) energy, emotional energy, and mental or intellectual energy. When (and if) the infinite potential (energy/power) of these three merge, then the cumulative force of "spirit" or "inspiriting" is said to take place and the performance is successful. Thus a Spherical Actor on stage (or off-stage) is an integrated and conscious human being in control of (1) the physicality of a performance, (2) the intellectuality of a performance, (3) the emotionality of a performance; and (4) their interrelatedness or Sphericality. The inspiriting intention behind any performance, viewed as a transference of that confluence of energies to audience members, involves the generation of an emotional response, an intellectual response, and a physical response within the audience. The confluence of these is the spiritual response: a successful performance.

The same Theater of the Sphere principles involved in the live performance of a play found application in the conception of those plays. The Theater of the Sphere informed all aspects of theatrical activity: performer training and performance, as well as the creation of performance pieces. In essence, the ensemble's collective productions sought to accomplish various things at once: the Teatro enacted or interpreted a slice of Chicana/o reality using characters and a style of acting from the oral tradition. The collective presented working-class themes typical of the Mexican carpa aesthetic, yet in combination with the Veinte Pasos. The Veinte Pasos shaped the artistic balance of the parts, the relationship between them, the interpretation of the slice of reality, and the performance philosophy and orientation of the piece. The overarching goal within plays was to cover the four aspects of life and human development represented by the Veinte Pasos and to transmit those four energies to audiences: energies of the body, the mind, the heart, and the spirit. These four aspects of energy were found in all performance pieces. In fact the creative process involved the design of performance pieces with the four energies in and working together. In the 1980 version of *Fin del mundo,* for example, the experiences of the main character—Reymundo "Mundo" Mata—to a large extent reflect the Veinte Pasos. The two-hour play is divided into two acts with ten scenes in the first act and thirteen in the second. Each scene epitomizes one of the steps of body, soul, mind, and spirit. In other words, the main thrust of the narrative in each scene corresponds to one of the Veinte Pasos. In addition, that performance (which toured Europe for six months) is grounded in indigenous philosophy concerning the complementarity of life and death. This comedic underdog farce takes place mainly in the "afterlife," blurring the two concepts: what is dead is shown to be alive, and vice versa. At the same time,

El Teatro Campesino, *El Baile de los Gigantes,* at the pyramids of Teotihuacán, Mexico, noon on June 24, 1974. (Photo by Theodore Shank.)

Mundo's personal journey through the afterlife serves as the context for satirizing world political scenarios.

Other Teatro Campesino plays manifest indigenous consciousness by other means. Plays such as *La gran carpa de la familia Rasquachi* integrate native mythologies through the active presence of divine figures such as Quetzalcoatl or Guadalupe (a reincarnated Mother Earth). At other times the Teatro Campesino enacted indigenous consciousness through pageants such as performance of the Chorti Mayan masked solsticial ritual known as *Baile de los gigantes,* through Conchero ceremonial dance (introduced by Andrés Segura Granados), or through the performance of the indigenous pageant *La virgen del Tepeyac* (The virgin of Tepeyac). Our Lady of Tepeyac reenacts the story of the Indian Madonna or earth mother Guadalupe, as she promises protection to the Indians besieged by colonization. The *Gigantes* is an ancient Mayan community solsticial dance, a physicalization of the Mayan sacred text, the Popol Vuh. As a ritual dance from the oral tradition it transmits scientific knowledge of astronomy, cosmogony, mathematics, and time-reckoning procedures. That knowledge is transmitted in the form of an allegorical struggle between the hero gods Hunhapu and Ixbalamque, who, with their parents, struggle against the giants.

For the benefit of many not directly involved with the Teatro Campesino, the ensemble also hosted Theater of the Sphere Workshops. As a model of humanism and human liberation, the Theater of the Sphere proposes that we cannot wait for the big social revolution and the new society before we begin conceiving of a new humanity. It places the beginning of a new humanity in the present and affirms that the process of human liberation will always have to begin from *within* oppression. The Teatro Campesino's Theater of the Sphere project sought to maximize the potential of the collective by trying to heal dehumanization and the degradation of work common in the theatrical mainstream and in the larger society. Through the Theater of the Sphere, the Teatro Campesino laid the foundation for a new model of cultural politics outside of dominant institutions. Performance was never conceptualized as something limited to stage work or as separate from daily life. Theater of the Sphere performance training was intended to foster and enhance Chicana/o humanistic ways of being and their concrete expression in all realms of life. As such, the Theater of the Sphere program affirmed the indigenous cultural axis as the center of Chicana/o decolonial visioning. While conceptualizing a Chicana/o distinctiveness Theater of the Sphere provided an important countercultural weapon against Euro-American cultural dominance and denigration that Chicanas/os experience daily at the job, in the schools and universities, the media, and related agencies of social control. With its insistence on the indivisibility of human being's faculties, the Theater of the Sphere fosters a utopian vision of humankind and a culture-bound program for cultivating human wholeness and self-awareness within the larger political struggle.

The concern with human wholeness and human regeneration and integration characteristic of the Theater of the Sphere must also be understood in the context of the sociohistorical era of violence and resistance in which it emerged: it was the height of the Vietnam War and of struggles calling for an end to that war. It was the height of the United Farm Workers' movement and of all civil rights struggles. The Teatro Campesino was deeply conscious of the human devastation visited upon Vietnamese (and other Third World) men, women, and children by the profit-seeking U.S. industrial-military complex. In fact the Teatro drew many parallels between the devastation of the Vietnamese people and the devastation at home of the largely minority farmworkers at the hands of agribusiness— ravages perhaps best illustrated by the farmworkers' life expectancy of fifty-four years. These two seemingly unrelated social struggles are shown in their interrelatedness in the Teatro's play *Vietnam campesino*. Another play, *Soldado razo*, similarly thematizes the trauma felt in U.S. barrios as a result of the Vietnam War. Thus the program of the Veinte Pasos affirms a new Chicana/o nonviolent humanism against the tide of U.S. genocidal and ecocidal practices of the Vietnam era.

Internal Contradictions and External Pressures: The Demise of El Teatro Campesino

Although the Theater of the Sphere's holistic model for life/stage performance needs to be counted among the most sustained and ambitious decolonial humanistic projects of its kind, the Teatro Campesino began to falter by 1980, and soon the collective dissolved. It ceased to function as a collective for multiple reasons. Like all visionary utopian movements, the nationalist organizations of the Chicano civil rights movement (such as the Teatro) contradictorily united both liberational and oppressive impulses. The Teatro Campesino's deeply inspirational and hard-hitting repertoire creatively challenged various social, racial, and economic oppressions while lamentably muting and replicating other forms of oppression, particularly of gender and sexuality.

What factors played into the collective's end? The 1980s ushered in twelve years of conservative Reagonomics and a backlash against the civil rights movement. Without the larger social context of the civil rights movement the Teatro lost much of its momentum. In addition to such external factors, internally the Teatro Campesino—along with the civil rights movement as a whole—suffered of its own contradictions. Among those internal contradictions were its long-standing and unresolved gender and sexual issues. Gender and sexual inequality were a direct outcome of the collective's strong patriarchal presence. The Teatro's enactment of indigenous collective structure fell short in two particularly notable and oppressive ways: much unlike indigenous social organization, the Teatro's patriarchal order marginalized women, lesbians, gays, the transgendered, the bisexual. The precolonial (and many postcolonial) indigenous societies of this hemisphere not only function cooperatively and collectively but also tend to be gynocratic or woman-centered. Native tribal society also traditionally honors all forms of sexuality, not just heterosexuality. In the Teatro Campesino *familia*, by contrast, there was no central powerful woman as a balancing force to the patriarchal Luis Valdez; and that patriarchal power grip occluded other forms of woman's power—woman as carrier of medicinal knowledge; woman as economic and political decision-maker; woman as lover of another woman; woman as visionary—and made such forms of women's power simply unimaginable.

The influence of heterosexual hierarchy is evident in the weak roles assigned to women. The value of the female body in Teatro Campesino productions is tied exclusively to reproductive functioning within a patriarchal social order. Women's multiple powers and sexualities—single, lesbian, bisexual, transgendered, heterosexual, and more—do not come into play. Generally speaking, women characters were narrowly circumscribed due to their positioning as satellites to male characters. Those women characters were clearly secondary to men on stage. Among those characters were the mother figure in *La gran carpa;* the "bad woman" sex worker, such as Chata in *Fin del mundo;* or the *vendida* (sellout) in *Los Vendidos.* Teatro Campesino productions on the one hand enacted ideologies and strategies of social critique, working-class survival, and revolution. Yet on the other hand the collective enacted an oppressive status quo of male power and male dominance.

Throughout its history Teatro Campesino female roles remained fairly constant and limited: women represented the same three or four types or categories: a familial category or an age category: mother, grandmother, sister, or wife/girlfriend. Women characters were furthermore dichotomized as "whore" or "virgin," as good or bad. As Antonia Castañeda has shown, this dichotomization dates back to the installation of patriarchy under early colonization. During that time, women (and the land) acquire devalued meanings associated with their reproductive work in a system of private ownership of both women and land. Women's value becomes attached to the patriarchal imperative of producing "heirs." Castañeda comments: "The woman who is defined out of social legitimacy because of the abrogation of her primary value to patriarchal society, that of producing heirs, is therefore without value, without honor. She becomes the other, the bad woman, the embodiment of a corrupted, inferior, unusable sex: immoral, without virtue loose."[16] The Teatro Campesino consistently replicated this gendered patriarchal imperative by dichotomizing women into "good" and "bad" based on sexuality.

Women in the Teatro Campesino responded by finding new outlets for their creativity. For example they created roles that were androgynous (the devil, the skeleton, death); others managed to play male roles (which were the axis of all productions); while others challenged Luis Valdez directly. In response to emergent feminist challenges from women members Valdez only seized the reins of control more and more tightly, to the extent that he actively divested and dissolved the collective when he went mainstream. Unaddressed gender and sexuality issues, including an unexamined heteronormativity, ultimately combined with an ascendant individualism (ego) born of Valdez's individual "mainstreaming" experiment. The dynamic of collective creation and cooperative survival ended by

1980 after Hollywood and then Broadway recruited Luis Valdez. Ultimately, the mainstream emphasis on individuals and not collectives drove a permanent wedge through the company.[17] In the end Luis Valdez both seized and refunctionalized the Teatro Campesino name, attaching it to his new production company. The ensemble members scattered. These internal and external dynamics combined to first limit and then dissolve the collective will and functioning of the Teatro Campesino ensemble. Nonetheless the Teatro Campesino productions from 1965 to 1980 remain an important landmark of what is possible under the auspices of a radical collective will.

NOTES

1. Luis J. Rodríguez, *Hearts and Hands: Creating Community in Violent Times* (New York: Seven Stories Press, 2001), 69.

2. Yolanda Broyles-González, *El Teatro Campesino: Theater in the Chicano Movement* (Austin: University of Texas Press, 1994).

3. For an excellent discussion of such rites of reciprocity within the context of religious/social festival see chapter six on the Prenda System in Olga Nájera-Ramírez's *La Fiesta de los Tastoanes* (Albuquerque: University of New Mexico Press, 1997).

4. Bonfil Batalla analyzes the rural indigenous arrangements of reciprocal relationships in his landmark book *Mexico profundo: Reclaiming a Civilization,* trans. Philip A Dennis (Austin: University of Texas Press, 1996).

5. Cited in Broyles-González, 57.

6. Diane Rodríguez, interview by the author, December 28, 1983, San Juan Bautista.

7. Although Hispanophile researchers have attributed the corrido genre to Spain, the evidence more strongly upholds its indigenous roots in Nahuatl epic. See the cogent argumentation advanced by Celedonio Serrano Martínez in his *El corrido mexicano no deriva del romance español* (Mexico: Centro Cultural Guerrerense, 1963). For a more detailed discussion of the Teatro Campesino's use of the corrido genre see chapter 1 of my book *El Teatro Campesino* and also my article "Women in El Teatro Campesino: '¿Apoco estaba molacha la Virgen de Guadalupe?'" in *Chicana Voices: Intersections of Class, Race, and Gender,* ed. Teresa Córdoba et al. (Austin, Tex.: Center for Mexican Studies, 1986), 162–87.

8. In chapter 1 of my book *El Teatro Campesino* I discuss the many indigenous forebears of the Cantinflas pelada/o underdog figure; see pp. 33–34. Other critics would perhaps like to credit European culture (commedia dell'arte) or even Euro-American culture (the San Francisco Mime Troupe) as precursors. Elizabeth C. Ramírez, for example, ignores campesino culture, the Mexican oral tradition, and indigenous heritage in her evaluation of the Teatro Campesino's early evolution. In *Chicanas/Latinas in American Theatre* (Bloomington: Indiana University Press, 2000) she occludes the creativity of the collective ensemble and of its campesino audiences. Ramírez proceeds to trace a direct masculinist and

individualistic genealogy between the Mime Troupe's Ron Davis as a key influence in "the shaping of a genius" (Luis Valdez). In this vision of the Teatro, Valdez is said to have single-handedly brought "commedia dell'arte" to the Teatro Campesino. I like to give Mexican campesino culture some credit, although it may well be that certain European elements were easily appropriated by the Teatro because of their similarity to some elements of indigenous culture.

9. Valdez's experiments in mainstream theater necessarily separated him from the collective. The mainstream absorbs individuals and not collectives. Valdez's success with *Zoot Suit* in California (and its failure on Broadway) motivated him to transform El Teatro Campesino into a production company, auditioning actors for occasional productions. Unlike the collective, the new production company sought grants for the first time, hired an administrative apparatus, and experienced a long-standing eclipse in artistic production. In the words of Jorge Huerta, "In effect, by 1999, no completely new play had come from Luis Valdez's pen since . . . 1986." *Chicano Drama: Performance, Society, and Myth* (New York: Cambridge University Press, 2000), 34.

10. Luis Valdez, Regents' Lecture, University of California, Irvine, November 1, 1984.

11. These titles are from the 1970s song album named *Mestizo* by Daniel Valdez, A & M Label (SP-3622), 1973.

12. In the Teatro Campesino's only published anthology of performance pieces entitled *Actos. El Teatro Campesino and Luis Valdez* (San Juan Bautista: Menyah Productions, 1971), 2. The idea to publish the actos was spearheaded by ensemble member Felix Alvarez. He tape-recorded the performances, which were then transcribed and published. This publication should not be regarded as "definitive" texts but as a snapshot in time: one rendition of those ever-evolving plays.

13. Olivia Chumacero, interview by the author, August 18, 1989, quoted from *El Teatro Campesino*, 97.

14. From an unpublished Teatro Campesino document entitled "Workshop," n.d. El Teatro Campesino Archives (San Juan Batista, CA).

15. From an unpublished Teatro Campesino document dated June 7, 1976. El Teatro Campesino Archives (San Juan Batista, CA).

16. Antonia Castañeda, "Sexual Violence in the Politics and Policies of Conquest: Amerindian Women and the Spanish Conquest of Alta California," in *Building with Our Hands: New Directions in Chicana Studies*, ed. A. de la Torre and B. M. Pesquera (Berkeley and Los Angeles: University of California Press, 1993), 27.

17. I describe this "mainstreaming" process and its effects on the collective ensemble after 1980 in great detail in chapter 4 of my book *El Teatro Campesino*.

THE LEGACY OF EL TEATRO CAMPESINO

Jorge Huerta

When I think about a theatrical legacy I usually imagine that the group that has left the legacy no longer exists. Indeed, my Webster's defines legacy as "anything handed down from the past, as from an ancestor." But what if that "ancestor" still exists? In fact, some of the theater groups that are being discussed in this volume are still operating. Yet teach has, indeed, left a legacy, and those that continue to do their work are perhaps creating new paradigms and newer legacies. El Teatro Campesino is one of those groups that is still functioning; however, it has gone through several incarnations since it was first founded in 1965. In its first fifteen years the troupe evolved from a farmworkers' theater to a community-based and student group, to an international touring company producing and publishing films, recordings and anthologies, and finally, to a professional producing organization. I believe that all of the theatrical activity of Chicanas and Chicanos today, from community and student *teatros* to professional theater companies and individual theater artists and filmmakers, owes its existence, directly or indirectly, to the Teatro Campesino.

I begin this discussion with the earliest examples of the Teatro Campesino's aesthetic and political legacies because these continue to hold sway with many community-based and student teatros working today. But Chicana and Chicano theater artists, playwrights, directors, designers, producers, and actors have come a long way since the early days of the Chicano theater movement. This "professionalization" of Chicano theater can be attributed to individual efforts, certainly, but one cannot ignore the impact of *Zoot Suit* in this evolutionary process. Another often-ignored fact is that the Teatro Campesino has always been listed as coproducer whenever the group performs in other venues. Thus, although *Zoot Suit* was produced in the Mark Taper Forum theater space and later in the Aquarius Theatre, the Teatro Campesino was also very much involved in the producing process.

Demographics and economics notwithstanding, *Zoot Suit* opened the doors to the "mainstream." And although that play has been attributed to Luis Valdez, it demonstrates the work of the collective as well. As I wrote in 1982, "[Valdez] combined elements of the acto, *corrido, carpa,* and *mito* with Living Newspaper techniques to dramatize a Chicano family in crisis."[1] With the exception of the Living Newspaper, all of the other genres I list were the result of Teatro Campesino workshops. Thus the Teatro Campesino members of that period can take pride in knowing that their collective exercises inspired the playwright and director to create the most important play written or directed by a Chicano to date, a formidable legacy.[2] I also believe that the successful eleven-month run of *Zoot Suit* in Los Angeles opened the doors of professional, nonprofit theaters across the country to other Latina and Latino theater groups and individual artists.

One can never really return to the past because conditions change. Yet, in some ways today's Teatro Campesino, which has been run by the children of the founders since 1994, is similar to the original.[3] The young people who make up today's Teatro Campesino are perhaps the original troupe's most vital living legacy. These descendants of the original founders were literally born into the Teatro Campesino. Their training was hands-on from the time they could speak. Unlike the original striking farmworkers in 1965, however, most of the young members of today's Teatro have formal educations. More importantly, all have benefited from the years of workshops, performances, and tours that their parents would take them on, diaper bags in hand. But the troupe is ever conscious of its humble beginnings. In an interview in 2001, Kinan Valdez, the new director of the Teatro, told me: "One of the most important things for us to build is an alternative grassroots network for touring and presenting."[4]

The new Teatro Campesino has created and performed *actos,* the early form of political sketch that defined the Teatro Campesino and all Chicano theater for several years. Most recently, the Teatro members created an acto about California's energy crisis, titled *Power to the People,* which they toured to various communities in California in 2001, often at no cost to the presenters. Following the typical acto model, California's governor, Gray Davis, called "Gravey Davey," is played as a bumbling idiot wearing a distorted mask and wig.[5] But the new generation has also produced non-

Chicano plays such as Alfred Jarry's *Ubu Roi* (1996) and produced a very successful revival of *Zoot Suit* in the fall of 2002, something the original troupe could never have dreamed of. With this in mind, cognizant of the fact that the Teatro Campesino is still a viable and vital theater company, my focus will be on the legacies of the group's first fifteen years, 1965–80. I will discuss the troupe's evolution from the earliest examples of the Teatro's aesthetics and politics to the mainstream success of *Zoot Suit,* and explore how those themes and forms are still being addressed by today's Chicano theater companies and artists.

I am treating the Teatro Campesino as a collective entity although, in fact, the Teatro and its founding director/playwright, Luis Valdez are sometimes interchangeable. Perhaps the Teatro Campesino could have emerged under the direction and tutelage of another person, but that would have been a completely different group. However collective the work of the Teatro may have been in the group's first fifteen years, Valdez guided the group with his own worldview, an aesthetic, spiritual and political vision that drove his creative spirit. However, my focus here is on the legacy of a performing troupe, its influence as a company rather than on the influences of one director, although Luis Valdez's contributions are similarly important. Equally significant are the many individuals who worked with El Teatro Campesino and other teatros over the years—individuals who have not only gone on to make their marks in Chicano communities as theater artists and cultural workers (as union leaders, educators, lawyers, medical doctors, and activists, etc.), but who also, as members of the Teatro Campesino, exercised a profound influence on Luis Valdez. Learning is a two-way process, and neither the director nor the Teatro members could have continued their artistic development without a dedicated and constantly evolving ensemble.

The *Rasquachi* Aesthetic and the Acto

In order to discuss what I believe to be the group's greatest influences, I have separated them into the general (and often interchangeable) categories of the aesthetic and the sociopolitical. I will discuss the group's political agenda, demonstrating how the Teatro inspired others to speak out against injustices by serving as a model to emulate. But even as I discuss the themes that the troupe was addressing, it is almost impossible to separate the aesthetic choices they made as well. After a chronological overview of the Teatro's aesthetic and political evolution I will give examples of how today's Chicana and Chicano theater artists are a logical extension of the Teatro Campesino's pioneering efforts.

The theatrical form that dominated the Teatro's presentations from 1965 to 1970 was the acto, so named by Valdez for expediency's sake. As indicated in *Power to the People,* the acto is a short, usually comical sketch, often created through improvisation, that is designed to be performed anywhere. The actos were ideally suited for the Teatro's initial efforts to get farmworkers to join the union. The heroes and villains are clearly defined, and a solution is either hinted at or unmistakably stated. The acto form is one of the most important aesthetic and political legacies from the early Teatro Campesino, a form that continues to be employed by that teatro as well as other contemporary teatros.

Although the aesthetic legacy is sometimes difficult to separate from the political, in the realm of aesthetics the Teatro Campesino developed what has sometimes been called the "*rasquachi* aesthetic." The Mexican term *rasquachi* is described by Tomás Ybarra-Frausto thus:

> Rasquachismo is brash and hybrid, sending shudders through the ranks of the elite, who seek solace in less exuberant, more muted and purer traditions. In an environment always on the verge of coming apart (the car, the job, the toilet), things are held together with spit, grit and movidas. Movidas are the coping strategies you use to gain time, to make options, to retain hope.[6]

Rasquachismo is a truly Chicano term, a product of the working class understood by the people who have had to negotiate the uncertainties of life *en el norte,* that is, north of Mexico. As an aesthetic, the earliest Teatro Campesino actos were truly rasquachi. Because the group had no money, they had to be prepared to perform anywhere, usually outdoors, and design elements came together by chance. The actos were simple but not simplistic, inventive by necessity. If you're going to perform outdoors, psychological realism is out of the question. Presentational theater is the norm, breaking the fourth wall to get the audience's attention because they are either working in the fields as scabs or at a park with the attendant noises and distractions. Even if the production is indoors, children will always be present, some supervised, others not. Therefore signs around the necks of the actors mark the characters clearly and masks further delineate the villain (pig face mask) from the heroes (no masks). Costumes are found and the exaggerated props are put together in somebody's kitchen. The rasquachi aesthetic cannot be "designed," it just happens.

During the first fifteen years of the Teatro Campesino's trajectory the group developed other performance genres, all reflecting the rasquachi aesthetic in one way or another. Those forms were the *mito,* or myth, the

El Teatro Campesino, *La Carpa de los Rasquachis,* October 14, 1973. La Muerta and El Diablo torment the Rasquachi. (Photo by Theodore Shank.)

corrido, and the *carpa.* The mito was more of a personal statement for Valdez in his efforts to rescue the Chicanos' indigenous heritage. Although the mito as a genre remains mostly Valdez's invention, his and the Teatro's invocations of indigenous thought and culture can be seen in the plays of many contemporary Chicana and Chicano playwrights. Indeed, most of the plays written by Chicanas and Chicanos since the emergence of the Teatro Campesino employ either actual indigenous symbols on stage or flutes and drums, as musical background, recalling the ancient Mesoamerican cultures that preceded the Spaniards.[7] These plays are not Valdezian mitos, certainly, but they are echoing a practice initiated by Valdez and his Teatro. Another genre that can be termed unique to the Teatro Campesino is the corrido, first explored as a performance technique in 1971. Mexican corridos are simply ballads that tell of lost love, violent retributions, and any number of human interventions in and out of the barrio that note repeating in song. Other teatros also dramatized corridos, but that genre is not evident in today's theatrical expressions, as far as I have seen. The genre that has continued to appeal to both producers and audiences alike is the carpa.

Although the Teatro Campesino did not invent the carpa style, the group did resuscitate it, revealing to the younger theater groups a style that was imminently Mexican in tone. The carpa genre is based on the early-twentieth-century Mexican tent shows that were very popular among the working classes in Mexico and the Southwest. *Carpa* literally means tent, the portable venues the companies would set up in the barrios and in which they would perform. The performances were a combination of comic, often satiric sketches, songs, dances, and other acts. The earliest farmworkers in the Teatro Campesino were well aware of the carpa tradition and emulated it with great skill. In effect, the actos were a product of the carpa sketches, another aspect of the rasquachi aesthetic. Teatro Campesino's opus magnum, *La carpa de los Rasquachi's,* became a staple for the group from 1973 to the end of the decade.

Sociopolitical Legacy

Teatro Campesino's initial sociopolitical legacy can be clearly seen in the themes that actos, songs, and other performance techniques exposed in presentations across the country and even abroad, bringing the plight of the Mechicano[8] to audiences in union halls, campuses, and community centers. The Teatro became a voice for the voiceless, giving Chicano audiences in particular a sense of belonging in a society that had ignored and suppressed them for generations. Sadly, every one of the issues the

Teatro exposed is still relevant. Those issues, in the order of their appearance in the collectively created actos, are farm labor, cultural denial, internal colonization, lack of equitable educational opportunities, inner conflicts in the Chicano movement, police brutality, an unjust judicial system, and the disproportionate number of Chicanos who were fighting and dying in Vietnam. Although strides have been made in some of these areas, every one of these issues, and more, still plague Mechicanos. Before discussing the evolution of the many teatros that were virtually the offspring of the Teatro Campesino, let me review the original actos and their sociopolitical goals.

Initially, the Teatro Campesino gave voice to farmworkers and to the union's cause. The first acto in their anthology, titled *Las dos caras del Patroncito* (The Two Faces of the Boss), created in 1965, comically exposes the powerful grower as just another human being not to be feared if the farmworkers unite against him with the union.[9] The next acto, *La quinta temporada* (The Fifth Season), created in 1966, is a modern-day morality play, complete with allegorical figures, that exposes the farm labor contractor as a parasite feeding off the workers he brokers for the grower.[10] The solution in both of these actos is "join the Union."

When the troupe separated from the union in 1967, they began to explore issues beyond the fields. Recalling a long tradition of Mechicano humor, they exposed the hypocrisy of the Mexican-Americans who deny their Mexican heritage with the now classic acto *Los vendidos* (The Sellouts).[11] In 1968 the troupe created a puppet play titled *La conquista de México* (The Conquest of Mexico), a hilarious satire on the Spaniards' conquest that juxtaposes the arrival of the Yankee/gringo with Cortés and his followers, who speak English with a Texan accent.[12] In contrast the natives speak Spanglish, the Chicanos' bilingual idiom, demonstrating the correlations between the first colonizers and the current hegemony: the Chicanos are the Indians and the Anglos are the Spaniards. The acto explicitly blames the conquest on the disunity of the natives, comparing those ancestral models to the present-day Chicanos who were, in fact, not united. The solution: "organize yourselves and unite against 'The Man.'"

In 1969 the Teatro created a critique of the educational system as it (negatively) affects Chicana/o and African-American students. Aptly titled *No saco nada de la escuela* (I Don't Get Anything Out of School), this acto shows the failures of the educational processes at the elementary, secondary, and postsecondary levels, satirizing the biases of the teachers as representatives of the system *en toto*.[13] The solution: demand better schools, bilingual education, and representative teachers.

Also in 1969 the Teatro took the bold step of critiquing the Chicano student movement itself with its brief but pertinent acto titled *The Militants*.[14] While the earlier *La conquista de México* employed the Aztecs and other natives as a metaphor for the Chicanos, this acto takes place in the present. In it we see two contemporary young Chicanos giving a public lecture, attempting to outdo each other as the "real" Chicano. In the men's zeal to prove which one is the true Chicano, they end up shooting one another, a metaphor for the divisions that were happening in the Chicano student movement at the time. This acto was truly prophetic. After Teatro Mecha at the University of California at Santa Barbara produced this acto for its parent Mecha student organization, the Mecha group split into two opposing organizations.[15]

The Teatro has always maintained strong ties to the farmworkers' union, and in 1970 created a brief acto titled simply *Huelgistas* (Strikers). This acto is actually based on one of the *huelga* (strike) songs the group's members had created over the years and pits several strikers against a grower, demanding justice in the fields. Again, the solution is clear: join the union. Also in 1970, with the Vietnam War in full swing and Chicanos dying or being wounded in disproportionate numbers, the Teatro created *Vietnam Campesino*, exposing the military-industrial complex in an effort to dissuade Chicanos from joining or supporting that war effort.[16] This was followed in 1971 by a very distinct antiwar statement, *Soldado razo* (Buck Private), a heart-wrenching tale, narrated by a shrouded Death, of a Chicano who goes to Vietnam and comes home in a box.[17] While *Vietnam Campesino* demonstrated the duplicities of the military-industrial complex at home and abroad, *Soldado razo*, by focusing on the family and the soldier who will die in Vietnam, becomes a much more personal and poignant statement. Though not a simple solution, the message in the antiwar actos is clear: "Don't support this charade of a war."

Taking Advantage of Technology: "I Am Joaquin"

Because most theater historians and scholars have focused on the theatrical activities of the Teatro Campesino, little attention has been paid to the troupe's use of multimedia, another important aesthetic and sociopolitical contribution. An example of the group's early venture into mixed media was inspired by a poem by noted Chicano leader Rodolfo "Corky" Gonzalez, titled "I Am Joaquin." After the Teatro left the farmworkers' union and began to dramatize other issues, Gonzalez's poem, epic in scope, was an excellent testimonial to put on stage. First published in 1967, the poem quickly became a paradigmatic statement about the evolution of the Chicano nation, beginning with the Mesoamerican cultures, through the Spanish conquest, into the northern reaches of Aztlán,[18] Manifest Destiny, the Treaty of Guadalupe Hidalgo,[19] and the marginalized existence of the Mechicanos today. While Luis Valdez narrated and brother Daniel and other musicians sang and played appropriate musical undertones, slides of various cultural images would appear on the screen as appropriate, underscoring the poet's words with pictures. Joaquin is both man and woman, child and adult, a universal "Everyone" designed to give the Chicanas and Chicanos a sense of their multilayered history. The poem begins with the following statement:

> I am Joaquín
> Lost in a world of confusion,
> Caught up in a whirl of a
>   gringo society,
> Confused by the rules,
> Scorned by the attitudes,
> Suppressed by manipulations,
> And destroyed by modern society.[20]

The poem ends with the following message of hope and renewal:

> I am Joaquín
> The odds are great
> But my spirit is strong
>   My faith unbreakable
>   My blood is pure
> I am Aztec Prince and Christian Christ
>   I SHALL ENDURE!
>   I WILL ENDURE!

(29)

In 1972 the Teatro produced a motion picture of their presentation of "I Am Joaquin" and sold or rented it to community groups, schools, colleges, universities, libraries, and so on. The film reached thousands of emerging Chicanas and Chicanos with its call for unity and pride.[21] Like the staged version of the reading, the motion picture is actually a series of still images reflecting the narrative. In other words, we see images of historic and contemporary photographs, paintings, sculptures, indigenous artifacts, and architecture that appear as we hear Luis Valdez's deep baritone voice narrating the poem. A feeling of motion is achieved by panning or zooming the camera, but in fact no live action is filmed, only stills.

As in the staged version, we hear Daniel Valdez and others singing and playing various instruments, from indigenous flutes and drums to Mexican corridos, to contemporary songs and rhythms. Having attended any number of political rallies and cultural events in the 1970s and 1980s I can assure the reader that this motion picture motivated thousands of people, especially the youth, to reclaim their indigenous, Mexican, and Chicano identities and demand better schools, improved working conditions, and so on.[22] The motion picture was a staple of Chicano political and cultural events and can be found in any library that caters to the Mechicanos.[23]

Other Teatros

When the Teatro left the union in 1967, the troupe relocated to Del Rey, California, not too far away from its birthplace, Delano. There, the Teatro rented a storefront space and founded El Centro Campesino Cultural (Farmworkers' Cultural Center), undoubtedly the first of its kind. In that modest space the Teatro offered workshops in various teatro techniques such as mask making, music, improvisation, and acting. The group would perform on the center's stage and would also tour to generate income. This first cultural center led to a second, larger center in Fresno, followed by the troupe's final move to San Juan Bautista, California, in 1971. The center in San Juan Bautista became a mecca for people interested in what the Teatro was doing. Scholars, theater artists, and students went to San Juan to observe the work or to participate in the ongoing workshops. Some people stayed and became members of the ensemble; others returned to their own teatros, renewed, invigorated and perhaps inspired to continue in theater or to take another professional path. From all accounts, no one left a residency in San Juan Bautista unchanged.[24]

Along with the members of today's Teatro Campesino, perhaps the troupe's most obvious legacy is found in the other Chicano theater troupes and individual theater artists that this company inspired. One of the earliest teatros that owed its genesis and its creative expressions to the Teatro Campesino was the Teatro Urbano, founded in San Jose, California, in 1968 by Luis Valdez's younger brother, Daniel. This urban counterpart to the farmworkers' theater became the second (documented) Chicano theater troupe. The younger Valdez was a member of the Teatro Campesino, but formed the new teatro in order to address the urban problems facing Mechicanas and Mechicanos living in one of California's largest Mechicano populations, San Jose. According to James Santibañez, the Teatro Urbano was composed of mainly "high school and college students as well as people who have made the theater their way of life."[25] Santibañez quotes from the Teatro's self-description:

> El Teatro Urbano was formed because of the need to . . . relate to our people the racism, bias and lack of understanding which was created by the Educational System. There was also a need to relate to our people the attitude with which the police, the judges, and various government agencies (welfare, unemployment, government funded programs) were dealing with our people.[26]

Daniel Valdez is a consummate musician, singer, and composer, and thus both the Teatro Campesino and his Teatro Urbano employed original music as well as traditional Mexican corridos, or ballads, to enhance their performances, telling their stories in song and narrative. The Teatro Urbano looked at urban causes, as stated in the preceding quotation, offering possible solutions. For some audience members, just seeing a satire of the police or biased judges and teachers was enough to satisfy their frustrations; for others, these actos added fuel to the fires that would break out, both literally and figuratively in state-run institutions such as schools and prisons.

While Daniel Valdez and others were forming the Teatro Urbano in northern California, poet and activist Guadalupe de Saavedra founded another urban teatro, Teatro Chicano, in East Los Angeles, also in 1968. According to Bernard F. Dukore, Saavedra was inspired both by the Chicano movement as well as by the Teatro Campesino, whose actos formed the aesthetic basis of Teatro Chicano's own pieces.[27] Dukore published one of the these actos, titled *Justice,* in 1971, the only acto from that period to be so recognized by a major scholar and press during that period.[28] *Justice* is an important example of an acto that, unlike the relatively nonviolent farmworker actos, promotes violent revolution.

Justice is a brief acto that centers on the exploitation of the Mexicans and Chicanos by "Honkie Sam," who the people eventually drive off the stage. They then appeal to the audience in Spanish: "Alright [*sic*], people, don't give in! Organize yourselves!"[29] Then one of the women goes into labor and produces a photo of Che Guevara, and the people shout: "It's a boy!" As Dukore comments, the image of Guevara points to "revolution: transforming society itself, perhaps along socialist lines."[30] And certainly, the acto calls for the people to resist the oppressive forces, the dogs, by killing them.[31]

Interestingly, although this acto calls for a violent response to "Honkie Sam," it was presented by the Teatro Campesino and other people attending a Chicano theater workshop in Del Rey, California, in 1968. Luis

Valdez told a group attending the Radical Theatre Festival at San Francisco State College later that same year: "Different people from San Jose and Los Angeles came down. And Lupe Saavedra . . . had a short story which he made into an 'acto.' It's about Honkie Sam and we performed it in the park."[32] *Justice* is very different from the early Teatro Campesino's farmworker actos, and in sharp contrast to Cesar Chavez's nonviolent philosophy. The aesthetics (the acto) can be attributed to the Teatro Campesino, while the politics are the product of a more radical aspect of the Chicano movement. Most importantly, these two examples of early offshoots of the Teatro Campesino demonstrate the reach that the Teatro was having. Members of both groups went on to form other teatros, which influenced other people, widening the circle and the legacy, as I will explore below.

By 1970 the Teatro had generated an untold number of teatros, student or community-based groups, in various parts of the country.[33] According to Bernard F. Dukore, "as of August 1969 there were nine Teatro [*sic*] Chicanos: three in Texas, three in southern California (two in Los Angeles, one in San Diego), two in Arizona, and one in New Mexico."[34] However, those are the teatros Dukore could locate; others undoubtedly also existed. In 1970 the Teatro Campesino hosted the first Chicano theater festival in Fresno, California, and fifteen theater groups attended. Twelve Chicano groups came from the Southwest, a Mexican troupe traveled from Mexico City and two Puerto Rican troupes came from New York City and Puerto Rico, respectively. In effect, Valdez and his troupe were "calling the disciples home," not in a paternalistic way, but in an effort to foster the continued artistic and political growth of the younger groups.

The following year the Teatro Campesino hosted the second festival, this time in Santa Cruz, California, with seventeen groups participating. A few weeks after the second festival, a group of directors and representatives gathered in the Teatro Campesino's headquarters in Fresno and founded TENAZ, El Teatro Nacional de Aztlán (The National Theatre of Aztlán) as a coalition of teatros. TENAZ remained a driving force in the Chicano theater movement well into the 1980s. The coalition sponsored yearly festivals and minifestivals, conferences, workshops, a newsletter, and other services dedicated to the evolution of the teatro movement. Because the Teatro Campesino was the only full-time teatro in operation, the troupe made its staff and offices available for a consistent administration of the national coalition. Without that benefit, TENAZ, and its constituent teatros, may not have flourished as they did.

By 1973 the number of teatros had swelled. Elizabeth C. Ramírez documented all of the extant Chicano theater groups she could find in 1973, and listed sixty-four active groups.[35] Of the groups founded before 1970, only four were still active, revealing the fact that many student teatros formed and folded within an academic year. Ramirez's chronological listing of teatros from 1965 to 1973 is a very valuable document of the period. However, because she only lists extant teatros, no one can really know how many "overnight" teatros formed and dissolved after a political rally or other community event prior to 1973. What is certain is the fact that within ten years of its creation the Teatro Campesino had almost single-handedly fostered a national theater movement. And although few of those teatros are still operating, the Teatro had a very real reach into the hearts and minds of the groups, their individual members, and the widening circle of audiences.

Economic Independence

While critical of unbridled global capitalism, the Teatro Campesino members accepted the contradiction and augmented their touring income through the sales and rentals of the film of "I Am Joaquin," and by producing and selling various items to help support their troupe. Indeed, their anthology, posters, T-shirts, record albums, and other memorabilia became immediate signifiers of a Chicano consciousness and could be seen on any campus and community where the troupe had performed. Following the Campesino's example, many other teatros also generated income through the sales of posters and other items such as folk crafts from Mexico.

The publication of the Teatro Campesino's first actos in 1971 served a twofold purpose, generating income and giving incipient teatros excellent and effective actos to produce, adapt, and emulate. The anthology was the first of its kind; until that book appeared, no other collection of actos had been published. Further, the Teatro gave any troupe permission to produce the actos free of royalties, reaching an even broader audience through the many productions that immediately followed publication of their anthology. Teatros throughout the country began to (re)produce those quintessential actos, changing locations, names, or other signifiers to best suit their audiences. Farmworker actos were transposed to urban workers' strikes; *Los vendidos* was adapted to suit a particular community's stereotypes. The educational issues exposed in *No saco nada de la escuela* led to many variations on the theme. The messages were clear: the Chicana/o had grievances, and they had better be addressed. Many people, especially students who witnessed those and other actos suddenly became active participants in demonstrations, boycotts, sit-ins, and other activities dedicated to improving the conditions of their people.

The publication of the troupe's actos was a very political act for the Teatro Campesino as well as an economic statement. Two years later, members of El Teatro de la Esperanza, of Santa Barbara, California, self-published their anthology, following the Campesino's example.[36] Other teatros soon followed with their additions to the growing bibliography, publishing their own original actos and short plays.[37] The Campesino was the only self-supporting teatro in the early 1970s and was showing by example how other troupes could liberate themselves from economic independence through hard work and self-sacrifice.

The Teatro Campesino's main source of income came from the troupe's national tours, especially on university campuses, where there were students eager to witness their own culture and politics on stage. This opened the doors for other teatros to generate income by following in the wake of the better-known but increasingly more expensive Teatro Campesino. In effect, the Teatro Campesino had created a touring circuit. If the Campesino could not accept a performance, they would contact other teatros and inform them of the potential performance opportunity. Throughout the Southwest, Northwest, and Midwest teatros could be found touring to campuses, community centers, and other venues away from home.

Teatro Chicano Today

Although only a handful of teatros from the early 1970's are still operating,[38] other companies have been founded in their wake. I would like to focus now on a few examples of theater companies, teatros, and individuals whose trajectories can be attributed to the Teatro Campesino. One prominent example of an early teatro that was inspired by the Teatro Campesino and that is still operating today is Su Teatro (Your Teatro), of Denver, founded in 1972 at the University of Colorado, Denver, by Rowena Rivera. Initially a student group, the teatro quickly involved community members from all walks of life: postal workers, teachers, social workers, and so on, and built a strong community support system. By 1989, under the artistic directorship of playwright/director Anthony J. Garcia, the group acquired an elementary school in the barrio and established El Centro, Su Teatro, a handsome facility that includes offices, classrooms, indoor and outdoor theater spaces and an art gallery. The company offers year-round activities including a nine-month season and classes and workshops in various artistic activities including folkloric music, dance, and drama. Su Teatro produces a variety of theatrical productions, with full-length plays for the mainstage season complemented by children's plays and actos for the youth. Taking their cue from the Teatro Campesino, Su Teatro has also produced cassettes and CDs of their plays.[39]

One of Su Teatro's most successful productions is *La Carpa Aztlán Presents: I Don't Speak English Only*, first produced in 1994. Written collectively by the ensemble and codirected by Anthony J. Garcia and the late José Guadalupe Saucedo, this production revives both the process of collective creation and the carpa tradition in songs and sketches (actos) that call into question the English-only initiatives being enacted across the United States. The proposal, of course, is that two languages are better than one, so why outlaw Spanish? The carpa is also critical of "Hispanics," recalling the earliest actos. This is yet another example of issues that were being exposed by the Teatro Campesino in the 1960s, problems that still resonate as the country has become more and more xenophobic, since September 11, 2001. The carpa/acto style is energetic and lively, satirizing the enemies in the typically bilingual dialogue and lyrics.[40] The premise is that this is a carpa, touring the countryside, presenting their production. And the Teatro does, indeed, tour this piece to various sites, including schools, universities, and community centers. Su Teatro is one of the few groups in the country that, like the Teatro Campesino, has its own facilities, unaligned with a larger community center. And although the company is not a full-time ensemble, there is a strong core of veterans, and even their children, involved in the operation. The tradition continues.

In California, two theater groups that can trace their beginnings to the direct influences of the Teatro Campesino are Teatro Vision, of San Jose, and the Latino Theatre Company, of Los Angeles. Although the companies are very different, the trajectories of both groups are similar, in that they evolved from former teatros that were products of the Teatro Campesino. Another California teatro that is also a living legacy of the Teatro Campesino, although less directly, is the Los Angeles–based troupe, ChUSMA.

Teatro Vision is a third-generation teatro, having evolved from Teatro Urbano (1968) to Teatro de la Gente (1970) to Teatro Vision in 1986. Teatro de la Gente was founded in 1970 by students at San Jose State College and San Jose City College. According to Ramírez, "Not any one person was responsible for the founding, but rather it was through members of Teatro Urbano organized by Daniel Valdez . . . that instigated the group."[41] The third-generation teatro was founded by Elisa Coleman Gonzalez, who had been a prominent member of Teatro de la Gente and an active participant in TENAZ. Gonzalez founded Teatro Vision along with other Chicanas (read women), eager to make women's voices heard. Gonzalez continues to lead the teatro, which employs three full-time staff members and several part-timers, including Gonzalez herself, who holds another full-time position outside the teatro. She runs her company much as the early teatros did, as a collective. Gonzalez has final say on all artistic decisions but is guided by a very active artistic committee made of up of core members of the company who are actors, directors, and so forth. They advise her on scripts and other matters relating to productions.

Teatro Vision maintains offices in the Mexican Heritage Plaza, a beautiful, multi-million-dollar complex of offices, meeting rooms, social services, galleries and an excellent 496-seat proscenium theater. Built with civic and private funds, the Plaza is in one of San Jose's largest barrios, making the Teatro easily accessible to its target audience: Mechicanas and Mechicanos. The Teatro produces a three-play season from the Chicano and Latin American repertoires, employing professional actors and directors. Plays range from Octavio Solis's family Christmas play, *La Posada Mágica,* to Manuel Puig's indictment of Argentine political oppression, *Kiss of the Spider Woman.* Unlike the Campesino or Su Teatro, Teatro Vision is a component of a much larger community center, but the group maintains artistic autonomy and benefits from the impressive facilities and community outreach of the Mexican Heritage Plaza.

The trajectory of the Latino Theatre Company is similar to that of Teatro Vision if one considers that the group's founding director, José Luis Valenzuela, had also been a member of San Jose's Teatro de la Gente. Valenzuela worked with Teatro de la Gente from 1973 to 1978, when he left to join the Teatro de la Esperanza in Santa Barbara.[42] With El Teatro de la Esperanza, Valenzuela was learning everything he could about the collective process, how to direct and create as an ensemble. While in Santa Barbara, Valenzuela worked with actor and future playwright Evelina Fernández, whom he would subsequently marry. Fernández and Valenzuela left the Teatro de la Esperanza in 1984 and moved to Los Angeles, where they formed a company of professional actors eager to perform in a play that spoke to their community. In 1985 the group produced Teatro de la Esperanza's collectively created play *Hijos: Once a Family,* about a Mechicano family that disintegrates as its members struggle to survive.[43] Valenzuela directed this domestic drama in a small theater space in East Los Angeles, winning popular and critical success. Valenzuela's professional directorial future was confirmed with that production, motivating the Los Angeles Theatre Center to hire him to head the Latino Lab later that same year.

When the administration of the Los Angeles Theatre Center hired Valenzuela, they were, in effect, hiring a company. Along with Valenzuela, the founding members of the Latino Lab were (in alphabetical order) Enrique Castillo, Evelina Fernández, Sal López, Angela Moya, and Lupe Ontiveros. Each of these actors had been in Valenzuela's production of *Hijos: Once a Family* and each of them had (and has) an impressive resume of acting experience in Hollywood as well as in Chicano theaters, having worked with Teatro Campesino, Teatro de la Esperanza, and other community-based groups. Like many other Latina/o actors working in Hollywood, Castillo, Fernández, Moya, and Ontiveros had all been in Luis Valdez's *Zoot Suit*, either in Los Angeles or New York (or both), as well as in the film of that play. Each brought a knowledge of professional theater and film to the Lab, and all were crucial to the success of the company, acting in almost all of the plays the Lab produced.

Evelina Fernandez is one of the professional actors and playwrights whose creative evolution was greatly influenced by the Chicano theater movement. Before joining El Teatro de la Esperanza she had been in two teatros based in East Los Angeles, Teatro Urbano and Teatro Movimiento Primavera, collective groups that were descended from Guadalupe Saavedra's pioneering Teatro Chicano. Fernandez was exposed to the Teatro Campesino aesthetics and politics through TENAZ festivals and workshops. Further, as a participant in the professional productions of *Zoot Suit*, she was working for the Teatro Campesino. Fernandez's odyssey from street theater activist to professional stage, television, and screen actor (she costarred in Edward James Olmos's film *American Me*) to playwright and screenwriter is an interesting example of the Teatro Campesino's legacy.

Evelina Fernandez discovered her playwright's voice while working with the Latino Lab and began to script plays for Chicanas. Her one-act comedy *How Else am I Supposed to Know I'm Still Alive?*[44] was first produced in Los Angeles in 1989. That same year, the Latino Lab was busy collectively creating a docudrama based on the life and death of Ruben Salazar, the *Los Angeles Times* reporter who was killed by a sheriff's tear gas projectile during the Chicano Moratorium of August 29, 1970. The play, titled *August 29*, premiered on August 29, 1990, the twentieth anniversary of that fateful day when tens of thousands of Mechicanas and Mechicanos marched in East Los Angeles to protest the war in Vietnam. This play had its roots in the earliest politics of "I Am Joaquin" and the many actos, like *Justice*, that called for an end to police violence. *August 29* was yet another exposé of police brutality, coupled with the issue of social responsibility by Chicanas and Chicanos. Fernandez was a major contributor to the script and took the leading role, all the while sharpening her writer's skills.

Fernandez continued to write her own plays after the success of *August 29*. Her next effort, *Luminarias,* is about a Chicana lawyer, her three professional girlfriends, and their trials and tribulations, especially with men. The play was originally commissioned by Hollywood producers, but, true to form, they believed "American" audiences would not accept a movie about professional Chicanas and passed on the option. When the Los Angeles Theatre Center folded in 1991, the Latino Lab became the Latino Theatre Company, working out of a Chicano cultural center, La Paza de la Raza, in East Los Angeles. *Luminarias* was produced by the Latino Theatre Company in the reconstituted Los Angeles Theatre Center in 1996, and in 1998 Valenzuela directed the full-length motion picture, premiering the movie in 1999 at various film festivals in the United States and abroad. By 2000 the film was being shown in movie theaters in select markets and is now available on video. In 2002 Fernandez's latest play, *Dementia,* was produced by the Latino Theatre Company at the Los Angeles Theatre Center to enthusiastic audiences. This play centers on a Chicano actor/director who is dying of the complications of AIDS, an important issue that was not an represented on stage in the first fifteen years of the Chicano theater movement. By dealing with women's issues, Fernandez and the Latino Theatre Company are expressing themes that were not immediately on the agenda of the Teatro Campesino. But their commitment to exposing women's issues and the ravages of AIDS is being communicated with the political zeal of early Chicano theaters. The difference is that the Latino Theatre Company is the only ensemble made of practicing professionals, people whose roots are clearly in the teatros but whose livelihoods are generated in regional theaters and in Hollywood.

The Next Generation: ChUSMA

In contrast to the older professionals who comprise the Latino Theatre Company, ChUSMA is composed of three actor-activists in their twenties who are a contemporary version of the earliest Teatro Campesino.[45] ChUSMA was formed in the late 1990s by Gustavo Chavez, Alberto Ibarra del Alto, and Marisol Torres. The trio counts Olivia Chumacero, a long-time member of the Teatro Campesino among the theater artists with whom they have worked. The following narrative from ChUSMA's program notes for their production of *The Naco Show* recalls what the earliest teatros were saying and doing:

The NACO Show 2001 is a brand new multi-media show fusing slides, video, and the best in *rasquachi* sketch comedy. With spoofs on characters such as Christina Aguilera, Oscar de la Hoya, Ricky Martin, this brings back the contemporary satire that *ChUSMA* is known for . . . we see *La MUJER* [the woman] and migrant workers battle it out with Violence, *la Muerte* [Death], and cowardly border vigilantes, police brutality, *y mucho mas*! [and much more!].[46]

Further, they place themselves directly in the tradition of the Chicano theater movement: "All this is done in a fusion of 'Neo-vaudevillian,' early Mexican carpa, and 60's teatro Chicano and performance art movement." *The Naco Show* exposes the problem of violence against women and the "Latin Invasion of Hollywood," themes that did not appear immediately in earlier Chicano theater. But the villains that paced the boards in the 1960s are still there: the police, border vigilantes, and the like. And although the troupe calls its short pieces "sketches," they are actos and rasquachi, as they proudly proclaim. The presence of La Muerte, the allegorical figure of Death, resonates with the Teatro Campesino's *Soldado razo*. As with Teatro Campesino's "I Am Joaquin," the ChUSMA members employ slides, but they've also added video, something the underfunded teatros could not have done. This is what I would call "rasquachi with technology," per-haps the next wave of Chicano theater as the new generation of Chicanas and Chicanos find their own ways of expressing their issues.[47]

Concluding Remarks: The Issues Remain Urgent

While one might think that the Vietnam actos would not maintain their relevance years after that conflict ended, they have, with slight modifica-tions. During the 1980s, when the Reagan administration began to wage war on the people of Central and Latin America through the CIA's covert terrorism, teatros immediately adapted *Vietnam Campesino* and especially *Soldado razo* to the new conflicts. One of the premises of both actos is that the humble Vietnamese and the Chicanos are both from an oppressed class, people working the land. Further, the "enemy" looked just like the Chicanos who had been sent to kill them. This parallel between two brown peoples was even more poignant when adapted to the jungles of Central America; the mestizos not only speak the same language, but they really do look just like their Mechicano counterparts.[48] As the United States wages war against the people of Iraq, teatros across the land are prepared to resurrect and adapt Teatro Campesino's and other early teatros' antiwar actos. And once again, "They look just like us." The legacy continues.

The Teatro Campesino lives today not only as a performing entity but also in the thousands of people whose lives were changed by one of their performances or a performance of one of their actos by another teatro. The Teatro lives in the continuing work of so many people who passed through the troupe's cultural centers, from Delano to Del Rey, Fresno to San Juan Bautista. It lives in the people who participated in workshops conducted by the teatro members either at home or on tour. The teatro continues to inspire through its publications, performances, videos and other materials that give the Chicana and Chicano a sense of place.

Hollywood refuses to acknowledge Latina/os' presence in this society despite the fact that this group is a majority in many cities and towns, especially in the Southwest. The Teatro Campesino members and others, like the Latino Theatre Company and Su Teatro, know all too well the machinations and constraints, the myopia and outright ignorance of Hollywood producers and have therefore taken to producing their own films and videos, all produced with minimal funding. Films like *Luminarias* and CDs such as *I Don't Speak English Only,* along with the Teatro Campesino's film of *Soldado razo* (2000), are living proof of the legacy of the Teatro Campesino.[49] The new generation's revival of *La carpa de los Rasquachi's,* which has been touring since 2001, is another reminder of the tremendous impact of the first version.[50] *La carpa de los Rasquachi* follows the trials and tribulations of one Jesus Pelado Rasquachi, a Mexican Everyman who crosses the border into this country and suffers indignities until his death. Jesus is a *pelado,* a rasquachi character right out of the original carpas, and he reminds us that Mexicans will keep coming to the land of their ancestors, and we'd better be ready for them. Echoing the words of Rodolfo "Corky" Gonzalez, first written in 1967, Chicano theater artists are still proclaiming with pride: "We will endure." That's a legacy.

NOTES

1. Jorge Huerta, *Chicano Theater: Themes and Forms* (Tempe: Bilingual Press, 1982), 177.

2. Yolanda Broyles-González points out that certain members of the Teatro Campesino could see the influences of their workshops with Valdez in the final production of *Zoot Suit.* Yolanda Broyles-Gonzáles, *El Teatro Campesino: Theater in the Chicano Movement* (Austin: University of Texas Press, 1994), 178–79.

3. For more on the new Teatro Campesino, see Jorge Huerta, "El Teatro Campesino: The Next Generation," *TheatreForum* 19 (Summer–Fall 2001): 33–39.

4. Kinan Valdez, interview by the author, San Francisco, February 16, 2001.

5. The Teatro Campesino's 2001 acto, *Power to the People,* is discussed in Huerta, "El Teatro Campesino."

6. Tomás Ybarra-Frausto, "Rasquachismo: A Chicano Sensibility," in *Chicano Art: Resistance and Affirmation, 1965–1985,* ed. Teresa McKenna and Yvonne Yarbro-Bejarano (Los Angeles: Wight Art Gallery, University of California, 1991), 156.

7. See Jorge Huerta, *Chicano Drama: Performance, Society, and Myth* (Cambridge: Cambridge University Press, 2000), chap. 1.

8. I use the term *Mechicano* when I am referring to both the U.S.-born or -bred Chicanos, as well as their Mexican counterparts, living in the United States. The two groups are usually interchangeable, although certain issues affect undocumented Mexicans in a way that they do not affect the "legal" Chicanos.

9. *Las dos caras del Patroncito* is in Valdez, *Early Works* (Houston: Arte Publico, 1990), 17–27. All subsequent references to the published actos refer to this volume.

10. Ibid., 28–39.

11. Ibid., 40–52.

12. Ibid., 53–65.

13. Ibid., 66–90.

14. Ibid., 91–94.

15. *Mecha* is Chicano jargon for match, used in lighting a fire. The acronym means "Chicano Student Movement of Aztlán" in Spanish. Mecha chapters could (and can) be found on any campus where Chicanas and Chicanos are enrolled. I directed *The Militants* with members of Teatro Mecha, the cultural arm of the Mecha chapter at the University of California, Santa Barbara, in the spring of 1971. Soon after, Mecha, did, indeed, split into two factions, and El Teatro de la Esperanza was born of that fracture when we left Mecha for the splinter group.

16. Valdez, *Early Works,* 95–97.

17. Ibid., 121–33.

18. Aztlán is the legendary home of the Aztecs, the land to the north, which Chicanos adapted to designate the Southwestern United States.

19. The Treaty of Guadalupe Hidalgo, ratified in 1848, transferred the northern reaches of Mexico (now the Southwest) to the United States. Although the treaty promised justice and equality for the mostly Spanish-speaking peoples living in the territory, those promises were soon abandoned. Most Chicano scholars see this date as the beginning of their people's dislocation, neither Mexican nor Anglo-American.

20. Rodolfo "Corky" Gonzales, *Message to Aztlán: Selected Writings of Rodolfo "Corky" Gonzales* (Houston: Arte Publico Press, 2001), 16.

21. When I asked Rodrigo Duarte-Clark, artistic director of El Teatro de la Esperanza, what he thought was the legacy of the Teatro Campesino, he responded: "The reading of 'I Am Joaquin' spoke to me so powerfully. Their legacy is in me because they made me see directly the effect of theater as a cultural and political force. It transformed audiences" (telephone interview by the author, August 23, 2002). Duarte-Clark joined Teatro de la Esperanza as a graduate student at the University of California, Santa Barbara, in 1973.

22. My first exposure to the Teatro Campesino was at the University of California, Riverside, in 1968. I was then teaching drama at a local high school. I was introduced to Chicano theater that night and knew that I would somehow get involved. I enrolled in the Ph.D. program at the University of California, Santa Barbara, two years later to research and direct Chicano theater.

23. The video of the Teatro Campesino's film of "I Am Joaquin" is available through the Escuela Tlatelolco Centro de Estudios, 2949 N. Federal Blvd., Denver, CO 80211.

24. For more on the lifestyle of the Teatro Campesino prior to 1980 see Broyles-González, *El Teatro Campesino*, chap. 2.

25. James Santibañez, "El Teatro Campesino Today and El Teatro Urbano," in *The Chicanos: Mexican American Voices*, ed. Ed Ludwig and James Santibañez (Baltimore: Penguin, 1971), 147.

26. Ibid.

27. Bernard F. Dukore, ed., *Drama and Revolution* (New York: Holt, Rinehart and Winston, 1971), 596.

28. Ibid., 589–98.

29. Ibid., 597.

30. Ibid.

31. De Saavedra also founded another teatro, the Teatro Popular de la Vida y Muerte (Popular Theater of Life and Death) in Long Beach, California, in 1969. According to Ramirez the group originally dealt with educational themes and later "began dealing with inter-cultural and political themes" (Elizabeth C. Ramírez, "The Annals of Chicano Theater: 1965–1973," masters thesis, University of California, Los Angeles, 1974, 186). De Saavedra left the group soon after its founding to initiate other teatros. See Dukore, *Documents for Drama*, 220.

32. "Radical Theatre Festival," published by the San Francisco Mime Troupe, (*Radical Theatre Festival* [San Francisco: San Francisco State College, 1968], 41). The three groups participating in that festival were Teatro Campesino, Bread and Puppet Theater, and the San Francisco Mime Troupe, all represented in this volume.

33. See Jorge Huerta, "When Sleeping Giants Awaken: Chicano Theatre in the 1960s," *Theatre Survey*, 43, no. 1 (2002): 23–35.

34. Dukore, *Documents for Drama*, 220 n. 3.

35. Ramírez, "Annals of Chicano Theater," 1.

36. Jorge A. Huerta, ed., *El Teatro de la Esperanza: An Anthology of Chicano Drama* (Goleta: El Teatro de la Esperanza, 1973).

37. For a list of plays and actos that were published by 1980, see the bibliography in Huerta, *Chicano Theater*.

38. None of the teatros founded before 1970 still exists. The oldest surviving teatros still operating are Teatro de la Esperanza (1971), originally of Santa Barbara, and now of San Francisco, and Su Teatro (1972) of Denver. None of the original founders of either teatro is still with these teatros.

39. For more information on Denver's Su Teatro, their season, publications, and recordings of their performances, see www.suteatro.org.

40. *La Carpa Aztlán Presents: I Don't Speak English Only* is available on CD from Su Teatro's website, cited in the preceding note.

41. Ramírez, "Annals of Chicano Theater," 110.

42. For an interesting account of the evolution of Teatro de la Esperanza, from its inception to 1990, see Mark S. Weinberg, *Challenging the Hierarchy: Collective Theatre in the United States* (Westport, Conn.: Greenwood, 1992), chap. 3.

43. The Teatro de la Esperanza's play *Hijos, Once a Family*, is unpublished. For an account of this play see Weinberg, *Challenging the Hierarchy*, 81–83.

44. Evelina Fernández's *How Else Am I Supposed to Know I'm Still Alive?* is published in *Contemporary Plays by Women of Color,* ed. Kathy A. Perkins and Roberta Uno (New York: Routledge, 1996), 158–67.

45. The term *chusma* is commonly used to refer to the "undesirables"; thus the trio is using a derogatory term as self-identifier, much like "Queer Nation." Of course, chusma is almost synonymous with rasquachi.

46. This narrative is from the program of the Festival of Chicano Theatre Classics held at UCLA, June 25–30, 2002. For more information on that event contact the Chicano Studies Research Center at the University of California, Los Angeles.

47. You can find some information about the group's productions, as well as many photos of their productions on tour, from Oregon to Chiapas, Mexico, on the their website, www.chumsa.com. The site also includes a few video clips. You can also order ChUSMA T-shirts.

48. I directed *Soldado razo* at the University of California at San Diego in 1985. By simply changing the location of the conflict, the message remained: "Do not fall victim to the government's lies."

49. The Teatro Campesino's film of *Soldado Razo,* retitled *Ballad of a Soldier* and directed by Anáhuac Valdez, directed by Anáhuac Valdez and Kinan Valdez. COTR Productions, 1999.

50. The Teatro Campesino performed *La carpa de los Rasquachi's* at the aforementioned Festival of Chicano Theatre Classics (see n. 46) to a thrilled audience of students and community members, recalling the premiere of that production in 1973. The energy was palpable, and the students, especially, told the organizers the next day that the performance changed their lives.

THE FREE SOUTHERN THEATER
Historical Overview

In 1963 the Free Southern Theater was born out of the civil rights movement through the efforts of three black activists at the Tougaloo College Drama Workshop in Jackson, Mississippi—Doris Derby, Gilbert Moses, and John O'Neal. All three were northerners who had come south to be part of the movement; O'Neal and Derby were field directors for SNCC (Student Nonviolent Coordinating Committee), and Moses was a journalist for the *Mississippi Free Press*. Besides El Teatro Campesino, no other collective in this anthology is as closely and integrally linked to a specific cause and political agenda as the Free Southern Theater. Finding a form of cultural expression that spoke directly to black experience in the rural and urban south and forging community for blacks through theater were the Free Southern Theater's primary goals.

In winter 1963, Derby, Moses, and O'Neal constructed a prospectus for the Free Southern Theater and enlisted the support of white Tulane University professor and *TDR* editor Richard Schechner. Schechner came on board initially as an advisor but within months joined O'Neal and Moses as a directing producer for the company. Free Southern Theater members often performed a variety of off- and onstage roles, but by 1965 Moses and O'Neal had the titles of executive producers of the Free Southern Theater, and Schechner was the chairman of the board of directors.

Reaching out to and connecting with rural and urban black audiences, filling the cultural and educational void for blacks, and "telling it like it is" were the Free Southern Theater's reasons for being—and since an expansive touring schedule and free admission to all performances were key tenets of the project, by necessity, fund-raising became a major and ongoing effort of the theater. Movement activists were not only the first creators of, and audiences for, the work, they also provided essential support by housing and feeding the three white and five black actors/theater workers in the company and providing performance spaces (meeting rooms and churches) for the Free Southern Theater's first summer tour (1964). It presented *In White America,* a documentary-style drama written by white Princeton University professor Martin Duberman, directed by Moses. The company toured to sixteen towns and cities; in New Orleans the audiences were integrated; in the Mississippi farming towns they were predominately black. After the murders of civil rights workers James Chaney, Michael Schwerner, and Andrew Goodman in August 1964, *In White America* was revised to reference this tragic event; the performance became "more militant," and freedom songs were added.[1]

During "Freedom Summer" (as summer 1964 was referred to thereafter) Schechner returned to New York to work on other projects and to raise money for, and interest in, the Free Southern Theater. Over the next five years, numerous Hollywood star-studded benefits in the North garnered support and money for the Free Southern Theater. In February 1965, the two productions of the company's second season and tour (1964–65) were presented in New York City as fund-raisers: Ossie Davis's *Purlie Victorious* (directed by Schechner) at the American Place Theatre and Samuel Beckett's *Waiting for Godot,* directed by James Cromwell, in which black and white actors performed in whiteface at the New School for Social Research.

Although the decision to perform in whiteface was challenged by some company members, audience response was often favorable (a regular practice of the Free Southern Theater was audience discussion after the performances). According to Free Southern Theater actress Denise Nicholas, "whiteface immediately stopped that first black-white reaction and forced the audience to deal with something else . . . the human heart of the play."[2] During these first few years the work of the Free Southern Theater reflected a central aim of the civil rights movement at the time—integration. Integrating anything in the South was crucial, and when he directed *Godot,* white actor-director Cromwell felt that whiteface was the best way to meld the goals of the movement, the Free Southern Theater, and Beckett—despite the complexities, conflicts, and (frequently) confusion arising out of this choice.

During the 1965 summer tour (Robert Cordier became artistic director at this time), the company produced Bertolt Brecht's *The Rifles of Senora Carrar* and remounted *In White America.* In addition, the company performed two improvisationally based works, created out of community workshops spearheaded by Gil Moses, *The Jonesboro Story* and *The Bougalusa Story*. These pieces encouraged audience participation.

After the tour, in fall 1965, the company suspended formal operations, and a number of performers left. Gil Moses and Denise Nicholas pushed for a "non-integrationist direction" for the Free Southern Theater; they were interested in creating an all black theater company.[3] In March 1966 Schechner resigned as chairman of the board of directors and was replaced by Tom Dent, a black writer-journalist who had recently moved from New York City to New Orleans, the city of his birth. Moses was named artistic director, but soon afterward he left the company and was replaced by Roscoe Orman, who helped set up the Free Southern Theater's Community Workshop Program in New Orleans. With Dent's extensive efforts (after Orman left, Dent became the artistic director of Free Southern Theater until fall 1970) the community workshop evolved into a year-round program of free classes (acting, creative writing, dance, black history and culture) providing local people with ongoing access to the educational and recreational enrichment of theater.

O'Neal also left the company at this time to serve out his Selective Service Board "sentence" for his conscientious objector status—two years of janitorial work in Chicago. Other landmark events of 1966 for the Free Southern Theater were receiving a $62,500 Rockefeller Foundation grant and the establishment of its headquarters in a former supermarket in the Desire Project of New Orleans, which was considered a "hard-core" black area of the city.[4] During summer 1966 the company toured Louisiana, Georgia, Alabama, and Mississippi with a performance of African-American poetry (some of these pieces had been developed in the community workshop), Gilbert Moses's *Roots,* William Plomer's one-act puppet play *I Speak of Africa,* and Brecht's *Does Man Help Man?*

In August, the Free Southern Theater was featured in a controversial segment of a CBS television show about six U.S. regional theaters, "Look Up and Live." The Free Southern Theater segment was filmed in the Desire housing project. Although the New Orleans Housing Authority tried to stop the segment from airing because of its sharp focus on the project's deplorable living conditions (it was successful in "blacking out" the show in New Orleans), the segment was otherwise shown nationally, bringing further recognition to the Free Southern Theater.

The fifth Free Southern Theater season, in 1967, consisted of *Happy Ending* by Douglas Turner Ward, an evening of poetry compiled by the company ("Uncle Tom's Second Line Funeral"), and Eugene Ionesco's *The Lesson*. Murray Levy was the one remaining white actor in the company; he directed and acted in *The Lesson*.

This was a time of changing focus and consciousness for the Free Southern Theater—working with new material by black artists and writers based on black experience became a consuming interest of the group. This shift was reflective of the emerging Black Arts Movement, which was connected to the black power phase of the civil rights movement. Black urban and rural communities were resituated at the center of the struggle for civil rights—it was these stories that needed to be told, performed, and exchanged. Throughout the early and middle 1970s small community theaters proliferated in New Orleans, and Dent, although no longer a member of the Free Southern Theater, worked hard to keep these companies alive and connected to each other through the establishment of the Southern Black Cultural Association (1974). Dent's play *Ritual Murder* was first performed by the Free Southern Theater in 1969; it was also produced by the Ethiopia Theatre, another black theater company in New Orleans, in 1976. Gilbert Moses returned to the Free Southern Theater to work with the company in 1969; productions included LeRoi Jones's *Slave Ship* and *East of Jordan* by Evan Walker. Throughout the 1970s, under O'Neal's leadership once again, the company produced a number of works by black writers, including Lorraine Hansberry's *A Raisin in the Sun* in 1972. Chakula Cha Jua adapted Langston Hughes's poetry into performances with the company during the 1974 and 1975 seasons.

Throughout the final decade of the Free Southern Theater O'Neal made a practice of using unpaid local people for the community-based work. In 1979, in part as a response to the claim that community-based theater work exploited the community, O'Neal used himself instead. The creation of his solo performance work heralded the beginning of Junebug Productions (see Jan Cohen-Cruz's essay in this volume).

The last chapter of the Free Southern Theater was marked in 1985 by a jazz funeral/reunion/conference in New Orleans organized by Free Southern Theater founders and others, which was an opportunity not to mourn, but to honor, preserve, and celebrate a Southern black arts tradition in signature New Orleans African-American style.

—C. R.

NOTES

1. Clarissa Myrick Harris, "Mirror of the Movement: The History of the Free Southern Theater as a Microcosm of the Civil Rights and Black Power Movements, 1963–1978," Ph.D. diss., Emory University, 1988, 28 n. 18.

2. Denise Nicholas in Annemarie Bean, *A Sourcebook on African-American Performance* (New York: Routledge, 1999), 108–9.

3. Gilbert Moses in Thomas C. Dent, Richard Schechner, and Gilbert Moses, *The Free Southern Theater by the Free Southern Theater* (Indianapolis: Bobbs-Merrill, 1969), 95.

4. Tom Dent in ibid., 104.

THE FREE SOUTHERN THEATER

Mythology and the Moving between Movements

Annemarie Bean

> Ideology and political statement either through documentary or contemporary application are one thing; we, however, are in search of mythology.
> —Thomas C. Dent, Richard Schechner, and Gilbert Moses, *The Free Southern Theater*

As Tom Dent asserted in 1967, the Free Southern Theater (1963–85) needed to "have its own thing, its own illustration, depiction."[1] Mythmaking and movements of black liberation have gone hand in hand in American history. Consideration of the civil rights movement and the Black Arts Movement reveals that mythmaking was intrinsic to the makeup of both. The Free Southern Theater was developed along the pattern of the civil rights movement, in that it was peopled and funded in its early years because of its commitment to the singular myth of integration. The aesthetics of an emerging Black Arts Movement, by contrast, purposefully and forcefully pursued many mythologies, as a "*moral* obligation to preserve that diversity and oppose conditions or compromises that deny the right of options and alternatives."[2] The Free Southern Theater only came to artistic fruition when it rejected the integrationist platform in favor of the multiplicity of the black experience espoused by the Black

Arts Movement. By doing so, the Free Southern Theater revealed what had become apparent as early as 1965: The integrationist movement of civil rights was divisive, not copacetic. This lack of unity, this laying bare of the failure of the promise of Reconstruction, stifled creativity because it did not have the energy and focus of an avant-garde artistic movement. The entry of the Free Southern Theater into the aesthetics of the Black Arts Movement—one that was steeped in making "its own thing," its own unique, multilayered, multi-influenced art—gave it an artistic voice, one that made it a black theater. However, the Free Southern Theater was neither a Black Arts Movement theater nor a civil rights movement theater. It moved between the two, creating mythologies around the ideas of integration and black power.

Aesthetics and the Civil Rights Movement: "The Black-White Question"

The performance of the civil rights movement happened in the streets, in the jails, and yes, also on the stage. Begun by three African-Americans, the Free Southern Theater started as an integrated theater company based in furthering black voter registration in Mississippi in 1963. With the addition of whites and blacks to the company, the formation of an integrated board of directors, the choice of producing plays written by white, Irish-born, France-residing Samuel Beckett and the African-American actor and activist Ozzie Davis, and the relocation from Jackson to New Orleans, the Free Southern Theater embodied the fruits and difficulties of maintaining a performance group fueled by what founder Gil Moses called "the black-white question."[3]

In the winter of 1963, the clear necessity to birth a free southern theater was conceived in the minds of Doris Derby, an artist; John O'Neal, a recent graduate of Southern Illinois University; and Gilbert Moses, an actor and director in Jackson, Mississippi. O'Neal and Derby were field directors for SNCC (the Student Nonviolent Coordinating Committee), and Moses was a journalist for the *Mississippi Free Press*. All were creative, educated northern African-Americans who saw Mississippi as redolent of a "Caste System in a Cultural Desert" and sought to culturally irrigate it through theater.[4] Not only was Mississippi a "cultural desert," it was a place of daily violence. The violence in retaliation for the SNCC Delta Campaign voter-registration drive in Alabama and Mississippi was encapsulated by SNCC field-worker and Mississippi native Fannie Lou Hamer, who said her home of Sunflower County was "the land of the tree and the home of the grave."[5]

Derby, O'Neal, and Moses's prospectus for a "Free Southern Theater" details the conceptual centrality of the terms *free, southern,* and *theater* in their project, which would "add a necessary dimension to the current civil rights movement through its unique value as a means of education."[6] "We wanted freedom," reflects Gil Moses in 1969, "for thought, and involvement, and the celebration of our own culture."[7] Their priorities were (1) the civil rights movement and (2) the theater as a means of (3) education about the movement. For the founders of the Free Southern Theater, civil rights, art making, and education were to intersect through their free(dom) theater, produced and performed in Mississippi and other southern states. Recognizing the southern African-Americans' "poise for drama," (as Zora Neale Hurston noted in her "Characteristics of Negro Expression"), the Free Southern Theater began with the idea that dramatizing the movement would be possible.[8] The political aim of the Free Southern Theater was dictated by the focus on integration by the civil rights movement, according to Gil Moses. But Derby, Moses, and O'Neal wanted the Free Southern Theater to "deal with black artists and the black audience." In an interview with Jan Cohen-Cruz, John O'Neal states that the Free Southern Theater was always a black theater, and argues that true integration cannot happen unless both whites and blacks share the balance of power. In the Free Southern Theater there were a few white actors, but, according to O'Neal, it was a black theater in its practice.[9] As Moses points out, these concepts were "in conflict from the beginning: The development of a black style of theater . . . and an 'integrated' theater, based on pre-existing structures."[10]

The civil rights movement gave the Free Southern Theater its southern legitimacy, its southern connections, its southern safe-havens. The "black-white question" of the 1964 Free Southern Theater paralleled the passage of civil rights legislation and was answered in 1966 with the establishment of the Black Panther party, when the Free Southern Theater became a black theater. However, in the interim, the Free Southern Theater looked to the civil rights movement for two aspects of their existence, survival and purpose. First, as Richard Schechner reports, the touring of Free Southern Theater was completely engineered by SNCC because a quick connection with the southern communities to which they were touring was a means of survival. "We needed safe places, especially since we were blacks and whites, men and women, traveling together."[11] He continues on to say that the "movement gave us a goal, a way of choosing our repertory."[12] According to Schechner, the civil rights movement gave the Free Southern Theater connections to communities and activist reasons to tour. But the civil rights movement did not give the Free Southern

Theater effective dramatic material, as they were to find out. The easiest way to measure at what points the Free Southern Theater favored an aesthetic based in an integrationist civil rights movement over an aesthetic based in the Black Arts Movement, and vice versa, is to look at what types of theater they produced. *In White America* by Martin Duberman, performed in the summers of 1964 and 1965, and *Roots* by Gilbert Moses,[13] performed in the summer of 1966, are two productions that demonstrate the group's artistic legacy in residing and moving between the two movements.[14] These productions may be placed on either end of this spectrum of movements, but through their content they are connected to black consciousness and the idea of community through cultural mythology-making in artistic forms such as theater. The Free Southern's black performance aesthetic was decidedly located in the Black Arts Movement by 1969; no longer did it exist on a cultural, creative edge. Already in 1964 the Free Southern Theater was seeking a black performance aesthetic imbued with *black consciousness,* arguably the theoretical core of both the civil rights and Black Arts Movements. But it was not until Moses's *Roots* was produced in 1966 that the group abandoned an aesthetic based in the integration project of the civil rights movement, in favor of the goals of black subjecthood of the Black Arts Movement.

This change had many causes; one was the absence of peer theater groups. The artistic edge was a lonely place, especially for a theater housed in a poor, urban southern neighborhood and wishing to question the cultural integrity of integration. The civil rights movement gave the Free Southern Theater its purpose, but not its aesthetic, because there was no aesthetic of integration. The reasons for integration—to quell the violent tide of violence on blacks and lack of representation—were more dramatic than the theater could realistically theatricalize. The struggle could not be staged. This inability to find theatrical material that dramatized the moment is also evident in the reportage of the civil rights movement. At first glance, the words of civil rights leaders seem well known (Dr. Martin Luther King Jr.'s "I Have a Dream" has become a classic of speechmaking). Yet the search for a dialog about the civil rights movement is often hampered by a sanitized, mediatized version of a nearly wordless movement. Consider a pictorial book from the period: *The Movement: Documentary of a Struggle for Equality.* Many of its pictures feature signature actions of the struggle for civil rights: sit-ins, voters registering, police barricades. Civil rights advocates hold signs with single words, "Justice," or short phrases, "Stop Segregation," "Register Now for Freedom," "Rent Strike for Freedom," "The Only Good Education is an Integrated Education." Under one photograph, a text by

Howard Zinn originally published in *The Nation*, recounts how a beating by police in Winona, Mississippi, left an educated, "tall, black-skinned and beautiful" woman, who was trying to register voters, able to utter only one word to friends, "Freedom."[15]

These images and others like them are stark, emotionally detached and nearly mute. The images of black civil rights leaders are more familiar than the words they uttered. Even less is known about most of the southern African-Americans who worked and sacrificed their lives and livelihoods in the struggle. Much of the news coverage of the civil rights movement was in the vein of the Zinn account: written by a white journalist or observer, reductive of a black participant. The entire story of the young black woman is defined by her utterance of one word, "Freedom." Therefore, the images are performative in the most limited sense of the word. Instead of transformative, the word "Freedom," by the very fact that it is not accompanied by other words uttered by its black speaker, is not freeing in its utterance, but limiting. Reading Zinn's account, we are told to applaud Annelle Ponder, the young black woman, for her devotion and her steadfastness to the civil rights movement, particularly because, in being young and educated, she is much like many of us. She altered her beaten and jailed status by remaining true to her cause of freedom through saying "Freedom" and not, "Get me the hell out of here." But we know very little about Ponder, and her narrative is culled as a powerful journalistic tool. Her utterance of "Freedom" may have transformed her status, but we do not see it. Our white media-conditioned interest has moved on, to another black face, black body in another picture, blurred by water hoses, chased by dogs.

Contrast the above with a recounting of a postperformance discussion after the Free Southern Theater's production of *Waiting for Godot* in Ruleville, Mississippi, in 1964. Local civil rights activist Fannie Lou Hamer compared the play's world to her own:

> Every day we see men dressed just like these, sitting around bars, pool halls and on the street corners waiting for something! They must be waiting for Godot. But you can't sit around waiting. Ain't nobody going to bring you nothing. You got to get up and fight for what you want. Some people are sitting around waiting for somebody to bring in Freedom just like these men are sitting here. Waiting for Godot.[16]

Hamer deftly recognized that the Free Southern Theater had finally achieved its goal of connecting with rural, black communities of the

South, albeit, in this example, through the material of Samuel Beckett. She notes that "Freedom" is a goal, obtained by pursuit. Her perception is similar to Annelle Ponder's, who utters the word "Freedom" in Zinn's story. However, what is markedly different between the two tellings is the articulation of the mythology. In Zinn's story, the protagonist role of the freedom-fighter, occupied by the black woman Ponder, is reduced to monosyllables, and the story is told by a white journalist. In Hamer's case, and this is crucial, the Free Southern Theater, through theater, gave her an image that was not reductive, but rich with a narrative. By utilizing the plot development of Samuel Beckett, to which she connected through the touring company of the Free Southern Theater, Hamer articulated a knowledge about black apathy toward the civil rights movement that, as readers of the Zinn article, we would have been unaware of. Duberman's *In White America,* in its documentary-style format, did not allow for inter-pretation and criticism by its audience. *Godot* did. The absurdity of Beck-ett allowed a transformative space for the audience, one in which they could construct their own mythologies. But *Godot* still was not *it* for the Free Southern Theater artistically. The form needed to be black-gener-ated, and out of the black southern experience. It would take Gil Moses's play *Roots,* performed during the summer tour of 1966, to give the Free Southern Theater an outlet for their interest in presenting the plays of the Black Arts Movement.

Subjecthood through the Black Community: The Black Arts Movement

Theoretical considerations of the (northern) Black Arts Movement, par-ticularly Black Arts theater, gain important nuances when reconsidered in light of the Free Southern Theater's parallel history. The founding events of the Black Arts Movement can be located in New York City in 1964 with the first performances of Amiri Baraka's (then known by the name LeRoi Jones) one-act plays *The Dutchman* and *The Slave,* and with the publication of Baraka's "The Revolutionary Theatre."[17] Even the name of this aesthetic movement (roughly extending from 1964 to 1975, ending with the impeachment of Richard Nixon and the end of the Vietnam War) came from a poem by Baraka: "Black arts we make / in black labs of the heart."[18] In an essay commissioned by the *New York Times* and then rejected by its arts editors, Baraka stated black revolution-ary theater would be a "theater of Victims . . . stagger[ing] through our universe correcting, insulting, preaching."[19] By means of the theater, *blacks, former victims, would achieve subjecthood through community.* Community was integral and essential to Black Arts drama's enactment, both in the subject matter (most often continual racism's effects on the black community) and in the practice of the play (rehearsals and staging in black community centers and neighborhoods).

The aesthetics of the Black Arts Movement were contemporary urban, with a historical backdrop of the circum-Atlantic, most notably West Africa, the Caribbean, and South America. Far-reaching globally and historically, Black Arts theater confronted a limited notion of the "ghettoized" or "plantation" black. The perimeters of the black community explored by black theater artists of the period intentionally reached beyond geographical borders. Playwrights of the Black Arts Movement, such as Sonia Sanchez and Ed Bullins, dramatically illustrated the widening scope of this 1960s black intellectual movement, connecting it with the negritude movement in West Africa, and the independence fights in the Caribbean and in Africa. Their plays also exhibit a diversity of dramatic form and content, supporting Mike Sell's assertion that a specific type of dramatic aesthetic was not the primary objective of the Black Arts Movement. Rather, there was a push toward an *unmarking* and *unmaking* of an aesthetic, allowing for a "release from object."[20] Sell perceptively reminds us that Black Arts dramatists were influenced by West African ritual and the Italian futurists, Antonin Artaud, and the Baptist Church. This "fluidity" was essential to the black artist rejecting the "white thing," the very "thingness" of arts materialism and commodification of (black) culture. The Black Arts Movement was not interested in marketing a black "thing" in order to satisfy white desire for it. And, in rejecting the marketing of blackness, the Black Arts Movement had, at its core, a responsive reaction to the leading story of (again, not by) black people of the 1960s, the civil rights movement in the South.

"Everything That Rises Must Converge"

The Free Southern Theater did not seek formal inclusion in the largely northern Black Arts Movement, but, rather, sought to bring it South, to reacquaint it with its roots, and to give it more stories to tell. The performance aesthetic of the civil rights movement is difficult to pinpoint because its practice was unable to reconcile the conflicts inherent in integration. This aesthetic derived from competing histories of white and blacks, highly educated and barely educated people, northerners and southerners, Jews and non-Jews, community and professional theater practitioners, all at a risen point of convergence, to borrow from the southern writer Flannery O'Connor.[21] All and all, the Free Southern Theater contained within its physical and artistic boundaries all the factions of the movement, all on tour (eating, sleeping, traveling) together. The integrated performances of the Free Southern Theater were volatile and combative, reflective of the external world. The power of live performance to overcome divisiveness was put to a supreme test during the tours of the Free Southern Theater in the South of the 1960s. This was due partly to the fact that plays that the Free Southern Theater needed to do—those of the civil rights movement—did not exist yet. The Free Southern Theater wanted to reflect the civil rights movement's goals of empowering the blacks of Mississippi to vote. There were no plays available that approached the power of the defiant statement of blacks such as Hattie Simmon. "Yes, I will register," she states in a 1962 CBS report on Mississippi and the Fifteenth Amendment, after her granddaughter and a young friend had been shot and critically wounded when Simmon's intent to register was published in the local paper.

The initial performance aesthetic of the Free Southern Theater was an integrated one, located in a theatrical space comprised of mixed locales, mixed religions, mixed classes, mixed genders, and mixed races.

An excellent and detailed journalistic account of the Free Southern's tour during the summer of 1964, "Theater of the Meaningful" by Elizabeth Sutherland, is filled with descriptions of the audience responses to the production, Martin Duberman's *In White America.*[22] Every performance began with the words "You are the actors." Sutherland describes the experimental nature of the production of *In White America,* serving as a means to find out "how Mississippi Negroes, most of whom had never seen a theatrical performance before, would react; and to ascertain what sort of theater should be developed." Audience reactions differed widely. Often, affirmation for speeches demanding equality sprang from audience members, "That's right!" "Amen!" "You tell it!" Local whites came to the production. In Indianola, the town where the White Citizens' Council had first organized with major funding from the state, twenty-five policemen, accompanied by the sheriff, showed up to see the play while the lights were still being hung. They sat in the back, and eventually the front of the theater was packed with African-Americans in unbearable heat. Sutherland listened in on conversations outside the theater between cops and a white volunteer about genetics. A few days later, the reporter returned to Indianola to talk to a white man, the county clerk, who had seen the production:

> That gentleman sat alone in a smallish room which had two entrances, for white and Negro. Quietly, with total hostility, he ex-

plained that he had gone to see the play to find out what the Summer Project was all about. He thought it was well acted, historically accurate as far as he could judge—and inflammatory. The production confirmed his suspicion that the project was Communist-infiltrated. . . . "The project was supposed to teach citizenship and voter registration. There's nothing in the play about those things. Anyway, there's no problem with voter registration in this county—Negroes can come down any time they want to."[23]

Sutherland makes the point that the federal government had decided to bring a suit against the local registrar, Theron Lynd, because only twelve of the seventy-five hundred adult blacks in the county had been judged eligible to vote in 1962.[24] To some of its white public, the early theatrical body of the Free Southern Theater was a social tragedy, a type of performance miscegenation. Like black citizens seeking their constitutional right to vote, the Free Southern Theater was silenced, regulated, and trapped.

Playing *White*

In White America begins with a preface by the playwright that states clearly, "My starting point was the wish to describe what it has been like to be a Negro in this country (to the extent that a white man can describe it)."[25] *In White America* sought to "document" the atrocities against blacks in America, and the meticulous Duberman includes his original sources in an addendum. The format of the play is somewhat like a living newspaper. In fact, the first scene opens with a white man reading a current newspaper. He states, "If God had intended for the races to mix, he would have mixed them himself. He put each color in a different place." The living newspaper format was reminiscent of the work of the Federal Theatre Project (1935–37), dependent on the hurried pace of an urban lifestyle with multiple characters, a type of life incongruous with the rural South. In two acts, the play requires three white actors and three black, along with a guitarist, to tell four hundred years worth of stories of black-white relations in America. All the actors shared the narrator role.

Essentially, *In White America* is a history lesson for those whites wanting to be sensitized to race issues. Given that the Free Southern Theater toured their production exclusively in the Black Belt of the South, this decision to produce a play intended for white, middle-class audiences should be explored. Clarissa Myrick Harris analyzes the choice as the result of the bind of double consciousness.[26] According to O'Neal, he and

John Cannon and Roscoe Orman in *In White America,* summer, 1964. (Photo by Bob Fletcher. Courtesy of Richard Schechner.)

Moses altered the play, inserting freedom songs and other forms of black music and giving it a "more militant focus."[27] When the murdered bodies of the civil rights workers James Chaney, Andrew Goodman, and Michael Schwerner were found, Moses and O'Neal added material about the murders to the script as well. Indeed, the August 7, 1964, performance of *In White America* in Meridian, Mississippi, was canceled, in deference to the memorial service for the three men. Ultimately, in the words of Gil Moses, to even have produced and toured so large and complicated a play was *the* achievement of the Free Southern Theater production:

> When I say *In White America* is important to us, I mean that O'Neal and I have a commitment to Mississippi. This production not only fulfills this commitment to Miss., and to the people who are interested in and working for the Free Southern Theater in New York, but to ourselves, as initiators of this idea.[28]

In the letter to Richard Schechner dated July 19, 1964, from which this excerpt comes, Moses describes the symbolic value of the play. O'Neal and Moses did not want, in Moses's words, to "play the fool," playacting that they were a touring theater company in Mississippi. In its simplistic staging and singular message, *In White America* was easy to put up and easy to tour. It proved the Free Southern Theater could artistically and financially manage to tour a play in Mississippi that dealt with issues of integration, something that had never happened before. And it gave the Free Southern Theater a very real manifestation of their idea to celebrate black culture's heroic responses to adversity.

In White America not only offered an example of what an "integrated performance aesthetic" might look like, it also laid bare the tensions of being the first and only theater of its kind. Schechner was in New York that summer, spreading the word about the company while conducting research for a book. As a creative black man, Moses knew of the doubts many had that the Free Southern Theater could carry out its plans; Schechner had told him as much when he communicated the inquiries he was getting in the North, "What are they doing now," "What will they be doing this summer."[29] The northern, urban potential patrons were already patronizing. In Mississippi, Moses identified that audiences needed to be cultivated, contacts made and locations established.[30] With the pressures mounting, the Free Southern Theater was threatened in what John O'Neal has called its "infancy" from the "spontaneous and chaotic" atmosphere.[31] Indeed, Moses, one of the proponents for becoming a true, all-black theater in a year or so, in 1964 was telling Schechner that O'Neal,

Moses, and Schechner were all together in this fight for a Free Southern Theater. *In White America* was probably chosen as the first production for its easy-to-produce form as much as content. Producing theater in the same area of Mississippi where southerners and northerners, black and white, were dying for suffrage, Moses's letter identifies the growing pains of a company about to play, with doubled meaning, "the most exciting theatrical circuit in America."[32]

To put a production of *In White America* on in rural Mississippi with black and white actors, even male and female actors, was a performative action imbued with politics and danger. In his valuable journal of the summer tour, the black actor Robert "Big Daddy" Costley recalls how, one and a half weeks after his arrival in New Orleans, the car and church of the Unitarian minister he was staying with were bombed. Five weeks later, other members of the company, one black and two white men, went to search for food in Jonesboro, Louisiana, and were stopped by two black policemen. Taken to the police station, the actors were harassed with questions from white policemen, concerning "what the Free Southern Theater really stood for." "How is that black pussy?" (to the white men), they asked, and "How does it feel to screw a white woman, boy?" (to the black man). The actors were released with a promise that the Ku Klux Klan would be told "two nigger lovers and a nigger were loose." "It was three hours of abject terror," Costley concludes.[33] Costley's accounts are important because he was not intricately tied up in the details of producing the tour. This meant that he could take bike rides through the towns they were touring, stay up late with his housing hosts, and record his observations and conversations. It is through these accounts that the environment of exhilaration and fear that fed the 1964 and 1965 tours of the Free Southern Theater can be accessed.

Roots and Black Consciousness

The triumph of *Roots* was to give its audience an interpretation of their own time and place. The place of the Free Southern Theater at the time of *Roots'* first presentation was an abandoned supermarket in Desire, a black and Creole ghetto in New Orleans. Gil Moses and Richard Schechner had left the company, and John O'Neal was in Chicago cleaning a hospital as a result of his 1-O classification.[34] A native New Orleanean who was a cofounder of the Umbra Writer's Workshop on the Lower East Side of New York (1961), Tom Dent had assumed the position of acting producer. Dent had also been a reporter for the *New York Age* and a press attaché for the NAACP Legal Defense Fund. Dent's ascendance was the direct result of the infighting that pushed Moses and Schechner out of the company. The choice of Dent by the board, and the presence of only one white in the company, Murray Levy, shifted the company to a truly black theater.[35] Dent literally bridged the gap between the South and the North, the civil rights movement and the Black Arts Movement, in that his past was in the South and his artistic and political present was in the North. He was black, educated, southern, politically sophisticated, and artistically engaged. His time as a producer for the Free Southern Theater (1966–70) was *the* transition period for the company, and given his multiple affinities, it might not have happened without him.

The transition was reflected in the group's program, which included African and African-American poetry; *Roots, I Speak of Africa,* a one-act puppet play by William Plomer; and Bertolt Brecht's *Does Man Help Man?* After previews in New Orleans, the tour schedule included sixteen locations in three months. Additionally, the Free Southern Theater sponsored a Community Writing Workshop in the summer, and held acting workshops and a seminar in creative writing and black literature. But the company continued to war about where to focus its attentions. As Dent observes in a letter to Denise Nicholas Moses in June 1966, "The company is now on the verge of psychic disintegration, because of the smoldering conflict over the course of the theater which has now broken into open flame."[36] The fight seems to have been between those in the company, such as Dent, who wanted to focus the primary energies on productions, and those in the company (Denise Nicholas Moses and Roscoe Orman) who wanted to conduct community outreach through workshops. There is very little documentation about how the touring season in 1966 went. Tom Dent writes that the group's program succeeded in "capturing for many the spirit of black pride and consciousness that the Movement was also undergoing at that time."[37]

Roots' premise is not dependent on presenting authentic "blackness" through representations of historical injustices against African-Americans, as *In White America.* It is based firmly in the avant-garde theater wing of the Black Arts Movement. Driven by black consciousness, the subjecthood of Dot and Ray is not seen as inspirational or revolutionary. They are unmasked. The characters of Dot and Ray, described by Moses as "an old Negro couple, to be played by young actors," are, respectively, dressed in a gas mask and adorned with a giant cotton bag. The entire one-act play is staged in their kitchen. Repetition fuels their lives. Dot asks Ray to wash up, Ray picks cotton everyday, even out of season, because that is what he does. Moses brilliantly constructs African-Americans who are defined through their ability to be constant, loyal, and silently present. At the end of the play, Ray uncharacteristically shouts, "I HAVE QUESTIONS, LORD," after which he slips on preserves and falls into a rat trap. Dot murmurs, "Do you think all old Negro men are like you?"—meaning, do you think all black men can do nothing, just like you? And, to the audience: Don't you think all black men can do nothing, just like Ray? Ray's weaknesses expose the audience's desire to see him fail. There is no triumph over adversity in *Roots* as there is in *In White America*.

Mythmaking and Community Building

I was born in 1965, yet I have no memory of the civil rights movement in the South, a surprising fact since I lived in Raleigh, North Carolina, from 1969 to 1972. My childhood southern playmates were reflective of the college town I lived in. Many ethnicities; none were southerners. But my mother tells one story. She worked part-time for a phone company that decided, in 1971, to integrate the workforce. One black man was hired, and he worked the second shift with my mother. During the dinner break, no one in the crowded dining hall would sit at whichever immense, communal table he chose to sit at. No one, except my German immigrant mother. Soon he was no longer there, to eat or to work. Of course, I have no true knowledge of why this man stopped working. Retrospectively, however, he gives me a secondhand experience of the failure of the phone company's institutionalized integration policy. They did not recognize the importance of fostering a *community* of African-Americans and progressive-minded whites within the company to create an integrated workforce. This lack of community-building could not challenge the historical formation of the two separate communities of the South, black and white. What the Black Arts Movement gave the Free Southern Theater was an artistic means of expression, a way of generating an identity that was not dependent on integration. The Free Southern Theater took their creative penultimate step in the path of the civil rights movement in order to jump into the Black Arts Movement. The theater company that became the Free Southern Theater was a product of both these movements. The Free Southern Theater was never formally part of the urban, northern-based Black Arts Movement. Its gestation occurred as part of the civil rights movement, and its artistic maturity was guided by the spirit of the Black Arts Movement. The spirit was one of cultural mythmaking that was inclusive of multiple sources, not racially, ethnically or geographically bound, and driven by the desire to create a new, southern black subjecthood through an artistic community.

NOTES

Many thanks to Jan Cohen-Cruz, James Harding, André Lepecki, and Cindy Rosenthal for comments on the manuscript and encouragement; to Leni McCollor, André Lepecki, and Mariah Ingwerson for childcare during a crucial period of writing; and to Robyn Cooper, Kristin Lombard, and Miles Simmons for helping me through.

1. Thomas C. Dent, Richard Schechner, and Gilbert Moses, *The Free Southern Theater by The Free Southern Theater* (Indianapolis: Bobbs-Merrill, 1969), 163.

2. Floyd Gaffney, "The Free Southern Theater: Not Just Survival," in *The Crisis*, January, 1978, 20.

3. Dent, Schechner, and Moses, *Free Southern Theater,* 99.

4. Ibid., 4.

5. David R. Goldfield, *In Black, White, and Southern: Race Relations and Southern Culture, 1940 to the Present* (Baton Rouge: Louisiana State University Press, 1990), 155.

6. Dent, Schechner, and Moses, *Free Southern Theater,* 6.

7. Ibid., 3.

8. Nancy Cunard, editor, *Negro: An Anthology* (1934; New York: Negro Universities Press, 1969), 39.

9. Jan Cohen-Cruz, "Comforting the Afflicted and Afflicting the Comfortable: The Legacy of Free Southern Theater," in this volume.

10. Dent, Schechner, and Moses, *Free Southern Theater,* 9–10.

11. Richard Schechner, quoted in Cohen-Cruz, "Comforting the Afflicted."

12. Ibid.

13. Not to be confused with the 1970s television miniseries of the same name.

14. For the first touring season of the Free Southern Theater in 1964, it was announced that the company would tackle a range of plays that reflect the integrationist tendencies of the board of directors. These were never produced by the Free Southern Theater: Langston Hughes's *Don't You Want to be Free?;* John O. Killens's *Lower Than the Angels;* Douglas Turner Ward's two one-act plays, *Day of Absence* and *Happy Ending;* Ann Flagg's *Great Getting' Up Mornin';* and an adaptation (by O'Neal and Moses, never completed) of *Antigone.* Like theater groups at traditionally black colleges in the late 1950s and early 1960s, black community and professional theater companies tended to gravitate toward the well-made classics such as *Antigone* and the propaganda/message plays of a past era. Tellingly, there were no published integration-themed plays written by African-Americans, with the exception of *A Raisin in the Sun* by Lorraine Hansberry (1959).

15. Lorraine Hansberry, *The Movement: Documentary of a Struggle for Equality* (New York: Simon and Schuster, 1964), 117. With the "cooperation and assistance" of the Student Nonviolent Coordinating Committee (SNCC). The Zinn essay, "The Battle-Scarred Youngsters," is reprinted in *Reporting Civil Rights* (New York: Library of America, 2003), 2:48–59. To read statements by Fannie Lou Hamer, Annelle Ponder, and June E. Johnson on beatings they received from sitting down at a segregated lunch counter in Winona, Mississippi, in June 1963, see *Reporting Civil Rights,* 1:836–44.

16. John O'Neal, "Motion in the Ocean: Some Political Dimensions of the Free Southern Theater (1968)," in Bean, *Sourcebook,* 119.

17. Kimberly W. Benston, *Performing Blackness: Enactments of African-American Modernism* (London: Routledge, 2000), 25.

18. Larry Neal, *Visions of a Liberated Future: Black Arts Movement Writings*, ed. Michael Schwartz (New York: Thunder's Mouth Press, 1989), 65.

19. LeRoi Jones, "The Revolutionary Theatre," *Liberator* 5, no. 7 (1965): 5.

20. Mike Sell, "The Black Arts Movement: Performance, Neo-Orality, and the Destruction of the 'White Thing,'" in *African American Performance and Theater History: A Critical Reader*, ed. Harry J. Elam Jr. and David Krasner (New York: Oxford University Press, 2001), 67. Sell is quoting James Stewart, a founder of the North Philadelphia Muntu reading group, along with essayist Larry Neal and playwright Charles Fuller.

21. The movement had brought black northerners Moses, O'Neal, and Derby to Mississippi, specifically SNCC's organizing around the issue of the Voter Rights Act. Soon, Derby faded out of the picture, and Richard Schechner, a white, Jewish, Tulane University professor of theater, joined the artistic cause. Though Schechner was not a member of SNCC, he could be said to represent many of the white, educated young people who came to Mississippi and Alabama in the Freedom Summer of 1964 to guarantee media coverage of the abuses served upon those states' black populations and on the black SNCC workers. Schechner also served as a double representative, as did the longtime Free Southern Theater actor Murray Levy, of liberal, second-generation Jewish participation in American social causes. In the beginning, O'Neal and Moses in particular wanted to have a professional theater touring company. Eventually, once the company moved to Desire in New Orleans in 1966, the company became a mixture of professionals and amateurs. It also became an almost all-black company, the exception being Murray Levy, who acted and directed with the company until 1967, leaving out of exhaustion.

22. There is very little description of the production itself, beyond "highly professional and compared very favorably to the original" (illustrating a determined New York bias nonetheless). Elizabeth Sutherland, "Theatre of the Meaningful," *The Nation*, October 19, 1964, reprinted in Dent, Schechner, and Moses, *Free Southern Theater*, 24–29. Sutherland also remarks that Denise Nicholas Moses does an admirable job with the Little Rock, Arkansas, scene of the play, done in New York by the great African-American actress Gloria Foster.

23. Ibid., 28.

24. Ibid., 26. Also see Fred Friendly, David Schoenbrun, and William Peters, producers, "Mississippi and the 15th Amendment," *CBS Reports*, 1962 (Princeton, N.J.: Films for the Humanities and Sciences, 2000).

25. Martin Duberman, *In White America: A Documentary Play* (Boston: Houghton Mifflin, 1964), vi.

26. Clarissa Myrick Harris, "Mirror of the Movement: The History of the Free Southern Theater as a Microcosm of the Civil Rights and Black Power Movements, 1963–1978," Ph.D. diss., Emory University, 1988, 27.

27. Ibid., 28 n. 18.

28. Dent, Schechner, and Moses, *Free Southern Theater*, 18.

29. Ibid.

30. Ibid.

31. Janet Rose Kenney, "The Free Southern Theater: The Relationship between Mission and Management," Ph.D. diss., University of Oregon, 1987, 65 n. 1.

32. Ibid., 19.
33. Dent, Schechner, and Moses, *Free Southern Theater,* 72–73, 86–87.
34. Ibid., 98–99.
35. Levy directed every segment of the evening except for *Roots.* Robert Costley directed *Roots.*
36. Dent, Schechner, and Moses, *Free Southern Theater,* 114.
37. Dent, Schechner, and Moses, *Free Southern Theater,* 133.

COMFORTING THE AFFLICTED AND
AFFLICTING THE COMFORTABLE

The Legacy of the Free Southern Theater

Jan Cohen-Cruz

A preacher and a storyteller have somewhat the same job: to comfort the afflicted and afflict the comfortable.
—Junebug Jabbo Jones

Picture four black-and-white photographs,[1] each portraying a stunningly bright New Orleans day in November 1985. In the center of the first, a black man in dark pants and a white blazer, a sash across his chest, holds a fringed umbrella up high. Behind him lies a casket, and to his right, five African-American musicians play brass and percussion. On the mouth of the tuba, spelled out with electrical tape, are the words Rebirth Jazz Band. Thus was the Free Southern Theater, inspired into existence by the civil rights movement, laid to rest.

The second image is a close-up of the casket with a folded piece of paper and a few roses on top. Mourners included members of activist theaters such as Carpetbag from Knoxville, Tennessee, Roadside from Whitesburg, Kentucky, Atlanta's Jomandi Productions and A Traveling Jewish Theatre from the San Francisco Bay Area. Past Free Southern Theater members including Chakula Cha Jua of New Orleans' ACT I and Albert Bostick with the Black Theatre Ensemble of Oklahoma City were invited to put items like old costumes, props, and scripts into the coffin. It also contained a broken mirror. Reflected therein, mourners could see that they were losing a part of themselves in the theater's demise. Music and dancing continued through the night. The next morning, following a eulogy, the funeral party traversed from the theater to the burial place in Armstrong Park in front of Perseverance Hall II in Congo Square. Jim O'Quinn recounts: "One of the bands strikes up a brass-heavy version of 'Just a Closer Walk with Thee' and the funeral marshal . . . begins the slow, bowing prance of the jazz funeral processional."[2]

The third photo depicts the slow procession to the grave site. Leading the way is Ben Stillman, a Free Southern Theater veteran and actual parade marshal, umbrella outstretched, followed by the musicians, pallbearers, and a long line of mourners, black and white. The last words are spoken for the departed before consigning the casket to the grave. The band begins the second line, upbeat and jazzy, leading everyone out of the cemetery to celebrate the deceased's life. The last photo is dominated by joyful faces singing; O'Quinn describes a "clamorous chorus of 'Ain't Gonna Study War No More' followed by 'We Shall Overcome,' giving way to 'Good Golly Miss Molly.'"[3] The central figure in the photo, a handsome, bearded African-American man in his forties, exudes energy. He is John O'Neal, who, as a sort of secular preacher, orchestrated the funeral (with a small committee guided by Wayne Coleman)[4] and eulogized the company, having cofounded it in 1963 with Doris Derby and Gil Moses.

The Free Southern Theater funeral had a dual purpose, reflected in its title: "A Funeral for the Free Southern Theater. A Valediction without Mourning: The Role of the Arts for Social Change." It marked the death of the Free Southern Theater at the same time that it affirmed the continuity of activist theater. The brilliant choice to do so via a jazz funeral—a southern, African-American ritual—underlined the Free Southern Theater's cultural role as a southern, African-American instrument of the civil rights movement. By marking the death of the theater *and* the movement by way of the funeral ritual, O'Neal articulated how intrinsically the Free Southern Theater had been sutured to the civil rights movement and how deeply both had been expressions of southern, African-American culture and spirituality. But the New Orleans jazz funeral also communicates the ongoing life of the departed's spirit, in the postburial phase of visiting all the places where that spirit flourished and collectively celebrating that life. In conjoining the funeral with a three-day conference of theater for social change, O'Neal celebrated the spirit of the Free Southern Theater and declared that though it was no more, its spirit lived on in activist theater.

The message did not fall on deaf ears. Caron Atlas, who later worked closely with O'Neal, described the event's impact:

> The funeral told me there was another way that art and politics connected beside what I was so familiar with—activism in the service of other causes but with artists as the primary constituents. The Free Southern Theater's notion of theater tied to a social movement went beyond artists. Theater companies inspired by the Free Southern were challenged to ask, rather than just being an ally with another group's struggle, how do you do this with your own people, within your own context and culture?[5]

With stunning prescience, the Free Southern Theater funeral marked the death of not only the civil rights movement but of many of the national political endeavors of the 1960s and 1970s. Still, as O'Neal "preached" through the "valediction without mourning" at the funeral, the integration of art and social change continued. The Free Southern Theater's legacy was manifested directly in Junebug Productions, the company that O'Neal had begun a few years earlier, and in the community-based theater movement more generally, which took up the torch from U.S. political theater of the 1960s and 1970s.[6] The question Atlas poses, how can a theater support struggles in its/our own context and culture, gave local direction to the next phase of art and activism in the United States. In the sections that follow, I shall examine the Free Southern Theater's legacy in Junebug Productions and U.S. community-based performance, tracing the theater's legacy as an artistic initiative allied directly to a political movement serving the interests of poor and oppressed people.

From the Free Southern Theater to Junebug Productions

The Free Southern Theater and its successor, Junebug Productions, are rooted in the rural culture of the Black-belt South and its proud traditions of resistance.

—John O'Neal, in *A Sourcebook of African-American Performance*

O'Neal's ability to grasp the big picture, evidenced in his construction of the Free Southern Theater funeral, manifested itself early on. Enrolling at Southern Illinois University, O'Neal had considered pursuing theology before committing to English and philosophy and deciding to become a playwright. Graduating in 1962, he took to heart Richard Burton's avowal that it takes at least twenty years to become a decent, "not even a good," actor. Aspiring to be an actor *and* playwright, O'Neal reasoned that he'd need at least twenty-five years. But he was consumed by dramatic developments in the civil rights movement. He believed that what was happening in the South was the most important thing in the world at that time, yet he'd devised a twenty-five-year plan that began in New York. O'Neal identified this dilemma within a religious context; defining sin as "the divergence between your ideas and your actions," O'Neal was compelled to conjoin his ideas and actions and head south to work with the movement.[7]

Settling in Mississippi, O'Neal became a field director for SNCC, the Student Nonviolent Coordinating Committee. He soon understood that the fight for civil rights was not going to be quickly resolved, followed by his return to New York: "I realized that this was not a problem of the south, though it had a particular vulnerability there, but of the whole system. This is a lifetime of work. So am I going to give up my ambition to write? Is there a coherent solution to the problem of being an artist and part of a movement for social change?"[8]

In 1963 O'Neal met Doris Derby, a painter who was also a field director for SNCC, and Gil Moses, a writer for the *Mississippi Free Press,* and together they founded the Free Southern Theater. Moses sent a copy of the theater's prospectus to Richard Schechner, at the time a drama professor at Tulane University in New Orleans, beginning a conversation that led to Schechner's becoming codirector in 1964.[9] Schechner recently articulated to me the theater's utter interdependence with the movement:

> SNCC was part and parcel of the theater. That's how we got our contacts and venues, knew where to go when we came into a town, who to see to help us get established. This was not like a conventional touring show; we needed to be immediately welcomed into the community. We needed safe places, especially since we were blacks and whites, men and women, traveling together. Without the movement we wouldn't have had the physical wherewithal. And then ideologically, the movement gave us a goal, a way of choosing our repertory.[10]

Schechner suggests that Free Southern Theater actors took not only emotional risks, as expected in theater, but also the physical risk that emanated from "blacks and whites, men and women" traveling together in the segregated South.

The Free Southern Theater was both part of a tradition and an innovator in U.S. activist art. In the 1920s and 1930s, for example, many U.S.

workers formed theater companies to support progressive causes. In contrast, Free Southern Theater members were trained theater people bringing their expertise to serve shared political goals. Though other companies of the time, like the San Francisco Mime Troupe and, even earlier, the Living Theatre, were committed to their art's relevance to contemporary political struggles, neither was as closely connected to a movement as the Free Southern Theater, as evidenced in O'Neal's and Derby's joint work for SNCC. Furthermore, although the relationship was complicated, the church held an important position within the movement as one of the few places that black people could gather without interference. The movement's link to the black church and more basically, the church's role in the cultural life of the black South, provided the Free Southern Theater with a particular moral and spiritual orientation. And while artists of the Harlem Renaissance (1919–29) also created work that served the African-American community (interestingly, Langston Hughes gave the Free Southern Theater its first contribution), the Free Southern was the first black-led theater of the South.

The Free Southern Theater was only possible because the 1960s and 1970s was a time of vigorous political engagement. SNCC's embrace of the ensemble is evidence of an appreciation of culture's role in a movement for social change. In the same spirit, El Teatro Campesino synchronized its efforts with César Chávez and the farmworkers' struggle, and Bread and Puppet accompanied the antiwar movement. Free Southern Theater's death says as much about the profound shift in the political climate as it does about a theater company's perennial struggle to survive. The movement itself splintered in the 1970s, as leaders died violently and different agendas were pursued by different factions. Though this essay is not the place to elaborate, internal tensions also tore the Free Southern Theater apart: what managerial and aesthetic style to embrace, whether to bring in professional actors or develop local amateurs, and whether to adapt a model of integration or of black nationalism. O'Neal avowed recently that the Free Southern Theater was always a black theater company. Just as African-Americans attending mainstream universities does not make those institutions integrated as long as they are controlled by white people, so a few white actors in the Free Southern Theater does not make it any less a black theater.[11]

Under Thomas Dent's leadership, the Free Southern Theater had frequently cast community performers, replacing Moses and O'Neal's earlier practice of hiring professionals.[12] In the last days of the Free Southern Theater, O'Neal felt it was exploitative to continue creating plays with unpaid local people who had to work day jobs and rehearse evenings, which was simply not enough time. So in 1979, O'Neal made a decision "to exploit myself" and make a solo show. Impressed by Hal Holbrook's *Mark Twain Tonight*, O'Neal considered basing his piece on W. E. B. DuBois. But he realized that he was too young to portray such a figure without extensive makeup. Then he thought to portray Paul Robeson, but James Earl Jones had recently opened a Robeson show on Broadway. So taking inspiration from Langston Hughes, who wrote about everyday characters as a result of listening to people in Harlem bars, O'Neal decided to create a character based on Junebug.

SNCC people had invented Junebug in the early 1960s as a representation of the wisdom of common people in the long tradition of cultural characters such as Anansi the spider and Uncle Remus, keepers of dreams, wily underdogs with strong survival mechanisms. These characters play a role parallel to O'Neal's own: passing on a rich cultural legacy. O'Neal began collecting stories about Junebug—dubbing him Junebug Jabbo Jones, and developing tales that emphasized such values as wit and humor to oppose power. O'Neal's characters speak right to the audience, telling stories and singing songs gathered from a broad cross-section of people. O'Neal has continued the Free Southern Theater's work through Junebug, celebrating the African-American community and supporting resistance to oppression, grounded in black oral tradition.

Junebug productions—three solo and two multicharacter plays featuring John as Junebug—are usually directed by freelancer Steve Kent.[13] The company is one of a number of progressive theaters capably managed by Theresa and Michael Holden. (Kent and the Holdens are white, reminding me that even as O'Neal considered the Free Southern Theater a black organization with white people in it, so is Junebug Productions.) Kent describes Junebug's aesthetic as "transformational theater" and "character-based storytelling."[14] Watching Kent and O'Neal working together on the solo plays in early 2002, I observed that Kent did not direct in the conventional sense but rather served as an adjunct to O'Neal's memory. "I think you sit on the plank at that line, John," Kent coached when O'Neal seemed unsure of where he was. Indeed, the degree to which O'Neal relies on his physical location to keep the lines flowing is strong, suggesting his body as a legacy of the work.

O'Neal's storytelling has a spiritual dimension. In keeping with his role as "secular preacher," his solo performances, each with its moral center, strike me as excellent dramatic sermons. Moreover, as Kent explains, the works' roots in African-American and African traditions are essential: "In all of the pieces, John sanctifies the space. We sprinkle water around the performance space every time we do it. We expect the audience, in

John O'Neal in *Junebug Jabbo Jones,* vol. 1, 1980. (Photo courtesy of John O'Neal.)

some way, to interact with the performers the way black audiences tend to do because of their church training."[15] O'Neal combines culturally syntonic forms, in this case oral tradition and ritual elements, with contemporary content, which has become a hallmark of the community-based performance aesthetic, also evident in groups like Roadside Theater and A Traveling Jewish Theatre.

O'Neal wrote the first Junebug play, *Don't Start Me Talking or I'll Tell Everything I Know; Sayings from the Life and Writings of Junebug Jabbo Jones* (1980) with help from Ron Castine and Glenda Lindsay. Its first production was directed by Curtis L. King. It introduces a world of cotton fields, church, and jails typical of the rural black South. In an epilogue, Junebug sums up the point of the play: "Can't nobody ride your back unless you first bend over." The second Junebug play, *You Can't Tell a Book by Looking at the Cover* (1985), written with Nayo Watkins, takes the audience through changing race relationships midcentury. With some resonance of Malcolm X, the main character, "Po' Tatum," stands for the many black youths who moved from their rural, southern homes to the cold northern cities. In the third, *Till the Midnight Hour* (2000), O'Neal tells stories about several kinds of villains and what it takes to straighten oneself out. He begins with the story of "Amazing Grace," written, amazingly enough, by a white slave ship captain. In a terrible storm, the captain promises

God he'll give up slaving if he makes it back to England. He does, and disregards his promise. At sea again, in an even worse storm, he promises again, writes this song, then back on land gives up slaving and becomes a preacher. Focusing then on a scoundrel called Bo Willie Boudreaux, the play meditates on a set of questions: "What would it take to save Bo Willie? How far would he and people like him have to go before we'd have to say he's irredeemable? When does the eleventh hour turn to midnight?" (undated Junebug publicity material). Structurally, the plays tease out themes through an assortment of stories, not one narrative line.

Approaches developed by the Free Southern Theater have become part of Junebug's process. Nayo Watkins, O'Neal's collaborator on *Junebug II,* descibes the significance of having started at Black Arts South, Free Southern Theater's writers' wing, directed by core Free Southern members Tom Dent and Val Ferdinand (Kalamu): "People were not writing in a vacuum. When you came to the weekly meetings with your writing, everyone had a piece about what just went down. I didn't think of myself as a writer but as a freedom fighter."[16] The sense of the writer expressing more than herself, continues Watkins, carried over to the 1980s and Junebug: "I've continued to ask, Where's the action? What am I supposed to be writing about? If I can't touch where the need is, address what things are really about, why would I write? Those of us who went through that training, so to speak, cannot get away from the fact that the work has to be relevant to something going on."[17] Watkins describes the Junebug playwrighting process as

> going to the people, doing in-depth interviews, making the play, taking it back to those people and asking, are we doing it right? Then revising and bringing it to the stage. My work has evolved from that, drawing on oral history, lore, folk story, and historical accounts, to build dramatic pieces with many voices and broad ownership. I've also been influenced by how John digs for political analysis; even if the story is gentle, it reflects a strong political statement.[18]

Watkins continues to embrace a model of playwright as voice of a people's aspirations and struggles.

The Junebug cycle teaches and preaches through storytelling. As Junebug Jabbo Jones puts it: "A preacher and a storyteller have somewhat the same job: to comfort the afflicted and afflict the comfortable." O'Neal connects these two cultural figures, suggesting that artists also have a moral dimension and preachers are also mindful of aesthetics. Similarly, the black church was dependent on the preacher's oratorical skills and the participants' embrace of the power of song to keep up their spirits. O'Neal is also talking about himself, as renowned for his steadfast commitment to art that makes a difference in the lives of poor and oppressed people—comforting the afflicted—as for the relentless standard to which he holds other activist-artists—afflicting the comfortable. And in explaining why he calls himself a storyteller, O'Neal as Junebug seems to chide his spectator-congregants to be vigilantly truthful: "A liar's somebody trying to cover things over, mainly for his own private benefit. But a storyteller's somebody trying to uncover things so everybody can get something good out of it. So I'm a storyteller. It's a heap of good meaning to be found in a story if you got a mind to hear." At times humorous, at other times unbearably sad, the world of actions and ideas into which O'Neal transports us emerges through the stories themselves, never devolving into political rhetoric.

Junebug also continues the Free Southern Theater's work by drawing on contacts from the civil rights era. The Environmental Justice Project, a multiyear effort begun in 1993 in O'Neal's home turf of New Orleans, brought together environmental and arts groups to highlight environmental racism, such as the high rate of cancer in poor neighborhoods of color. This work is in a great tradition of art to support, encourage, and celebrate "those things that are good for a community, and to expose those things that are bad for a community."[19] Environmentalist Robert Bullard, a project participant, believes that the images and stories facilitate an understanding of environmental justice as a major issue: "I can talk and talk about the number of toxic particulates in the air, but you see a photograph of children playing next to leaking chemicals and it is clear."[20] Longtime Free Southern Theater associate Ron Chisolm, now director of the People's Institute for Survival and Beyond, facilitated workshops in undoing racism for the artists and partners. M. K. Wegmann, a former managing director of Junebug Productions, states that although there is "no civil rights movement nationally anymore, there is ongoing civil rights work. The people Free Southern Theater touched and influenced continue to be leaders."[21]

A Legacy in Southern, African-American, and Community-Based Theater

There are those who view art as . . . all about giving individuals . . . the prerogative to express their feelings and views. There are others who see art as part of the process of the individual in the context of community and the community coming to consciousness of itself.

In the first case, the artist is seen as a symbol of the antagonistic relationship between the individual and society. In the second case,
the artist symbolizes the individual within the context of a dynamic
relationship with a community. . . . Obviously the latter view is the
one that I identify with. . . . That gives basis to the notion that the
artist is a vehicle for a force greater than him- or herself . . . it includes the whole spirit life that we participate in, as well as the
whole political, social and economic life.
> —John O'Neal, in Kate Hammer, "John O'Neal,
> Actor and Activist"

The Free Southern Theater became the prototype for the contemporary
community-based arts movement by virtue of its hyphenated identity. Its
commitment to art integrated in a movement for social change meant considerable attention had to be paid to strategies of both art and movement.
Companies that have drawn inspiration from the Free Southern Theater
have gone beyond the conventional boundaries of aesthetics in defining
their relationship to their audiences and communities.

According to Thomas Dent, the Free Southern Theater introduced the
idea of black community theater in the South, "that coming together, the
ensemble quality of theater, the interaction of performers with audiences,
that made community theater a very fine medium for carrying forth cultural questions and ideas."[22] Dent identifies a number of theaters that developed in New Orleans as descendants: Dashiki, Nat Turner, Ethiopian,
Congo Square, and Act I Theater and Festival. M. K. Wegmann believes
that the Free Southern Theater's political stance challenged both black
and white theaters in New Orleans: "They didn't exactly replicate the little
theater model."[23] That is, in contrast to regional theaters' emulation of the
little theaters' focus on new European techniques, the Free Southern
chose plays for their relevance to civil rights. Wegmann describes the
1960s and 1970s as a renaissance for New Orleans theaters—black, white,
traditional, experimental—which have usually had a hard time surviving
there. Most important was access to a range of companies with different
aesthetics and politics. The legacy of the Free Southern Theater, adds Wegmann, was also passed on through classes that company members taught
at local schools: "A number of people involved in New Orleans theater
now were in high school or college then. Chakula Cha Jua—he studied
with the Free Southern Theater and is still directing in town."[24]

While appreciating the Free Southern Theater as the first integrated,
in the familiar sense of the word, theater in the city, O'Quinn notes that
it also "spun off successful [commercial] careers like that of director
Gilbert Moses and television actress Denise Nicholas."[25] Perhaps the

greatest number of people were affected by Moses, who, as director of two episodes of *Roots,* based on Alex Haley's famous 1976 book, was the only highly placed African-American in the creation of the $6 million miniseries that told American history from an African-American point of view. One of the most watched miniseries in TV history, the concluding episode was seen by 130 million viewers, nearly half the national population. Though it did not lead immediately to the expansion of black TV, it did lead to more television specials with black participation.[26] James Cromwell, the Oscar-winning actor (for best supporting actor in *Babe*) and director, always acknowledges the Free Southern Theater's importance to his development.

The Free Southern Theater's work with the civil rights movement also influenced black artists and companies in the North. Beth Turner, founder-editor of *Black Masques,* asserts, "Probably most black theater started as community initiatives—a Mobilization for Youth project in New York City became New Federal Theatre when they hired Woody King Jr. New Lafayette, also in New York, was allied to an antipoverty agenda. Charles Fuller came out of Philadelphia, writing skits for community action organizations to get people to deal with community problems."[27] Turner describes one project in which Fuller's actors staged a robbery, chased the supposed thieves into the theater, and then talked about the issue with the audience.

O'Neal helped found three organizations to support politically progressive artists. The point, states O'Neal, was that "the problems of oppressed and exploited people exceed the capacity of any one of those people to solve by themselves. They can only be solved by collective action, which includes aggregating our resources."[28] The purpose of the first, the Southern Black Cultural Association (1974), was to facilitate support among black theaters. Although plagued with money problems, the SBCA played a positive role in the growth of activist artists, as Nayo Watkins recently reflected.

> Several of us from the Free Southern Theater moved away. The SBCA kept a group of us who were doing, as Tom Dent said, "this work which tries to move communities," in touch with each other. We met once a year, and in between time communicated through newsletters and the phone, sharing original work. Young people were brought in to meet the older ones. In New Orleans it evolved into the Congo Square Writers. McNeil [aka Chakula Cha Jua] was part of it; he founded ACT I—Association of Community Theaters, Inc.—which became a younger generation of folks doing the same

thing. When I went back to New Orleans, I found young people reading and performing my poetry.[29]

Connecting communities segregated by race and class characterizes the two other organizations that O'Neal helped shape, Alternate ROOTS and American Festival Project. Like the Free Southern Theater, both groups have also emphasized partnerships with organizations committed to the same political goals. The first gathering of what would become Alternate ROOTS—Regional Organization of Theaters South—took place in 1976 at the Highlander Research and Education Center in New Market, Tennessee. Highlander was already a renowned grassroots activist organization with an appreciation of culture's role in social change. Representatives of about a dozen companies including O'Neal's met to discuss how they could best share their resources and skills. Dudley Cocke, director of the Appalachian Roadside Theater, just a year old at the time, remembers their focus as southern theater sharing "a history in the civil rights and anti-war movements and a feel for rural life."[30] O'Neal recounts that he was drawn in to ROOTS because of Cocke's responsiveness to O'Neal's concern about the national increase in Ku Klux Klan activities. Ruby Lerner, executive director during ROOTS' formative years, describes the new association as both an arts organization and "a grass roots cultural movement, peculiar to the South, whose aim is to be part of the transformation of the region—by acknowledging and critically assessing its past, particularly with regard to race, uncovering its buried history and untold stories, and celebrating its heroes."[31] Such a model is resonant of the mission of the Free Southern Theater, which went beyond the creation of theater.

ROOTS' stated mission is "to support the creation and presentation of original art that is rooted in a particular community of place, tradition or spirit. As cultural workers, we strive to be allies in the elimination of all forms of oppression. ROOTS is committed to social and economic justice and the protection of the natural world and addresses these concerns through its programs and services."[32] ROOTS features an annual meeting where members share performances, workshops, and discussions of the issues they address separately the rest of the year. They publish newsletters and, funds permitting, provide financial and touring support. The Community/Artist Partnership Program, for example, "supports artists developing healthier relationships in their communities, whether at home or on the road."[33] According to Steve Kent, the common denominator at ROOTS was people who were "antiracist, antisexist, alternative, grassroots, weird, fun, kooky, playful, and had that delicious southern-style gift of gab and generosity of spirit. I don't think it's an accident that linguistically, the South is the only place with a plural inclusive in the English language: 'y'all.'"[34] Kent affirms the peer-to-peer validation ROOTS provided. According to Nayo Watkins, "ROOTS is the only place we find the intersection of white and black activist artists. It's stated, intended, and sometimes even practiced."[35]

Despite the fact that O'Neal chaired ROOTS for three years and Cocke did so for two, in recent years both have distanced themselves from the organization because of theoretical and strategic differences. The breakpoint for O'Neal was his perception that most people involved in ROOTS were on a different road: just wanting to do their work and not taking the time to seriously argue out the direction of the community-based arts movement. He also believed that ROOTS did not focus enough on the role of race in the development of American culture, especially in the South. O'Neal sums up: "To get people involved, we cast too broad a net and backed away from clarifying the central principles around which we are organizing. All these people's good intentions were taken for the work."[36]

Though O'Neal has stepped back from ROOTS, he hasn't quit; he recognizes that *some* valuable conversations go on there and still often attends the annual meeting. He spoke highly of the last executive director, African-American writer Alice Lovelace, and of newly elected Euronne Vaughn. From my perspective, ROOTS plays a unique role in connecting community artists from the southeast United States and elsewhere. Many ROOTERs are rural artists, marginalized during the rest of the year, who need a community with which to connect socially as well as politically. And politics is still on the ROOTS agenda; an 'undoing racism' committee, for example, regularly offers workshops at the annual meeting. But O'Neal sees three contingents of artists at ROOTS these days: new vaudevillians, the political, and the avant-garde. This raises a question that regularly accompanies legacy—how can a field sustain a range of members, necessary for its ongoing existence, while continuing to nurture those focused on the original emphasis?

In 1982, Cocke and O'Neal developed the idea of the American Festival Project (AFP) as an expression of their desire to work with artists who had a sharper political focus. According to O'Neal, "The fact that we also produced what we called back then 'world-class art' was a fortunate coincidence."[37] The first AFP was produced by Bob Martin at the People's Center in San Francisco and also included the Traveling Jewish Theatre. Over the years other companies—such as El Teatro de la Esperanza, Liz Lerman Dance Exchange, and Urban Bush Women—also based in particular constituencies and with compatible political goals, joined the initiative. The festivals address social issues through performances and workshops via long-term residencies in small towns across the United States. Caron Atlas, first director of the AFP, elaborates: "The AFP is committed to shining a light on local culture . . . where you are from has a profound effect on what you have to say. . . . Cultural and geographical diversity go together."[38]

Significantly, AFP is not reliant on national political activity. In the absence of an active national movement for social justice, Atlas sees the AFP's work around local concerns as building toward a national dialogue. O'Neal quotes Tip O'Neill to assert that "all politics is local"; the local contributes to the broader effort.[39] People on a micro-level can decide what is important to them and act accordingly. But they must be ever mindful of others who share such struggles, to avoid what O'Neal describes as a kind of chauvinism, while taking advantage of organizing possibilities on every local horizon. Examples of AFP residencies include Junebug Productions' Environmental Justice Project in New Orleans, a project initiated by the University of Louisville to deal with incidents of ethno-violence and rape; and a project in the multiethnic working-class towns of Lewistown and Auburn, Maine, focused on economic difficulties and plant closings.

Through residencies all across the nation, AFP has also played an important role in propagating community-based art techniques. The most pervasive is the story circle, a process of story collecting, sharing, and exchanging that takes place in a circle. O'Neal emphasizes that everyone is equal in a circle, and each person must be able to see everyone else.[40] Typically, a group generates a theme, and then each person takes three to five minutes to tell a personal tale that the theme evokes. Most important, everyone else listens. Then there's cross-conversation about what's come up and some time for summing up at the end. Story circles frequently lead to other activities, such as collective creation of plays.

It is impossible to identify any one originator, but certainly O'Neal has played a role in the story circle's dissemination. For him, it is philosophically rooted in Free Southern Theater's principle of dialoguing with the communities that they were supporting. Rather than tell people what to do, the Free Southern Theater strove to create performances that stimulated discussion and development. Junebug Productions' partnership with Roadside also emphasized discussion with the community rather than setting themselves up as authorities. The exchange of stories has proved to be a better way of having dialogue than argument, explains O'Neal.

Adversarial debates reward people who are trained in their techniques. Those tend to be people who have the largest vocabularies
and largest egos and most willingness to claim ground and hold it.
Which merely affirms the problem you're starting with in the first
place. How can we get past this? I knew the power of the circle itself. So instead of standing on stage and answering questions, I
moved off the stage and sat in the audience and said, "Let's talk.
What do you think?" And then I asked, "Why don't you tell me a
story that the experience of the theater evoked in you?"[41]

To equalize the dynamic between extroverts and introverts, they made a
circle and took turns.

Presently, AFP is in the throes of an organizational shift precipitated
by the inclusion of some new artists, not all performance-based, and a
new director. O'Neal left because of a disagreement with the new leadership and the direction of the organization. Initially, AFP was a collaboration among people who thought they had a shared political perspective
and vision. But O'Neal now contends that they hadn't had sufficient discussion, leaving the basis of their politics implicit, not explicit. Atlas also
identifies tensions that the AFP has wrestled with from the beginning.
Should they stay a small coalition or open up? Should Appalshop, located
in Whitesburg, Kentucky, remain AFP's organizational home? On the one
hand, Appalshop can provide the necessary infrastructure, is the home of
AFP cofounder Dudley Cocke and Roadside Theater, and was Atlas's operational base as its developmental director. On the other hand, though
AFP has always acted autonomously, O'Neal found it problematic for an
organization of color to be based somewhere that hiring people of color
is nearly impossible.

O'Neal sees the ideas that came to characterize all three organizations—the Southern Black Cultural Association, ROOTS, and the AFP—
as too broad to be useful:

We say we're progressive, and yet we have such diverse ideas in the
arts about what it is we're supposed to do. For me, the arts are an instrument for a people's consolidation—to identify what's important
to us and celebrate and advance those things that contribute to our
abilities to live more effectively and better, to identify those things
that are dangerous to us and push those to the side, and to help
people come to grips and clarify those things. So our political goals,
what would be helpful to our collective best interests, must take priority and stand at the center of the artistic enterprise.[42]

In contrast, O'Neal perceives that most of his colleagues in the field see politics as coincidental: "If I have a political idea and think it's the center of the world, it's okay, but they don't agree with that for them and believe that's okay. They think they should do what they want to do, and I should do what I want to do, and if we can help each other, fine."[43] The struggle against oppression and exploitation remains central to O'Neal, whereas many community-based artists see neither him nor themselves as oppressed, nor do they find that to be an impediment in being part of the organizations he cofounded. O'Neal sees pragmatism, that is, helping each other raise money and the like, as the basis for their participation rather than higher principles.

Particularly flawed from O'Neal's perspective is the notion that if people like someone's art, that's necessarily a good thing. He explains: "People respond to an aesthetic product when it strikes an emotional chord and they feel an identity with it. But you can feel identity with work that you aren't identified with. Through the aesthetic instrument, an artist gets past the critical apparatus and attacks the gut instead of going through the head." O'Neal gives the example of Tarzan's popularity. A strong white man, he was made king of the apes, playing into the assumption that white people are supposed to be in charge, the assumption "that even an uneducated idiotic white guy who was shipwrecked as a child and raised by apes is going to be stronger, smarter, and better than all those black people who'd been living in the jungle all that time." The story may be popular but is not the less dangerous for being so, even as Amos and Andy may amuse even as they propagate racism. O'Neal is interested in alliances with artists not simply content with their work's popularity but concerned about "the direction to go in, membership criteria, the historical moment we're part of, and what makes our work valuable or not. Not in the SBCA, Alternate ROOTS, or American Festival did we ever answer those questions clearly."[44]

Although appreciating the dilemma that O'Neal raises, I wonder about a generational divide, based not on age but on when people became politically active. Although civil rights, labor organizing, and the women's movement continue to inspire, people who entered the field since the late 1980s may be more influenced by models such as ACT UP and strategies of opposition to the World Trade Organization.[45] Activist artists face the classic legacy question—is the next generation meant to be true to the spirit or the letter? How to strike a balance between upholding the most important principles discovered by a previous generation and allowing each cluster of artists to define its own priorities for its own times?

From Atlas's perspective, O'Neal's main role in the AFP was as a visionary,

> a clear, political voice, uncompromising, speaking up for what he believed, proposing a lot of the ideas for the projects. In meetings when we'd be arguing over minutiae, he'd keep us focused on the bigger picture. He'd raise the hard issues that folks didn't always want to talk about, like racism within our own group and on the part of some of our collaborators—university people, arts presenters, and staff of community organizations. He had a very firm perspective about working on behalf of poor and oppressed people that he didn't always feel the people involved in the project itself were doing. He was the conscience for the original vision.[46]

Steve Kent also describes O'Neal as a visionary, but questions if he's as good a leader, in the sense of "motivating the people on their team":

> He overloads them. He's a highly educated man and even people his age haven't had his experiences. We have to find a way to transmit those experiences, aesthetics, and approach to other people. If you're going to be in Duke Ellington's band, you're going to do it the way Duke Ellington does. It doesn't mean that the Duke's way is the only way. When you're with John, that's the way to do it. He's going to have a right to set the arrangement and be the leader. Not waste time finding consensus when we're here to find out what he wants to do. That's why we were pulled here together in the first place.[47]

Although Junebug Productions no longer participates with the AFP, it collaborates with other ensembles in the same production. Wegmann sees the space this makes for artists to continue their own struggles with stereotypes as a major contribution. Roadside Theater and Junebug Productions made *Junebug/Jack* together; with Brenda Aoki and Mark Izu, O'Neal and Michael Keck made *Ballad of the Bones* about African-American and Asian-American relationships. A Traveling Jewish Theatre and Junebug Productions made *Crossing the Broken Bridge. Promise of a Love Song* incorporates three cultural perspectives—African-American via Junebug Productions, Appalachian via Roadside Theater, and Puerto Rican via Teatro Pregones.

And Now . . .

I asked John O'Neal what *he* sees as the greatest legacy of his work emanating from the Free Southern.

> JO: The ideas. I don't have anything unique to contribute to the technique of making theater. But I have come along at a time when certain ideas were in place and I encountered people and experiences that put those ideas into a certain level of action: the idea that in this time, art is in its proper place when it is an instrument for social and political development. It's not a new idea but it's an idea that has been dishonored for this time, by its advocates as well as by its opponents. We've had so many advocates that reduced the idea to agitprop—not that there's anything wrong with propaganda. Everyone seeks to propagate his own view. But propaganda does not reach the level of high art because it is addressed to such narrow concerns, this initiative or that campaign; things that by their nature are short term. Once that campaign achieves its objective, the material that has been developed around it is dated and no longer useful.
>
> JC-C: In other words it takes so much energy, why make a piece that will have such a short shelf life?
>
> JO: Right. Not that one shouldn't make beautiful posters to get people to do things. But that's not the limit of what you do when you make art. I think the big challenge is how to make this global culture that will afford the best possibilities for complementary developments of all living things. The principles to guide it have to include respect for everything from plants, to bugs, way up to the most grand and wonderful things imagined. I think of the universe as a living thing, a single organism bound together by forces that we can only speculate about.
>
> JC-C: Has that been a vision you are trying to work through your theater?
>
> JO: My whole life is about that.[48]

O'Neal is currently focused on *The Color Line*. Participants gather stories of people who were involved in the civil rights movement and use them in their playmaking. They are not necessarily overtly political when they begin; O'Neal's hope is that this experience will "draw them into a dialogue and open up the doors of experience that were invisible to them before." He compares this process to people who grew up singing gospel, a tradition of truth telling, and the power they gained from it: "When you're singing in a choir and the sound of the whole choir comes out your mouth, you can get to a new level of consciousness." He warns against perjuring this experience; people do claim it for their own and get a lot of mileage out of it. But through listening and creating work that integrates the legacy of civil rights, O'Neal believes people will get a similarly powerful collective experience and we'll get a new movement.[49]

At the core of the legacy of the Free Southern Theater is a model of the artist-preacher grounded not in the church of a particular religion but of a particular moral and political philosophy. That philosophy would hold America to the promise of the rhetoric: all of us are created equal. The leader of such a project needs faith, because this is an epic struggle that evokes our country's unresolved racist past, takes place in the present, and extends well into the future. It requires connection to ancestors, the ability to stay the course, and commitment to the future beyond one's own days on earth. Such a leader serves a spiritual goal—what O'Neal articulates in his dedication to "everything from plants, to bugs, way up to the most grand and wonderful things imagined." The preacher-storyteller draws wisdom from the community, as epitomized in the Junebug cycle, and is at ónce oral historian, moral arbiter, political activist, and entertainer, held between frustration with the world as it is and a vision of how to improve it through our efforts.

NOTES

1. The photos, by Jackson Hill, appear with a brief essay," A Farewell without Mourning: A Jazz Funeral for Free Southern Theater," *Changing Scenes* 14, nos. 3–4 (1987).

2. Jim O'Quinn, "Free at Last," *American Theatre*, March 1986, 27.

3. Ibid.

4. The funeral was a project of Junebug Productions, whose fiscal agent at the time was the local Contemporary Arts Council. CAC and the National Presenters Network cosponsored the performance component. Coleman, who'd been involved with the Free Southern Theater when Tom Dent led the company, is now the director of a civil rights museum in Birmingham, Alabama. Each of these organizations is thus part of the Free Southern Theater legacy.

5. Caron Atlas, interview by the author, New York City, 7 April 2002.

6. Community-based theater is not, however, strictly political. Its goals are as likely to be educational or therapeutic.

7. John O'Neal, interview by the author, Lavarne University, Calif., January 22–25, 2002, and telephone interview, August 6, 2002.

8. Ibid.

9. According to O'Neal, Moses and he argued so much that they needed a tiebreaker. They also needed someone with good theater credentials. Third, O'Neal and Moses understood that the American theater is a white institution and thus it would be good to have a white associate.

10. Richard Schechner, interview by the author, 2002.

11. O'Neal, interview.

12. Volunteerism is still an issue in community-based arts. Plays are typically made with community participants and given how hard money is to come by, usually only the professional artists are paid.

13. Kent also founded and directed a formidable theater company, The Provisional, in 1976 in Los Angeles.

14. Steve Kent, interview by the author, Los Angeles, January 22–25, 2002.

15. Ibid.

16. Nayo Watkins, telephone interview by the author, April 4, 2002.

17. Ibid.

18. Ibid.

19. Mat Schwarzman, "Something Big," *Inside Arts,* November 1998, 32.

20. Ibid., 35.

21. M. K. Wegmann, telephone interview by the author, April 5, 2002.

22. Tom Dent and Jerry W. Ward Jr., "After the Free Southern Theater: A Dialog," *TDR* 31, no. 3 (1987): 121.

23. Wegmann, interview.

24. Ibid.

25. O'Quinn, "Free at Last," 27.

26. Donald Bogle, *Primetime Blues* (New York: Farrar, Straus and Giroux, 2001).

27. Beth Turner, interview by the author, New York City, February 4, 2002.

28. O'Neal, interview.

29. Watkins, interview.

30. Dudley Cocke, "CAPP: A New Posture?" *High Performance* 16, no. 4 (1993): 13.

31. Ruby Lerner, "Searching for Roots in Southern Soil," in *Alternate ROOTS: Plays from the Southern Theater,* ed. Kathie deNobriga and Valetta Anderson (Portsmouth, N.H.: Heinemann, 1994), xvi.

32. See www.alternateroots.org.

33. Kathie deNobriga, "An Introduction to Alternate ROOTS," *High Performance* 16, no. 4 (1993): 14.

34. Kent, interview.

35. Watkins, interview.

36. O'Neal, interview.

37. Ibid.

38. Quoted in Jan Cohen-Cruz, "The American Festival Project," in *But Is It Art?* ed. Nina Felshin (Seattle: Bay Press, 1995), 119.

39. O'Neal, interview.

40. See www.npn.web.org/our_partners/profiles/junebug/ for this and more on O'Neal's approach to story circles.

41. O'Neal, interview.

42. Ibid.

43. Ibid.

44. Ibid.

45. Eric Rofes, foreword to *from ACT UP to the WTO,* ed. Ben Shepard and Ronald Hayduk (London: Verso, 2002), x–xii.

46. Atlas, interview.

47. Kent, interview.

48. O'Neal, interview.

49. Ibid.

THE PERFORMANCE GROUP
Historical Overview

Although every ensemble inevitably adds or loses members, the Performance Group is unique among the collectives examined in this volume because it was more of a sequence of Performance Groups than its name initially suggests. Generally speaking, the Performance Group went through three manifestations during its thirteen-year history: the first and arguably most famous (1967–70), which produced the legendary *Dionysus in 69*, began as a workshop and survived just over two troubled years. The second group (1970–72) was less tumultuous than the first, but is likewise remembered for a major production, *Commune* (1972). The third Performance Group (1972–80), which is remembered primarily for its early productions, *The Tooth of Crime* (1972) and *Mother Courage and Her Children* (1974), had a number of members from the second group but was much more fluid, adding new members as old members came and went. Over the course of the Performance Group's thirteen-year history, only Richard Schechner, Joan Macintosh, and Jerry Rojo remained. But it was Schechner who was the group's center of gravity. As executive and artistic director, Schechner was the indisputable, albeit controversial, guiding force of the Performance Group.

Indeed, the Performance Group grew, in many respects, out of the work that Richard Schechner began in the early 1960s as a young professor at Tulane University, where he cultivated a relationship with the Free Southern Theater and where, together with Franklin Adams and Paul Epstein, he subsequently founded the New Orleans Group (1964–67). Much of the work of the New Orleans Group, which included an important production of Ionesco's *Victims of Duty,* involved experiments with "intermedia, Happenings and environmental theatre,"[1] and when Schechner left Tulane for New York University in 1967, he wanted to build upon the work he had done with NOG. Once in New York, Schechner directed *Guerrilla Warfare* (1967), a street theater piece that was staged simultaneously in multiple areas of Manhattan. Shortly thereafter, Schechner began a workshop that was based in part on his earlier work with NOG, on encounter group techniques, and on exercises he had learned from the Polish director Jerzy Grotowski, who was teaching a small acting class at NYU that same fall.[2] Somewhere between twenty-five and forty people initially attended the workshop, many of whom had participated in *Guerrilla Warfare* and wanted to continue working with Schechner. As the workshop grew in intensity and demands, it also decreased in size, and by January 1968, strict attendance standards had reduced the group to a core of about ten participants meeting three to four times a week. It was from this core that the Performance Group ultimately emerged. Along with Schechner, the group included Remi Barclay, Samuel Blazer, Jason Bosseau, Richard Dia, William Finley, Joan MacIntosh, Patrick McDermott, Margret Ryan, William Shephard, and Ciel Smith.

The turning point for the workshop came when internal and external events radically transformed the direction of the group, gave it a new sense of identity and purpose, and, in a very literal sense, set the stage for the Performance Group's seminal contribution to American experimental theater. At Schechner's behest, the workshop began in January to focus on Euripides's *The Bacchae,* ostensibly working "in terms of a 'project' not a production."[3] Almost simultaneously, the group was forced to locate a new space for its work, having worn out its welcome at the community center near Tompkins Square Park where the participants had met since shortly after the workshop had begun. Their work on *The Bacchae* began to move seriously toward production when, with the help of a bank loan secured by Schechner, the group was able to convert an old garage on Wooster Street into a permanent theater. Located in what is now called Soho, the Performing Garage, which is roughly fifty feet by thirty-five feet, proved to be an ideal working space for Schechner's interest in environmental theater. Using an innovative design that blurred the lines separating the spaces of performance and audience, Michael Kirby and Jerry Rojo transformed the Performing Garage into a site where the group could realize what it had heretofore only conceptualized in workshops. The group's work on *The Bacchae* in their new theater culminated in the phenomenally successful production of *Dionysus in 69,* a production which is perhaps *the* paradigm of environmental theater.

As the production of *Dionysus in 69,* which "ran for 163 performances over more than a year,"[4] drew to a close, the Performance Group fell under immense pressure. Expectations and tensions were running high, and a period of turmoil ensued. Rehearsals for their next production, *Makbeth,* were not going well, and internal conflicts between members became more pronounced. After they voted one of their founding members out of the group solely for financial reasons, there was a lingering sense of betrayal both with regard to their commitment to each other and with regard to their theatrical ideals. Indeed, there was a strong feeling that they had devolved into "a production company," a feeling that, for better or worse, Schechner's own actions did little to dispel.[5] Amid conflicting organizational visions that were exacerbated by deep anxieties about the pending production of *Makbeth,* Schechner had boldly asserted his legal authority as executive and artistic director of the Performance Group— authority that included the power: to hire or fire individual members; to select which plays to produce; and, to make casting and directing assignments. Some new members were added to the group and some founding members left. But the turmoil continued and only reached a head in the aftermath of the poor critical reception of *Makbeth* (1969).

While *Makbeth* furthered the ideals of environmental theater in an innovative mise-en-scène that encouraged audience members to move about freely even as the simultaneous staging of three or four scenes denied them the possibility of observing the production as a whole, the production itself received poor reviews from the critics and had to close for lack of an audience. The failure of *Makbeth* signaled the end of the original Performance Group, which splintered into three factions. Punctuated by legal battles, the end was contentious and bitter. But for Schechner, it also signaled a new beginning. Maintaining control over the Performing Garage and the name of the group, Schechner rebuilt the Performance Group in March 1970. From the founding members only Joan Macintosh and Jerry Rojo (the scene designer) remained. They were joined by Stephen Borst, who had joined the production of *Makbeth* and, among others, by Spalding Gray and Elizabeth LeCompte. both of whom would later become founding members of the Wooster Group (the much celebrated experimental successor to the Performance Group). Although Gray had taken a role in *Makbeth* shortly before its closing, he and LeCompte only really began to contribute to the group once work on *Commune* (1970) began—Gray as a performer and LeCompte as an assistant director. Others joined the group as well, some only for the production of *Commune.* Among the latter were Bruce White, Jayme Daniel, Patricia Bower (now Cooley), Converse Gurian, Maxine Herman, Mik Cribben, and Patric Epstein. Those who

stayed on after *Commune* and contributed to subsequent productions included Stephen Borst, Joan MacIntosh, Spalding Gray, Elizabeth
LeCompte, James Griffiths, and Timothy Shelton.

Working with a series of group improvisations, the newly reconstituted Performance Group departed from the earlier group's focus on
dramatic texts. With *Commune,* the Performance Group opted instead to
develop a collage of images that were culled from American history and
centered around "the killing of film actress Sharon Tate and her friends
by members of the Charles Manson commune."[6] In many respects, the
piece addressed an American idealism that had gone awry and that was
slipping towards fascism, a point underscored by the coercive bent in the
approach to environmental theater that was adopted for the production.
Unlike previous Performance Group productions where the audience
was invited to participate *(Dionysus)* or set in constant motion *(Makbeth),*
Commune was structured around compulsory participation that began,
among other things, with audience members having to give up their
shoes for entry into the Performing Garage. Neither were they allowed
to enter the garage with their friends or companions, and once escorted
individually into the theater, they discovered, often to their own bewil-
derment, that the performance would not go on unless selected members of audience were willing to sit in a circle that designated them as the
village of My Lai (the village that was massacred by American troops in
the Vietnam War). When they resisted, the entire production came to a
standstill. Though not always well received, the production of *Commune*
marked the return of the Performance Group as a critical force, and
after its premier in 1970, the show continued in at least three variations
through 1972.

As far as that basic principles of environmental theater are concerned,
theater historians tend to cite *Dionysus in 69, Makbeth,* and *Commune* as the
works that make up the core vision of the Performance Group. Nonetheless, it continued to produce innovative works for almost another decade,
disbanding only after Schechner left in 1980, shortly after the production
of *The Balcony* (1979). By the time of his departure, the group was already
in its third phase, having served, over the course of the 1970s, as a spring-
board for some of the most creative talent to emerge in the New York experimental theater during the final decades of the twentieth century. In
this regard, one needs to be careful about writing off the Performance
Group's work too early. Though the production of *Commune* may have explored the outer parameters of the group's vision of environmental theater, the productions that followed, especially *The Tooth of Crime* (1972)
and *Mother Courage and Her Children* (1974), marked a refinement of the

aesthetics of that vision. That refinement coincided with a gradual retreat from giving the audience too large a role in the productions themselves.

By 1975, when the Performance Group produced David Gaard's *The Marilyn Project* in the upstairs studio space of the Performing Garage, Elizabeth LeCompte and Spalding Gray had already branched out "with two other members of The Performance Group and other friends" to produce *Sakonnet Point,* the first piece by the Wooster Group.[7] Though *Sakonnet Point* marked a major departure from the performance aesthetic that Schechner had cultivated within the Performance Group, the two companies coexisted during the last half of 1970s, during which the Performance Group produced a version of Seneca's *Oedipus* (1977), Terry Curtis Fox's *Cops* (1978), and finally Genet's *The Balcony* (1979). By that time the Wooster Group had produced *Rumstick Road* (1977) and *Nayatt School* (1978). In the same year that the Wooster Group produced *Point Judith* (1980), it assumed the lease for the Performing Garage, as the thirteen-year history of the Performance Group came to a close.

—J. M. H.

NOTES

1. Richard Schechner, *Environmental Theatre* (New York: Applause, 1994), 256.

2. Ibid., 256–57.

3. The Performance Group, *Dionysus in 69,* ed. Richard Schechner (New York: Farrar, Straus and Giroux, 1970), n.p.

4. Theodore Shank, *Beyond the Boundaries: American Alternative Theatre* (Ann Arbor: University of Michigan Press, 2002), 96.

5. William Hunter Shephard, *The Dionysus Group* (New York: Peter Lang, 1991), 224.

6. Shank, *Beyond the Boundaries,* 99.

7. David Savran, *Breaking the Rules* (New York: Theatre Communications Group, 1988), 3.

THE PERFORMANCE GROUP
BETWEEN THEATER AND THEORY

Martin Puchner

Accounts of the Performance Group, as of many other theater collectives active in the 1960s and 1970s, have been heavily inflected by the polemics that still surround this period in American history. Many of the old adversaries are still alive and in positions of power. Mark Rudd, the leading member of the Students for a Democratic Society (SDS), is a college professor in New Mexico; members of the Weather Underground Bernadine Dorn and Bill Ayers teach at Northwestern and University of Illinois at Chicago; and Angela Davis, of the Black Panthers, holds a professorship at the University of California at Santa Cruz. The presidential race of 2004 was a battle between a Vietnam vet turned antiwar protester and the offspring of an anti-1968 dynasty. Since our political, cultural, and artistic life is still shaped by those active in the late sixties and early seventies, it is not surprising that the debates about this era are determined by the values associated with it, including personal liberation, autonomy, collectivity, and authenticity, which were set against social control and capitalism. Histories of 1968, in other words, are often replays of 1968 itself, with the same terms, the same dilemmas, and the same protagonists.[1]

This is nowhere as true as in the case of the Performance Group. The group's director, Richard Schechner, is widely acclaimed as the theorist and founder of a new discipline, performance studies, over which he continues to hold much sway. This also means that he has had a strong—even dominant—voice when it comes to writing the history of the Performance Group, which plays a significant role in the canon of performance studies.

This history of the Performance Group, as articulated by Schechner and performance studies more generally, maintains that the group revolutionized the theater by searching for authentic bodily expression instead of training actors in elaborate artifice.[2] Workshops and exercises were meant to profoundly transform the actors and eventually the audience as well. Detractors, by contrast, have derided such projects as a nostalgic search for the "real" and the "authentic."[3] Equally contested is the group's proclaimed unwillingness to bow to the dictates of the dramatic text, which in the eyes of some led to a haphazard tinkering with works of great literature (for example *Makbeth*) or a misguided attempt to fabricate texts in the rehearsal process *(Commune)*.

What both friends and detractors seem to agree on, however, is that the Performance Group was indeed focused on authentic bodies, transformative exercises, and collective actions. This consensus has obscured what I take to be the single most significant feature of the Performance Group, namely the close connection, in the work of its founder and director, Richard Schechner, of polemical texts, performance practices, and theoretical arguments. Commentators have been too quick to accept a hierarchy that places the corporeal over the cerebral, the authentic over the analytic, and the performance over the various textual genres that surrounded and permeated the group's work. The critical perspective I am offering emphasizes the latter terms, insisting that the group's theater work must be seen as part of a nexus of activities that include Schechner's editorship of *The Drama Review* (*TDR*), the theater journal that printed many of his missives, polemics, and manifestos, as well as the theoretical work that ultimately led to the full-fledged formulation of performance theory.[4] I will call this connection between manifesto, theater work, and theory the *manifesto-performance-theory nexus*. Far from judging the Performance Group's performances as either successful or unsuccessful realization of some previously conceived theory, I suggest that manifesto, performance, and theory should be considered as alternative forms of manifestation, none of which can claim superior status.

Even though most commentators emphasized the group's interest in ritual, immediacy, and corporal expression, some did recognize that there was something conceptual and abstract driving the Performance Group's productions. Sam Shepard, for example, wrote an angry letter to Schechner concerning the group's production of *The Tooth of Crime*. While unjustly accusing the company of offering a "random interpretation," his final, equally angry, observation, that the production was driven by "theory," captures a glimpse of the manifesto-performance-theory nexus: "I have had it with theory and idealized theatre."[5] William Hunter Shephard, one of the original members and an otherwise avid supporter of Schechner, equally complained about what he perceived as the dominance of theory over acting: "Like Grotowski, I felt that the actor's creative process was the core of the theatrical event, but I began to suspect that Schechner's interest in such details was secondary to his more general theories about environmental theatre."[6] Stefan Brecht, although supportive of the group, used a related vocabulary, noting that the performers had a quality of "abstraction."[7] And Schechner himself foregrounds the theoretical and conceptual agenda driving the last production of the Performance Group, Genet's *The Balcony:* "On conceptual grounds especially—in what the production suggested but could not entirely realize—I am proud of the work."[8] What these remarks describe, either as flaws or as strengths, characterizes the Performance Group throughout, namely that the performance never stands on its own, but is informed by something that can be alternatively described as a theory, an ideal, a tendency toward abstraction, or a concept that is never fully realized in any given production but by which all productions are somehow informed.

The formative impact of the manifesto-performance-theory nexus is not unique to the Performance Group. It is a prevalent, though often overlooked, dynamic within twentieth-century avant-garde theater, from E. G. Craig and the futurists through Antonin Artaud to theater movements in the fifties and sixties, including fluxus and the situationists. Despite their significant differences, they all share one feature: their theater practice was driven by manifestos and often immediately translated into theory. The nexus thus points not only to a central feature of the Performance Group but also to the group's modernist inheritance.

There are four key words, or concepts, that were put into circulation by the manifesto-performance-theory nexus and that therefore stand at the center of my analysis: (1) environmental theater; (2) group theater; (3) ritual; and (4) transcultural performance.

Environmental Theater

Environmental theater is a term that was launched by one of Schechner's best-known manifestos, "Six Axioms for Environmental Theater" (1968), in the pages of *TDR*.[9] However, not content with formulating his axioms in the form of a manifesto, Schechner also translated it into theater. This translation was immensely successful in that both positive and negative reviewers never questioned this new label. The group sometimes advertised its productions as "environmental" stagings of a given text. Environmental theater, in other words, was a label that stuck; one of the most successful attempts at branding a theatrical style. And after emerging in a manifesto and being translated into performance, environmental theater finally became a central component of performance studies, to the point where Schechner applied this term to all kinds of performances, activities, and rituals such as the Ramlila at Ramnagar, India.[10]

Environmental theater, in other words, is a textbook example of the manifesto-performance-theory nexus and therefore allows us to analyze this nexus in detail. The first component is the manifesto. Almost as soon as Schechner took over the editorship of *TDR*, he became dedicated to the creation of a new theater and, more important, to the creation of the new ideas and theories that were to give rise to it: "new theatres ask for new ideas, and if we are to have a real theatre on this continent, one which readily translates art and theory, ideas will necessarily emerge that recognize the particular historical, political, and social facts of American life as well as the unique aesthetics of our own theatre practice."[11] However, if new ideas were to give rise to a new theater, *TDR* had to actively intervene in, and not just describe passively, the theater scene. Hence, Schechner adopted a polemical style centered on the manifesto. For this purpose he instituted the "*TDR* Comment" and began to encourage the publication of manifestos and manifesto-like texts, over the opposition of the former editor, who found the newly shrill tone of *TDR* unseemly. "Six Axioms for Environmental Theater" was thus not an individual case but the first culmination of a whole new style that would dominate *TDR* for decades.

But Schechner not only formulated the new ideas that theater artists were supposed to then translate into performance. He decided to take matters into his own hands and founded, for this purpose, the Performance Group. The group's work was explicitly dedicated to the task of turning the "Six Axioms" into performance. Indeed, the term *environmental theater* describes the most successful aspect of the Performance Group's productions. While many contemporary reviewers, theorists, and observers, including Schechner's guru Grotowski, often expressed dissatisfaction with the Performance Group's performances, they praised its work in the narrow area of environmental theater, namely set design. These designs—relabeled "environments" in the playbills—have left a lasting impact on theater history. Schechner himself coedited a book showcasing these designs and the theory behind them. And through the work of theater historians, such as Arnold Aronson and his *History and Theory of Environmental Scenography* (1981), these designs have acquired an important place in the history of stage design.[12]

Particularly notable about these designs was the way in which they positioned performers and audiences in relation to one another. In many productions, including *Dionysus in 69, Makbeth, The Tooth of Crime,* and *Commune,* each audience member was allowed to choose his or her own place, either on the floor or on the various platforms and scaffolds that became the signature design of the Performing Garage, the performance space found and formatted by the Performance Group (and which still serves the Wooster Group, the successor of the Performance Group, today). In *The Tooth of Crime,* for example, ushers and members of the cast directed the audience to clear spaces needed by the performers; and audience members could follow individual actors or otherwise alter their position in the course of the performance within a delimited public space, which was separated from a private space. In *Makbeth,* a production based on a heavily edited version of Shakespeare's *Macbeth,* the audience had to enter individually through a maze set up above the main theater space. Often, scenes were set in a pit, which would require the audience to draw near in order to be able to catch as much as a glimpse of what was going on below. For *Mother Courage,* Jerry Rojo decided against the traditional wagon and instead turned the entire performance space into an abstract semblance of a wagon. And for *Commune,* he built what he called a pueblo-style structure that turned the audience into "cliff-dwellers."[13] Only on occasion would the designers, or "environmentalists," place the audience in a more traditional space, as they did in *Oedipus,* where the audience was seated in a small Roman-style arena. In most shows, however, audiences were dispersed throughout the Garage. The effect Schechner tried to achieve through this dispersal of the audience was a "multi-focus" experience that would, at the same time, encourage "selective inattention."[14] This way, the perception and experience of theater was supposed to be altered and enhanced.

The project of dispersing audiences and performers was part of a larger agenda, namely of erasing the boundaries defining the traditional theatrical event, including the boundaries between the actors and the role, between the theater space and set design, between the theater and the street, between the text and the lives of the performers, and between rehearsal and performance. What Jon McKenzie has called the "liminal norm," the search for the in-betweenness in performance studies, defines already the manifesto and then the productions mounted in the name of environmental theater, which was singularly devoted to the explosion of boundaries and the search for a space in-between traditional divisions.[15]

The boundary between actors and audiences, so central to Schechner's manifesto, proved the most difficult to break. The first and most far-reaching production in this respect was *Dionysus in 69,* through which

Schechner hoped to draw the audience into various kinds of ritual acts. For this purpose, actors would at various moments involve individual audience members and then hope that the general ritualistic atmosphere would turn them into veritable coperformers. The results were not always encouraging. At times audience members felt harassed and sexually assaulted, especially when the group toured in the Midwest. And conversely, actors felt assaulted by audience members. Instead of breaking down the boundary between actors and audiences, *Dionysus in 69* in fact reasserted it.

Critics have been tempted to dismiss these experiments as quixotic attempts to erase the difference between audience and actors. Rather than following such dismissals, I propose to consider these experiments as effects of the manifesto-performance-theory nexus that propelled the Performance Group beyond what was considered theater and into a terrain with few rules and experiences, where individual productions would be no more than hesitant attempts at translating concepts that had been launched as manifestos into theatrical form. Such translations were sometimes highly successful, and at other times less so. Both successful and unsuccessful theatrical translations were subsequently retranslated into performance theory, where they enjoyed different kinds of successes and failures. It is important to recognize here that the theatrical performances, the translations of manifestos into theater, should not be seen as the ultimate goal of these concepts, nor did the success or failure of these concepts in theatrical productions say anything about their ultimate importance and power. The theater was simply one form of manifestation among others, including the manifesto and theory, and each of them requires a different set of standards for judging the success or failure of a given project.

Group Theater

While the idea of an environmental theater dictated the elimination of the boundary separating performers from the audience, the erosion of internal boundaries separating the director from the performers answered to a different concept: group theater. Rather than simply implementing a director's interpretation of a dramatic text, the Performance Group ventured to generate a performance, sometimes even a text, in an elaborate and lengthy process that included various kinds of psychophysical exercises, often inspired by Grotowski, as well as games, improvisations, and other activities. The Richard Schechner archive at Princeton testifies to the significance of this aspect of the group's work. Some of these exercises were meant to enhance the flexibility of the body, but most of them targeted the intangible intersection of physical movement and psychological states.

These exercises and games were the core of the group's emphasis on collaboration and the process through which it asserted its dominance over a dramatic text. Group theater was a way of undoing the single dominance of the dramatic text. Breaking the rule of dramatic literature over theatrical production was one of the most notorious projects of the Performance Group. Most reviews of its productions scrutinized whether and to what extent Schechner and the group had altered or distorted the dramatic texts. This very scrutiny demonstrated just how right Schechner was in targeting the fixation of theater reviewers on dramatic detail. Given the explicit desire for demoting drama, it may be surprising how many of the Performance Group's productions used classics in the dramatic canon, from Shakespeare's *Macbeth* to Brecht's *Mother Courage*. In both cases, however, the dramatic texts were edited heavily, especially in the case of *Makbeth*, whose new spelling was meant to signal the departure from Shakespeare's text.

One of the productions that was not based on a given dramatic text was *Commune*, a show about Middle America and its communal practices. Schechner and the group assembled a host of texts, scenes, and music ranging from *The Bible* and *Moby-Dick* to various kinds of country music and English hymns. The most important thematic elements, however, were current events. One was the My Lai massacre committed by American troops in Vietnam, whose representation was based on interviews with soldiers who had participated in the massacre. Another was the Charles Manson gang's murder of the twenty-six-year-old actor and wife of Roman Polanski, Sharon Tate. This episode, one of the longest in the show, was staged through a ritual reenactment of Tate's murder. The Manson episode became charged, throughout the show, with all the additional material gathered in this multilayered and collage-like production. Manson resembled Jesus, for example, and provided a domestic echo of the violence committed in Vietnam. The My Lai theme was environmentally marked by a burial ditch, which served as the counterpart to a water barrel labeled, in a Brechtian fashion, "El Dorado." Instead of being based on a dramatic text, *Commune* thus consisted of a wild collage extracted from contemporary life in America.

The central target in *Commune*, however, was the question of the myth and the reality of community in America. Both the group dynamic of the My Lai massacre and the Charles Manson "family" constituted forms of collective excess, the one consisting of young army recruits committing unspeakable horror and the other of the notorious guru who had convinced his followers that he was the fifth rider of the apocalypse (with the Beatles constituting the other four) whose mission it was to start a race war. At the same time, the notion of community was something dear to the heart of the Performance Group and its group ideal. The group had formed through explicit community-building exercises and understood itself as a closely knit collective. However, not content with its own internal collectivity, the Performance Group also gauged the possibilities and limits of drawing the audience into its community as well. For this purpose, *Commune* framed the audience from the very beginning by requiring that all spectators take off their shoes so that cast members could try them out and thus redistribute these small, but significant, pieces of private property.

Given the communal aspirations of the Performance Group, *Commune* was thus one of the most self-referential productions, even as it was also one of the most problematic. Audience members were invited to join various kinds of circles formed by the actors, and the whole production was premised on the willing cooperation of the audience. But the limits of community, of communal theater, became evident all too quickly, for the audience was not only invited, but also required, to participate at certain moments in order for the show to proceed. Schechner himself describes one evening when some audience members refused to participate and the show thus ground to a halt for many hours. Most of the audience and also some of the cast left, and the remaining actors and spectators were able to finish the show only much later, with Schechner reading the lines of an actor who had long since left. It is unclear whether this battle of wills between the Performance Group and the passive (and increasingly passive-aggressive) spectators was a triumph or a failure. No matter how one may wish to judge this particular moment, it certainly revealed the limits of community, unsurprisingly, perhaps, since the show was as much about the violence as it was about the utopian promise of communal organization and group dynamic.

The Performance Group's campaign against the dominance of dramatic literature, which had led to the collectively assembled *Commune,* became particularly difficult in the case of *The Tooth of Crime,* when the group had to deal with the opinions and reactions of the author of the play, Sam Shepard. In his correspondence with Shepard, Schechner emphasized that he was not approaching the text of *The Tooth of Crime* with a specific concept or interpretation in hand. Rather, the material for the production would emerge from the elaborate rehearsal process, whose results no one, not even he, the director, could predict. In the end, Schechner left Shepard's text more or less intact and also declared that the playwright's inventive language had been one of the reasons why he and the group had wanted to stage the play in the first place.

The Tooth of Crime is based on something close to a private or semi-private language. The action of the play revolves around the competition between an aging rock star who finds himself being challenged by a new-comer refusing to play by the rules of the game. The rockers, however, speak in a made-up language that seems to be drawn from gang warfare and street combat, almost anticipating the wars between East and West Coast rap musicians in the late nineties. The language of challenge and honor is mixed with a discourse surrounding cars, machinery, and weapons. The central values, however, around which the competition be-tween the two protagonists revolves are authenticity and drive, the killer instinct that the established rocker has lost to the outsider and upstart, who inevitably wins in the end. The actual battle, however, takes place not so much as physical combat but as a battle of speech and oratory, of po-etic challenges and quick repartees.

Rather than disassembling the dramatic text as it had done in other cases, the Performance Group left Shepard's text alone and focused pre-cisely on the physical aspects of the combat, which the dramatic text had relegated to a second place. The Performance Group's production was in-ventive, taking place in typical environmental fashion on several levels and between different zones, and it made the direct man-to-man combat immediate by having the audience draw near and around the two fight-ers. In the hands of the Performance Group, *The Tooth of Crime* became an undoubtedly physical play, a play about fighting and killing. This meant, however, that the production was out to challenge the imposing domi-nance of Shepard's language that had given the action of the play its pe-culiar and mysterious character. In the end, the Performance Group's production can be seen as a kind of battle between a powerful dramatic text and a performance group out to challenge this text's dominance by insisting on the particular dynamic of group theater.

In his exchange with Shepard, Schechner had emphasized the partic-ularly collaborative rehearsal process as that upon which the group the-ater ideal was based. What did this process look like? In a comment on *Dionysus in 69*, Schechner described the beginnings of the rehearsal or workshop process in greater detail:

> We knew something of each other and of the exercises I had taken from my work with the New Orleans Group, Grotowski, and else-where. The root of that work was exploration. And exploration, as we understood it then, meant exchange. We exchanged touches,

places, ideas, anxieties, words, gestures, hostilities, rages, smells, glances, sounds, loves.[16]

Physical and psychological exchanges, open-ended exploration—these are the key words associated with the process that for many constituted the heart of the group's activities. The passage also emphasizes the importance of group members getting to get to know one another intimately. William Hunter Shephard calls this dynamic the "Group Mind."[17] As Shephard makes clear, however, the Group Mind was a fragile state. Throughout the existence of the Performance Group, very few members remained constant, and its history can be subdivided into relatively short phases, each marked by a substantial change in the composition of the company. Indeed, Schechner attributed the ultimate failure of *The Balcony* to the fact that too many new members, who had not participated in exercises, explorations, and exchanges, had joined, while several key members, including those who would split off and become the Wooster Group, were pursuing their own projects simultaneously. One limit to the group theater ideal was thus the constant fragmentation of the group itself.

The open-ended, collaborative, and explorative project as it is described by Schechner captures an essential element of the Performance Group's work. But it is also misleading. It is misleading in that it obscures precisely the manifesto-driven, "idealized theater," which Sam Shepard and others had detected. This discrepancy was made possible by the fact that even though the Performance Group did work collaboratively and placed an almost unique emphasis on exercises and rehearsals, Schechner remained in control of the most important artistic and strategic decisions. After *Makbeth,* Schechner posted a text on the door of the Performing Garage stating his claim to almost absolute authority and spelling out the decisions he would reserve for himself. This was a manifesto in the older sense of the word, namely the declaration of a king or a head of state, the manifestation of a sovereign.

Despite this "manifesto," the power struggles continued. It was during the group's tour in India, with the production of *Mother Courage,* that Schechner wrote down, in a kind of diary, his vision of his own leadership over the group: "I want administrative and artistic control: what (I suppose) Richard Foreman and Robert Wilson have: the ability to listen to all opinions but myself to make all decisions, selections, deep-rhythm choices."[18] What I would like to emphasize is that Schechner's drive for dominance was not just a question of personality, but a dynamic fueled by the significance of the manifestos and theories surrounding and permeating the group's work, an area over which Schechner exerted significant control as editor of *TDR*. The reference, in the quotation above, to Richard Foreman is particularly telling in this respect, for Foreman's control over the Ontological-Hysteric Theater followed the same logic. Even more so than Schechner, Foreman considered the theater a venue for manifesting his own manifestos and theoretical speculations. While the question of control is thus not specific to the Performance Group, it erupted here with particular violence since the Performance Group, as opposed to Foreman's troupe, explicitly presented itself as group theater. The history of the Performance Group thus remained a history of power struggles, which erupted with particular vehemence after those performances that were seen as failures. After *Makbeth*, for example, only Richard Schechner, his wife Joan MacIntosh, Spalding Gray, Steve Borst, and the designer Jerry Rojo continued (Steve Borst had joined the group only after *Dionysus in 69*). The final breakup and the formation of the Wooster Group were the result of a struggle between Schechner and Elizabeth LeCompte, who is still the director of the Wooster Group.

While the group theater ideal both worked and did not work in the theater, it was translated into a different venue: theory. Schechner's exercises and exchanges, processes and explorations have become central elements in performance theory, where they continue to influence our understanding of movement, rehearsal, and group dynamics. The paradox of collaboration and control should not be seen as proof that the group theater ideal somehow failed in practice. Indeed, this paradox was in part caused by the significance of theory, by Schechner's control over his own theory. The significance of Schechner's manifestos and theories also meant that he would have a dominant role in the group's theatrical work and thus impose limits on the Group Mind.

Ritual

The concept that is closely connected to both environmental theater and group theater is that of ritual. No term has been evoked more often in conjunction with the rehearsals and performances of the Performance Group, and none has triggered more heated polemics. The debate surrounding this term has been often unproductive because it is located at the intersection of a number of competing projects, programs, and traditions. The new emphasis on exercises, games, and the rehearsal process, for example, was something that could be couched in ritualistic terms, since elaborate forms of preparation are often as important to ritual as its performance. Indeed, many of Schechner's exercises were derived from non-Western ritual theater. And the participation of the audience, the very fact that ritual does not know disinterested and distanced observers, could be used to describe the project of drawing the audience into the process of performance.

In addition, Schechner's frequent evocation of ritual was part of a modernist inheritance, a yearning, seemingly inextricably intertwined with twentieth-century art, for an art located historically prior to Western industrial societies, for a time when the division of labor, the bureaucratic state, and an autonomous sphere of art did not yet exist. In the theater, this inheritance often led to a renewed fascination with the supposed ritualistic origin of Greek drama. For others, including Antonin Artaud, ritual implied an all-out attack on dramatic texts and written literature in general, and a new emphasis instead on a new physical theater, a theater of cries and gestures.

Artaud is a good lens through which to analyze the Performance Group not only because he influenced, directly and indirectly, the group's productions, but also because Artaud was caught up in a manifesto-theater-theory nexus of his own. For while he called for a theater of bodies and without text, these calls were uttered not in the theater, but in a series of texts and manifestos collected in a book called *The Theater and Its Double*. Artaud never managed to fully translate these manifestos into performance, so that instead he had to retranslate them into theory.[19] The manifesto-performance-theory nexus has been overlooked, in the case of Artaud as much as in the case of the Performance Group, because the notion of ritual signified precisely a rejection of a textual, cerebral, and theoretical theater and instead an embrace of a corporeal, spontaneous, and unmediated one. What the manifesto-performance-theory nexus reveals, however, is that these values are themselves produced not by something corporeal and unmediated, but, on the contrary, by the textual genre of the manifesto and by the cerebral mode of theory.

The paradoxical status of ritual emerged nowhere as clearly as in the production that has stood at the center of most histories of the Performance Group: *Dionysus in 69*. This production foregrounded the paradox of ritual not so much by demonstrating how difficult it was to actually create a ritualistic theater, although these difficulties occurred as well. Rather, Schechner and the group had chosen a play that like no other was itself obsessed with the ritualistic origins of Greek tragedy, namely Euripides' *The Bacchae*.

Euripides was the youngest and most cerebral of the great Greek tragedians. As a consequence, his tragedies irreverently contained comedic and other improperly "tragic" elements that signaled his distance from Aeschylus. *The Bacchae* thematizes this distance; it is in fact an early version

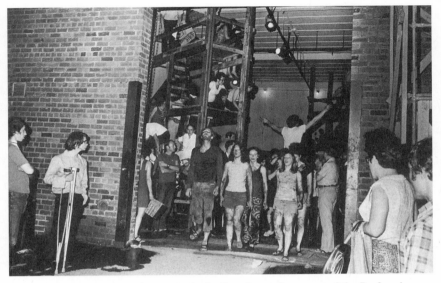

After performance of *Dionysus in 69,* leading the audience out of the Performing Garage. (Photo courtesy of Richard Schechner.)

of metatheater. Thebes is caught between the new, Eastern ritualistic cult of Dionysus and the law-and-order king of Thebes, Pentheus. The ritual, fueled by the rejection, ends bloodily, teaching Thebes to accept the ritual without fully falling prey to it. Schechner recognized and foregrounded Euripides' ambivalence toward ritual and claimed the same ambivalence for himself.[20] At various moments, for example, the actors would interrupt the performance by shedding their roles and identifying themselves by their real names. Indeed, the production ended with the actor playing Dionysus leaving the Performing Garage as if he were running for political office. *Dionysus in 69* thus did not try to hide the difference between 1968 New York, Euripides' Athens, and the presumed ritualistic origin of tragedy that was unavailable to Schechner and Euripides alike. The success of *Dionysus in 69* seemed to stem from the fact that Schechner apparently shared Euripides' recognition that the ritualistic origin of Greek tragedy was a thing of the past.

Despite Schechner's declared ambivalence about ritual, however, the production sought to actually create a number of rituals, including an opening "birth ritual" and a closing "death ritual," in which the actors formed a kind of tunnel, with the men lying on the ground and the women, standing astride them, creating the opening through which an actor could be hoisted. The Performance Group developed several other ritual dances and interactions through which Schechner hoped to elicit the participation of the audience. At various moments, the actors formed piles of interlocking human bodies moving to the rhythm of drums and other instruments. The climactic scene in which Agave kills her son added an ample supply of stage blood to this mix. Nudity, eroticism, physical contact, bloody violence: these were the strategies that animated the production. They were also the ways in which the Performance Group signaled its distinct, physical approach to a classical text. Indeed, many of these ritualistic scenes had grown out of the exercises and rehearsal techniques through which the group had first constituted itself.

All this implied that the group was asserting its own distinct approach to the text, feeling free to add new material to Euripides' text not only through the invention of these various rituals but also, for example, by casting the relation between Dionysus and Pentheus in terms of homosexual desire and the struggle for sexual domination. All this meant that *Dionysus in 69* tilted the balance between ritual and cerebral metatheater, so carefully maintained by Euripides, toward ritual. The best measure for this imbalance is the fact that many of the rituals that the Performance Group instigated on stage had actually been off stage in Euripides. Moving true ritual offstage had been Euripides' main technique for signaling his distance from ritual. Schechner's decision to put these rituals on stage, and to engage the audience in them, thus reveals how strong the desire for actual ritual at work in this production really was. The designer Rojo even reported that members of the Performance Group were beginning to think that they had in fact created a new religion.[21] Somewhere underneath Schechner's ambiguity there operated the modernist yearning for ritualistic origins that accompanied the art of modernity in the twentieth century.

Like Artaud's theater of cruelty, Schechner's theater of ritual was destined to celebrate its greatest success in the form of a book, or rather in several books. The first of them was a book about the production, including Euripides' text and many evocative photographs. Eric Bentley wrote: "DIONYSUS IN 69 is a brilliant job of book making. Even better than the show was. Proving that the non-literary theatre is really better as literary theatre."[22] The success of the book registers not so much the dominance of literature over performance, as the extent to which the book version of *Dionysus in 69* managed to capture the manifesto-performance-theory nexus. For in addition to containing the adapted Euripides text and production photographs, the book included theoretical commentaries that explained the idealistic and manifesto-driven agenda for which the production was supposed to be the theatrical form. In this way, the Dionysus book, like Artaud's collection of manifestos, managed what the production has only partially achieved: a relation to ritual as distanced as that of Euripides.

At the same time, the rituals that were only partially realized in performance became a central component of performance theory. Many of Schechner's publications revolve around ritual, and the work of the Performance Group functioned as a constant point of reference, even as a kind of proof, of the usefulness of Schechner's theoretical discussions of ritual theater. Once more, the theatrical manifestation of a key term had been translated into theory. The book version of *Dionysus in 69* paved the way for many similar projects, including a book entirely devoted to *Makbeth* as well as to a collection of environmental designs by Rojo.[23] The success of these books was not just an effect of the advantages of print. In an added twist to the manifesto-performance-theory nexus, Schechner turned his theory seminars at NYU into workshops resembling rehearsals of the Performance Group, inspired by the classroom work of the anthropologist Victor Turner.[24] In a way, ritual had come full circle: from manifesto to performance and theory, it was then translated back into performance.

Transcultural Performance

In the modernist imagination, ritual was not only something located historically prior to the modern West, but also outside its geographic domain. In fact, most influential theater-makers and visionaries of the early twentieth century had been obsessed with East Asian theaters, including Noh theater (Meyerhold, Brecht, Yeats, Pound), Chinese theater (Meyerhold, Brecht), or Balinese theater (Artaud). Here too, the Performance Group proved to be an inheritor of the modernist theater, funneled through the manifesto-performance-theory nexus. In his manifesto "Transcultural Performance," Schechner openly embraced this modernist inheritance, including its most contested aspect, namely primitivism: "I am arguing for both an experiment and a return to traditional, even ancient, values. This argument has been implicit in experimental art for a long time: it is the root of that art's 'primitivism.' Transculturalism is a predictable, even inevitable, outcome of the avant-garde, its natural heir."[25] Although the crucial term, primitivism, is set in quotation marks, it nevertheless signals how much Schechner understands himself to be the natural heir of the early twentieth century. Again, however, it is not only the content that ties the Performance Group to modernism, but the very fact that it was driven by manifestos, one of the central genres of the twentieth-century avant-gardes.

Although the "Transcultural Performance" manifesto was not published until 1982, when the Performance Group had just broken up, Schechner had been dedicated to non-Western theater since the sixties. The production most visibly dedicated to the intercultural performance agenda was Brecht's *Mother Courage,* which the group took on an extended tour to India. Just as *The Bacchae* had been a good occasion to examine ritualistic origins, so *Mother Courage,* a play about avoiding starvation in a poverty-stricken continent, was a good occasion to try out the possibilities, and the limits, of transcultural performance.

From the beginning, the Performance Group was determined to apply the lessons of Brecht to their own theater practice. Schechner, for example, used Mother Courage's cash register to take tickets before the performance, thus confronting audiences with the fact that theater, like the objects sold by Mother Courage, were part of a business transaction. More importantly, the same cash register was used, during intermission, to sell food to the audience, which was invited to participate in a communal feast with the actors. In addition, many tenets of Brechtian theater, including the breaking of illusion, the exposing of the difference between actor and role, had been part of the Performance Group's approach to acting. While Brecht achieved these effects by means of an estranged acting, the Performance Group did so by breaking the frame of the theater and by using the actors' actual biographies. In his *New York Times* review, Clive Barnes objected to the group's decision to translate epic theater into their own terms, for example by not using an actual wagon: "Mother Courage's Wagon is not a theoretical dramatic idea, but a tangible theatrical metaphor";[26] again the dichotomy between theory and theater asserts itself in this opposition between a theoretical, if also dramatic, idea and a theatrical metaphor. The most important "theoretical" idea behind the production, however, emerged when the show traveled to India, where it participated in the project of transcultural performance. The production's emphasis on monetary transactions, the necessity for survival, all this would, so the group hoped, resonate doubly in South Asia.

From the beginning, the group was concerned about its privileged status and what it would mean for them to come to India in order to make theater about starvation. Schechner had made it clear from the outset that all surplus would be donated to "hunger relief."[27] The whole tour thus stood under the ominous sign of food and starvation. In the diary kept during this trip, Joan MacIntosh noted:

I know I am tense and upset. The talk at Adal's about the starving villagers was very upsetting. What to do, what to say. Munera has an outburst based on Badal's play. She accuses us of just sitting and talking but not doing anything about the peasants. We eat. And then, after that full delicious Bentgali meal we sit on loaded bellies and talk about starving villagers. They must be fed before they can even have the brains and energy together to revolt. It is the middle classes who want them to revolt. Us. All the poor can do is worry about the next meal. How to eat, how to feed their children. Revolt, change, doesn't occur in their vocabularies. Hence Badal's Rural Development Project, I couldn't sleep that night.

While MacIntosh observed the collision of *Mother Courage* with India's harsh reality, Schechner felt the dream of transcultural performance threatened from another side: where he and the group had hoped not only to play for different audiences but to immerse themselves in various kinds of Indian theater, they found that the organizers were primarily interested in *Mother Courage* and therefore had put the group on a tight schedule that did not allow for much encounter and exchange.[28] Indeed, Brecht had exerted an immense influence on Indian theater, certainly comparable to his influence on American theater.[29] The "trans" in transcultural performance proved a difficult goal to achieve.

Once more, however, what found only a partial realization in theater was then translated into theory. Of all the key terms associated with the Performance Group, transcultural performance is the most significant for the formation of performance studies. Schechner's most important theoretical texts, *Between Theater and Anthropology* and *Performance Theory*, proceed through a technique of juxtaposition, alternating between analyses of non-Western theater and detailed descriptions of the Performance Group performances. And performance studies seminars became alternative places for enacting transcultural performance.[30] As part of the manifesto-performance-theory nexus, transcultural performance has remained a project with lasting impact.

*   *   *

In the eighties and nineties, those associated with the term *postmodernism* have tended to regard many of the values and projects driving the Performance Group, such as immediacy, authenticity, communalism, and ritual, as Romantic throwbacks. The point, however, is not to critique these particular values, but to excavate the structure that brought them into existence in the first place. Recognizing this structure, what I have called the manifesto-performance-theory nexus, requires that we abandon the assumption, frequently held by practitioners and theorists alike, that the sole goal of manifestos and theories about theater is the creation of better performances, the assumption that the proof of the pudding lies only in the eating. What I am suggesting is rather that the proof lies also in the receipt, the cooking, the eating, the restaurant review, and the theory of the pudding. This approach, it seems to me, is methodologically, if not in its values, consistent with performance studies, which has argued for an expanded understanding of the theatrical event registered precisely in such concepts as environmental theater, group theater, ritual, and intercultural performance. However, the significance of these concepts can only come into view when we recognize that they were put into circulation by something altogether different, namely the manifesto-performance-theory nexus. Analyzing this nexus requires an expanded notion of theater as well, but in a different dimension, one designated by the genre of the manifesto and the mode of theory. It is in this dimension that the modernist heritage of the Performance Group emerges.

NOTES

1. This problematic has been analyzed very acutely by Janelle Reinelt in her article "Approaching the Sixties: Between Nostalgia and Critique," *Theatre Survey* 43 (May 2002): 37ff.

2. Michael Kirby, *A Formalist Theater* (Philadelphia: University of Pennsylvania Press, 1987). See also Philip Auslander, *From Acting to Performance: Essays in Modernism and Postmodernism* (New York: Routledge, 1997).

3. See Philip Auslander, *Liveness: Performance in a Mediatized Culture* (New York: Routledge, 1999).

4. See, for example, Marvin Carlson, *Performance: A Critical Introduction,* 2nd ed. (New York: Routledge, 2003). Peggy Phelan challenges this origin in the introduction to *The Ends of Performance,* ed. Peggy Phelan and Jill Lane (New York: New York University Press, 1998). More recently, Shannon Jackson has reexamined the disciplinary history of performance studies, in *Professing Performance: Theatre in the Academy from Philology to Performativity* (Cambridge: Cambridge University Press, 2004).

5. Richard Schechner Archive, Princeton University Library, Rare Books and Manuscripts, Series 5, subseries 1, box 168.

6. William Hunter Shephard, *The Dionysus Group* (New York: Peter Lang, 1991), 34.

7. Stefan Brecht, *TDR* 43 (1969): 156–68.

8. Richard Schechner, *Between Theater and Anthropology,* with a foreword by Victor Turner (Philadelphia: University of Pennsylvania Press, 1985), 263.

9. Richard Schechner, "Six Axioms for Environmental Theater," *TDR* (1968): 41–64.

10. Schechner, *Between Theater and Anthropology,* 175.

11. Richard Schechner, *TDR* 8, no. 2 (1963): 10.

12. Arnold Aronson, *The History and Theory of Environmental Scenography* (Ann Arbor, Mich.: UMI Research Press, 1981).

13. Brooks McNamara, Jerry Rojo, and Richard Schechner, *Theatre, Spaces, Environments: Eighteen Projects* (New York: Drama Book Specialists, 1975).

14. Schechner, "Six Axioms," 58.

15. Jon MacKenzie, *Perform or Else: From Discipline to Performance* (New York: Routledge, 2001).

16. *Dionysus in 69: The Performance Group,* edited by Richard Schechner, designed by Franklin Adams, photographs by Frederick Eberstadt, with additional photographs by Raeanne Rubenstein and two folios of photographs by Max Waldman (New York: Farrar, Straus and Giroux, 1970). Text is not numbered. Page 11.

17. Shephard, *The Dionysus Group,* 44.

18. Schechner Archive, Series 5, box 167, folder 3.

19. See my "Manifesto=Theater," *Theatre Journal* 54 (2002): 449–65, and my *Poetry of the Revolution: Marx, Manifestos, and the Avant-gardes* (Princeton: Princeton University Press, 2006).

20. To Joel Schecter, Schechner said: "Euripides is at once fascinated and repelled by the Dionysian." Schechner Archive, box 66, folder 1.

21. Rojo writes: "As audiences projected a religion on us, some in the Group began to wonder whether it wasn't religious" (McNamara, Rojo, and Schechner, *Theatre, Spaces, Environments,* 94).

22. Schechner Archive, letter from Eric Bentley to Robert Grioux, box 166, folder 1.

23. *Makbeth After Shakespeare,* adapted by Richard Schechner (Schulenburg, Tex.: I. E. Clark Publishers, 1978).

24. Victor Turner, *From Ritual to Theatre: The Human Seriousness of Play* (New York: PAJ Publications, 1982).

25. Richard Schechner, "Transcultural Performance," *TDR* 26, no. 2 (1982): 4.

26. Clive Barnes, "The Theater: A Disappointing 'Mother Courage,'" *New York Times,* February 25, 1975, 30.

27. Schechner Archive, box 167, folder 3.

28. Schechner, notebook, March 19: "For the most part, our sponsors concentrated on making *Mother Courage* a success and few arrangements were made for us to see modern, folk, traditional, or ritual performances." Schechner Archive, Box 167.

29. See, for example, Utpal Dutt, *Towards a Revolutionary Theatre* (Calcutta: M. C. Sarkar and Sons, 1982).

30. Turner, *From Ritual to Theatre.*

A DIFFERENT KIND OF POMO

The Performance Group and the
Mixed Legacy of Authentic Performance

Mike Vanden Heuvel

We've all seen them: the grainy black-and-white photographs, slightly am-
ateurish to begin with, suffering the further indignation of being copied
into scholarly books and the pages of *TDR* (not known in those days for
providing the finest grade of paper). When the images contain the then-
notorious nudity featured in *Dionysus in 69,* the look is disconcertingly of
cheap porn, pre-Internet and therefore both less real and more insidious.
There is little in Frederick Eberstadt's snapshots that convey the posed
look we associate with production stills from the "legitimate" theater,
none of the refined visual kitsch that remains one of the great pleasures
of conducting visual archival work in theater studies. Instead, the camera
angles are obtuse, the focus sometimes blurred, composition is lacking,
the whole thing conveying that peculiar carnivalesque tawdriness that the
era of Woodstock, Be-Ins, and Yippie Nation seems now to evoke in the
collective memory.

The means by which the work of the Performance Group and other
experimental group theater companies of the 1960s and 1970s is
recorded visually has a good deal to do with how they are remembered
and how their legacy is to be interpreted. Especially given Richard
Schechner's own comment in his necrology of experimental theater of
the period, *The End of Humanism,* that "my generation failed to develop its
own means of training—of getting performance texts across to the fu-

Dionysus in 69. (Photo by Max Waldman. 1969. Max Waldman Archives. All Rights Reserved.)

ture," the matter of photo documentation assumes some importance because it registers one of the few remaining public traces of what, exactly, those contorted and heaving bodies were *doing* in performance.[1] However, it's also transparently the case that the context in which such images are read has changed substantially in the thirty years since American experimental theater dominated the New York scene and occupied the minds (and bodies) of some of the most original thinkers and practitioners American theater has produced. Whereas in the 1960s the unfinished look of the production photos communicated many of the most prized aesthetic aims of the period—immediacy, authenticity, "poor theater," and a directness suggesting forms of countercultural political engagement—such rawness is not likely today to suit the eye of a generation weaned on ever more densely pixellated images routinely Photoshopped through several revisions (I've even heard these called "revivals") before being presented (in an irony Schechner might relish) as thoroughly simulated versions of "Actuals."

The discrepancy between these different ways of interpreting the visual record left by experimental collectives like the Performance Group dramatizes both the divided legacy they have handed down and the discordant nature of contemporary theater and culture. Strangely, however, the disparity may also help to explain why so little actual work from the group's theatrical practices and productions is seen in the cutting edge of contemporary theater. One can hardly imagine today any of the Performance Group's works being revived, much less received, in an unironic manner that would leave any measure of its original earnestness intact. This absence of direct manifestations of earlier group theater aesthetics in today's work may indicate a sharp rupture between modern and postmodern forms of theater, or at least a breach between a past counterculture heavily invested in community-making and a post-Reagan America characterized by discrete individuals absorbed into temporary affiliations of culture, media, and capital.

Certainly the Performance Group, perhaps more forthrightly than most other theater collectives of the period, propelled to an emphatic last gasp some of modernism's intransigent (and perhaps irresolvable) crises—regarding the humanist subject, the relation of avant-garde art to popular culture and to high art institutions, and the place of ritual in the modern world—thereby pushing forward by the very limitations of their agenda the process of rethinking such practices and reconfiguring them into what today has become normative in postmodern culture and theory. Robert Brustein once wrote of the Living Theatre that it "had performed an unintentional service by marking the territory beyond which it was fruitless and unproductive to tread."[2] Whether or not this assessment is fair in regard to either the Living Theatre or the Performance Group (and there are good reasons and sufficient evidence to suggest it is not), the overwhelming triumph of a late capitalist or postmodern sensibility that defers or negates virtually all stable forms of community and the unmediated authenticity upon which such community can be based has rendered group theater's aesthetic legacy and its cultural politics ambivalent at best, and at worst retrograde. It may well prove, then, that the Performance Group's most enduring legacy will be the means by which its work is deployed, sometimes rather disparagingly, by contemporary theater historiography and performance theory as a mainly negative example to be used in forging some understanding of key issues in the fields, such as the history and problematics of authenticity in performance, the relation of performance to contemporary politics, the temporal and aesthetic relations of modernism to postmodernism, and so on.

In such narratives, the Performance Group's failure to come to grips with a changing cultural and theatrical context and to incorporate these changes into its training and productions will likely be highlighted, after which critics will then be free to argue that the company's derelictions (and more generally group theater as a movement) produced a counter-response that catalyzed the development of a new generation of alternative theater artists prepared to explore different directions in accord with an emerging "postmodern condition." Schechner's troupe provides a tidy frame for such a genealogy because of dramatic schisms that opened up between the director and elements of the company, many of whom—Elizabeth LeCompte and Spalding Gray, for instance—used these clashes to forge new styles of alternative theater and performance that sought to address changing notions of textual instability, the actor's authentic presence, the use of environmental design, and the relationship of performer to audience.

However, even if group theater work of the 1960s and 1970s will find itself at times portrayed as an embarrassing bloodline to postmodern theater ("accursed progenitor!")—and it almost certainly will—there exist as well more positive legacies that emerge, if not directly from the Performance Group's performances or the nature of its collectivity, then from the retrospective imagination exercised upon it by many of its former members. Schechner, most publicly, has used the period following his work with the Performance Group and his continued association with academia and East Coast Artists to develop an increasingly expansive theory of "performance" as a cross-disciplinary subject constituting a confederated field of academic inquiry. While it would be an overstatement to argue that Schechner "invented" performance studies out of his experiences with the Performance Group, he certainly laid the groundwork for one of its most vital realizations by his early championing (and unique interpretations) of Grotowski, Barba, Brook, and others at a time when Harold Clurman's Group Theatre aesthetics still dominated directorial styles and actor training in the United States. As well, the Performance Group's elaboration of environmental staging (developing Schechner's earlier work with the New Orleans Group and the Free Southern Theater) as both a theatrical practice and the basis for theories of audience participation, the ritual use of space, and the decentering of the dramatic text, have proved central to developing the more anthropological forms of performance theory.

The influence of the Performance Group's work is not of course limited to theoretical or academic developments alone, nor can its entire legacy be traced only through Schechner's role in it. The characteristic qualities of the Performance Group productions—environmental design, the use of ritual and shamanism in performance, the reconfiguration of canonical pre-texts by the company (acting as "final arbiters" of the production), pre-expressivity and group therapy in actor training and performance, and so on—has considerably influenced the development of contemporary activist, community-based theater in America, which, lacking the same communal organization and politics as the Performance Group, has perhaps positioned itself to better address the social and cultural milieu of an increasingly fractious society. And so, even as the Performance Group's legacy as a negative example must be recognized and analyzed, it is a mistake to assume that the desires and needs that its practices engaged have been displaced entirely from contemporary culture and theater.

The Negative Legacy: A Failed Politics of Presence?

The next generation of students and scholars will likely first encounter the Performance Group's work in such comprehensive secondary studies as Margaret Croyden's *Lunatics, Lovers and Poets,* Christopher Innes's *Avant Garde Theater, 1892–1992,* C. W. E. Bigsby's *Critical Introduction to Twentieth-Century American Drama,* Arnold Aronson's *American Avant-Garde Theatre: A History,* and (specifically related to the Performance Group's actor training) in Phillip Zarilli's *Acting (Re)Considered.* Interestingly, as well as providing descriptive and contextualizing material on the work, each of these sources includes rather sharp critiques of the Performance Group's aims and practices. The company's dependence on canonical literary pre-texts, while it simultaneously polemicized for a nonliterary theater of an Artaudian "affective athleticism," is often presented as evidence that the Performance Group was not willing to go far enough in destabilizing the dramatic canon or function of the author (as, for instance, Grotowski and Chaikin were to do). In terms of actor training, Schechner's inclinations toward what Zarilli calls "immediate expressivity and 'presence' in the theatrical moment" have been interrogated as part of the larger examination of logocentric presence initiated by Derrida and carried on by many others.[3] As Elinor Fuchs succinctly summarized this critique in an important early essay, "Presence and the Revenge of Writing: Re-thinking Theatre after Derrida":

> The Presence cultivated by such theatre practitioners as the Becks, Richard Schechner, Joseph Chaikin, and Peter Brook . . . was staked on the revelations of the self and a corresponding suspicion of the text. To the positive value assigned to improvisation, audience participation, myth, ritual and communion they opposed a view of the author's script as a politically oppressive intruder, demanding submission to author-ity. The speech that bubbled up from the inner depths was more trustworthy than the alien written

word, and many of them experimented with efforts to slip the con-
stricting knot of language altogether.[4]

As part of a related critique, Aronson points to the Performance
Group's failure to recognize the lack of communal foundations and
shared myths in American culture, and declares that experimentation
with environmental scenography has ended.[5] Bigsby begins his account of
the Performance Group by relating some of Grotowski's criticisms of
American experimental theater in general (itself a rather suspect tactic),
and mentions in particular the questionable dynamics of the collective.
Foremost among these is the use of group therapy as a means to reach a
collective identity that produced, not just the desired state of collectivity
but "a sense of exclusiveness, a condescension with respect to the experience of those outside the magic circle who could be alternately wooed
and patronised."[6] Bigsby argues that this leads inevitably, as many commentators have mentioned, to forms of participation always already
tinged with manipulation. More deeply, Bigsby and others locate a senti-
mentalism and romanticism at the core of the Performance Group's theoretical and practical work that produces a troubling ahistoricism and an
increasing fascination with myth and metaphysics, a point to which I will
return, with a different twist, later in this essay.

These critiques of the Performance Group's work generally point to defects in its aesthetic and its flawed conceptualization of how a countercultural group theater ought to produce its work in relation to hegemonic
culture. Such arguments, although manifestly important in launching theoretically sophisticated and historically grounded analyses of forms of collective theater-making (forms that seem sometimes amenable to neither
theory nor history), are themselves certainly open to countercritique.
Aronson, for instance, announces the end of environmental theater as if
this were owing to flaws in Schechner's original axioms and the Performance Group's scenographic practices, or as if it were an idea whose potency has simply waned. But if one roots the decline of interest in environmental theater, as Steve Nelson and Schechner himself have done, in
cultural and ideological terms, then one not only understands how the
forces of late capitalism and consumer culture have co-opted Schechner's
original notions to (as Nelson says) "redecorate the fourth wall," but also
that environmental theater's demise has been greatly exaggerated by lack
of attention to how it continues to influence mass spectacles and entertainments.[7] Not only should performance studies analyze mass cultural
uses (and abuses) of environmental scenography, it should also turn away
from the practice's manifestations solely in high-art, avant-garde theater

practice located in traditional urban centers, and consider as well its continued widespread appearance in community-based, activist performance work.

More recently, however, in addition to criticisms of particular practices of mise-en-scène, the work of experimental theater artists of the 1960s has also been judged negatively in terms of its cultural politics, especially as these relate to the pivotal changes taking place in Western economic and social spheres during the period of group theater's renaissance. In an exemplary deconstruction, for instance, Philip Auslander focuses on the Performance Group's "politics of ecstasy" and the theatrical presentation of authenticity and performative "presence" that undergirds such a politics. With experimental companies like the Living Theatre and the Performance Group forcefully emphasizing the theater's direct presentation of behavior rather than literary drama's foregrounding of representation, argues Auslander, the weight of meaning was thrown naturally on the live presence of the performer, her existence in shared space and time before the audience. As Schechner describes it, "Behavior is marked by qualities of presence and contingency, both contested terms. *Presence* means that the author or producer of the behavior is there actually behaving, actually doing at the same moment and in the same space as the receivers. *Contingence* [*sic*] means that no score is perfectly reenacted time and again. Every instance is either an original or there is no original anytime."[8] In the Performance Group's best-known works *(Dionysus in 69; Commune; Makbeth),* both presence and contingency were emphasized in order to promote a radical politics of liberation by situating the fully present, vulnerable, and therefore existentialized (even spiritualized) performer before an audience meant to see the actor as an exemplar of authenticity in all its freedom. As Auslander argues, such an actor performs as "charismatic Other" to the repressed spectators, reminding them that they do not yet live in the moment according to their own desires, but exist instead in various stages of inauthenticity where contingency is abolished in favor of the masks and plots imposed upon them by a repressive society.[9] The existential aura of the successful performer, it is surmised, will be sufficient to draw the spectator into the direct experience of his or her own potential presence and contingency, thus establishing community with the audience based in like feeling and freedom (one is always shocked to remember that, in 1970, there were over two thousand communes operating in the United States). Such moments were most directly sought in the audience participation exercises and caresses of *Dionysus in 69* and, less manipulatively, in the request that spectators contribute their shoes to a growing pile that would become, in *Commune,* a synecdoche for the corpses left at My Lai.[10]

In order to distinguish a "transgressive" experimental theater of the 1960s and 1970s from a postmodern theater of "resistance," Auslander situates the Performance Group's performances in a strictly modernist "Artaudian/Grotowskian/Beckian line of thought" that manifests the belief that "because the presence of the actor as one living human being before others is spiritually and psychologically liberating in itself, [the] pure presentation of performer to audience is the best means available to the theater to make a radical spiritual/political statement."[11] The truly authentic actor (or experimental theater company), therefore, retains the modernist belief that art may stand autonomously outside the commodity culture that organizes and constrains play, and may even threaten capitalism's hegemony by presenting embodied proof of its alternative. This notion of presence, however, is claimed by Auslander to have been put to the test during the Vietnam War years and to have been invalidated by an emerging postmodern condition. Describing the social context in which the Performance Group performed (the war and, after the Paris strikes and occupations of 1968, the emergence of a counterculture characterized by its use of political spectacles such as street demonstrations and guerrilla theater), Auslander concludes that experimental group theaters still caught up in a politics of ecstasy were soon to find themselves fighting a rearguard action. As more and more "authentic" spectacles of protest (motivated by both the Left and Right) revealed the hands of "spectacle managers" and other very unplayful and uncarnivalesque mediations, the very notion of pure presence was undermined. As a result:

> Postmodernist theater and performance artists and theorists implicitly and explicitly rejected the premises of the ecstatic political theater of the 1960s: its reliance on the presence of the performer, its reluctance to engage commodity culture by entering into it, its dramatistic model of political art and action, its communitarianism.[12]

Adopting the language of the postmodern, Auslander then goes on to describe artistic activities—stand-up comedy, performance art, and the early work of the Wooster Group (including LeCompte and Gray)—that, foregoing artistic autonomy, ecstasy, and revolution, have explored instead a politics of "radical complicity" and "resistance."

The Performance Group's rather public demise in the late 1970s and its slow transformation into the Wooster Group often plays a large part in narratives relating the shift from modernist to postmodernist sensibilities in American group theater.[13] As LeCompte (who joined the Performance Group in 1970 after seeing *Dionysus in 69*) increasingly became disaffected by Schechner's focus on a ritualized environmental design and his use of group therapy and other psychoanalytical methods to develop actor training in ever more vulnerable and cathartic directions,[14] she began to develop her own work within the Performance Group's collective framework, working closely with Gray and other performers.[15] Even in her own appearances with the company, the notoriously stage-shy LeCompte distanced herself from her roles with elaborate masks, wigs, makeup, and task-oriented acting preparations. As a director, by as early as 1975 she was moving resolutely away from the performance of actorly presence and evolving a style—influenced by the work of Richard Foreman, Stuart Sherman, and Robert Wilson—that emphasized the phenomenological "breaks" and brackets that mediate "liveness" and performance.[16] Speaking of *Sakonnet Point,* for instance, LeCompte insisted that the performance was in no way thematically driven to present the past of Gray's childhood in any direct, present way: "The piece isn't about the past, it's really about us thinking about the past."[17]

By 1980, with Schechner's interest in the group (and perhaps his control over it) waning steadily after trips to India and East Asia, and interest in the "cooler" approach to training and composition gaining ground steadily, LeCompte and those members of the Performance Group interested in working with her formally constituted the Wooster Group and separated from Schechner and other performers from his company (the first Wooster Group trilogy, *Three Places in Rhode Island,* and its epilogue, *Point Judith,* had already premiered under the auspices of the Performance Group). Although relations between LeCompte, Gray, and Schechner have appeared strained publicly over the years, LeCompte acknowledges the formative influence of the Performance Group's experiments with environmental design and the use of the text as material to be confronted by the collective rather than simply "done" in its entirety.

But the notion that the Wooster Group should be solely credited with bringing these practices more "up to date" with a postmodern sensibility, and thus relegating the Performance Group's work to the dustbin of theater history is, however, difficult to support. Certainly the coincidence of the Wooster Group's rise to national prominence after the events surrounding the use of blackface in *Route 1 & 9 (. . . the Last Act . . .)* (1981), and the sudden (but belated) arrival of poststructuralist theory to a wide readership of theater scholars and critics around the same time, allowed the use of multiple and disarticulated texts to lend greater cachet to

Wooster Group performances than the very similar practices of the Performance Group were ever granted.[18] No doubt LeCompte's painterly aesthetic and her more intellectualized sense of the ironies arising from the juxtaposition of texts (linguistic, spoken, amplified through microphones, as well as imagistic and mediated through video monitors) places her compositional style more in line with the "free play" and "always already" mediated notion of textuality propounded by Barthes, Derrida, and Foucault.[19] Most importantly, LeCompte's willingness to develop training techniques in a more ad hoc and improvisational manner, as opposed to what she claims was Schechner's insistence on "working backward" by "perpetra[ting] training for his own legitimacy/propaganda even when the results of the training stood in direct antagonism to his ideas," makes the work of the Wooster Group "experimental" in an open-ended and thus postmodern way that the Performance Group's was never intended to be.[20]

However, given the eventual backlash against the dominance of poststructuralism in the academy, and of endless ironizing and apolitical indeterminacy in postmodern performance, it is by no means a fait accompli that the modernist aesthetics and practices of the Performance Group have been left behind in a postmodernist wake. Nevertheless, the Performance Group's legacy will forever be bound up with the rise of the Wooster Group as one of the most successful and enduring group theaters to emerge in America. Although this is in a very true sense an accurate summary, it is not complete. Thus, in order to wrest the modernist patrimony of group theater from such a constricted, dead-end narrative, I will now consider some potentially more positive legacies that have hitherto been eclipsed by the dominance of postmodern theories and theaters.

Constructing the Positive

The critiques of American group theater I have thus far recounted have stood up well and have proved useful in pointing to various ruptures between modern and postmodern theater forms, and between the cultural politics of the collective past and localized present. Together, they forcefully make the case that the Performance Group's legacy is largely negative, that is, a tradition of honorable experiments (in actor training, collective performance, audience participation, environmental scenography, and so on) that have ultimately failed except in their unintended role as forebears of postmodern performance. Moreover, these failures are often posited as evidence of the larger dereliction of modernity itself, the final incapacity of that discourse to sustain itself in theatrical terms by grasping after the vestigial remains of the humanist subject, depth psychology, transcendental signifieds, and collective audience response. What waits over the horizon of these failures is the decathected and libidinal pleasures of postmodern performance, seemingly better positioned to address art's relationship to the constant transformations of late capitalism and to the position of the individual as an unstable signifier whose desires are always contained within the hegemony, ceaselessly circulated among innumerable and temporary conversions of capital, information, and imagery. As Roger Copeland once described it, like the wide-eyed Wallace Shawn over his *My Dinner with André* (Gregory), we listen attentively while the fantastic exploits of high modernist theater purists like Grotowski and Schechner are related in all their zaftig detail before we politely bring our napkins to our mouths to conceal the smirk.[21]

However, it seems necessary to complicate this single, and largely negative, narrative of 1960s group theater's legacy for several reasons. First, such a perspective tends to render theater history genetically, as if previous forms, once vitiated, give way to more advanced organisms that are better able to adapt to present circumstances. Such a simplified Darwinian model distorts a much more complicated reality in which residual elements of prior and seemingly defunct theatrical forms may take on new life in other guises, even as they give place to newer and more culturally dominant forms. Bruce McConachie's alternative to genetic history, what he calls the "theatrical formation" ("the mutual elaboration over time of historically-specific audience groups and theater practitioners participating in certain shared patterns of action"),[22] is useful here because it allows us to follow the legacy of the Performance Group beyond the modernist cul-de-sac it is said to have culminated in to see how it continues to operate within a theatrical formation that, although dominated and to some degree erased in academic scholarship by certain types of postmodern theater, nevertheless maintains variations on the practices explored by the Performance Group.

Second, the periodization suggested by Auslander and others in order to create a genetic theater history is open to interrogation because it assumes a rather sharp break between modernism and postmodernism that is, from current perspectives, difficult to justify. It is possible, for instance, to position the Performance Group, not at the dead end of a modernist avant-garde, but rather as heralding what Richard Sheppard calls a "first phase" of postmodernism, one characterized by "counter-cultural opposition and celebratory affirmation, and includ[ing] such writers and artists as Robert Rauschenberg, Jasper Johns, Jack Kerouac, Allen Ginsburg and the Beat Poets, John Cage, William Burroughs, Donald Barthelme, Andy

Warhol, Susan Sontag, the Fluxus Group, the Conceptualists of the Situationist International (1957–72), Joseph Beuys, and Henri Chopin."[23] Operating at the apex of a cultural moment when immersion in the dominant culture was seen neither to void the possibility of critical distance nor to signal what Fredric Jameson would later call the more pessimistic, second phase of postmodernism's "experience of defeat" and its devolution into "blank irony," this affirmative version of postmodernism has generally been absent from most theoretical discourse.[24] As we shall see, however, it survives as a viable alternative (although not beyond critique) to the more ludic and nihilistic formulations of the postmodern condition, which themselves have been questioned for being reactionary and quietistic.[25]

Third, as Auslander himself points out, the argument that postmodern theater and performance should work toward being resistant rather than transgressive in the old avant-garde sense is predicated upon conditions of commodity capitalism and mediatization specific to Western, and particularly American (even suburban), culture.[26] Even as globalization makes these conditions increasingly prevalent across the globe, the fact remains we are decidedly *not* "all postmoderns now." In fact, nascent social movements like antiglobalization make it clear that, for activists who still believe that critical distance (and dissidence) is possible despite the "society of the spectacle," it is not clear that even suburban America is emptied of residual and emergent discourses that might turn against the dominant paradigm of postmodernism and its concomitant narrowing of politics to acts of "transgression."

Against such assumptions we must consider comments such as those Schechner made to James Harding in a recent interview:

> Some of the radical experiments in space, environmental space for example, were made by people interested in what I call the backward-looking and the intercultural avant-garde (Grotowski and myself for example). We found our models for staging—as well as other aspects of our theater—in nontechnological cultures as well as in earlier versions of Western culture, in archaic and ritual practices.[27]

A "backward-looking and intercultural avant-garde" differs in some respects from the avant-garde that assumes a genealogical relation to what Auslander and other academics describe as Western postmodernity and postmodernism. By exploring what Schechner understands to be the unique conditions involved in being "backward-looking and intercultural," it becomes possible, I think, to trace a more positive legacy of the Performance Group's work in both theory and practice today.

Recently there have been attempts to reconfigure definitions of post-modernism (and sometimes modernism as well) so as to avoid the endgame scenarios suggested by prominent theorists such as Baudrillard and Žižek. Most relevant to the issue at hand here is the recent emergence of what some critics insist is a "constructive postmodernism" set in opposition to a "deconstructive postmodernism."[28] Against the perceived radical nihilism of the latter, constructive postmodernism attempts an ecological and phenomenological response that seeks patterns in the deconstructed free play of meaning and origins. Although the ideas associated with constructive postmodernism are transparently an attempt to refute the more extreme claims of postmodern theory, and to recuperate in modified form the ideologies of humanism, science, and spiritualism that most postmodern theory attempts to evacuate, there is no denying that these ideas attract a number of important thinkers from across the disciplines (perhaps most prominently the art historian Suzi Gablik). As well, constructive postmodernism offers a critical language and set of topoi that allow artists and thinkers normally marginalized by academic discourse (which tends to focus almost exclusively on deconstructive post-modernism) such as radical feminists, community arts activists, postmodern humanists, and the like, to reemerge as important nodes in the network of practices that make up the increasingly wide arena of what Andreas Huyssen calls postmodernism's "field of tension."[29]

As part of the more general reaction against the extremes of poststructuralist and postmodern theories that begins with Habermas's *The Philosophical Discourse of Modernity* (1985), constructive postmodernism argues, in N. F. Gier's somewhat overwrought formulation, that "the French deconstructionists are throwing out the proverbial baby with the bath water. [They] wish to reject not only the modern worldview, but any worldview whatsoever."[30] Sharing deconstruction's suspicion of logocentrism and the dominance of Cartesian rationalism and the Enlightenment faith in science, the constructive postmodernists would attempt, not simply to affirm this state of radical multiperspectivism, but to join forces with the "new sciences" of nonlinear systems theory, cybernetics, and other forms of pattern-based thinking to rediscover and "re-enchant" the world by divining orders of meaning and value hidden to linear and logocentric thinking. The New Age rhetoric of much constructive postmodernist thought arises from its desire to forge an integrated concept of humankind and social reality out of "the best" elements of premodern and modern societies, seeking a union of gemeinschaft and gestellschaft that will "avoid the liabilities of both premodernism and modernism."[31] As expressed in cultural terms by Gablik in *The Reenchantment of Art,* the hope is for a new art "ushered in by twentieth-century physics, ecology and general systems theory, with its call for integrative and holistic modes of thinking."[32]

Schechner's work with the Performance Group was certainly "backward-looking" in its own way, but less as a nostalgia for the communal nature of premodern society ("There's no way back to a genuine premodernism. Who wants it anyway? Human life then was threatened by the environment. Today human life threatens the environment. What we need is balance")[33] than as a desire to find the performative means to reinvoke a premodern *mode of thinking* that intuitively seeks pattern and continuity rather than rupture, discontinuity, and fragmentation for its own sake. The "future of ritual," then, as Schechner names it in a recent book title, meant for the Performance Group the use of ritual not as a dance back to some forgotten tribal morn, but as an alienating device to reawaken forms of global thinking and social interaction that he senses are nearly lost from contemporary culture. In this context, the reawakening of ritual is a means to bring about the "end of humanism" with its Cartesian dualisms and linear thinking, and to prepare the way for a constructive postmodern consciousness: "A consciousness that relies on bundles and networks, on spheres, modes, and relations. It is a performance world reminiscent of medieval totalism, where actions are instantly transformed into relations."[34] Taking the postmodern notions of decentering and the loss of sustaining metanarratives at face value, Schechner follows the constructive postmodernist's impulse to see these as calling forth, not the free (and empty) play of difference, but "the construction of holistic, global systems":

> Because there is no center there must instead be an order of relations, not a hierarchy or a pyramid or a circle with a center point, but more like what the earth's atmosphere looks like from close space: whorls, constantly shifting but totally interrelated patterns or movements.[35]

This postmodernism produces, not the Baudrillardian "precession of the simulacra" in which passive and unresponsive monads are overwhelmed by the multiplicity of information and imagery and rendered incapable of experiencing the Real, but rather an information-rich environment that quickly breaks down linear thinking and provokes a multidimensional, performative imagination in order to discern texture and pattern in the matrix. For that reason, as Schechner points out, "his" avant-garde has always been "intercultural" and anthropological as well.

Like other constructive postmodernists, he uses the decentering of Western hegemony emphasized in deconstructive postmodernism as a means
to supersede existing geographical and cognitive maps defined by hierarchies and impermeable borders with "a lot of sponging up and down—
transfers, transformations, links, leaks. . . . One very complicated system."[36] Although he remains wary of the potential for globalization to
become just another form of neocolonialism, Schechner takes postmodernism's claims to decenter the West from its historical position as First
World as a sign of opportunities for complex and multileveled performative interactions around the globe. And, in perhaps the most important
legacy that group theater in America has left to the future, these ideas
have called forth new paradigms for understanding performance as it operates in contemporary cultures.

First, in its more theoretical manifestation, the influence of a constructive postmodernism within the performance practices of group theaters
like the Performance Group and the Open Theater have profoundly affected certain strands of performance studies—not always positively, to
my mind, but one cannot ignore their significance. Although the definitions, methodologies, and future paths of this still-emerging field are uncertain and often contested, the Performance Group's "backward-looking
and intercultural avant-garde" indisputably played a foundational role in
determining the global approach necessary to any formulation of the
field. Without the open laboratory format and process-oriented work utilized by the Performance Group and others (such as inviting the anthro-
pologists Edith and Victor Turner to rehearsals), it is doubtful that the re-
ceptiveness to anthropological theory and fieldwork methods that
characterizes many forms of performance studies today would have
emerged. Similarly, the Performance Group's actor training and its incor-
poration of methods drawn from transactional analysis played a significant
role in opening up exchanges between sociological disciplines and theater
studies, forcing the latter to confront a wider field of human performance
than the mere enactment of dramatic scripts. Perhaps most importantly,
the Performance Group's work in environmental staging was to produce
effects ranging far beyond Jerry Rojo and Jim Clayburgh's unique
scenographies for *Dionysus in 69, Commune, Mother Courage,* and other productions. Not only did Schechner's elaboration of Allan Kaprow's ideas
from *Assemblages, Environments, & Happenings* (1966) bring painterly discourse into the remit of theater practice and studies (with profound results for former Performance Group members like Elizabeth LeCompte),
it also helped prepare the way (along with reader response theory from literary studies) for consideration of performance as space, time, and behav-

ior that is given meaning only within a dynamic that includes the audience. From there, it was not a long step to begin thinking about how this expanding and ever more complex web of interactions mimicked in important ways the "environment" as it was being discussed by ecologists; and, as Schechner was to write in the "Re-Introduction" to the 1994 reissue of *Environmental Theater,* "The theatrical and the ecological meanings of environment are not antithetical. An environment is what surrounds, sustains, envelops, contains, nests. But it's also participatory and active, a concantination [*sic*] of living systems."[37]

It's perhaps not surprising, then, that the "other legacy" of the Performance Group's work is found in forms of theater devoted to holistic and communitarian values, as well as to what Mat Schwarzman refers to as "the growing authority of 'Third World,' Environmental, Feminist and Queer social theory and social change models that view art and culture as important sites of struggle."[38] The language of constructive postmodernists like Schechner is more holistic than what many of us may be comfortable with because it prioritizes but does not limit itself to analyzing (and sometimes resisting) the effects of the information that we associate with a mediatized (and mostly Western) postmodern culture. That is, while recognizing the importance of the flow of representational signs, commodities, and images as both bearers of information and iconoclasts of continuity in the modern world, constructive postmodernism also acknowledges the effects produced within this dynamic by objects and processes both more tangible and sometimes less so: the body, behaviors ranging from breath to speech to emotional release, landscape both inhabited by human communities or bereft of them, healing, festivals, game playing, and so on. Because of its focus on such "concatenations of living systems," the constructive approach to postmodernism's rich overload of information and its propensity to mix cultures indiscriminately through travel both physical and virtual has proved itself especially useful to forms of theater whose primary (and generally optimistic) goal is healing and the shaping of continuity and meaningful pattern.

Among those groups and organizations currently following some version of the constructivist postmodern agenda, one might list community-action theaters, theater for development projects around the world, neighborhood workshops addressing local issues of gender, language, race and class difference, feminist-based community-building narrative performance in California, prison theater in Argentina, Suzanne Lacy's categories of "new genre public art," and other instances where the efficacy of performance is intended to be more than simply transgressive and ironic.[39] From Joe Varga's environmental designs for Richard Owen

Geer's community-based work *(Swamp Gravy)*, the continued importance of ritual structure in feminist performance, and the group psychology work taking place in theater-in-education classrooms in Britain and around the world, the legacy of American group theater in general, and the Performance Group in particular, remains vibrant despite its long absence from most academic discourse.[40] Similarly, Eugenio Barba's "horizontal interculturalism" and the activities of ISTA (International Schools Theatre Association) and other professional organizations stubbornly maintain an insistence that pattern, rather than difference, is the emergent paradigm within which to practice meaningful performance and to share performance traditions across cultures.[41]

Schechner can display, as Patrice Pavis has written, "a resolute optimism, perhaps excessively so" in his drive to mix cultures in a dynamic that he believes must eventually level them and thereby yield greater understanding.[42] Such are the hazards, it seems, of believing in our time that pattern, rather than difference, is the emergent paradigm within which to understand our place in a global and information-saturated world. But if the legacy of American group theater is to be made visible, one cannot accomplish this by writing genetic history alone, focusing on how the new is different and more suitable than the old. One must look for more complicated patterns, and in doing so, one might conclude, we are still influenced by that legacy.

NOTES

1. Richard Schechner, *The End of Humanism* (New York: Performing Arts Journal Publications, 1982), 36.

2. Robert Brustein, "Contemporary American Theatre: The Impotence of Freedom," *Theatre Quarterly* 3, no. 10 (1973): 34.

3. Phillip Zarrilli, *Acting (Re)Considered: Theories and Practices* (New York: Routledge, 1995), 15.

4. Elinor Fuchs, "Presence and the Revenge of Writing: Re-thinking Theater after Derrida," *Performing Arts Journal* 26–27, nos. 2–3 (1985): 164.

5. Arnold Aronson, *American Avant-Garde Theatre: A History* (New York: Routledge, 2000), 101–2.

6. C. W. E. Bigsby, *Beyond Broadway,* vol. 3 in *A Critical Introduction to Twentieth-Century American Drama* (Cambridge: Cambridge University Press, 1985), 126.

7. Steve Nelson, "Redecorating the Fourth Wall: Environmental Theatre Today," *TDR* 33, no. 3 (1989): 72–94.

8. James M. Harding, "An Interview with Richard Schechner," in *Contours of the Avant-Garde: Performance and Textuality,* ed. James M. Harding (Ann Arbor: University of Michigan Press, 2000), 203.

9. Philip Auslander, *Presence and Resistance: Postmodernism and Cultural Politics in Contemporary American Performance* (Ann Arbor: University of Michigan Press, 1992), 44.

10. Schechner wrote in regard to the European production of *Commune* that "dancing with the audience was archaic by 1972." Cutting out the March to Death Valley that opened the original American production, Schechner believed, "gave the audience a chance to decide whether or not the murders would be re-enacted." He called this "the first thematically relevant, wholly conscious audience participation during the two years of playing *Commune.*" See Richard Schechner, *Environmental Theater* (1973; New York: Applause Books, 1994), 301.

11. Auslander, *Presence and Resistance*, 37.

12. Ibid., 42. To Schechner's credit, he soon became aware of both the darker side of an ecstatic politics (possibly because, in the wake of *Dionysus in 69*, some audience members asked to join the the the Performance Group "cult") and the lack of a foundation for communal culture in post-Eisenhower, late capitalist America. The work following *Makbeth*, for instance, shows much greater concern for using environmental space as a tool for complementing textual meaning and affect, rather than for inspiring direct audience participation.

13. See, for instance, David Savran, *Breaking the Rules: The Wooster Group* (New York: Theatre Communications Group, 1986); and Michael Vanden Heuvel, *Performing Drama/Dramatizing Performance: Alternative Theater and the Dramatic Text* (Ann Arbor: Uninversity of Michigan Press, 1991).

14. In an interview with Joan MacIntosh, Arnold Aronson commented that "MacIntosh's approach to performing might best be described as a mixture of physical training, traditional theatrical technique and psychological character development. In talking about creating a role, she occasionally will slip into jargon more often associated with so-called 'method' actor than a 'new theater' performer." *TDR* 20, no. 3 (1976): 31. Timothy Wiles characterizes acting influenced by Artaud and Grotowski as moving toward "theater as a separate reality" through the catharsis, not of the spectator primarily, but of the actor. See *The Theater Event: Modern Theories of Performance* (Chicago: University of Chicago Press, 1980).

15. In LeCompte's first directed work, *Sakonnet Point* (June 1975), she joined Leeny Sack and Alexandra Ivanov, along with Gray and the eight-year-old Erik Moskowitz, in performing the piece. Sack and Ivanov were replaced in later performances (October 1975) by Joan MacIntosh and Libby Howes.

16. For discussion of LeCompte's early directing motifs, see Lenora Champagne, "Always Starting New: Elizabeth LeCompte," *TDR* 25, no. 3 (1981): 19–28; and Alexis Green, *Contemporary American Theater*, ed. Bruce King (New York: St. Martin's Press, 1991), 117–34.

17. Arnold Aronson, *"Sakonnet Point,"* *TDR* 19, no. 4 (1975): 35.

18. For discussion of early carryovers from poststructuralist theory to New York alternative theater, see Fuchs, "Presence and Revenge"; Gerald Rabkin, "Is There a Text on this Stage? Theater/Authorship/Interpretation," *PAJ* 26–27, nos. 2–3 (1985): 142–59; Michael Feingold, "North Pedantic," *Village Voice*, February 7, 1984. For a retrospective look at the mutual influences of academic theory and the work of the Wooster Group, see Mike Vanden Heuvel, *"L.S.D. (Let's Say Deconstruction!): Narrating Emergence in American Alternative Theater History,"* in *The*

Wooster Group and Its Traditions, ed. Johan Callens (New York: Peter Lang/Presses Interuniversitaires Européennes, 2004).

19. Although LeCompte has often gone on record to express her disregard for contemporary theory, Euridice Arratia reports that while preparing *Brace Up!* she read aloud to the performers essays on Noh and *kyogen* theater from Barthes's *Empire of Signs.* See "Island Hopping: Rehearsing the Wooster Group's *Brace Up!*" *TDR* 36, no. 4 (1992): 138.

20. Elizabeth LeCompte, "Who Owns History?" *PAJ* 6, no. 1 (1981): 52.

21. Roger Copeland, "A Post-Mortem for the Post-Modern," *Theater* 22, no. 3 (1991): 67.

22. Bruce McConachie, *Melodramatic Formations* (Iowa City: University of Iowa Press, 1992), 232.

23. Richard Sheppard, *Modernism—Dada—Postmodernism* (Evanston, Ill.: Northwestern University Press, 2000), 359.

24. Douglas Kellner, "Introduction: Jameson, Marxism, and Postmodernism," in *Postmodernism/Jameson/Critique,* ed. Douglas Kellner (Washington, D.C.: Maissonneuve, 1989), 23.

25. For an overview of such critiques of postmodern theory, see Sheppard, *Modernism—Dada—Postmodernism,* 364–65.

26. See Auslander, *Presence and Resistance,* 11, 169.

27. Harding, "Interview with Richard Schechner," 208.

28. See especially Suzi Gablik, *Has Modernism Failed?* (1984; New York: Thames and Hudson, 1986), and *The Reenchantment of Art* (New York: Thames and Hudson, 1991); David Ray Griffith, John B. Cobb Jr., Marcus P. Ford, and Pete A. Y. Gunter, *Founders of Constructive Postmodern Philosophy: Peirce, James, Bergson, Whitehead and Hartshorne* (Albany: SUNY Press, 1993); Frederick Ferre, *Being and Value: Toward a Constructive Postmodern Metaphysics* (Albany: SUNY Press, 1996), and *Knowing and Value: Toward a Constructive Postmodern Epistemology* (Albany: SUNY Press, 1998).

29. Andreas Huyssen, *After the Great Divide: Modernism, Mass Culture, and Postmodernism* (London: Macmillan, 1986), 217.

30. N. F. Gier, *Spiritual Titanism: Indian, Chinese, and Western Perspectives* (Buffalo: SUNY Press, 2000), 13.

31. Ibid., 14.

32. Gablik, *Has Modernism Failed?* 6.

33. Schechner, *The End of Humanism,* 119.

34. Ibid., 119.

35. Ibid., 120.

36. Ibid., 125.

37. Schechner, *Environmental Theater,* iv.

38. Mat Schwarzman, "It's About Transformation," *High Performance* 64, no. 4 (1996): 32.

39. See Suzanne Lacy, ed., *Mapping the Terrain: New Genre Public Art* (Seattle: Bay Press, 1995); and Schechner, *Performance Studies: An Introduction* (New York: Routledge, 2002).

40. Perhaps it is more specifically absent from theoretical discourse. Recent exchanges in academic journals such as *TDR* regarding the efficacy of community-based performances attest to continued interest in such constructive postmod-

ernist work. See, for example, the exchange over Sara Brady's essay on the "Non-Radicality" of *Steelbound* (a community-based performance set in Bethlehem, Pennsylvania) in *TDR* 45, no. 3 (2001).

41. For "horizontal interculturalism," see Schechner, *Performance Studies*, 245–51.

42. Patrice Pavis, "Interculturalism and the Culture of Choice: Richard Schechner Interviewed by Patrice Pavis," in *The Intercultural Performance Studies Reader*, ed. Patrice Pavis (New York: Routledge, 1996), 41.

THE BREAD AND PUPPET THEATER
Historical Overview

The highly visible presence of its gigantic puppets accompanied by grotesquely masked performers parading through antiwar demonstrations drew international attention to the work of the Bread and Puppet Theater in the mid-1960s and made it one of the seminal guerrilla theater troupes to emerge during that turbulent decade. Enormously influential, the Bread and Puppet Theater not only redefined how theater is done in the streets but also how mass demonstrations are conceptualized and staged. Today, variations on its puppets and masks remain a staple ingredient in major political demonstrations throughout the world, and Bread and Puppet itself is still active as a theater after four decades of work and numerous transformations. The one constant in these transformations has been Peter Schumann, Bread and Puppet's undisputed artistic director, whose work has remained so closely associated with that of Bread and Puppet that distinctions between the two are often difficult to make. Indeed, throughout the sixties, the group was repeatedly identified in advertisements and reviews as "Peter Schumann's Bread and Puppet Theater"—something, as Stefan Brecht has noted, other collectives like the Performance Group, the Living Theatre, and the Open Theatre "scrupulously avoided or prevented" despite having dominant directors.[1]

This close association between Schumann and Bread and Puppet has generated some confusion among scholars as to the precise year in which the Theater began. Depending on the scholar, the dates vary among 1961 (Shank), 1962 (Bread and Puppet Archives, UC Davis), and 1963 (Brecht, Bell).[2] What is certain is that shortly after Schumann's arrival in

New York from Germany in 1961, his previous experience in sculpture, choreography, and puppetry quickly led him to the circle of avant-garde artists who lived in the city's Lower East Side and who, in a wide variety of artist expressions, were challenging conventional notions of theater and performance in formats like the Happenings, in groups like the Living Theatre, and in venues like the Judson Memorial Church, where in the spring of 1962 Schumann himself conceived and directed a ritual dance of death appropriately entitled *The Totentanz*.

Although the rudimentary characteristics of Bread and Puppet performances were a part of *Totentanz*, general consensus tends to locate the beginning of the Bread and Puppet Theater in October of the following year in a Lower East Side loft on Delancy Street, where Peter Schumann along with Bruno Eckhardt and Robert Ernstthal began a small experimental theater troupe. In works like *The King's Story* (1963), they produced performances that combined sculpture, puppetry, music, and dance. Other members of this original core group, which remained intact until early in 1968, included Elka Schumann, Eva Eckhardt, Charlie Addams, and Irving Doyle. They named the group Bread and Puppet Theater, in part because of the now legendary practice initiated by Schumann of distributing his own freshly baked dark bread at the beginning of each performance—a gesture that not only carried with it the communal-ritualistic import of "breaking bread together" but also the symbolic suggestion, according to Schumann, that theater ought to be as substantial, nourishing, and commonplace as bread itself.[3] Indeed, the sharing of bread with the audience is, in many respects, an outgrowth of what Françoise Kourilsky has characterized as a basic communal spirit that Bread and Puppet owed to the circus tradition of being a "self-supporting commune." As Kourilsky notes, the Bread and Puppet Theater is about "making things, baking bread, building puppets, and putting on shows" while "trying to live off what it produces with little outside financial aid."[4]

Throughout the sixties, Bread and Puppet was located in New York, touring widely but working out of the Lower East Side. Although the group continued to do indoor theater, Schumann affirmed in a 1968 *TDR* interview that the heart of their theater was "performance in the streets."[5] At the time of this interview, Bread and Puppet performances were closely associated with the politics of protest and the growing resistance to the Vietnam War, and much of Bread and Puppet's most significant work during this period involved a creative, choreographed, and highly visible presence at major antiwar demonstrations, where they paraded large anti-industrialist puppets like "Uncle Fatso" and donned shrouded masks like Schumann's Vietnamese women. Even indoor theatrical pieces like *Fire* (1966) took an antiwar stance. Among the more significant examples of Bread and Puppet's street theater during this period were outdoor works like *A Man Says Goodbye to His Mother* (1968) and *The Cry of the People for Meat* (1969). In the former a young man takes leave of his mother and goes to a distant, dangerous land where as an armed soldier he participates in a variety of atrocities before being killed himself. The latter combines biblical imagery with a highly critical depiction of imperialism and violence.

As the sixties drew to a close, the Bread and Puppet Theater had grown sizably, in part because its considerable international reputation allowed for the planning of larger spectacles and larger tours. But the increased size also began to lead to tension within the group and to difficulties reconciling the processes of its artistic direction with the group's democratic collectivism. These tensions came to a head toward end of the 1969 European tour, and when Bread and Puppet returned to the United States, Schumann began splitting the theater into smaller groups in an effort to manage its size. An invitation in 1970 for the Bread and Puppet Theater to become the theater in residence at Goddard College in Plainfield, Vermont, gave Schumann a more fundamental opportunity to rethink both Bread and Puppet's structure and its aesthetics. Taking only two members with him (Harvey Spevak and Bill Dalrymple), Schumann, his wife Elka, and their children left for the facilities on Cate Farm, which Goddard College had placed at his disposal.[6] In a larger sense, this move "coincided with the 1970s 'back to land' movement,"[7] and while it afforded Schumann the opportunity to explore new modes of artistic expression beyond "the aggressive-moralistic mode of street theatre,"[8] it also left Bread and Puppet divided between the Goddard residency, a Coney Island project, and a traveling circus. Neither the Coney Island project nor the traveling circus proved to be particularly successful, and gradually attention shifted entirely to the new base in Vermont.

Bread and Puppet's residency at Goddard lasted four years (1970–74), during which time, in addition to working on its own pieces, Bread and Puppet offered a wide variety of workshops to Goddard students. Since Goddard was never in a position to offer much financial support, Bread and Puppet had to rely on touring to generate revenue, and this necessity caused the theater to grow once again in size. Even in the early part of the residency at Goddard, when Bread and Puppet started touring *Birdcatcher* (1971) and *Simple Light* (1972), it was already back up to about twenty members, many of whom were new Goddard recruits.[9] As the years progressed, student interest in the theater dwindled, exacerbated in part by the college's refusal to facilitate Schumann's work with students.[10] After a

1973 European tour, the theater's residency at Goddard came to a end when Schumann announced that the group would do a final big circus and then disband.[11]

Far from marking the end of the Bread and Puppet Theater, the plans for that final circus were the harbinger of a new beginning. Schumann left Goddard College for Vermont's Northeast Kingdom, where, by way of his in-laws, he and his wife Elka had an old dairy farm in Glover. The Schumanns were followed to "the Dopp Farm" by a select group of performers who settled in the area and took up their own theatrical projects while also working with Schumann. This new group included John Bell, Trudi Cohen, Barbara Leber, and Michael Romanyshyn, among others. Although they worked on a number of different individual pieces, the most notable performances to emerge from Dopp Farm were the productions of the *Domestic Resurrection Circus*—an early version of which was first performed in 1970. These productions became annual Dopp Farm events. Beginning in 1975 and continuing until 1998, each of these outdoor productions focused on a different theme, for example, *Ishi* (1975), *The United States Bicentennial* (1976), *L'Histoire du pain* (1980), *Central American and Liberation Theology* (1984), *Theatrum Mundi* (1990) and *Unite!* (1998). As the years passed, the *Domestic Resurrection Circus* began to attract larger and larger audiences. By the late 1990s, it was a major tourist event, attracting audiences of forty to sixty thousand people, "who attended as seekers of entertainment and 1960s nostalgia."[12]

After the final production of the *Circus* in 1998, which had been marred by the murder of an audience member by another in a senseless fight, Schumann shifted to a format in which Bread and Puppet performed smaller pieces throughout the summer and thereby effectively cut the overwhelming and unmanageable onslaught of tourists to a single event.

Bread and Puppet continues to tour, and recently performed two antiwar pieces, *How to Turn Distress into Success: A Parable of War and Its Making* (2003) and *Standing-In-The-Way-Bystander Commemoration* (2003) at their annual engagement at the Theater for the New City in New York.

—J. M. H.

NOTES

1. Stefan Brecht, *Peter Schumann's Bread and Puppet Theatre*, 2 vols. (London: Methuen, 1988), 1:202.

2. See Theodore Shank, *Beyond the Boundaries: American Alternative Theatre*

(Ann Arbor: University of Michigan Press, 2002); Brecht, *Bread and Puppet Theatre*, John Bell, "Beyond the Cold War: Bread and Puppet Theater and the New World Order," p. 35.

3. Brecht, *Bread and Puppet Theatre*, 1:169.

4. Françoise Kourilsky, "Dada and Circus," *TDR* 18, no. 1 (1974): 107.

5. Peter Schumann, "With the Bread and Puppet Theatre," interview by Helen Brown and Jane Seitz, *TDR* 12, no. 2 (1968): 66.

6. Brecht, *Bread and Puppet Theatre*, 1:240.

7. John Bell, "Beyond the Cold War: Bread and Puppet Theater and the New World Order," in *Staging Resistance: Essays on Political Theatre*, ed. Jeanne Colleran and Jenny S. Spencer (Ann Arbor: University of Michigan Press, 1998), 36.

8. Brecht, *Bread and Puppet Theatre*, 2:14–15.

9. Ibid., 1:240.

10. Ibid., 2:259.

11. Ibid., 1:250.

12. John Bell, "The End of *Our Domestic Resurrection Circus:* Bread and Puppet Theater and Counterculture Performance in the 1990s," *TDR* 43, no. 3 (1999): 77.

"GO HAVE YOUR LIFE!"

Self and Community in Peter Schumann's Bread and Puppet Theater

Sonja Kuftinec

The inclusion of Bread and Puppet Theater in an anthology focused on collectives and group performance might seem at first oddly misplaced. The company emerges from the convictions and artistry of a single individual, choreographer/sculptor/designer/director Peter Schumann, who at times seems to productively discourage the formation of a stable group associated only with himself. When surrounded by young interns several years ago at his Glover, Vermont, home, Schumann reportedly shouted, "You all have to leave. Leave me alone. Go have your life!"[1] Yet, these very principles of resistance to group formation around an iconic individual, the call to "have a life," even the anecdotal source of a perhaps apocryphal historical fragment, grounds a critical overview of this artistically compelling, politically engaged, and in many ways community-based theater.

Over forty years, the Bread and Puppet Theater has remained a resilient presence on the American alternative theater scene, animated by ongoing interactions between the individual artist and community engagement, political sophistication and accessibility, commitment to the sacred and popular, and to Marxist and humanist ideologies. Rather than deconstructing these somewhat tenuous binaries, this essay positions the exchanges between them as essential to the development and critical situating of the theater, particularly to the intertwining of art and ideology in the company's outdoor parades, pageants, puppetry, and indoor performances "for the Insides."[2] The call to "go have your life," to rethink the material conditions and communal myths through which we live our lives, infuses this analysis, particularly the selection of sites to examine, all of which share in common my personal encounters with the theater.

Personal engagement might seem entirely too subjective a critical approach, while also excluding events and performance practices prior to my initial contact with the theater in 1986. The selection of sites, however, also encompasses existing archival documentation of a theater that does not publish its own performance scripts.[3] An approach that embraces the arc of the company to the present day additionally resists tendencies to moor the theater in the 1960s context from which it first emerges, and wrests Bread and Puppet from a linear theoretical narrative that stagnates the theater in a pre-postmodern realm.[4] Finally, emphasis on live encounters alongside archival analysis embraces the multisensory experience of the theater, one that complements its own nonliterary aesthetic. Each of the performance sites I focus on—a gallery exhibition in Soho, early indoor performances, and circus pageantry outdoors in Glover—emphasizes various aspects of the theater's aesthetic and ideological tensions.

Inside at the Exit, 2002, 1972, 1969

From May through August 2002, Soho's Exit Art Gallery showcased six "visually oriented" theater artists who began their careers in lower Manhattan.[5] "Show People: Downtown Directors and the Play of Time," juxtaposed installation spaces designed by and featuring the personal artistic journeys of Anne Bogart, Richard Foreman, Meredith Monk, Peter Schumann, Robert Wilson, and Reza Abdoh.[6] While bringing together these artists in a single conceptual space proves historically important and compelling, the choice to highlight individual artists potentially limits understanding of their relationships to ensemble. The focus on visionary (visually oriented as well as avant-garde and auteur) directors also frames the individual within a particular radical aesthetic context of 1960s New York.

Though trained in sculpture and dance, since founding the theater in 1963 Schumann has expressed ambivalence about this radical context and, at least in its early New York years, about the status of the theater as a company. In a 1968 interview he explained, "I wouldn't really consider us a company. There's a large turnover—and the size of each production is different."[7] While the nature of the company would change over time, particularly as individuals moved to Vermont year-round to organize and perform with the theater, some ambivalence exists within the quote itself. The plural pronoun referring to "the company" implies an existing group beyond Schumann's "I." Yet, its "turn-over" posits a fluctuating membership. As former *TDR* editor Erika Munk commented in 1970, "The people in the company may come and go, the masks [designed by Schumann] remain."[8] A present-day view again shifts the emphasis on group participation under Schumann's direction. "We always call it 'the company,' meaning those working full time," elaborates John Bell, a full-time member from 1975 to 1985, and part-time thereafter; but "Peter Schumann has always been the artistic director . . . a 'Bread and Puppet' show is one directed by Peter."[9]

According to many who have worked with Schumann, this arrangement produces profound artistic effects, embracing both his artistic leadership (the masks) and the collective contributions of various members over time (their animation), participants who also contribute music, costumes, characterization, and text. Longtime former company member Michael Romanyshyn allows that the ease of working creatively with Schumann's leadership may be generational.[10] One of Schumann's contemporaries (Schumann was born in 1934), radical activist Jules Rabin, acknowledged about his earlier work with the theater, "As a father of a family, I found it demeaning to subordinate myself to Peter, as one does working with him. He is the absolute master of his theater."[11]

Within Rabin's assertion, the pronoun slips again to a singular possessive "his," as it does in Stefan Brecht's prolific writing on the company's early years, referred to always as "Peter Schumann's Bread & Puppet Theatre." In a detailed depiction of *The Cry of the People for Meat* (1969) Brecht inscribes Schumann's individual artistry in an almost parodic excess of accreditation. "Conceived, produced, directed & narrated by Peter Schumann, performed by his Bread & Puppet Theater. Masks, costumes, lighting & music by Peter Schumann, with much help & a little inspiration from the company."[12] The company in this case seems little more than a loose group of helpful, mask-animating inspirers; an assumption that ongoing members quite cheerfully refute.[13]

Despite the refutation of past and current company members, the figure of the solitary and quite often male director persists in historical narratives of American experimental theater. James Roose-Evans's 1984 *Experimental Theatre from Stanislavsky to Peter Brook* places Bread and Puppet within a linear trajectory of alternative theaters that moved away from group creation "and owe their success to the ingenuity and decisions of their creator."[14] By focusing more on individual than on collective creation, "Show People" seems at first to lie within this trajectory.

Yet, Schumann's self-styled exhibition, re-creating a corner of the compelling and chaotic Bread and Puppet museum in Glover, resists individual focus. Where many of the other installations contain textual explanation by the artists describing or evoking their personal aesthetic journey, Schumann's more performative texts conjure the aesthetic and ideological drives of the Bread and Puppet Theater: anticapitalist, prohumanist, cheap art.[15] Constructed entirely of cardboard, paint, a wooden wind wheel, ropes, and papier-mâché, the space consists of a series of haunting and often comical figures, manifestos, and lyrical slogans.

A naked pink figure hovers high on one wall reading the "Naked Truth." Below, painted airplanes threaten sculpted miniature horses caged in barbed wire fences, as painted people fall from the sky. A sheet of paper emerging beneath them from a totemic masked tree announces: "Depleted uranium is the radioactive waste left after the extraction of weapons grade uranium. The depleted population of the U.S. government is a population left after the original grade life has been extracted from it." On the corner of a nearby wall a figure lies comatose under the title "The American Sleep," surrounded by more seated naked-truth readers, blind to the destruction around them. Perhaps they are part of the "regimented industrial sleep." Perhaps they have taken "pills for disengagement," leading to "drowsy participation democratic . . ." (the slogan trails off under the sleeping figure). Across the room two sculpted puppets sit facing each other and a wooden cross, as a figure above them wraps cardboard arms around his tortured body. Words wrap around the seated puppets' naked paper bodies below in never quite completed sentences of inaction: "We are very upset, we are, we are very, we are," "We are going, we are going, we are . . ." Hanging above in rows from hanging-open cardboard mouths, more figures in dunce caps submit their pious admonishments: "Thou shalt eliminate." "Thou shalt terrorize." Below and opposite to them, oppositional, if somewhat ambiguous, slogans appear to answer the dunces. "All holy cows and paper maché Gods unite against the supremacy of the Ruling Class God." Other slogans call for "Insurrection against the Existing order of life."

"Go have your life!" I remember Schumann (perhaps) advocating far away in his Glover workshop. Based on a body of work represented in the art gallery, and available on video in the exhibit, I surmise that this "life" must be oppositional to existing systems, the ruling class, to disengagement: he calls for the "original grade life," that which resists "drowsy participation."

Schumann has asserted that the Marxist theory conjured by these slogans against the ruling class had less influence on his thinking than pup-

Bird Catcher in Hell, 1971. (Photo by Etienne George.)

petry itself, a European folk tradition he declares "more radical than those sixties radicals."[16] Schumann critiques what he saw as apolitical hedonism. In contrast, he asserts, "Puppets are insurrectionists."[17] As iconic but somehow alienated beings, manipulated by but separate from human subjects, they exist in a liminal realm between representational and real, and can counter that real with perhaps greater effectiveness.

Schumann's figures enact a heterotopic space; what Michel Foucault refers to as a countersite in which "the real" is recognized, contested, and inverted. Schumann cites documents from a South American prison next to representational church figures, constituted by the words they say, while they do nothing. Inaction becomes a contested site inscribed on the body of the puppet. The contestation lies exactly within the gap between the representational and the real. In this kind of radical puppetry the figures are not consumable and "cute like muppets," they become instead "effigies and gods."[18] With these sculpted and painted cardboard figures Schumann consciously conjures a new reality, "a reality that first of all defines reality."[19] In doing so, he resists another "reality" in which "the arts are the privilege of the rich,"[20] and instead constitutes a countermetaphysics grounded in individual consciousness as well as particular material histories.

This intertwining of metaphysics, myth, and materiality through evocatively sculpted, and thus distancing, masks and puppets emerges in sharp detail within early Bread and Puppet indoor productions such as *Fire* (1966), *The Cry of the People for Meat* (1969), and *Gray Lady Cantata #2* (1972), the latter available on video at the exhibition. I settle into a bean-bag chair in the gallery café to view the piece, presented through a series of powerful tableaux, silent save for a chime that signals the end of each scene and a cello that sweeps under the stillness of select moments. The minimal action unfolds at a leisurely but compelling pace. Two women sit, figures masked by enormous sculpted faces and flowing robes: the eponymous gray ladies. A masked man drinks coffee. The plates, cups, and finally the chairs of this pseudodomestic scene are jerked off the shallow stage by attached strings. A jewel tear falls from the eye-hole of a masked figure, without sentimentality. Like the domestic props, the jewel is attached to a string, an object obviously manipulated into its staged signification, more powerful because of this rough doubling. In other scenes, a black cardboard plane moves against a painted backdrop by a seated gray lady. Strobe lights flash, bodies crawl across the stage pulled by ropes, by rope-creatures. The gray lady of the title is gently picked up. Schumann walks onto the stage and snaps off a light. A chorus of community participants enters and sings harmonically down the scale, "The sun it rises every day, and in the evening goes away," repeating the scale with a verse about the moon.

The images seem both easily readable and beyond absolute interpretation. We are nowhere in particular, but an outside world of planes, bombs, and destruction is clearly evoked. The final chorus both refers to and moves beyond this outside world. Verses speak of the cyclical order of life, of a natural rhythm beyond human action. Yet the embodiment through (finally) unmasked individuals seems strikingly "real." The humanness of the chorus becomes more visible when it follows the prior masked enactment: a Bertolt Brechtian de- and re-familiarization.

Beth Cleary refers to the "reduction of the self" that occurs in Bread and Puppet theater.[21] The performer's energy moves outside of the ego-self through the animating effigy. In the *Gray Lady's* communal chorus, as in a similar production I witnessed in 1999, the unmasked performing self reemerges only in relation to others. The theater seeks a reunion of individuals with a natural, almost sacred order, and at the same time recognizes the everyday destruction that works against this radical utopia. So in its aesthetic syntax, the theater seeks something greater than the quotidian and yet accessible to a popular audience—a quality Schumann feels that religious narratives once attained. "What we are looking for finally," he explained in 1972, "is a language, a mythology that is to everybody's understanding."[22] Combining Christian myth with European folk traditions with material history, shows such as *The Cry of the People for Meat* attempt to constitute that language.

The 1969 production, exquisitely documented by Stefan Brecht, brings together biblical narrative with Vietnamese testimonial, Mother Earth with Uncle Fatso (a cigar-smoking ur-capitalist), beast masks and tiny hand puppets. The action unfolds through a kind of circus-barker-meets-medieval-pageant aesthetic, most of it stage-managed by Schumann in full view of the audience, and accompanied by such "cheap" sound as pot-lid cymbals, kazoos, cowbells, crickets, horns made of washing machine agitators, and a tape of Second Avenue (New York City) traffic. Thirty years later, the printed, copied evocation still conveys a sense of the production's dense hybridity. In one extraordinary scene, the beatitudes emerge as slogans of resistance, images accompanying the parables of Jesus point up the present-day Vietnam-era hypocrisies in a rapid-fire vaudevillian pace.

While it is difficult to comment only briefly about this rich remnant, I want to mention three main points that emerge in relation to some of the aesthetic and ideological tensions earlier outlined. Rather than dismissing its authority as an opiate, the piece emphasizes the resistant power of some Christian narrative tropes, highlighting their anarchist and socialist elements. Stefan Brecht refers to this focus as transitioning from a "transcendentalist father-principle to an immanent life-principle,"[23] from authoritative power to individual human potential. Thus the recovery of the mythic within the sacred is balanced with a popular humanist sensibility. Early in the show's narrative, Schumann steps onto the stage to breathe life into Adam and Eve, but he does so as himself, or rather in his role as puppeteer. As Brecht explains, "Schumann's role is that of God, but he does not in any way act God: God is not there."[24] The creation myth here is clearly conjured by, rather than simply enacted through, human beings. Finally, the piece resists not only status quo politics but also assumptions about political theater. "Political theater tends to be slogan theater," explains Schumann in one manifesto. "[It] bores the equally-minded and offends precisely those customers whose hearts it wants to win."[25] While *Cry* both affirms the power of and resists certain precepts of religious myth, Bread and Puppet's theater offers what Friedrich Schiller referred to centuries ago as a new kind of unifying power, a "'form of communication' that engages inter-subjective relationships between people."[26]

Yet, despite this image of a radical artistic utopia, a new metaphysics of human relations, audiences might still view the theater as an aesthetic artifact. In reference to performances of *Fire*, Schumann reminisces, "Sometimes the play was performed where the audience simply took it as another example of modern, avant-garde theatre. They were viewing it for its aesthetic rather than its content."[27] For a piece that George Dennison in his well-known 1966 *Village Voice* review cited as a prayer for life and its vulnerability, a service for the dead that allowed the audience to "respond to the horrors of Vietnam,"[28] this less politically engaged response can seem especially inappropriate. But as Schumann himself notes, the indoor performances in theatrical spaces suffered from a disciplinary system and context that could precondition audience reception. "It's too comfortable, too well known," he ruminated in 1967. "People are numbed by sitting in the chairs in the same way."[29]

Baz Kershaw locates a production's effectiveness in the difference between the discursive limits of theater and the expressive excess of performance. The commodification of theater, of most theater-in-a-theater-building, limits its potential to provoke reflection and change.[30] Recognizing these limitations, Bread and Puppet complemented its quieter indoor pieces with popular, outdoor, mainly urban parades, along with rural pageants. Performed annually in the company's Glover, Vermont, setting for over twenty years, *Our Domestic Resurrection Circus,* its sideshows, ding-dongs, and derivatives, together offer another site to examine the interaction of theater, community, and notions of a better world over three decades in small-town Vermont.

"A Complete Other World": The Circus Comes to (and stays in) Town, 1986, 2002

Bread and Puppet's indoor shows, produced for the most part during the company's New York years from 1963 to 1970 and later on tour throughout the United States, Europe, and Latin America, contrast with Glover's outdoor pageantry in a number of ways. While both sites focus on clearly articulating "Good against Evil,"[31] the quieter, more intimately focused indoor shows require a different kind of attention and aesthetic than the bigger, bolder, more participatory outdoor pieces. Set into the environment of northern Vermont, these consciously carnivalesque and free productions strive to enact in their resistant content and exemplary context what George Dennison referred to as a "fragment or image of a better world."[32]

Schumann himself posits the circus as "a complete other world,"[33] and the production's rural context animates this possibility. Living as cheaply as possible, Peter and Elka Schumann, along with a year-round Bread and Puppet company, follow the tenets of Elka's grandparents, Scott and Helen Nearing, whose 1954 book *Living the Good Life* provided guidelines for later back-to-the-land movements.[34] The company continues to refuse corporate and foundation grants, subsisting on commissions, donations, and poster sales. They work with local carpenters and artist-plumbers, student interns and theater professors-cum-dishwashers. Yet, this ongoing effort to animate a utopian community of inclusion has still had to combat the pervasive forces of postindustrial capitalism—particularly an entertainment-oriented, nostalgia-driven consumer culture. John Bell's "The End of *Our Domestic Resurrection Circus*" offers a particularly astute analysis of counterculture-as-commodity and its role in the demise of the large-scale annual circus in 1998.[35] I will focus here on the dynamics of community formation and cultural critique through symbolic, ideological, and participatory associations.

I first encountered Bread and Puppet Theater as a college student in 1986 when I took the equivalent of a theater road trip with a few actor friends. I remember the vastness of the puppets operated by hundreds of participants, and of the outdoor audience—thousands of temporarily transplanted New Yorkers, hometown Vermonters, and curious college kids—all milling around the woods to view what seemed to me at the time politically simplistic agitprop about Latin America.[36] As twilight approached and the audience drifted to the natural outdoor amphitheater, my judgment shifted, and I became awed by both the enormity of spectacle and participation (including hundreds of puppeteers and local Glover residents). The starkness of pageantry framed against and framing the natural space drew me into the landscape aesthetically and topographically, as the act of sharing slices of hearty, redolent, aioli-smeared rye bread viscerally connected me to the audience community. The vast scale of the performance, its requisite mobility and spatial embracing of its audience, contributed as much to a sense of community formation as the symbolic associations animated by the pageantry.

Particular symbolic moments also contributed to this communal sensibility, inviting moments of mass booing (for personified symbols of political or corporate control) and cheering (the vanquishing of said foes). A temporary sense of what Victor Turner terms *communitas*,[37] a falling away of status structures seemed to permeate the crowd. But as Anthony Cohen points out, symbols prove effective in animating community only because of their openness to interpretation.[38] Representations of "butchers" (featureless, white-faced, black-suited male puppets) provoke a unified feeling of condemnation among the audience in part because they remain undefined as specific oppressive forces. Complicating this multifaceted symbolic reading, through the late 1980s and 1990s, the circus became as much a site of countercultural consumption as political provocation. Coming together to witness a satirical pageant did not necessarily activate audience members or nurture those already activated. When the Domestic Resurrection Circus shifted to the Insurrection Circuses after the 1998 pageant, a different kind of provocation ensued, one marked as much by continuing resistance to consumer culture and globalization as by a shift in nuance and scale.

I returned to Glover in 2002 to witness the *What Is to Be Done?* circus and *Where Are We Going?* pageant, both inspired by Joel Kovel's *The Enemy of Nature,* an "eco-socialist" manifesto denouncing capitalism as a global apocalyptic system of oppression.[39] While the performance, production process, and audience had shifted in the ensuing years, elements of circus agitprop that critiqued the particular political landscape and of pageant spectacle that took on more abstract systems of human relations continued. Taken together, the performance field additionally enacted tensions between structural modernist notions of binary power relations and their postmodern and poststructural critiques.

Peter Schumann has celebrated and denounced aspects of modernism, but almost always within an enlightenment framework, in which the grand narrative of capitalism continues to hold sway. According to a 1991 essay by Schumann, the tragedy of modernism is that its liberatory aspects, such as destroying taboos of perception, remained confined to art and did not penetrate the oppressive structures of capitalism.[40] Thus, in the spirit and style of early-twentieth-century workers' theaters, the 2002 circus acts and preceding "ding-dongs" (sideshows developed by summer interns) posit a bifurcated society in which those who own the means of production oppress the wage laborers and easily manipulate the general populace. Performance style relies on bold connections between behavior and power rather than psychological motivations of individual characters. As in the indoor performances, large-scale puppets and masks contribute to the psychological distancing of human character and behavior, pointing toward its more material motives.

In one early circus act the "Rotten Idea Theater Company" appears from behind the Bread and Puppet school bus "curtain" to present a piece on "how to beat a recession." Masked characters identified by signs hung around their necks include individual signifiers of power (President B), nation-states (Iraq), and allegorical, anthropomorphized groups (the American Electorate) and institutions (the Stock Market). A narrated sequence of events, presented in a broadly physical slapstick style, underlines links between economics and politics and their collateral manipulation of power. The Stock Market crashes (the masked character falls over). "The electorate doesn't like it!" announces the narrator. The President gets an idea (The President looks at "Iraq" and calls "Look!" to the

Electorate, who turns its head.) With their attention diverted from the Stock Market, President B pushes "Iraq" down with the cry of "Bush!" The Stock Market rises up, the electorate reelects President B, and the narrator posits a cyclical repetition of these events linked to historical precedent as the actions repeat at a quicker pace: "Repeat faster as in history." While the symbols remain somewhat open, the audience is encouraged to align the actions of two generations of Bush presidencies in a way that reduces and at the same time potentially clarifies the material and political forces contributing to and constituting historical events.

While these tactics may seem politically simplistic, they follow a conscious strategy of popular theater. Joan Holden of the San Francisco Mime Troupe draws out the activating possibilities and pleasures of this kind of political melodrama. "The fact is that most people have never been much attracted by morally ambiguous plays and unpleasant families who torture each other psychologically."[41] The more popular theater taps into the kinds of emotions generated by a sporting event, encouraging an audience to "really, deeply, take sides."[42] Popular theater takes on the genres that attract an audience not generally drawn to more conventional theater, often derided as low culture: circus, soap opera, vaudeville, pageantry. Like other socially engaged populist theaters, Bread and Puppet then inserts political content into these forms, drawing on such diverse sources as found text from newspapers (a quote from Donald Rumsfeld), public documents (the Declaration of Independence), and ancient Babylonian verse. Attorney General John Ashcroft's insistence on civilian surveillance is lampooned via a stream of "ear" puppets that disperse themselves among the audience, listening into potentially subversive conversations, as well as by a troupe of "Homeland Security Forces" who capture a Thomas Jefferson figure and force him to read aloud from his "insurrectionist document," the Declaration of Independence, which urges a popular revolution against oppressive state forces.

But if the *What Is to Be Done?* Circus emphasizes particular political satire, the *Where Are We Going?* pageant offers a more meditative and at the same time grander-scale metaphysical and material contemplation of an ethical society. The audience moves from somewhat distanced observers seated together en masse, to a more loosely grouped, site-specific processional performance field in the woods. Echoing a shift in content and focus, this space is both marginal to and frames the more politically specific circus. The narrative opens up a structural binary that assumes stable forces of Good and Evil, implicitly acknowledging the social construction of various archetypes, while also positing a possible future beyond the conflict for material goods and power.

The pageant strips the circus down while opening up the historical and physical scale of events. The jazz instruments of the circus band transform to junk sounds, sticks beating against scrap metal, and to a capella voices. Two women who introduce the pageant don their washerwomen masks, kerchiefs, and aprons in front of us, marking the construction of these characters, and their separation from the more particular women's bodies beneath the mask. Within the woods where we move and watch, memorial houses built for dead friends, relatives, and members of the company conjure the more metaphysical realm of the journey that this pageant asks us to contemplate. "Where are we going?" takes on a more resonant meaning in the midst of these reminders of immanent death.

The pageant also addresses the material history of the question "Where are we going?" through Peter Schumann's storyboard lecture. In a familiar ideological pattern, this history encompasses Christian myth alongside a critique of institutional religion, individual choice and the social structuring of choice. We begin in Paradise, where according to Schumann, "The question 'Where are we going?' doesn't exist." Instead of an expulsion from paradise leading to knowledge, Schumann posits a history of "manipulators and directors" that divide choice, creating distinct pathways for the human journey (heaven and hell), which seem to negate the question's complexity. Yet the question remains even in unified populations (illustrated by a question mark in a jar), "like sourdough," the starter for bread baked by Schumann each morning. Schumann proposes that the question continues to emerge in resistance to a shallow kind of unity, particularly that imposed by "modernists and post-modernists who pronounce 'peace' and 'harmony,' without contemplating their resolution."

While one may take issue with how Schumann uses the terms *modern* and *postmodern*, his critique remarkably complicates the more dualistic reading of the circus that sets up Good against Evil. The pageant does not propose a new paradise or utopia, or even a structurally bifurcated society, but instead advocates a constant questioning of individual choice. Schumann elaborates on the consciousness hopefully provoked by this insurrection pageant. "To insurrect means to allow people to see that their manner is invented, comes down to them from the top, is given to them as something didactically unchangeable." Schumann posits a move from the hierarchical to the horizontal and communal, a space where "messaging with each other is cultural insurrection."[43]

As if to illuminate this realignment from the vertical, the last part of the pageant moves from the woods into an open field where we witness the staging of a possibility of human engagement beyond top-down conflict. Using the topography of a gently sloping hillside and naturally shallow amphitheater, the pageant stages a battle based on a Babylonian text discovered by Schumann's daughter Maria. A troupe of earth-toned "barbarians" wielding a magnificent war puppet confront a similarly equipped troupe of silvery-blue "aliens." As though traveling through the landscape of history, as well as that of the field, the two troupes emerge from the distant horizon and move steadily toward us. The leaders of each group call out justifications for the ensuing battle: the need for land, power, and icons to their leadership, while the masses destroy each other. The battle's choreography then challenges a simple reading of this violent conflict as stage fight. Emerging from one layer of costuming, a group of dancers in red arise and disappear into the landscape behind them as the leaders continue to pronounce rationales for these deaths. Finally, a link is made to the circus, as a group of "possibilitarians" emerges from the bodies remaining on the ground. These possibilitarians had been introduced in the circus prologue challenging the forces of "Homeland Security," and later saving a stampeded crowd at a "World Cup" soccer match in which the IMF (International Monetary Fund) and WTO (World Trade Organization) compete, using the globe as a ball. The possibilitarians now literally and figuratively rise up from the battle and cite a manifesto for a new kind of world beyond a history inscribed in conflict. Denouncing "the battlefield that killed us" and history itself "which is a battlefield," the possibilitarians repeat pronouncements we had heard first in the circus. They demand "total consumer non-confidence," "hands returned to owners in improved condition," and "life and lower wages." These slogans figure an anticapitalist, eco-socialist possible future in opposition to alienated labor. At the same time, their symbolic impact becomes more shaded.

In the circus, the possibilitarians performed within a structural narrative clearly defining right and wrong, chanting, "We see a blight we put it right!" Within the pageant context, the group posits a more nuanced understanding of material history, refusing a historiography marked by large-scale clashes, instead proposing possible microhistories, a recording of events from the perspective of the ground rather than the heights of power.

In their enunciations of new relationships of labor to power, the possibilitarians as actors also animate the complex negotiations of power within Bread and Puppet Theater. Peter Schumann had led us to the field. He had introduced a series of scarecrow-like figures representing obstacles to individuals "having a life": effigies such as Humdrum, Normality, Morality, Reality. Then he had stepped aside from the battle, choreographed by his daughter Tamar Schumann, and from the manifestos written by a company of summer interns. He then reappeared at the end of the pageant to stage-manage the manifesto's articulation. When the first performer stumbled over her lines, he stepped out to encourage her to say the lines as composed. He later reminded the group to speak together with their arms raised. Rather than detracting from the experience, Schumann's intervention made visible and transparent the negotiation between artistic direction and group development, between individual will and communal formation.

The circus and pageant necessarily unfolds in a linear manner and seems to posit a structural binary of power relations. But an aesthetic and ideological impulse toward recycling and communal participation complicates both of these readings. Cardboard boxes become puppet outfits, newspapers providing initial use as sources for quotations are later transformed to papier-mâché. Puppets reappear in various pageants and parades over the years, resisting a stabilization of their symbolic meaning. Insurrection suggests resurrection with a signal difference; it is concerned with how power operates as a way to engage resistance. This power is not locatable in a single individual, but in an understanding of the nature of production and surveillance. While on the field, Schumann shares control and creation with a community of participants, in the furthest margins of the farm, in the outhouses, an intern project from a previous summer offers a poststructural critique of how power operates. Though Schumann has dismissed postmodernism as "solution seeking," and Joel Kovel rejects poststructuralism as "without hope,"[44] I find another set of ideas in the bathrooms: a series of quotes from Foucault about the principles of unverifiable and omnipresent power.

Peter Schumann and others have situated the company's New York productions, participatory work with communities in Spanish Harlem and the South Bronx, and antiwar and antinuclear parades as "more politically involved." After moving to Vermont the company recognized that overt antiwar spectacles did not make sense in the Vermont village parades and Glover fields. "It changed our ideas about how to get to people," admits Schumann.[45] The company and Schumann maintain resistance to society, but in a way that encourages active choice on the part of the multigenerational pageant participants and the audience for and with whom they play. The company animates what Alan Read refers to as an ethics of "good" theater. "When it is good, it enables us to know the everyday in order better to live everyday life."[46] To create a better world, to go have your own life. These two pronouncements seem to resonate with each other like the two slightly off-key notes that emanate from the double trumpets Schumann blows to announce the circus each year. Like the horn at Jericho, these trumpet calls make things happen, he explains. And one horn is not enough.[47] They must talk with each other, perhaps question each other about what it means to create a better world, to have one's life. As the Bread and Puppet Theater continues to reflect and perform, these and other questions will persist in arising, like sourdough in a jar.

NOTES

1. Larry Bogad, telephone interview by the author, July 22, 2002.

2. In comments at the Newport Folk Festival in 1967, Schumann stated, "Some of our shows are in the street and some are inside. The inside shows are meant for the Insides, the outside shows are meant to be as big and loud as possible." "Streets and Puppets," in Arthur Sainer, *The New Radical Theatre Notebook* (New York: Applause, 1997), 122.

3. Most of the theater's performances, particularly parades, pageants, and rituals, escape the boundaries of scripted text. Otherwise, performance records exist in manuscript versions owned by the company, including "Very Small Books" of images associated with recent Domestic Resurrection Circus pageants. Some particular performances have been publicly archived. "With the Bread & Puppet Theatre: An Interview with Peter Schumann," by Helen Brown and Jane Seitz, *TDR* 12, no. 2 (1968): 62–73, depicts in sidebars three brief outdoor pieces, *A Man Says Goodbye to His Mother, The Dead Man Rises,* and *The Great Warrior.* Stefan Brecht's extensive "Peter Schumann's Bread & Puppet Theatre," *TDR* 14, no. 3 (1970): 44–95, includes a moment-to-moment performance description of *The Cry of the People for Meat* (1969). John Bell's "Beyond the Cold War: Bread and Puppet Theater and the New World Order," in *Staging Resistance: Essays on Political Theater,* ed. Jenny Spencer and Jeanne M. Colleran (Ann Arbor: University of Michigan Press, 1998), 31–53, details a 1995 production of *Mr. Budhoo's Letter of Resignation from the IMF.* A script for *A Nicaraguan Passion Play* was published in *New Theatre Quarterly* 5, no. 17 (1989): 15–21. George Dennison's 1966 review of *Fire,* reprinted in *An Existing Better World,* ed. Geoffrey Gardner and Taylor Stoehr (Brooklyn: Autonomedia, 2000), 89–93, offers a lyrically detailed account of this anti–Vietnam War piece. Green Valley Media recorded three Domestic Resurrection pageants in 1993, 1994, and 1998. Jeff Farber's 1992 video, *Brother Bread, Sister Puppet,* documents the 1988 circus and pageant.

4. In "Beyond the Cold War," John Bell argues that companies such as Bread and Puppet tend to get limited to their sixties work and its context. According to Bell, this allows for a "clearer evolutionary narrative" placing postmodern theater and performance art at a further point along a progressive continuum (35).

5. Francise Russo's review of the exhibition, "The Artist as Young Dog," *Village Voice,* June 11, 2002, cites Exit cofounder Papo Colo referring to "these directors whose aesthetic is so strongly visual."

6. Curator Norman Frisch explained, "We asked them to portray themselves as young artists first starting to make a career in New York and to trace how these early ideas are still present in their work—or not" (qtd. in Russo, "Artist as Young Dog"). Reza Abdoh died in 1995, and Frisch worked with Abdoh's estate to curate his installation space.

7. Schumann, "With the Bread & Puppet Theatre," 70. Company members from various eras posit slightly different histories. In an e-mail (July 31, 2002), Beth Cleary, associated with the theater since the late 1980s, offers one performance lineage. A company did exist in the early New York years, though with more loose association with the theater (the "turnover" Schumann discusses). When the theater moved to Plainfield in 1970, another group of individuals became associated with it through Goddard College, many of whom continued to work with the Domestic Resurrection Circus through the 1990s. Another group joined in the late 1970s, not necessarily affiliated with Goddard, many of whom have also stayed connected with Bread and Puppet, though later founding their own independent companies. Cleary also refers to artists in Europe and other places, whom Schumann calls upon when he's putting together a show or going on tour. "So 'company'—?" She concludes, "No." John Bell and Michael Romanyshyn modify this account somewhat, explaining that a company of full-time and salaried members works year-round with the theater, though concurring that the relation of Peter to the company has always been fluid (Romanyshyn, e-mail to the author, August 1, 2002).

8. Erika Munk, "TDR Comment," *TDR* 14, no. 3 (1970): 33.

9. Bell, e-mail to the author, July 30, 2002. Adds Michael Romanyshyn, "For a show to be a Bread and Puppet show, I would say Peter had to have had a direct hand in it at some point" (e-mail).

10. Michael Romanyshyn, interview by the author, Otisfield, Maine, July 3, 2002.

11. Rabin, qtd. in Nat Winthrop, "Rad Company: Vermont's Oldest Activists are Still Talking 'bout a Revolution," www.uvm.edu/~jmoore/sixtiesonline/vermontrads.html, 4.

12. Brecht, "Schumann's Bread & Puppet Theatre," 52.

13. John Bell explains, "Part of Peter's creative genius is to inspire his collaborators to invent and contribute various elements of performance, which he puts together in the productions" (e-mail). As witnessed by Stefan Brecht's writings, these contributions may not be credited by outsiders, perhaps because they occur mainly at the level of animation rather than direction. George Dennison cites a company member's genial critique of Schumann. "You never saw a guy had less mechanical ability than Peter. I mean, he'll put things together with scotch tape, and he'll say, 'It looks great!' Other people have to make things work" (91). Bell acknowledges this imbalance in his article "Beyond the Cold War." He calls for criticism that "could valorize the contributions of its members (women and men) as fundamental elements of a cultural mix that, together with Peter Schumann's European sense of moral theater and his Brechtian confidence in the techniques of popular theater, created a unique theatrical hybrid" (37).

Elka Schumann's role in the company has a fascinating history. Schumann stayed at home to care for the couple's five children while her husband traveled throughout Europe and the United States, and she has served a supportive function as the company's accountant, additionally running the company's printing and press. Schumann also plays saxophone with the band, and has quietly developed a number of creative pieces for the company, many based on children's nursery rhymes and songs, sometimes with an ensemble of women investigating their social roles. The realm of the domestic may be perceived as limiting; in Schumann's case it seems to have also served as a site of creative inspiration (interview by the author, Glover, Vermont, August 18, 2002). The role of gender and performance in Bread and Puppet Theater deserves further consideration than this essay allows.

14. James Roose-Evans, *Experimental Theatre from Stanislavsky to Peter Brook* (London: Routledge, 1984), 113.

15. According to a 1987 lecture to SUNY students (*A Lecture to Art Students at SUNY/Purchase, New York* [Glover, VT: Bread and Puppet Press, 1987]), Schumann started a company called Cheap Art designed to resist art as an ally for business. Cheap Art is "light, quick and easy to do, mostly made from scraps and junk." Designed to "provide the correct thought at the right moment," or the "inappropriate symbol for an event or chore," or as "Universal thank-you to existence" (3–4). Cheap Art synthesizes much of Schumann's anticapitalist ideology and aesthetic.

16. Schumann, qtd. in Eugene Van Erven, *Radical People's Theatre* (Bloomington: Indiana University Press, 1988), 58.

17. Schumann, "Puppetry and Politics," *American Theatre,* November 1986, 56.

18. Schumann, qtd. in Kerry Mogg, "A Short History of Radical Puppetry," www.geocities.com/CapitalHill/Senate/7672/puppet.html, 1.

19. Schumann, "With the Bread & Puppet Theatre," 62.

20. Schumann, "Puppetry and Politics," 33.

21. Beth Cleary, e-mail to the author, August 1, 2002.

22. Schumann, qtd. in Françoise Kourilsky, "Dada and Circus," *TDR* 18, no. 1 (1974): 108.

23. Brecht, "Peter Schumann's Bread & Puppet Theatre," 87.

24. Ibid., 58.

25. Schumann, "Puppetry and Politics," 32.

26. Jürgen Habermas, "Excursus on Schiller's 'Letters on the Aesthetic Education of Man," in *The Philosophical Discourse of Modernity,* trans. Frederick G. Lawrence (Cambridge: MIT Press, 1991), 45.

27. Schumann, in Sainer, *New Radical Theater Notebook,* 199.

28. Dennison, review, 89.

29. Schumann, "With the Bread & Puppet Theatre," 70.

30. Baz Kershaw, *The Radical in Performance: Between Brecht and Baudrillard* (New York: Routledge, 1999).

31. In "Streets and Puppets," his 1967 speech at the Newport Folk Festival, Schumann asserts, "Some of our shows are good and some are bad. But all of our shows are for Good and against Evil" (Sainer, *New Radical Theater Notebook,* 122).

32. Dennison, review, 83.

33. Schumann, qtd. in Kourilsky, "Dada and Circus," 107.

34. Helen Nearing and Scott Nearing, *Living the Good Life: How to Live Sanely and Simply in a Troubled World* (New York: Schocken, 1970).

35. John Bell, "The End of *Our Domestic Resurrection Circus:* Bread and Puppet Theater and Counterculture Performance in the 1990s," *TDR* 43, no. 3 (1999): 62–80. Bell's *Landscape and Desire: Bread and Puppet Pageants in the 1990s* (Glover, Vt.: Bread and Puppet Press, 1997) provides a detailed critical overview of pageants in the 1990s, drawing links to and contrasts with the early-twentieth-century

pageantry movement. Several other excellent critical essays on the Domestic Resurrection Circus document and critically engage the pageant's aesthetics. See in
particular Kourilsky's "Dada and Circus." Beth Cleary's "Negation Strategies: The
Bread and Puppet Theater and Performance Practice," *New England Theatre Journal* 9 (1998): 23–48, compellingly reads the 1991 pageant *The Triumph of Capitalism* through Frankfurt School critical theory.

36. The focus of the pageant shifted after Bread and Puppet's 1987 trip to
Nicaragua. In an interview following this experience, Schumann reflected on the
past few circuses and their overemphasis on "ladies in bathing suits jumping
around." The theater hoped to restructure what had become a division between
"all that silly stuff" and the serious content to follow. "I think we did that enough,
and now we are going to create some other form. I don't know yet exactly how, but
I'm sure we'll have a very different *Circus* next year. Thanks to Nicaragua." Interview by Rosa Luisa Márquez, "The Bread and Puppet Theater in Nicaragua, 1987,"
New Theatre Quarterly 5, no. 17 (1989): 6. It was this different circus that I saw.

37. Victor Turner, *From Ritual to Theatre: The Human Seriousness of Play* (New
York: Performing Arts Journal, 1982), 45–46.

38. Anthony Cohen, *The Symbolic Construction of Community* (New York: Young-
stock, 1985), 55.

39. Joel Kovel, *The Enemy of Nature* (New York: Zed, 2002).

40. Peter Schumann, "The Radicality of the Puppet Theater," *TDR* 35, no. 4
(1991): 82.

41. Joan Holden, "In Praise of Melodrama," in *ReImaging America: The Arts of
Social Change,* ed. Mark O'Brien and Craig Little (Philadelphia: New Society,
1990), 279.

42. Ibid., 281.

43. Peter Schumann, interview by Marc Estrin, www.theaterofmemory.com/
art/bread/inter_ps.html.

44. Joel Kovel, lecture on *The Enemy of Nature,* Glover, Vermont, August 18,
2002.

45. Schumann, qtd. in David Sterrit, "Many-Sided Bread and Puppet Man,"
Christian Science Monitor, February 9, 1973, 20.

46. Alan Read, "Theatre and Everyday Life," in *The Routledge Reader in Politics
and Performance,* ed. Lizbeth Goodman with Jane de Gay (New York: Routledge,
2000), 189.

47. Schumann, in *Brother Bread, Sister Puppet.*

BREAD AND PUPPET AND THE
POSSIBILITIES OF PUPPET THEATER

John Bell

Like Bread & Puppet, we believe in a theater that is created
cheap and is cheap to see.
—Theater Oobleck, Chicago, 2002

When Peter Schumann and his colleagues first performed as Bread and
Puppet Theater in 1963, they immediately defined what they were doing
in a manner unique for the American stage and for New York City culture.
As drama, Bread and Puppet shows vigorously rejected dependence on
playwrights, actors, and the whole superstructure of Broadway and off-
Broadway that had developed over the past six decades of American theater. As puppet theater, Schumann's rough, expressionist shows were the
exact opposite of the cuteness and feigned innocence pursued by mainstream American puppetry, then focused on children's shows and fascinated by the medium of television and the commercial possibilities of advertising. As avant-garde performance, Bread and Puppet shows directly
benefited from the support of such already established innovators as the
Living Theatre, Merce Cunningham, and the variety of projects flourishing under the umbrella of Judson Church, but Schumann felt the avant-
garde scene was limited by a certain elitism, and took his puppets into the
streets of New York City to play for rent strikes and antiwar demonstrations

and in community centers and city parks. So, while Schumann's work definitely had connections to contemporary forms of innovative sixties art and performance, and shared a great commonality of purpose with many aspects of that work, at the same time Bread and Puppet Theater had ambivalent ties to drama, puppet theater, and avant-garde performance as they were generally understood in the sixties. Bread and Puppet's work never comfortably fit into any of those categories.

As it developed and emerged from the sixties onward, Schumann's Bread and Puppet Theater combined unrealistically high ideals for art (which Stefan Brecht so insightfully connects to the German romantic tradition) with the lowest methods of execution (papier-mâché, cardboard, and plentiful amounts of New York detritus), to make rough, simple statements with dance, music, and sculpture: "cheap art," as Schumann later defined it, which would attempt to address the most basic contradictions of United States life, straight on.[1]

Over its forty-year history, Bread and Puppet has developed an overlapping array of strategies for making accessible, politically conscious live performance in the United States and around the world. These strategies are essentially based on two concepts:

> Puppet theater and other traditional forms of popular performance offer viable and appropriate means of making thoughtful and effective contemporary art.
> It is indeed possible to make good art and good theater that consciously and unabashedly connect to political events and ideas.

Bread and Puppet has created political theater in and for particular communities throughout the world, based on these two interlocking concepts, that traditional popular theater techniques are viable means of making modern art, and that modern political art can serve a helpful purpose in our world. At this point let me define "political art" and "community" more clearly. By political art I mean artistic works whose content, methods, or contexts seek to engage both artists and viewers in an overt or implied consideration of the economic, governmental, and social forces at work in the societies in which the art is created and presented. By community I mean any self-identified body of individuals who consider themselves connected to one another by geographical, social, or political affinities. In premodern, or contemporary rural societies, communities are generally marked by geographical proximity, but in modern urban or suburban societies of the electronic age, communities can be self-determined by individuals who define their existence in particular ways (i.e., the community of Red Sox fans; the gay and lesbian community of Boston; the Phishhead community).

Since 1963 Schumann's theater has developed a variety of specific performance methods related to these two concepts, methods that have determined sites, theatrical techniques, dramaturgical structures, economics, and the social and cultural contexts of its theater. These methods include the following:

Performing outdoors on streets and sidewalks, in parks, plazas, town squares, pastures, and forest clearings, in churches, lecture halls, galleries, warehouses, and museums, as well as in traditional proscenium-arch stages and black-box theaters.

Inventing and developing performance techniques based on dance, vocal and instrumental music, mask and puppet manipulation, solo performers and choruses, and the various combinations of these forms in freely invented stagings.

Turning away from the dramatic structures of high-culture Western plays (except for some forays into Greek and Shakespearean tragedy and expressionism) and basing its plays on traditional dramatic structures of puppet theater including Punch and Judy, Kasperle, and epic Sicilian puppet theater; as well as the dramatic structures of Noh drama; medieval passion plays, mystery plays, and martyr plays; baroque cantatas and oratorios; the Catholic mass; variety shows, sideshows, circuses, and pageants; and an array of processional forms including Fourth of July parades, political demonstrations, religious processions, military marches, and funeral parades.

Utilizing economies of collective living, low income and low expenses, and seeking as much as possible to exist outside of what Schumann calls "the money economy."

Developing audiences for its work by connecting to the worlds of "avant-garde" performance, political activism, puppet theater, music performance, community-based theater, and to educational communities from elementary schools to universities; and by creating its own performance venues and audience communities, particularly in the twenty-seven-year development of the Domestic Resurrection Circus at Bread and Puppet's home in Glover, Vermont.[2]

Above all, these various Bread and Puppet strategies of direct, live performance are conceived as opposites to corporate-controlled television,

film, radio, sound recordings, and computer communication—"dead theater," as Taylor Stoehr puts it—which have dominated American culture
at least since the end of World War II.[3] Bread and Puppet's work insists
upon the power and importance of live theater, in a mass-media environment that presents itself as the true medium and arbiter of ideas, beliefs,
and desires. Bread and Puppet's point of view declares that truth and
artistry are not authenticated by electric and electronic media emanating
from corporate power centers in New York and Los Angeles, and that instead the essential art of our times can be created a few feet in front of
our faces, in moving images easily concocted from, say, papier-mâché,
cardboard, a bass drum, and a violin. Above all, this is an argument
against the idea that performance is primarily commerce ("show business"), and for the ideal of performance as essential cultural activity
wherein the most important ideas of a particular society are enacted, celebrated or condemned, and analyzed.

Of course, Bread and Puppet's definition of its work in essential opposition to mainstream cultural forms has all the while been locked in a sym-
biotic, binary, and inevitable (and perhaps contradictory) embrace with
that dominant culture. This parallels the similar stance of Peter Schumann's grandfather-in-law Scott Nearing, whose utopian proposal of the
1920s that workers should leave their jobs and the cities for "the good life"
of rural subsistence farming was ever connected to the urban and suburban cultures constantly expanding into farmland.[4] Importantly, both Nearing and Schumann have acknowledged this inevitable contradiction: despite his back-to-the-land practices, Nearing consistently used a pickup
truck to do necessary chores, and Schumann has likewise not ignored the
structural realities of contemporary life. In both cases, the challenge has
been to create alternatives to dominant culture, and yet to maintain specific points of contact with certain aspects of that culture, all the while
maintaining a critical analytical viewpoint—a difficult balancing act.

The Obvious Appropriateness of Avant-Garde Traditions

In 1987, in an essay about the politics of "postmodern theater" inspired
by Hal Foster's analysis of postmodern art, Philip Auslander sensed a crisis in contemporary theater practices arising from widespread "uncertainty as to just how to describe our cultural condition under multinational capitalism." Auslander was quite certain that the situation of
multinational capitalism in the 1980s was absolutely different and separate from the situation of multinational capitalism over the preceding
hundred years, and that the most salient characteristic of "political art

strategies" that were "left over" from "the historical avant-garde of the early twentieth century and from the 1960s" was their "obvious inappropriateness."[5] Auslander wanted to explain the uncommitted and apolitical stance of such celebrated postmodernist performers as Robert Wilson, Richard Foreman, and the Wooster Group by asserting a certain uniqueness to the United States (or more specifically, Manhattan below Fourteenth Street) in the late 1980s, and his premise was built upon a rejection of the entire Euro-American avant-garde tradition from the 1880s onward, since, above all, that tradition was characterized by an unabashed commitment to particular aesthetic, social, or political ideas. Auslander's rejection of the avant-garde as a useful tradition was later echoed by the editors of *Staging Resistance,* a 1998 collection of essays on political theater, who, quoting Fredric Jameson, declared that "we are facing a 'new and historically original dilemma' for which adequate aesthetic or cognitive maps do not exist," a dilemma necessitating a "much-needed remapping of contemporary political theater."[6]

Certainly the last hundred years in the development of culture and politics around the world have been marked by enormous changes, most specifically the rise and fall of totalitarian states in Europe and Asia, and, at the end of the last century, the triumph of global capitalism that made the United States the world's dominant power. Soon after its inception, Bread and Puppet Theater found a specific political inspiration for its productions within the discourse of opposition to the Vietnam War (1964–75), but that period constitutes only eleven years of the theater's work, and not all of Schumann's output during that time was even focused on the war. Underlying the argument that engaged political theater is an "obviously inappropriate" tradition for post-Vietnam theater-makers is, I think, a belief that the postmodern situation both politically and aesthetically no longer allowed the kind of certitude or point of view that, in classic avant-garde works, especially those of Brecht and Piscator, supposedly led to obnoxiously didactic propaganda that reduced or eliminated all doubt or contradiction. But the avant-garde tradition of political art was, in fact, never so uniformly configured, and even in the case of Brecht, its foremost exemplar, it has been filled with ambiguity, uncertainty, and contradiction.

What is consistent in the tradition of avant-garde theater is that artists over the past hundred years have found themselves in one of two situations: either the reasons for making political art appear to be obscure or nonexistent, in which case political art might be an option but certainly not a necessity; or the reasons for making political art are obvious and compelling, in which case such art becomes not simply an option, but a necessity. In the

United States, political art was considered a necessity by feminist artists of the 1890s; by W. E. B. DuBois and other African-American artists from the 1910s onward; by the Provincetown Players in the 1920s; by the Federal Theater Project, the Group Theatre, and scores of other companies in the 1930s; by the Living Theatre beginning in 1947, by the San Francisco Mime Troupe, Bread and Puppet Theater, El Teatro Campesino and others in the 1960s and 1970s; by ACT-UP and other AIDS activists in the late 1980s; by antiglobalization activists since the Seattle demonstrations of 1998; and by thousands of groups and individuals around the world who opposed the United States' invasion of Iraq in 2003.

The cultural scene of the United States today has changed somewhat from the 1960s, in that electronically mediated means of communication play an even more compelling role in cultural life, and because after the end of the Vietnam War a unified antiwar movement fractured into separate and sometimes competing political factions based on specific aspects of race, gender, and lifestyle. But the arguments for low-level, immediate, grassroots communication of ideas—especially those ideas that are not articulated by mass-media outlets—remain the same, and all post–Vietnam political movements in one way or another took advantage of such concepts, developing them in particular ways to respond to the changing nature of the cultural landscape.

A sense of this coexistence of continuity and change is evident in the context of a Bread and Puppet tour to Paris in the spring of 2003, in response to which the newspaper *Le Figaro* asked "Où sont les hippies d'antan?," rightfully connecting Schumann's political theater to an idealism that might seem to have gone the way of the vanished lifestyle.[7] And yet the Bread and Puppet performances of *Insurrection Mass with Funeral March for a Rotten Idea*—"a full frontal attack on the United States's war against Iraq," according to another Paris journalist—took place within months of the largest unified antiwar protests the world has ever seen.[8] With these kinds of events in mind, I would argue that the greatest cultural change since Philip Auslander's 1987 essay is that the realities of the post–September 11 world have made the tentative "uncertainties" and exquisitely nuanced "dilemmas" that appeared to characterize the "postmodern" moment now seem like unaffordable luxuries. Which is to say that for artists' organizations such as THAW (Theaters Against War), a consortium of over 160 theater groups and organizations in New York City and around the world that suddenly coalesced on the eve of the U.S. invasion of Iraq, making politically conscious art is not simply an option, but, once more, a necessity. In this situation, the traditions of political theater that Bread and Puppet have used and developed since 1963 are obviously appropriate, serving as valuable models for many young theater artists, just as they did for Peter Schumann forty years ago.

In what follows, I would like to consider some of the various artists who have been influenced directly by Peter Schumann and his theater, and the strategies they have adopted and developed as they have created their own methods of art and performance. This analysis suffers from the perennial drawbacks of categorization: actual artists and actual artworks don't neatly respect the boundaries superimposed upon them by academic writers. In the present situation, this means that different groups and individuals sometimes employ a variety of different strategies in their work, reflecting their multiple influences (which are of course not limited to Bread and Puppet). Another variable in the discussion that follows is that some of the artists mentioned had only limited (if intense) exposure to Bread and Puppet's work; some participated occasionally or infrequently in Bread and Puppet productions; while still others were intimately involved in the creation and development of the theater's work for many years before finding their own paths.

Puppets and Popular Theater Forms Legitimate Modern Theater

What unifies the first group of artists I want to consider is the sense that such traditional low-culture theater forms as puppetry, mask theater, circus, and ritual are entirely appropriate alternatives to the supposed dominance of actor's theater, "the drama," and mediated performance. The politics of such performances arise not so much in the content of these artists' works themselves, but in the radicality of their assumptions about low-culture techniques.

Guillaume Lagnel's Théâtre Arche de Noé began in southern France in 1968, inspired by American avant-garde companies such as the Open Theater and the Living Theatre, but particularly by Schumann and Bread and Puppet, who were instantly celebrated in French cultural circles when they arrived in Paris in the midst of the student uprisings of 1968. Théâtre Arche de Noé (whose name reveals a sense of the apocalyptic, quasi-biblical urgency typical of French youth culture in the sixties) invented its own particular style of intense, visual-based ritual theater that it has pursued consistently almost as long as Schumann's company. In 2002 a Catalan critic reviewing a performance of the company's *Le Livre de Nos Jours* saw in the Arche de Noé production an approach still consistent with a Bread and Puppet sense of performance as modern community ritual:

The artists of l'Arche de Noé are not actors from whom you buy a performance, but officials, always at risk, who offer themselves to the theater. . . . This art—almost entirely without words—does not respond to cerebral, intellectual perceptions, and instead cancels those senses in order to open itself to the heart. A popular art, with magnificent rigor![9]

Another artist affected by Bread and Puppet's early productions in Europe is the celebrated American puppeteer and director Roman Paska. Paska first worked with Bread and Puppet in France in the seventies, but his own puppet creations were also strongly influenced by early-twentieth-century art puppeteers like the Austrian Richard Teschner, as well as by the *wayang golek* rod puppet tradition of Java. Paska's work has involved the creation of small, one-man shows as well as larger productions (such as his *Moby Dick in Venice,* or Strindberg's *Ghost Sonata*) that have contributed to the continuing development of puppet theater as a respected modern theatrical form throughout Europe. While Paska's work has been celebrated in the international milieu of world puppet festivals, including the Jim Henson Foundation's International Puppet Festivals of the 1990s, some of his most important contributions have been in France, where he served as the director of the Institut International de la Marionnette, in Charleville-Mézières, one of the foremost institutes of puppet study in the world.

A contemporary of (and sometime collaborator with Paska) is Massimo Schuster, who joined Bread and Puppet in Italy in the early seventies, but who then began to create his own puppet shows in collaboration with painters, sculptors, and musicians starting in 1975. Although Schuster later said that "Peter [Schumann] is such a strong, volcanic, invading personality that actually it's very difficult to find your own way," and that after he left the company "for almost ten years, my shows were bad copies of Bread and Puppet," Schuster's Théâtre de l'Arc-en-Terre quite definitely developed its own particular style of puppet theater.[10] Like Paska, Schuster's work has been a noted contribution to the post-1960s European development of puppet theater as art theater. As such, Schuster has made productions of classic dramatic texts, such as *Le Cid, Richard III, Macbeth, The Iliad, Ubu Roi, The Three Musketeers,* and *The Corsican Brothers,* using forms ranging from toy theater to large-scale stage productions, and has also pursued puppet work as a visiting director in theaters throughout western Europe.[11]

In Florence during the late 1970s, the Bread and Puppet company met a group of student singers and musicians caught up in the renaissance of Italian folk music (spearheaded by the Nuova Compagnia di

Canto Popolare), and decided to collaborate. Peter Schumann subsequently came to develop a Bread and Puppet show, *The Ballad of Masaniello* (1977, based on a folk song and folktale about a Neapolitan fisherman who became a failed revolutionary) with that group of Italian students in Vermont during the summer of 1977. By the time *Masaniello* toured northern Italy the following year, the students had formed their own company, Pupi e Fresedde ("puppets and bread" in the dialect of Puglia), under the direction of Angelo Savelli, who still heads the group. Now based in Florence, Pupi e Fresedde has developed its own style of reinventing traditional Italian performance techniques (although for the most part leaving puppets behind), and has become an established element of theater life in Tuscany.

In North America, scores of puppeteers, performers, musicians, and visual artists have come into contact with Bread and Puppet. In the early 1980s director Guy Laliberté and other members of a street-theater and stilt-walking group called Le Club des Talons Hauts (The High-Heel Club) regularly crossed the Canada–United States border in August, part of a large contingent of vibrant Québécois theater-makers and theatergoers who made an annual pilgrimage to northern Vermont to see Bread and Puppet's Domestic Resurrection Circus. Inspired by Schumann's example of an avant-garde theatrical circus pursuing a particular theme and point of view, the Club des Talons Hauts reinvented itself on a much grander and higher-budget scale (with the help of substantial funding from the Quebec government) as Cirque du Soleil, creating its own dramatic circus, whose early iterations included masks, stilts, and puppets. Quite unlike the Bread and Puppet Circuses, Cirque du Soleil focused on "real" circus performers and circus techniques, not the cheap papier-mâché puppet versions prized in Glover. For the most part, Cirque du Soleil stepped away from the political content of the Bread and Puppet Circus, a decision that helped the Quebec group achieve success with more mainstream audiences, and create a highly profitable global entertainment corporation. And yet, a 2003 *New Yorker* advertisement for Audi automobiles featuring Laliberté described the Cirque du Soleil aquatic production *O* as "deeply concerned about the state of our planet," and Laliberté as "profoundly committed to creating works that are powerful expressions of hope."[12]

In the early seventies, after she had trained with Jacques Lecoq in Paris, and worked with Herbert Blau's Kraken company, director Julie Taymor worked one summer with Bread and Puppet when the company was in residence at Goddard College's Cate Farm, in Vermont. "At night I would go into the barn and sculpt," Taymor later said, "and [Peter Schumann would] come over and give me some guidance. And then I said, 'Well, I'm gonna do this. What do you suggest? Who should I be with?" And he said, 'Don't do, just watch."[13] Taymor subsequently went on to "just watch" various forms of traditional Javanese puppet theater on an extended trip to Indonesia, which inspired her to return to the United States and create her own forms of puppetry as "serious," legitimate, and commercially successful theater. Taymor's sense of the possibilities of puppet theater became as fervent as Schumann's commitment to the form, and eventually, with the support of the Walt Disney Corporation, she reintroduced spectacle and puppet theater to Broadway with the landmark appearance of *The Lion King* in 1997.

Like Massimo Schuster and Roman Paska, Chris Hardman worked as part of the Bread and Puppet company before striking out on his own, in Hardman's case in San Francisco, where he created Snake Theater in the early 1970s. For years the company developed its own forms of mask, puppet, and object shows, more as avant-garde performance than activist theater. In 1980 Hardman began to pursue a somewhat different focus with Antenna Theater, which, in his words, "combines cutting-edge audio technology with interview-driven sound designs, puppetry, masked movement, 3-D projections, sensor-tripped animation, sculptural objects, features of the natural landscape, and prefabricated environments," not only in theater productions, but also in installations and museum audio tours, which now are a central aspect of the company's work.[14]

A very recent Asian theater connection to Bread and Puppet is evidenced by the work of Parvathy Baul, a young Bengali singer and painter who, together with her husband, puppeteer Ravi Gopalan Nair, worked with Bread and Puppet during its five-month-long *Seven Basic Needs* exhibition and performances at Expo 2000 in Hannover, Germany. Both Baul and Nair also subsequently worked with Bread and Puppet at the company's farm in Glover. Although Parvathy Baul was already well trained in various Bengali folk styles, after working with Schumann she began to perform traditional Baul songs in tandem with large canvases she painted to illustrate them. This directly reflected the Schumann's picture performance techniques, although the connections are more complicated, since the Bread and Puppet forms are themselves variations on European *bankelsang* and *cantastoria* traditions, which, as Victor Mair points out, are connected to various Indian picture performance forms that preceded them.[15] Thus, Parvathy Baul's embrace of cantastoria marks not only a connection to Bread and Puppet, but a specific integration back into the worldwide network of picture performance traditions.[16]

Bread and Puppet's frequent performances in Latin America have taken place both in the context of international avant-garde theater festivals, and as part of North American movements in solidarity with liberation theology and with the leftist Central American uprisings in El Salvador, Nicaragua, and Guatemala that dominated the 1980s. One of Peter Schumann's early sixties New York collaborators, Enrique Vargas (who also worked at Ellen Stewart's La Mama theater, and established his own Gut Theater in Harlem), returned to his native Colombia to produce theater there, and is now the director of Teatro de los Sentidos, which often uses puppets in its work. Although Bread and Puppet subsequently toured in Colombia, Venezuela, and Brazil, its more intensive and extensive Latin American connections have tended to center on Central America and the Caribbean (i.e., in Puerto Rico, Nicaragua, Costa Rica, Mexico, Cuba, and Martinique), fueled by workshops and tours. In Puerto Rico, especially rich connections were developed in the 1970s and 1980s with theater director and teacher Rosa Lusia Marquez, whose own productions in Puerto Rico have reflected not simply her intensive collaborations with Schumann, but her substantial work with Augusto Boal, and with such Puerto Rican artists as Antonio Martorell.[17]

What links all these artists, besides their connection to Bread and Puppet, is their commitment to theatrical forms that lie outside the nexus of actors' theater and "the drama," their sense of the appropriateness of puppets, masks, circus, folk theater, and other traditional techniques as functional tools for making modern theater. Schumann's commitment to political content, or to noncommercial functions of theater, resonates to a different degree in these artists' work. Certainly every performer discussed in this chapter has had to deal with the hard economics of live art in the multimedia era, and their strategies of survival have all followed different paths since their encounters with Bread and Puppet.

Articulating the Legitimacy of Political Performance

The second group I want to consider includes Bread and Puppet–related artists who, while pursuing their own performance forms after their encounter with Schumann's theater, have remained committed to the idea that political content or a sense of political context is an appropriate and reasonable, as well as sometimes necessary element of their work

A good example of this is Dee Dee Halleck, who after working with Bread and Puppet in New York in the sixties, began to make video documentaries with New York–area schoolchildren. Halleck extended the idea that art making can and should be accessible to all elements of society into the new technology of videotape, and in 1981 these efforts led her to help create Paper Tiger Television, which describes itself as "an open, non-profit, volunteer video collective" based in New York City, which works "to challenge and expose the corporate control of mainstream media."[18] Following the success of Paper Tiger, Halleck went on to help found Deep Dish TV, a national satellite network of "access producers and programmers, independent video makers, activists, and people who support the idea and reality of a progressive television network."[19] Halleck's work is fascinating because of its consistency with Peter Schumann's grassroots, hands-on approach to art making, and because of its insistence on political content and context, for example in the ten-part *Gulf War TV Project* series that Halleck helped create in 1990. Halleck has also continued her relationship with Bread and Puppet, especially through her documentation of years of Domestic Resurrection Circuses, some of which recently emerged in her documentary film *Ah! The Hopeful Pageantry of Bread and Puppet* (2002).[20]

Unlike Halleck, director Peter Sellars was never part of a Bread and Puppet company, but he experienced an intense exposure to Bread and Puppet's work when he was living and studying theater in Paris in the mid-1970s. Sellars saw multiple performances of Bread and Puppet's three-hour-long *Domestic Resurrection Spectacle* at the Théâtre des Champs-Élysées in 1976, and although he had already been exposed to puppetry during his apprenticeship with Margo Lovelace in his hometown Pittsburgh, he was profoundly struck by the theatrical possibilities Schumann's troupe explored, and especially by Bread and Puppet's ability to create astoundingly effective stage spectacle with quite simple—even crude—uses of masks, puppets, objects, light, music, and movement.[21] Sellars's own work has developed especially on the proscenium stages of established theaters, often as the daring reinterpretation of traditional work (Bach cantatas, Mozart operas, or a Russian futurist epic), and also as the first appearance of new works of high-culture performance, such as his production of John Adams's *Nixon in China* at the Brooklyn Academy of Music in 1987. Sellars works with actors, singers, dancers, and musicians rather than puppets, but in all his work he persistently argues the need for a political sense of theater. This has extended to his curatorial efforts, for example as the director of the 1990 Los Angeles Festival, which featured a stunning array of high-culture and traditional performance work from all parts of the Pacific Rim, and his sense of political context persists in the way he conceives such projects as his production of Aeschylus's *Children of Herakles* in 2003. In his staging of the play at the American Repertory Theater in Cambridge, Massachusetts, Sellars reenvisioned the tragedy of Herakles' orphaned children in connection to the contemporary plight of refugees, and in particular the situation of teen-aged refugees in the Boston area, whom Sellars cast in the play in largely silent roles as Herakles' orphaned children, who seek refuge in Athens. In addition, Sellars augmented the performances of the play with preliminary question-and-answer sessions about the contemporary politics of refugee immigration, film showings after each performance, a dinner break (much like the all-day structure of the Bread and Puppet circuses), and, during the run of the show, special afternoon performances for high school students. In a radical departure from ART's normal production methods, Sellars attempted to insert Aeschylus's play right into the political and cultural life of Boston, echoing the role of tragedy in ancient Athenian culture, but also the parallel efforts of Bread and Puppet. A few months later, on National Public Radio, Sellars articulated his point of view even more strongly. "Right now producing weapons drives the American economy and the American economy of death is not sustainable," he said in an interview on the *Marketplace* program; "Rethinking sustainability is crucial. Artists are the ones to do that thinking—out loud."[22]

A similar sense of the appropriateness of a political perspective in art often characterizes the work of jazz trumpeter Dave Douglas, who performed with the Bread and Puppet brass band in a number of Domestic Resurrection Circuses and toured in Europe with the company in the early 1990s, but has since emerged as one of the United States' most popular and respected younger jazz musicians. In 2001 Douglas released a compact disc entitled *Witness,* which, in a gesture rare for mainstream American jazz, was an explicitly political effort. In notes about the album posted on his website, Douglas wrote the following:

Angered by a newspaper article on the rising fortunes of weapon makers during the NATO war on Yugoslavia, I decided to write music celebrating positive protest against the misuse of money and power. Each piece is inspired by and dedicated to artists and activists who have creatively challenged authority, sometimes endangering their own lives, but inspiring the rest of us to resist.

Echoing a phrase that Peter Schumann earlier used on a popular antiwar banner of the eighties, Douglas said, "At this time, I feel even more strongly that as citizens we need to be especially vigilant of the decisions made in our name and with our money."[23]

A more distant, and yet perhaps more intense connection to the outspokenly political aspect of Bread and Puppet's work is described by Eugene Van Erven in his book *The Playful Revolution,* an analysis of "theater and liberation in Asia," which explains that as early as 1971 members of the influential Filipino theater group PETA (Philippines Educational Theater Association) employed Bread and Puppet–style techniques in their own emergent forms of political community performance in the Philippines. PETA's grassroots training activities of the early seventies, according to member Lutgardo Labad, took the form of a four-week workshop teaching a variety of theater techniques: "movement theatre, bread and puppet theatre, realistic theatre, and expressionism."[24] In other words, at this moment in the early seventies, Schumann's techniques were so commonly understood and accepted in this South Asian context that they could slip into lowercase, common parlance, as a particular type of engaged theater, an impressive measure of the cross-cultural range of political theater at the end of the twentieth century. PETA does not focus specifically on puppet techniques, although it does incorporate them as one of many options. But underlying all of PETA's work from the seventies through the nineties is the urgency with which it embraces political theater as a cultural and political necessity for change in the Philippines.

A closer link with a "third world" activist arts organization has developed since the eighties between Bread and Puppet and MECATE (Movimiento de Expresion Campesino Artistica y Teatral), a Nicaraguan campesino community arts organization headed by Nidia Bustos. Beginning in the years of the Sandinista revolution, MECATE began to create activist theater and music performances throughout Nicaragua that articulated campesino social and political issues, and criticized the ruling Somoza dictatorship. Numerous workshop and performance collaborations between Bread and Puppet members and the *promotores culturales* of MECATE led to the development of puppet, mask, and picture performance shows in Nicaragua, although the work of MECATE remains primarily focused on traditional Nicaraguan folk forms, and activism on behalf of campesino concerns.[25]

These various artists, in different fields, in different countries, using very different means (and at one point or another all linked with Bread and Puppet), have persisted in analyzing culture and creating new artworks with politics in mind, and with a sense that it is entirely appropriate to do so—a strategy of normalizing the presence of political discourse in arts. This is a difficult feat in the midst of mainstream ideologies that by and large reiterate the opinion once voiced (according to Spalding Gray) by director Robert Wilson in the 1980s: "'I just don't think art has any, should have any, connection with politics, morality, grinding social axes.'"[26]

Puppet Pageants and Parades

A particular aspect of Bread and Puppet's work has been its reinvention of the American community pageant, a particularly modern innovation that began in New Hampshire in 1905, and spread across the United States in the decades that followed. Its creator, Percy MacKaye, considered these outdoor community spectacles to be examples of "democracy in action"—political theater, in other words, whose stories and contexts embodied and enacted essential national ideals.[27] The early-twentieth-century American pageants had much in common with their processional forebear, the patriotic community parade celebrated on the Fourth of July or on other significant holidays, and Bread and Puppet has regularly utilized both forms to create new versions of locally generated political theater, still examples of "democracy in action," but with a different political context than MacKaye's celebrations. The influence of Schumann's pageants and parades can be found in performers who have been inspired to create such community-based events with larger-than-life puppets, masks, and music in order to create an accessible, participatory, and local "alternative" theater. In what follows I would like to focus on the number of companies who have worked successfully with pageants and parades (although most of the following companies are not simply limited to these forms).

Foremost among the Bread and Puppet–influenced pageant and parade makers are Sara Peattie and the late George Konnoff, puppeteers who worked with Bread and Puppet in New York City in the late 1960s, and in Vermont in the early seventies, but who emerged from Schumann's company to create their own Puppeteers' Cooperative in 1976. The Puppeteers' Cooperative came to specialize in creating community-based pageants and puppet shows across the United States. Aside from Peattie's development of a series of toy theater political satires *(The NewsSharks)*, the work of the Puppeteers' Cooperative has not focused on specifically political topics, as Schumann's work has. Instead, Peattie and Konnoff have created a profoundly political body of work by teaching communities how to create their own outdoor puppet spectacles and processions, usually leaving the content of such shows up to the decisions of the local group. As part of this work, Peattie and Konnoff have worked for many years with mid-Manhattan community organizations such as the Lincoln Square Neighborhood Center, to invent and perform pageant versions of *King Lear* and other classics (which Peattie characterizes as "massive, barely rehearsed extravaganzas") for the Lincoln Center Out-of-Doors Festivals.[28] Peattie's *68 Ways to Make Really Big Puppets* and her how-to videotape *How to Make Giant Puppets* nonchalantly propose that almost any group of people can design, build, and perform visual theater on a grand scale with modest means.[29] This by itself alone is an extremely powerful statement, and together with the company's work, a significant example to make in a society that has increasingly defined spectacle as the legitimate purview of corporate, government, and mass-media performance practices alone. The Puppeteers' Cooperative's efforts to open up puppet performance to anyone extend to their "Puppet Free Library" in the basement of Emmanuel Church in downtown Boston, where community groups or individuals can borrow over-life-size puppets and masks to use however they wish.[30] In 2003 Peattie expanded the Puppet Free Library to New York City, with a branch in Brooklyn.

A most successful example of Bread and Puppet community pageant making has been In the Heart of the Beast Puppet Theater of Minneapolis, which Sandy Spieler and Ray St. Louis created in the mid-1970s after briefly working with the Bread and Puppet company in Glover. Bread and Puppet's "magnificent and soulful work," Spieler wrote, "ignited the first spark of inspiration for the theater's founding."[31] In the Heart of the Beast's annual May Day Parade and Festival has become an annual feature of the Minneapolis–St. Paul ritual year, and is most clearly inspired by Schumann's sculptural styles, puppet techniques, and dramaturgical structures. In addition to this now-traditional festival, In the Heart of the Beast also develops new indoor puppet theater productions dealing with local and national political issues, such as Ku Klux Klan racism and the arrival of Columbus in the Americas. By imbedding itself in the life of its community, incorporating community members in its productions, and performing clearly for that community, Spieler's company has become an essential feature of Minneapolis–St. Paul culture, which is a difficult feat for a theater company to achieve anywhere.

Similarly, if on a somewhat smaller scale, Marlena Marallo and Patrick Wadden created Arm-of-the-Sea Puppet Theater in Saugerties, New York, during the early 1980s. This Bread and Puppet–influenced company has managed to survive over the following two decades, at first connected with Pete Seeger's Clearwater campaign to clean up the Hudson River, but then expanding into its own realm. Arm-of-the-Sea sees its outdoor shows with life-size and giant puppets and masks as efforts "simultaneously to confront the turbulent strata of our historical moment, defend the integrity of the planet's life support systems and suggest the possibilities of personal and social transformation."[32]

Chicago's Red Moon Theater presents another complex example of multivalanced puppet theater with a particular focus on pageants and parades. The community puppet workshops that Blair Thomas, Jim Lasko, and Clare Dolan started in Chicago's Logan Square neighborhood in 1990 grew out of the work all three had done at Bread and Puppet circuses, and in fact Dolan was a full-time Bread and Puppet company member during the nineties. Under Thomas and Lasko's direction, the Red Moon Theater first focused on creating neighborhood pageants and parades, but then grew into a respected mainstream Chicago theater company with a series of full-length productions incorporating "masks, physical performance, and an international range of puppetry styles."[33] With such shows as *Moby Dick* (1995) and *Frankenstein* (1996) at the Steppenwolf Theater, and the giant shadow-puppet spectacle *Galway's Shadow* (2001) at Chicago's Museum of Contemporary Art, Red Moon established itself as the city's preeminent puppet-oriented theater, and yet still prizes its community theater work in Chicago neighborhoods.

Matthew Hart, an ACT-UP activist from Philadelphia, started Spiral Q Puppet Theater in that city following numerous summers of work on the Domestic Resurrection Circus, where his already keen sense of political activism and theater connected with the techniques of large-scale puppet theater and street performance practiced by Bread and Puppet. In a 2002 Canadian Broadcasting Corporation radio documentary by David Cayley, Hart articulated his sense of Bread and Puppet's influence on other puppeteers:

> In many ways, it's like the mother ship. People go there to get schooled, and meet other people who are doing similar types of work within that theater tradition. And then they go back. People go back and do their own work or whatever. I came back to Philadelphia, and I chose to come back to the city and do a theater project that was in the same vernacular as Bread and Puppet but that was really urban-based.[34]

Hart is not uncritical of what he considers the drawbacks of Bread and Puppet's rural setting, and his experience in Glover made him feel that "the whole [Domestic Resurrection Circus] enterprise was divorced from the urban environment, and there was a disconnect between the mostly middle-class, white performers and their subject matter (rebels in Chiapas)."[35] Spiral Q reflects quite clearly how Hart's energy has succeeded in creating a political community puppet theater in an urban environment, and like In the Heart of the Beast Theater and Red Moon Theater, Spiral Q offers a wide scope of activities to the city in which it lives. Hart's theater offers community puppet-making and performance workshops, organizes festivals, invents and performs its own mask, puppet, and toy theater shows, and has established an annual Philadelphia ritual entitled People-hood: An All-City Parade and Pageant.

While the above companies have tended to create a variety of different forms of community-based puppet theater, Chris Wells and John McCleod concentrated on community-oriented street processions with over-life-size puppets when they created the ecology-oriented All Species Day Parade in Santa Fe, New Mexico, in the late 1970s. This was a period during which Wells and McCleod both learned puppet techniques while working at Domestic Resurrection Circuses, although in addition they also studied and were influenced by Latin American pageant traditions, which also employ masks and oversize puppets. A recent description of All Species Day events (which now occur in San Francisco and Kansas City as well as in Santa Fe) speaks of "using pageantry to strengthen conscientious val-ues toward Earth, nature, and our fellow humans," but adds that such the-atrical events are "not new," and have "probably been here as long as hu-mans have."[36]

Like Hart and McCleod and Wells, Felicia Young returned home from summer work with Bread and Puppet to start a home-grown community parade tradition. In Young's case, the community is New York City, and specifically the same East Village neighborhoods where Bread and Puppet began its work in the sixties. In 1991 Young started Earth Celebrations to organize large-scale community-supported puppet parades and pageants to celebrate the many autonomous community gardens that New Yorkers in the Lower East Side created in rubble-filled vacant lots throughout the 1970s and 1980s. These performances have grown to include a yearly Win-ter Pageant as well as the now-annual Rites of Spring Procession to Save Our Gardens. Earth Celebration's community garden performances nec-essarily became politicized during the administration of Mayor Rudolph Giuliani, who initiated a battle against the gardens, claiming it was neces-sary to destroy many of them in order to build new housing. At that point, Giuliani's campaign began to play a theatrical role as an added antagonist in Young's parades and pageants, and Young and her colleagues re-sponded by deepening their activist efforts in support of community gar-dens, with ecology workshops, community organizing projects, art exhibi-tions, videos, and Internet projects.

A quite different type of modern pageant making influenced by Bread and Puppet has developed in the context of the alternative music world of improvised rock music. In the mid-1980s a second-generation wave of "hippie" culture emerged that increased the popularity of the Grateful Dead in the last years of its existence, as well as a whole "Deadhead" lifestyle based on following the band during its many extensive tours of the United States. After the death of Grateful Dead guitarist Jerry Garcia in 1995, this subculture gave rise to the phenomenon of the "jam band" music scene, centered particularly on the decidedly "alternative" music, spirit, and atmosphere of the Vermont band Phish. Following the example of Deadheads, Phish fans became known as "Phishheads," and in the mid-nineties there was a considerable overlap between Phishheads and aficionados of *Our Domestic Resurrection Circus,* sometimes termed "Breadheads."[37] Phish had come together at Goddard College in Plainfield, Vermont (where Bread and Puppet had been in residence from 1969 to 1974); and members of the band had joined thousands of other young "alternative" Vermonters trekking to the annual Bread and Puppet Circuses. It's clear that the experience of the Glover events helped inspire Phish to create its own rural music and art festivals from 1996 to 2000, as part of its overall efforts to design the context of its performances outside the traditional bounds of commercial American rock-and-roll performances in arenas and stadiums. Phish's carnival-like events have been a cross between Woodstock music festivals, Bread and Puppet Domestic Resurrection Circuses, and the alternative "Gatherings" of the Rainbow Family. Taking place in large, unused rural spaces such as decommissioned Air Force bases, the Phish festivals attracted thousands of young fans who camped for two or three days at the sites to experience not only Phish's trademark concerts of extended jams, but also sideshows, art installations, and various pageant-like performance events, from giant spectacle (the lighting of a twenty-five-foot-tall match at the 1997 "Great Went" festival) to informal street parades of New Orleans–style music.[38] These particular elements of the giant Phish concerts were to a large extent designed, built, and performed by longtime Bread and Puppet members and volunteers, such as building contractor Russ Bennett and Bread and Puppet bandleader Ron Kelley, who turned their decades of experience producing massive participatory outdoor pageants and circuses to the creation of the more commercial and less political Phish spectacles. In fact, the overlap in personnel between the large-scale Phish concerts and Bread and Puppeteers were so extensive that many Phishheads believed that the Bread and Puppet Theater itself performed at the events. The example of Phish spectacles, whose over-life-size pageantry anchored temporary communities of young audiences interested in the momentary creation of pleasure-seeking counterculture, has in turn inspired more such events, like the Bonnaroo festivals of Tennessee, to which Bennett has also contributed his efforts.

By themselves alone the artists and events mentioned above constitute a new American pageant movement of the late twentieth century; they also stand out because of their clear and developed connections to Peter Schumann's work. But Schumann's influence is undoubtedly even more widespread, not only as a result of Bread and Puppet's Domestic Resurrection Circuses, but because of its workshops around the United States and all over the world and the almost anonymous effect they consequently have had on local pageant and parade practices. I happened upon one such instance by accident in Mexico City in 1999, when theater activists, including Jesusa Rodriguez of the Coyoacan theater group El Habito, used a giant Bread and Puppet cloth sailboat (featuring a huge skeleton painted on the sail) in a massive street demonstration in support of the burgeoning Zapatista movement. Schumann and other Bread and Puppeteers had made the boat as part of a 1996 Day of the Dead workshop with the Casa del Teatro in Coyoacan, leaving it behind in hopes that it would continue to be used in parades and pageants, and so it was.

All over the world, although especially in the developed societies of the northern hemisphere, corporate conglomerates seek to convince us that all important culture and communication takes place by means of the mass-media systems they own and control. Live, community-based events such as the pageants and parades noted above strongly counter the ideology of mass-media substantiation, and thus by their simple existence are profoundly political events. They become even more politically important when, as in many of the cases above, specific political ideas are articulated through pageant and parade techniques. The possibilities of immediate and grassroots communication are stunningly powerful, as anyone who has ever participated in a political demonstration, Fourth of July parade, or community pageant can attest, and the continuation of MacKaye's concept of "democracy in action" by means of pageant and parade has become, in the past few decades, profoundly subversive and impressively powerful.

A Network of Political Puppet Theaters

Unlike many twentieth-century directors, Peter Schumann has never focused his work on the creation of a particular system or training regimen as a means of expanding the influence of his performance techniques. Instead, the scores of Bread and Puppet company members over the past forty years have taken part in what veteran puppeteer Michael Romanyshyn has termed a "master-apprentice" relationship more redolent of Old World guild traditions than modern professional training.[39] Scores of company members have emerged from their work with Bread and Puppet

The Puppeteers' Cooperative, 1998. (Photo by Orlando Marra.)

to create their own particular versions of puppet theater with community connections and a political context. Many puppet theaters growing out of and inspired by Schumann's enterprise have come and gone since the sixties: Murray Levy's 1970s Stomache Ache Theater in Boston, Antoinette Dalrymple's Bread Bakers' Puppet Theater of Vancouver, the Whole Loaf Puppet Theater of Toronto, and the Barking Rooster Theater of central Vermont, to name simply a few.[40] Still others, such as Puppeteers' Cooperative, Arche de Noé, and Théâtre l'Arc-en-Terre, mentioned above, have survived, combining ideas and techniques learned from Bread and Puppet together with their own explorations and experiences, to create an array of performance practices amounting to a network of modern political puppet theater.

Amy and Andy Trompetter began their Blackbird Theater in Maine in 1975, and like many post–Bread and Puppet companies, as Massimo Schuster related, Blackbird's early work closely followed Schumann's example, and even performed Bread and Puppet's *Christmas Story* as part of its repertoire. Blackbird Theater invented community pageants and parades in the United States and Europe, as well as more contained puppet theater productions, which were marked by Amy Trompetter's distinct painting and sculpture style. The Trompetters separated in the late 1970s, at which point Andy Trompetter moved the Blackbird Theater to Maryland, where it performed puppet shows until his death in 1977. Amy

Trompetter, now a theater professor at Barnard College, recently revived the Blackbird Theater in Rosendale, New York, and also works as an independent director, whose work has included a spectacular puppet production of Rossini's *The Barber of Seville* at the St. Ann's Warehouse in Brooklyn in 2003.[41]

Sue Bettman, a Bread and Puppet alumna from the theater's Goddard College era, started Dragon Dance Theater in central Vermont together with her husband Sam Kerson in the mid-1970s. Dragon Dance Theater developed a typical post–Bread and Puppet range of performances, including parades, pageants, indoor and outdoor shows, workshops, and exhibitions. In the 1990s, Bettman and Kerson began to pursue different projects, and Kerson has continued as the director of Dragon Dance, developing a particular focus on cross-cultural exchanges with Mexican and Canadian artists. Dragon Dance's summer workshops and recent productions such as *Sol y Luna,* a collaboration with the Mexican company Comparsa, based on Zapotecan legends, reflect that pan-American interest.

Performance artist Paul Zaloom, perhaps the best-known American performer to emerge from the Bread and Puppet company, became a solo performer in the late 1970s, making puppet shows with found objects, slide projections, and shadow images created with an overhead projector. All of these techniques are forms that Peter Schumann's work has eschewed, and by embracing them, Zaloom has created a visual style particularly distinct from Bread and Puppet practices, and yet still closely tied to the cheap art aesthetics and possibilities of political content central to Schumann's work. Zaloom specifically connected himself to the solo performance scene that developed in New York City during the late seventies, in the company of Spalding Gray, Eric Bogosian, Karen Finley, Holly Hughes, and others, but then later worked in network television as the host of a CBS children's science show, *Beakman's World.* His recent work as a solo performer and political satirist has returned to such fundamentals as handpuppet theater in his *Punch and Jimmy* (a gay version of the traditional Punch and Judy handpuppet show) while also continuing his trademark tabletop object performances in such puppet extravaganzas as *Velvetville, Mighty Nice,* and the futuristic *2222.*

Great Small Works is a New York–based company formed in 1995 whose members have had varying degrees of involvement with Bread and Puppet from the seventies onward. The company's monthly spaghetti dinners at P.S. 122 continue a twenty-five-year East Village tradition of community-based avant-garde dinner theater inspired, in part, on Bread and Puppet's concept that "theater is more like bread, more like a necessity."[42]

Great Small Works has also made shows in the Bread and Puppet mold, incorporating oversize masks and puppets, political circuses, street processions. But, in addition, the company has turned to forms of theater completely outside the varieties of puppet theater embraced by Schumann's company, by spearheading an American "toy theater revival" through its International Toy Theater Festivals and by creating shows based on musical cabaret, vaudeville, dance theater, machine performance, and Yiddish music, such as *The Memoirs of Glückl of Hameln* (1999) and *A Mammal's Notebook: The Erik Satie Cabaret* (2001).

In 1993 Puerto Rican puppeteers Pedro Adorno and Cathy Vigo, who were members of the Bread and Puppet company in the early 1990s, founded Agua, Sol y Sereno, a San Juan–based theater group that has combined puppets, masks, stilts, and dance to make theater pieces and community-based workshop productions in Puerto Rico, the United States, Canada, Nicaragua, and Cuba. Agua, Sol y Sereno's work has developed its own particular character by combining forces with performers whose previous work may not include intensive work with puppets and masks. For example, the company's performance of *Una de Cal y una de Arena,* in the summer of 2002 at Boston's Puerto Rican Day festival in Franklin Park, was a critique of real estate development in Puerto Rico as an environmental, social, and cultural catastrophe, but the show did not use puppets or masks. Instead, Adorno, Vigo, and the other members of the group used *Stomp*-style percussion music made from found objects, combining it with dance and dialogue to address thousands of Latino Bostonians at an otherwise decidedly apolitical cultural event. The intent of the show—to add a sense of the political aspects of the Puerto Rican situation to a fairground celebration—was clearly in line with Bread and Puppet–style motives; but Adorno's production did not at all look like a Bread and Puppet show.

A more recent Bread and Puppet–influenced company in Italy is Damiano Giambelli's Teatro del Corvo, based in Padua. Giambelli, a puppeteer, painter, and sculptor who has worked often with Bread and Puppet both in the United States and in Europe over the past decade, has focused his company's work on handpuppet theater, toy theater, street processions, and community theater. Giambelli's puppets and parading elements were part of demonstrations against the World Trade Organization in Genoa, Italy, in 2001, and a letter he wrote about the violence that came to mark that event became the text for a Bread and Puppet show that year, *Public Participation Uprising: The Red Zone of Genoa Denunciation Oratorio.* Giambelli's work with other members of the Bread and Puppet network includes his participation in Great Small Works's toy theater festivals, and continuing collaborations with director Amy Trompetter.

Michael Romanyshyn actually began his puppet work with Blackbird Theater, before becoming an integral member of Bread and Puppet in the seventies. Romanyshyn continues to work with Schumann's theater on occasion, and yet has also devoted his energies to the creation of a variety of activist, community-oriented theater enterprises. Romanyshyn cofounded the Shoestring Theater in Portland, Maine (together with sixties Bread and Puppet alumnus Charlie Addams); and in 1996 created Los Kabayitos Puppet Theater, which at that moment became the only full-time puppet theater in New York City. More recently, Romanyshyn and Susie Dennison (a Bread and Puppet veteran whose mother, Mabel, played a central role in Schumann's theater in the early sixties) have run puppet workshops for teenagers from international regions of conflict at the Seeds of Peace summer camps in Maine, and in 2001 created the Temple Stream Theater in an old church in Temple, Maine.

A Bread and Puppet mainstay in the midnineties, Emily Anderson, went out on her own in 1998 and started the Awareness Theater Company in nearby Burlington, Vermont, to make theater productions—mostly with puppets—with developmentally disabled men and women, along with her own puppet and toy theater shows. Anderson's colleague in Bread and Puppet in the nineties, Clare Dolan, has since taken her theater work in the direction of solo performance, developing an ongoing series of semiautobiographical cantastorias, *The Story of Go-Go Girl,* as well as various other puppet shows. Another nineties Bread and Puppet company member, Jason Norris, together with Adam Cook, created Insurrection Landscapers, a rough-aesthetic puppet troupe whose work I would like to consider below in the context of the recently developed "puppetista" movement in the United States.

If the array of Bread and Puppet–connected theater work around the world over the past four decades amounts to a network of performance practices, the productions created by Bread and Puppet alumni amount to a particularly strong ring in close vicinity to Schumann's own work. By this I mean that the work of Bread and Puppet alumni most consistently makes use of the concepts and methods Schumann has pioneered, and all these puppeteers pursue low-cost, intellectually and spiritually rigorous puppet theater with a political context, in the belief that live performance creates the best medium for the profound exchange of ideas. The consistency of this work still stands in contrast to mainstream puppet practices in the United States, where political context is often suspect, and high budgets are often considered the inevitable correlative of good art.

Puppetistas and the Antiglobalization Movement

In an interview broadcast on the BBC's World Service on June 1, 2003, global eco-activist Dr. Vandana Shiva articulated her sense of the current state of the world by saying that

> everyone knows democracy is in crisis. Under globalization, representative democracy must necessarily become anti-people, therefore must create police states, therefore must become more militaristic, and must destroy human rights and civil liberties everywhere.

Interviewer Fergus Nicoll responded that the antiglobalization movement that has emerged since the late nineties in opposition to the forces Shiva described is characterized by middle-class leftists with a "touchy-feely" weakness, but Shiva responded to him by citing a recent example of First World performance activism:

> It's not touchy-feely, it's about the young kids. For example, at a meeting where I had gone recently, in St. Louis, the headquarters of Monsanto, young kids cycling to a conference [were] arrested, on absolutely fictitious grounds of not having licenses. You don't need a license for cycling. They are taking a cycle march across the corn belt of the United States for a GM-free America [i.e., free of genetically modified crops]. This arbitrary arrest is not about a touchy-feely middle class, it's about life-and-death matters for the poor, the tribals who are being shot at as their land [is sought] by mining companies, timber companies in India. Women, denied their right to water. But it's also about life-and-death issues for those who seek a free life and freedom in everyday matters and their civil liberties in the north.[43]

The "cycle march" Shiva referred to was the bicycle-powered Caravan Across the Cornbelt, which traveled crossed the Midwest in May and June 2003 and was organized by Chicago puppeteer Ben Majchrzak, one of the many activist puppeteers to recently emerge from the Bread and Puppet Theater. The caravan featured performances by the Flying Rutabaga Circus Review, an ad hoc collective consisting of Majchrzak, members of the Puppetual Motion Cycle Circus, the Liberty Cabbage Theater Revival, and other performers, and it is interesting to note that news of this combination of activism, low technology, puppets, and political theater would appear on a worldwide radio broadcast as an example of global activism. To a great extent, it is a sign of the continuing presence and relevance of Bread and Puppet–style political performance in twenty-first-century global culture.

The Caravan Across the Cornbelt was an interesting development in the ongoing efforts of the worldwide antiglobalization movement, because instead of staging street demonstrations during the meetings of international organizations (such as the ones Giambelli's Teatro del Corvo puppets had joined in Genoa two years earlier), Majchrzak and the other caravan activists communicated their ideas about what Shiva calls the "earth democracy movement" directly to audiences in small towns and on farms across the heart of middle America. Puppets (for example, Majchrzak's *Jack the Giant Killer* handpuppet show) were central to this work.

The high theatrics of the antiglobalization movement, including the return of political puppet street spectacle, began four years before the Caravan Across the Cornbelt, in the fall of 1999 at massive protests against the World Trade Organization in Seattle. A variety of arts activist groups contributed to the events, including the Ruckus Society, Art and Revolution, and Wise Fool Puppet Intervention from San Francisco; and, from Bread and Puppet, company members Jason Norris and Ben Majchrzak, as well as activist Mabel Dennison (a central supporter of Bread and Puppet, and a Bread and Puppet veteran from the early 1960s). The puppet-building workshops Majchrzak and Norris organized led to the creation of puppets, masks, banners, flags, costumes, and instruments used in parades and pageants during the week of protest. The intensity of opposition to the World Trade Organization and the World Bank at Seattle stunned the United States and the rest of the world, and certainly the extensive theatricality of those protests was an important element of the surprise they generated in governments, corporations, and mass media around the globe. This renewed sense of the possibilities of puppets as political street theater has since become an important part of reinvigorated international antiglobalization and antiwar movements, which later expanded to include worldwide opposition to the United States invasion of Iraq in 2003. In the United States in particular, a number of young puppet companies and individual puppeteers have shared this commitment to political puppet theater, including Insurrection Landscapers, the Puppetual Motion Cycle Circus, the RPM Puppet Conspiracy, and the Shoddy Puppet Company. Many of these puppeteers took part in the Radical Cheese Festival, a conference of new political puppet theaters that Jason Norris, Ben Majchrzak and others organized at Bread and Puppet Theater in 2001, and which marked a particular coalescence of the new movement.

Late in July 2000, just prior to the Radical Cheese Festival, Norris, Cook, Majchrzak, Matthew Hart's Spiral Q Theater, and Morgan Fitz-patrick's Shoddy Puppet Company all took part in puppet-building work-shops in Philadelphia, to create street spectacles on the occasion of the Re-publican Party's presidential convention. Their workshops, in two separate warehouse buildings in the city, were open to anyone interested in partic-ipating, and undercover agents of the Philadelphia police department soon joined in, keeping track of the puppeteers' activities, and, in the role of *agents provocateurs,* urging them to take part in illegal activities. On the afternoon of August 1, 1980 Philadelphia police officers (without a search warrant), surrounded one of the workshops, arrested all those inside, in-cluding Norris and Cook, and destroyed four hundred recently built pup-pets and banners in a trash compactor. Majchrzak and his colleagues, who had escaped arrest, were still able to perform bicycle-mounted puppet shows in the coming days, as part of the large anti-Republican street demonstrations, even though the protesters' possibilities of expression through images had been greatly reduced by the police raid. More impor-tantly, the police repression of the puppeteers galvanized their political activism, and in emulation of the Mexican Zapatista movement they started to call themselves "puppetistas," spray painting on their T-shirts the slogan "Puppetry is not a crime!"

The governmental fear of puppets since the Seattle WTO protests and their ubiquitous presence at demonstrations around the world have made political puppet theater more noticeable now than at any time since the Vietnam War era, when Bread and Puppet reinvented the political protest as an art form.[44] To get a sense of the different facets of this reinvigorated political puppet theater network, in the summer of 2002 I interviewed David Solnit, an activist puppet maker from San Francisco's Art and Revo-lution collective, who had just returned to the United States from puppet and street theater workshops he had led in Israel and Argentina. Since I had never come across Solnit's work in a Bread and Puppet context, I was hoping to discover some source of political puppet theater completely un-connected with Bread and Puppet. However, when I asked Solnit about his impetus for making over-life-size cardboard and papier-mâché puppets, he cited B. Ruby Rich of San Francisco's Wise Fool Puppet Intervention, and added that she had learned such techniques at Minneapolis's In the Heart of the Beast Puppet Theater, thus tracing a network linkage that inex-orably led to Bread and Puppet. Are such connections inevitable? Prob-ably, in the sense that by 2002 the idea of making political puppet theater has spiraled around the world so many times and in so many ways that at-tribution to some originary effort is futile and senseless.

"Indigenous Puppeteers of the World Unite!"

Indigenous puppeteers of the world unite!
Be unmodern and unmodernize the world! Be as little as
the big puppets of this typical indigenous puppet theatre and
PULL OFF THE MODERNIZATION SUIT AND TIE
AND LET THE NAKED SUN SHINE ON YOU!
    —Peter Schumann, "Indigenous Puppetry
                    Manifesto No. 1"

The question raised by the emergence of a new generation of political puppeteers is whether the artistry of their work can match the energy of their political convictions. Peter Schumann raised this issue at the 2001 Radical Cheese Festival by urging the puppetistas to be even more radical, not simply in their approach to politics, but in their approach to the entire means and functions of art making. I believe that what Schumann was asking the the younger puppeteers to consider was not simply the project of creating insightful political positions and well-functioning performances that support them, but the challenge of reimagining society completely, and finding ways to live that reimagining, including the creation of puppet shows that are good theater fully integrated into their community.

In the aftermath of September 11, 2001, Bread and Puppet continued doing what it has always been doing. It developed a new antiwar processional piece for demonstrations in Washington, D.C., and New York City against the U.S. war on Afghanistan, which began October 7. On October 14, the Battery Park City Parks Conservancy presented the first outdoor theatrical event in lower Manhattan after the World Trade Center attack: Bread and Puppet's *Public Participation Uprising: The Banquet* at Robert Wagner State Park. This performance (a version of *The Red Zone of Genoa Denunciation Oratorio*) received an overwhelmingly positive response from New Yorkers desperate to communicate with each other in some kind of direct manner. The following month, in a sign of developing post–September 11 cultural changes in the United States, the organizers of the annual Greenwich Village Halloween Parade, who had annually solicited Bread and Puppet's involvement in that event previously, refused to allow the theater to participate in that year's parade because of the political content of Schumann's work.[45] In the months to come, Bread and Puppet continued its annual December performances at New York's Theater for the New City, and in May 2002, an installation of Schumann's work was included in Norman Frisch's *Show People* exhibit at the Exit Art Gallery in New York, together with installations by Reza Abdoh, Anne Bogart, Richard Foreman, Meredith Monk, and Robert Wilson. In June, Bread and Puppet once again began its summer program of circuses and pageants in Glover.

The pageant that summer included a "Battle of Good and Evil." The music for this spectacle was a typical Bread and Puppet selection of fascinating pieces of compelling artistic interest: four-part Sardinian a capella religious music, and a brass-and-vocal setting of a chorus from Henry Purcell's 1689 opera *Dido and Aeneas*. The action of the pageant, centered on a large-scale conflict on a pristine green meadow between two giant armies, Barbarians and Aliens, was characterized by extravagant comic bluster but also deftly countered by the chilling sobriety of the ancient Babylonian texts the Alien and Barbarian leaders used to describe their battles, a minatory reminder of the coming U.S. invasion of Iraq. The Barbarian leader, for example, roared:

> I turned the city into ruined hills and heaps of debris. I placed images of myself and my gods in his palace and declared them to be henceforward the gods of their country. As for Menahem I overwhelmed him like a snowstorm and he fled like a bird, alone, and bowed at my feet. I received tribute from him: gold, silver, and multicolored trimmings.[46]

The armies' battles ended with all the warriors dead on the field, but after a pause the performers arose, shed their motley battle uniforms, and were now "Possibilitarians," who chanted:

> We are the Possibilitarians!
> What do we say?
> We can do it, it's ok!
> What's good, what's bad?
> What's fun, what's sad?
> What blinks, what stinks?
> What's up, what's down?
> And what is totally ready to drown?
> We are the Possibilitarians.
> And not necessarily vegetarians!
> We see a plight, we put it right;
> To stop a fight is our delight!

The appearance of the illogically optimistic Possibilitarians was quite in line with one of Schumann's most basic movement sequences: falling, and then rising; choreography inevitably linked to one of Schumann's favorite thematic sequences: from death to resurrection; a very old dramatic arc indeed.

In 1967 Guy Debord wrote that in the modern world "everything that *was* directly lived has moved away into a representation," a "spectacle" consisting of "images detached from every aspect of life fuse[d] in a common stream in which the unity of this life can no longer be reestablished."[47] In a way, the argument here has been that Bread and Puppet Theater, over its years of experiments, has from time to time succeeded in making theater that is truly a part of the life of the community in which it is performed, and that those puppeteers and other artists who have crossed paths with Bread and Puppet have seen how such "situations" (as Debord might put it) could be created. As these people have continued on their own paths, they have created their own works that, in various ways, in their particular strategies, have acknowledged the importance of Schumann's efforts. It's not the case that Schumann invented political puppet theater as an essential art form, because that tradition is actually quite old. But certainly he turned to it at an important moment in the twentieth century, and the strands of related work that have followed Schumann's efforts are a Bread and Puppet legacy.

NOTES

1. See Stefan Brecht, *Peter Schumann's Bread and Puppet Theatre,* vol. 1 (New York: Routledge, Chapman and Hall, 1988), 14–23; and Peter Schumann, *Cheap Art Manifesto* (Glover, Vt.: Bread and Puppet Theater, 1984).

2. See John Bell, "The End of *Our Domestic Resurrection Circus:* Bread and Puppet's Counterculture Performance in the 1990s," in *Puppets, Masks, and Performing Objects,* ed. Bell (Cambridge: MIT Press, 2001), 52–70.

3. Taylor Stoehr, "Angels and Devils: Live Theater and Dead," *Antioch Review* 60, no. 2 (2002): 188.

4. On Schumann and Nearing, see John Bell, "Uprising of the Beast: An Interview with Peter Schuman," *Theater* 25, no. 1 (1994): 41–42.

5. Philip Auslander, "Toward a Concept of the Political in Postmodern Theatre," *Theatre Journal* 39, no. 1 (1987): 21.

6. Jeanne Colleran and Jenny S. Spencer, introduction to *Staging Resistance: Essays on Political Theater,* ed. Colleran and Spencer (Ann Arbor: University of Michigan Press, 1998), 2. The Jameson quotation is from "Cognitive Mapping," in *Marxism and the Interpretation of Culture,* ed. Cary Nelson and Lawrence Grossbert (Urbana: University of Illinois Press, 1988), 351.

7. Pierre Marcabru, "Où sont les hippies d'antan?" *Le Figaro,* May 11, 2003, 26.

8. Molly Grogan, "Bread & Puppet Insurrection," *Paris Voice,* May 2003.

9. "J.G.," in *Le Travailleur Catalan,* review of *Le Livre de nos Jours,* quoted in

"Perpignan: La Catalane; Théâtre Saison 2002/2003," http://www.mairie-perpignan.fr/theatre/livre_des_jours.asp, September 20, 2002.

10. Quoted in David Cayley, *Ideas: Puppet Uprising* (Toronto: CBC Ideas Transcripts, 2002), 28. This is a transcript of a *CBC Ideas* radio broadcasts of December 9, 10, 16, and 17, 2002.

11. See Massimo Schuster's twenty-fifth anniversary catalog of his work, *Ave marionnette* (Marseille: Théâtre de l'Arc-en-Terre, 1995).

12. "Eight Individuals Who Never Follow," special advertising section for the Audi A8L, *New Yorker,* June 16 and 23, 2003, 29–40.

13. Richard Schechner, "Julie Taymor: From Jacques Lecoq to *The Lion King,*" in Bell, *Puppets, Masks, and Performing Objects,* 31.

14. "Chris Hardman: Artistic Director/Founder, Antenna Theater," Antenna Theater home page, http://www.antenna-theater.org/chris.htm, September 20, 2002.

15. See Victor Mair, *Painting and Performance: Chinese Picture Recitation and its Indian Genesis* (Honolulu: University of Hawaii Press, 1988).

16. See the documentary DVD by Ravi Gopalan Nair, *Vastuvadi Baul-1: Documentation on a Group of Singer Performers of Bengal, India,* Kerala, Ravi Parvathy, 2001.

17. See Rosa Luisa Márquez, *A-saltos: El juego como disciplina teatral* (Humacao: Ediciones Cuicaloca, 1996).

18. "About Paper Tiger," Paper Tiger home page, http://www.papertiger.org/index.php?name=about, June 19, 2003.

19. "About Deep Dish TV," Deep Dish home page, http://deepdish.igc.org/aboutus/index.html, June 19, 2003.

20. Tamar Schumann and DeeDee Halleck, dirs., *Ah! The Hopeful Pageantry of Bread and Puppet,* Bread and Puppet Film Project, Willow, N.Y., 2002.

21. Peter Sellars, remarks at an Emerson College Performing Arts Forum, Boston, February 14, 2001. On Sellars's apprenticeship with Margo Lovelace, see Norman Frisch, "Snails Surround the Stage: Opera Director Peter Sellars Recalls his Years in Puppetry," *Puppetry International* 12 (Fall 2002): 28–32.

22. Peter Sellars, "Commentary," *Marketplace* June 9, 2003, produced by Public Radio International, http://marketplace.org/shows/2003/06/09_mpp.html, June 12, 2003.

23. Dave Douglas, notes on *Witness,* on his website, http://www.davedouglas.com/witness.html, October 27, 2002.

24. Eugene van Erven, *The Playful Revolution: Theatre and Liberation in Asia* (Bloomington: Indiana University Press, 1992), 20. In addition, see Brenda Fajardo and Socrates Topacio, *PETA Theater Workshop Manual Series 1, BITAW Basic Integrated Theater Arts Workshop* (Quezon City: Philippine Educational Theater Association, 1989), which lists Susan Green's *Bread and Puppet: Stories of Struggle and Faith from Central America* (Burlington, Vt.: Green Valley Film and Art, 1985) as an important reference source for PETA community workshops.

25. On the collaboration of Bread and Puppet and MECATE in the creation of a Sandinista passion play, see John Bell, "The Bread and Puppet Theater in Nicaragua, 1987," *New Theatre Quarterly* 5, no. 17 (1989): 8–22. See also Ross Kidd, "Testimony from Nicaragua: An Interview with Nidia Bustos," *Theaterwork,* September 1982, 32–40.

26. Robert Wilson, qtd. by Spalding Gray in David Savran, *The Wooster Group, 1975–1985: Breaking the Rules* (Ann Arbor, Mich.: UMI Research Press, 1986), 152.

27. On the development of the American pageant movement, see Naomi Prevots, *American Pageantry: A Movement for Art and Democracy* (Ann Arbor, Mich.: UMI Research Press, 1990).

28. Sara Peattie, "George Konnoff," Puppeteers' Cooperative website, http://www.gis.net/~puppetco/gk.htm, June 19, 2003.

29. Puppeteers' Cooperative, *68 Ways to Make Really Big Puppets: A Patternbook of Parades and Pageants* (Somerville, Mass.: Puppeteers' Cooperative, n.d.); and Puppeteers' Cooperative, *How to Make Giant Puppets* (Boston: Puppeteers' Cooperative, 1994).

30. The Puppeteers' Cooperative offers a wide variety of free diagrams, puppet plays, and instructions for puppet building on its website, http://www.gis.net/~puppetco, which has helped puppeteers as far away as Pakistan.

31. Sandy Spieler, "Acknowledgments," in *Theatre of Wonder: Twenty-five Years in the Heart of the Beast*, ed. Colleen J. Sheehy (Minneapolis: University of Minnesota Press, 1999), viii.

32. Arm-of-the-Sea Theater, "Mission Statement," at the Arm-of-the-Sea Theater web page, http://www.armofthesea.org/history.html#mission, September 20, 2002.

33. "About Red Moon Theater," Red Moon Theater website, http://www.redmoon.org/redmooninfo/aboutred.html, November 1, 2002. Blair Thomas left Red Moon and now performs solo puppet shows; Lasko remains the artistic director of the company.

34. Cayley, *Ideas,* 29.

35. Spiral Q Puppet Theater home page, http://www.spiralq.org/aboutHome.html, October 27, 2002.

36. "All Species: A Brief Introduction," All Species Project: Environmental Education & Action home page, http://www.allspecies.org/about/overview.htm, September 20, 2002.

37. On the final years of the Domestic Resurrection Circus, see Bell, "End of Our Domestic Resurrection Circus."

38. The Phish festivals included "The Clifford Ball" at the Plattsburgh, New York Air Force Base, 1996; "The Great Went," at the Loring, Maine Air Force Base, 1997; "The Lemon Wheel," at Loring AFB, 1998; "Camp Oswego," in Oswego, New York, 1999; and "Big Cypress," a New Year's Eve festival at the Seminole Indian Reservation in the Everglades on December 31, 1999.

39. Cayley, *Ideas,* 28.

40. David Anderson, a member of Bread Bakers' Puppet Theater, and founder of the Whole Loaf Puppet Theater, started another puppet company in Toronto, the Clay and Paper Theater (see www.clayandpapertheatre.org, November 1, 2002).

41. See Trompetter's description of this production in "The Barber of Seville," *Puppetry International* 12 (Fall 2002): 36–39; as well as Anne Midgette's review of the production, "Adding Shtick to Opera in a Play for Belly Laughs," *New York Times* May 9, 2003, E3.

42. Peter Schumann, "We give you a piece of bread" manifesto from 1960s, New York City; reprinted in 2002 by Bread and Puppet Press, Glover, Vermont.

43. Fergus Nicoll, interview by Vandana Shiva, on *Agenda,* BBC World Service, June 1, 2003, http://www.bbc.co.uk/worldservice/programmes/agenda/shtml, June 3, 2003. See also "Arrests and Weapons Allegations Spark Activists' Anger," *St. Louis Post-Dispatch,* May 17, 2003, 8.

44. In Stefan Brecht's opinion, by showing up "so consistently in New York City peace parades" and providing those events "with a consistent image," Bread and Puppet "invented a new art form, the puppet parade" (*Peter Schumann's Bread and Puppet Theatre,* 489). On the importance of puppets to post–September 11 street protests, see Philip Kennicott, "Borne in Effigy. If Protest is Theater, Its Biggest Actors Are Puppets," *Washington Post,* March 17, 2003, C1-2.

45. On Bread and Puppet participation in the Greenwich Village Halloween parades, see John Bell, "Louder Than Traffic: Bread and Puppet Parades," in *Radical Street Performance: An International Anthology,* ed. Jan Cohen-Cruz (New York: Routledge, 1998), 271–81.

46. *The Oratorio of the Possibilitarians* (program), Bread and Puppet Theater, 2002, 10.

47. Guy Debord, *Society of the Spectacle* (Detroit: Black and Red, 1983), secs. 1, 2; emphasis added.

The resource section lays the foundation for further research by providing readers with crucial information on material for each theater collective. It provides information on archives, a list of published material by members of each collective, a list of material published about each collective, and a list of available audiovisual material documenting their performances.

THE LIVING THEATRE

Archives

The Living Theatre Archive
New York Public Library for the Performing Arts
Theatre Research Division
Dorothy and Lewis B. Cullman Center
40 Lincoln Center Plaza
New York, NY 10023-7498
Phone: (212) 870-1630

Publications by Living Theatre Members

Beck, Julian. "Storming the Barricades." In *The Brig: A Play*, by Kenneth H. Brown. New York: Hill and Wang, 1965.

———. "Money, Sex, Theatre." In *Counter-Culture: The Creation of an Alternative Society*, ed. Joseph Berke. London: Peter Owen, Ltd., 1970.

———. *The Life of the Theatre*. San Francisco: City Lights, 1972.

Beck, Julian, and Judith Malina. "Containment is the Enemy." Interviewed by Richard Schechner. *TDR* 13, no. 3 (1969): 24–44.

———. "*PARADISE NOW*: Notes." *TDR* 13, no. 3 (1969): 90–107.

———. "Paradise Later: An Interview with Judith Malina and Julian Beck." Interview by Erika Munk. *Performance* 1 (1971).

———. *Paradise Now.* New York: Random House, 1971.

The Living Theatre. "The Avignon Statement." *TDR* 13, no. 3 (1969): 45.

Malina, Judith. "Directing *The Brig.*" In *The Brig: A Play,* by Kenneth H. Brown. New York: Hill and Wang, 1965.

———. *The Enormous Despair.* New York: Random House, 1972.

———. *The Diaries of Judith Malina, 1947–1957.* New York: Grove, 1972.

Preface to Sophocles' *Antigone* by Judith Malina. Adapted by Bertolt Brecht. New York: Applause, 1984.

Malina, Judith, and Hanon Reznikov. "Living on the Street: Conversations with Judith Malina and Hanon Reznikov." Interview by Cindy Rosenthal. In *Radical Street Performance: An International Anthology,* ed. Jan Cohen-Cruz. New York: Routledge, 1998.

Rostagno, Aldo, Julian Beck, and Judith Malina. *We, The Living Theatre.* New York: Ballantine, 1970.

Publications on the Living Theatre

Biner, Pierre. *The Living Theatre: A History Without Myths.* Trans. Robert Meister. New York: Avon, 1972.

Brecht, Stefan. "Revolution at the Brooklyn Academy of Music." *TDR* 13, no. 3 (1969): 47–73.

Brown, Kenneth H. *The Brig: A Play.* New York: Hill and Wang, 1965.

Gelber, Jack. *The Connection.* New York: Grove/Atlantic, 1960.

———. "Julian Beck: Businessman." *TDR* 30, no. 2 (1986): 6–29.

McDermott, Patrick. "Portrait of an Actor, Watching: Antiphonal Feedback to the Living Theatre." *TDR* 13, no. 3 (1969): 74–83.

Rosenthal, Cindy. "Antigone's Example: A View of the Living Theatre's Production, Process, and Praxis." *Theatre Survey* 41, no. 1 (2000): 68–87.

Sainer, Arthur. *The New Radical Theatre Notebook.* New York: Applause, 1996.

Silber, Irwin. "To: Julian Beck, Judith Malina, and the Living Theatre." *TDR* 13, no. 3 (1969): 86–89.

Tytell, John. *The Living Theatre: Art, Exile, and Outrage.* New York: Grove, 1995.

Yale/Theatre 2, no. 1 (1969). Issue devoted to the Living Theatre.

Film and Video

The Brig. A film by Jonas Mekas, 1964. Mystic Fire Videos.

The Connection. A film by Shirley Clarke, 1961. Mystic Fire Videos.

Emergency! A film by Gwen Brown, 1968. Mystic Fire Videos.

Frankenstein. Staged for German TV, 1965. Available at Lincoln Center Library for the Performing Arts, New York.

Mysteries and Smaller Pieces. Camera Three videotapes, produced and directed by Merrill Brockway, 1968.

Paradise Now. Filmed in Brussels, 1970. Mystic Fire Videos.

Resist: To Be with the Living. Documentary film by Dirk Szuszies, 2003.

Signals Through the Flames. A film by Sheldon Rochlin and Maxine Harris, 1983. Mystic Fire Videos.

THE OPEN THEATRE
Archives

The Open Theatre Papers
The Joseph Chaikin Papers
The Jean-Claude van Itallie Papers
Department of Special Collections and Archives
Box 5190
Room 1212
Kent State University Libraries
Kent State University
Kent, OH 44242-0001
(330) 672-2270
http://speccoll.library.kent.edu

Publications by The Open Theatre Members

Chaikin, Joseph. "The Actor's Involvement: Notes on Brecht." Interview by Erika Munk. *TDR* 12, no. 2 (1968): 147–51.
———. "Fragments." Ed. Kelly Morris. *TDR* 13, no. 3 (1969): 141–44.
———. *The Presence of the Actor.* New York: Atheneum, 1972.
———. "Closing the Open Theatre." Interview by Richard Toscan. *Theatre Quarterly* 4, no. 16 (1975): 36–42.
Open Theater. *Three Works by the Open Theater.* Ed. Karen Malpede. New York: Drama Book Specialists, 1974.
———. *Terminal.* Created by the Open Theatre ensemble, codirected by Joseph Chaikin and Roberta Sklar, text by Susan Yankowitz. *Scripts* 1 (November 1971): 17–47. First, large-company version.
———. *Terminal.* In *The Radical Theatre Notebook,* by Arthur Sainer. New York: Applause Theatre Books, 1977. First version, with stage directions adapted for small company.
Terry, Megan. *Viet Rock.* In *Four Plays.* New York: Simon and Schuster, 1967.
van Itallie, Jean-Claude. *America Hurrah.* New York: Coward-McCann, 1966.
van Itallie, Jean-Claude, and the Open Theatre. *The Serpent.* New York: Atheneum, 1969.

Publications on the Open Theatre

Blumenthal, Eileen. *Joseph Chaikin: Exploring at the Boundaries of Theatre.* New York: Cambridge University Press, 1984.
Copeland, Roger. "Remembering the Real Open Theatre." *New York Times,* December 25, 1983, 11.
Hulton, Dorinda. "Joseph Chaikin and Aspects of Actor Training: Possibilities Rendered Present." In *Twentieth Century Acting Training,* ed. Alison Hodge. New York: Routledge, 2000.
Malpede, Karen. "The Open Theatre." In *People's Theatre in Amerika.* New York: Drama Book Specialists, 1973.

Pasolli, Robert. *A Book on the Open Theatre*. New York: Avon, 1970.

Shank, Theodore. *Beyond the Boundaries: American Alternative Theatre*. Ann Arbor: University of Michigan Press, 2002.

Video

The Mutation Show. CBS *Camera Three* videotape, 1973. Distributed by New York State Education Department, Albany, N.Y.

Nightwalk. CBS *Camera Three* videotape, 1973. Distributed by New York State Education Department, Albany, N.Y.

The Serpent. Educational Broadcasting Corporation Film for Public Television, 1969. Distributed by Arthur Cantor, Inc., New York, N.Y.

Terminal. CBS *Camera Three* videotape, 1970. Distributed by New York State Education Department, Albany, N.Y.

AT THE FOOT OF THE MOUNTAIN

Archives

Records of At the Foot of the Mountain
Manuscripts Division
213 Elmer L. Anderson Library
222 21st Avenue South
University of Minnesota
Minneapolis, MN 55455
(612) 625 3550

Publications by Members of At the Foot of the Mountain

Boesing, Martha. *The Pimp*. In *A Century of Plays by American Women,* ed. Rachel France. New York: Richards-Rosen Press, 1979.

———. *The Web*. In *Plays in Process* 4, no. 1. New York: Theatre Communications Group, 1981.

———. *Journey Along the Matrix: Three Plays by Martha Boesing*. Minneapolis: Vanilla Press, 1981.

———. *The Story of a Mother, a Ritual Drama*. In *Women in American Theatre*, ed. Helen Krich Chinoy and Linda Walsh Jenkins. New York: Theatre Communications Group, 1987.

———. "Process and Problems." In *Women in American Theatre*, ed. Helen Krich Chinoy and Linda Walsh Jenkins. New York: Theatre Communications Group, 1987.

Publications on At the Foot of the Mountain

Canning, Charlotte. *Feminist Theaters in the U.S.A.: Staging Women's Experience*. New York: Routledge, 1991.

Dolan, Jill. *The Feminist Spectator as Critic*. Ann Arbor: University of Michigan Press, 1988.

Flynn, Meredith. "The Feeling Circle, Company Collaboration, and Ritual Drama:

Three Conventions Developed by the Women's Theater, At the Foot of the Mountain." Ph.D. diss., Bowling Green State University, 1984.

Gillespie, Patti. "Feminist Theatre: A Rhetorical Phenomenon." In *Women in American Theatre,* ed. Helen Krich Chinoy and Linda Walsh Jenkins. New York: Theatre Communications Group, 1987.

Greeley, Lynne. "Martha Boesing: Playwright of Performance." *Text and Performance Quarterly* 9 (July 1989): 207–15.

———. "Making Familiar: Martha Boesing and Feminist Dramatic Structure." In *Theatre and Feminist Aesthetics,* ed. Karen Laughlin and Catherine Schuler. Teaneck, N.J.: Fairleigh Dickinson University Press, 1995.

Jenkins, Linda Walsh. "At the Foot of the Mountain." In *Women in American Theatre,* ed. Helen Krich Chinoy and Linda Walsh Jenkins. New York: Theatre Communications Group, 1987.

Leavitt, Dinah. *Feminist Theatre Groups.* Jefferson, N.C.: McFarland, 1980.

Natalle, Elizabeth. *Feminist Theatre: A Study in Persuasion.* Metuchen, N.J.: Scarecrow Press, 1985.

Roth, Martha. "Here Come the Sisters: A Profile of Martha Boesing." *Sojourner,* October 31, 1996, 29–31.

Film and Video

"Going to Seed." Part of Showtime's Search for Excellence Series. Shot in Minneapolis, Minnesota (no date). Lincoln Center Library for the Performing Arts, Theatre on Film and Tape Archive.

THE SAN FRANCISCO MIME TROUPE

Archives

The San Francisco Mime Troupe Archives, 1959–99
University of California, Davis
General Library, Dept. of Special Collections
Collection number: D-61
100 North West Quad
Davis, California, 95616-5292
(530) 752-1621

Publications by Members of The San Francisco Mime Troupe

Alexander, Robert. *I Ain't Yo' Uncle: The New Jack Revisionist "Uncle Tom's Cabin."* Woodstock, Ill.: Dramatic Publishing, 1996.

Davis, R. G. *The San Francisco Mime Troupe: The First Ten Years.* Palo Alto, Calif.: Ramparts Press, 1975.

Holden, Joan. "The San Francisco Mime Troupe a Quarter of a Century Later: An Interview with Joan Holden." Interview by William Kleb. *Theatre* 16, no. 2 (1985): 588–61.

Holden, Joan, et. al. "The San Francisco's *Mozamgola Caper.*" *Theatre* 20, no. 1 (1988): 55–71.

San Francisco Mime Troupe. *By Popular Demand: Plays and Other Works by the San Francisco Mime Troupe.* San Francisco: San Francisco Mime Troupe, 1980.

San Francisco Mime Troupe and Friends. *Factwino Meets the Moral Majority. Humanist* 42, no. 4 (1982): 5–43.

Publications on the San Francisco Mime Troupe

Baxandall, Lee. "The San Francisco Mime Troupe Perform Brecht." *Praxis* 1 (1975): 116–21.

Cohn, Ruby. "Joan Holden and the San Francisco Mime Troupe." *TDR* 24, no. 2 (1980): 41–50.

Malpede, Karen. *People's Theatre in Amerika.* New York: Drama Book Specialists, 1973.

Orenstein, Claudia. *Festive Revolutions: The Politics of Popular Theater and the San Francisco Mime Troupe.* Jackson: University Press of Mississippi, 1998.

Reinelt, Janelle. "Approaching the Sixties: Between Nostalgia and Critique." *Theatre Survey* 43, no. 1 (2002): 37–56.

Schechter, Joel. Performance review of "The Arrest of the Anarchist Keith Henry" by the San Francisco Mime Troupe and the San Francisco Police Department. *Theatre Journal* 47 (1995): 541–42.

Shank, Theodore. *Beyond the Boundaries: American Alternative Theatre.* Ann Arbor: University of Michigan Press, 2002.

———. "Political Theatre as Popular Entertainment." *TDR* 81, no. 1 (1974): 110–17.

Wolf, Stacy. "Politics, Polyphony, and Pleasure: The San Francisco Mime Troupe's *Seeing Double.*" *Journal of Dramatic Theory and Criticism* 8, no. 1 (1993): 61–81.

Film and Video

Silber, Glen, and Claudia Vianello. *Troupers.* Icarus Films, 1985.

EL TEATRO CAMPESINO
Archives

El Teatro Campesino Archives
705 Fourth St.
San Juan Bautista, CA 95045
(831) 623-2444

Publications by Members of El Teatro Campesino

El Teatro Campesino and Luis Valdez. *Actos.* San Juan Bautista, Calif.: Menyah Productions, 1971.

Valdez, Luis. "Brecht: The Intellectual Tramp: An Interview with Luis Valdez." Interview by Yolanda Broyles-González. *Communications from the International Brecht Society* 12, no. 2 (1983): 33–44.

———. *Luis Valdez' Early Works: Actos, Benabé and Pensamiento Serpentino.* Houston: Atre Publico Press, 1990.

———. *Zoot Suit and Other Plays.* Houston: Arte Público Press, 1992.

Publications on El Teatro Campesino

Broyles-González, Yolanda. "Women in El Teatro Campesino: '¿Apoco estaba mo-lacha la Virgen de Guadalupe?'" In *Chicana Voices: Intersections of Class, Race, and Gender,* ed. Teresa Córdoba et al. Austin, Tex.: Center for Mexican Studies, 1986.

————. *El Teatro Campesino: Theater in the Chicano Movement.* Austin: University of Texas Press, 1994.

Elam, Harry J., Jr. *Taking It to the Streets.* Ann Arbor: University of Michigan Press, 1997.

Huerta, Jorge. *Chicano Theatre: Themes and Forms.* Tempe, Ariz.: Bilingual Press, 1982.

————. *Chicano Drama: Performance, Society, and Myth.* New York: Cambridge University Press, 2000.

————. "El Teatro Campesino: The Next Generation." *Theatre Forum* 19 (2001): 33–39.

————. "When Sleeping Giants Awaken: Chicano Theatre in the 1960s." *Theatre Survey* 43, no. 1 (2002): 23–35.

Malpede, Karen. *People's Theatre in Amerika.* New York: Drama Book Specialists, 1973.

Ramírez, Elizabeth C. *Chicanas/Latinas in American Theatre.* Bloomington: Indiana University Press, 2000.

Santibañez, James. "El Teatro Campesino Today and El Teatro Urbano." In *The Chicanos: Mexican American Voices,* ed. Ed Ludwig and James Santibañez. Baltimore: Penguin, 1971.

Shank, Theodore. *Beyond the Boundaries: American Alternative Theatre.* Ann Arbor: University of Michigan Press, 2002.

Video

I Am Joaquin. Directed by Luis Valdez. Escuela Tlatelolco Centro de Estudios, 1969.

Zoot Suit. Directed by Luis Valdez. Universal Films, 1981.

La Pastorela: A Shepherd's Tale. Directed by Luis Valdez. PBS *Great Performances,* 1991.

Ballad of a Soldier. Directed by Anáhuac Valdez and Kinan Valdez. COTR Productions, 1999.

THE FREE SOUTHERN THEATER

Archives

The Free Southern Theater Archives
John M. O'Neal Papers, 1957–72
Amistad Research Center
Tilton Hall
Tulane University
6823 St. Charles Avenue
New Orleans, LA 70118
(504) 865 5535

Publications by Members of The Free Southern Theater

Dent, Thomas C., Richard Schechner, and Gilbert Moses. *The Free Southern Theater by the Free Southern Theater.* Indianapolis: Bobbs-Merrill, 1969.

Dent, Thomas, and Jerry Ward Jr. "After the Free Southern Theater: A Dialogue." 1987. In *A Sourcebook on African-American Performance,* ed. Annemarie Bean. New York: Routledge, 1999.

Moses, Gilbert, John O'Neal, Denise Nicholes, Murray Levy, and Richard Schechner. 1965. "The Free Southern Theater." In *A Sourcebook on African-American Performance,* ed. Annemarie Bean. New York: Routledge, 1999.

O'Neal, John. "Motion in the Ocean: Some Political Dimensions of the Free Southern Theater." 1965. In *A Sourcebook on African-American Performance,* ed. Annemarie Bean. New York: Routledge, 1999.

———. "A Road Through the Wilderness." 1988. In *A Sourcebook on African-American Performance,* ed. Annemarie Bean. New York: Routledge, 1999.

Publications on the Free Southern Theater

Bean, Annemarie, ed. *A Sourcebook on African-American Performance.* New York: Routledge, 1999.

Hammer, Kate. "John O'Neal, Actor and Activist." In *A Sourcebook on African-American Performance,* ed. Annemarie Bean. New York: Routledge, 1999.

Harris, Clarissa Myrick. "Mirror of the Movement: The History of the Free Southern Theater as a Microcosm of the Civil Rights and Black Power Movements, 1963–1978." Ph.D. diss., Emory University, 1988.

Film and Video

No known footage.

THE PERFORMANCE GROUP

Archives

The Richard Schechner Papers (including the Performance Group papers)
Department of Rare Books and Special Collections
Princeton University Library
One Washington Road
Princeton University
Princeton, NJ 08544
(609) 258 3184
http://www.princeton.edu/~rbsc/

Publications by Members of The Performance Group

McNamara, Brooks, Jerry Rojo, and Richard Schechner. *Theatre, Spaces, Environments: Eighteen Projects.* New York: Drama Book Specialists, 1975.

The Performance Group. *Dionysus in 69.* Ed. Richard Schechner. New York: Farrar, Straus and Giroux, 1970.

Schechner, Richard. *Public Domain*. New York: Bobbs-Merrill, 1969.
———. *Makbeth after Shakespeare*. Schulenburg, Tex.: I. E. Clark, 1978.
———. *Environmental Theatre*. 1973. New York: Applause, 1994.
Shephard, William Hunter. *The Dionysus Group*. New York: Peter Lang, 1991.

Publications on the Performance Group

Aronson, Arnold. *The History and Theory of Environmental Scenography*. Ann Arbor, Mich.: UMI Research Press, 1981.
———. *American Avant-Garde Theatre: A History*. New York: Routledge, 2000.
Brecht, Stefan. "*Dionysus in 69*, from Euripides' *The Bacchae:* The Performance Group." *TDR* 43 (1969): 156–68.
Clemons, Leigh Ann. "The Power of Performance Environmental Theatre and Heterotopia in *Dionysus in 69*." *Theatre Studies* 37 (1992): 66–73.
Croyden, Margaret. *Lunatics, Lovers, and Poets: Contemporary Experimental Theatre*. New York: McGraw Hill, 1974.
Innes, Christopher. *Avant Garde Theatre, 1892–1992*. New York: Routledge, 1993.
Malpede, Karen. *People's Theatre in Amerika*. New York: Drama Book Specialists, 1973.
Shank, Theodore. *Beyond the Boundaries: American Alternative Theatre*. Ann Arbor: University of Michigan Press, 2002.

Film and Video

Dionysus in 69. Directors Brian De Palma and Richard Schechner, 1970.
Tooth of Crime. Director Ken Kobland and James Mccarthy, 1973.
Extensive photography and film, including outtakes of Brian de Palma's film *Dionysus in 69*, raw footage of *Oedipus*, and other videos is held in the Richard Schechner Papers, Princeton University Libraries.

THE BREAD AND PUPPET THEATER

Archives

Bread and Puppet Theater Archives, 1962–81 (bulk 1964–75)
University of California, Davis
General Library
Dept. of Special Collections
Collection number: D-136
100 North West Quad Davis, CA 95616-5292

The Bread and Puppet Theater Collection (1962–85)
Special Collections
Bailey/Howe Library
University of Vermont
Burlington, Vermont 05405

Bread and Puppet Collections (1967–88)
Archives and Special Collections

Thomas J. Dodd Research Center
University of Connecticut Libraries
405 Babbidge Road, Unit 1205
Storrs, CT 06269-1205

Publications by Bread and Puppet Members

Bell, John. "Bread and Puppet Theater's 'Rites of Winter.'" *Puppetry Journal* 35, no. 4 (1984): 5–8, 16.

———. Review of *Peter Schumann's Bread and Puppet Theatre,* by Stephan Brecht. *Puppetry Journal* 41, no. 2 (1989): 14–15.

———. "The Bread and Puppet Theatre in Nicaragua, 1985." *New Theatre Quarterly* 5, no. 17 (1989): 8–22.

———. *Landscape and Desire: Bread and Puppet Pageants in the 1990s.* Glover, Vt.: Bread and Puppet Press, 1997.

———. "The End of *Our Domestic Resurrection Circus:* Bread and Puppet Theater and Counterculture Performance in the 1990s." *TDR* 43, no. 3 (1999): 62–80.

———. "Beyond the Cold War: Bread and Puppet Theater and the New World Order." In *Staging Resistance: Essays on Political Theatre,* ed. Jeanne Colleran and Jenny S. Spencer. Ann Arbor: University of Michigan Press, 1998.

Bread and Puppet. *Bread and Puppet: Stories of Struggle and Faith from Central America.* New York: Norton, 1985.

Schumann, Peter. "With the Bread and Puppet Theatre." Interview by Helen Brown and Jane Seitz *TDR* 12, no. 2 (1968): 62–73.

"Bread and Puppets." *TDR* 14, no. 3 (1970): 35.

———. *Puppen und Masken: Das Bread and Puppet Theater: Ein Arbeitsbericht.* Frankfurt am Main: Fischer-Taschenbuch-Verlag, 1973.

———. "Puppetry and Politics." *American Theatre,* November 1986, 32–33.

———. *A Lecture to Art Students at SUNY/Purchase, New York.* Glover, Vt.: Bread and Puppet Press, 1987.

———. "The Bread and Puppet Theatre in Nicaragua, 1987." Interview by Rosa Luisa Marquez. *New Theatre Quarterly* 5, no. 17 (1989): 3–7.

———. *The Radicality of the Bread and Puppet Theater.* Glover, Vt.: Bread and Puppet Press, 1990.

———. "The Radicality of the Puppet Theatre." *TDR* 35, no, 4 (1991): 75–83.

———. *Puppetry and the New World Order.* Glover, Vt.: Bread and Puppet Press, 1993.

———. "Five Reasons Why I Support Air Strikes to Lift the Siege of Sarajevo." *TDR* 38, no. 2 (1994): 10–11.

———. "Uprising of the Beast: An Interview with Peter Schumann." Interview by John Bell. *Theatre* 25, no. 1 (1994): 41–42.

———. *Fiddle Sermons from Insurrection Masses with Funeral Marches for Rotten Ideas.* Glover, Vt.: Bread and Puppet Press, 1999.

Publications on Bread and Puppet Theater

Blanc, Eric. "A Domestic Resurrection Circus for Frogs." *Puppetry Journal* 46, no. 2 (1994): 10–11.

Brecht, Stefan. *Peter Schumann's Bread and Puppet Theatre*. 2 vols. London: Methuen, 1988.

———. "Peter Schumann's Bread and Puppet Theatre." *TDR* 14, no. 3 (1970): 44–90.

Cleary, Beth. "Negation Strategies: The Bread and Puppet Theatre and Performance Practice." *New England Theatre Journal* 9 (1998): 23–48.

Dennison, George, Geoffery Gardner, and Taylor Stoehr. *An Existing Better World: Notes on the Bread and Puppet Theater*. Brooklyn: Autonomedia, 2000.

Kourilsky, Françoise. "Dada and Circus." *TDR* 18, no. 1 (1974): 104–9.

Malpede, Karen. *People's Theatre in Amerika*. New York: Drama Book Specialists, 1973.

Munk, Erika. "TDR Comment." *TDR* 14, no. 3 (1970): 33–34.

Nichols, Robert. "Christmas Story, 1962." *TDR* 14, no. 3 (1970): 91.

Simon, Ronald T., Marc Estrin, and Bread and Puppet Theater. *Rehearsing with Gods: Photographs and Essays on the Bread and Puppet Theater*. White River Junction, Vt.: Chelsea Green Publishing, 2004.

TDR 14, no. 3 (1970). Special issue on Bread and Puppet Theater.

Towsen, John. "The Stations of the Cross." *TDR* 16, no. 3 (1972): 57–70.

Toy, Judith. "Bread and Puppet Theatre Workshop Intensive." *Puppetry Journal* 45, no. 3 (1994): 13–14.

Film and Video

Farber, Jeff. *Brother Bread, Sister Puppet—Street Theatre and Political Satire*. Insight Media, 1993.

Halleck, DeeDee, and George Griffin. *The Green Meadows*. 16mm film, 1975.

Halleck, DeeDee, and Tamar Schumann. *Ah! The Hopeful Pageantry of Bread and Puppet*. Viewing Habits / Bread and Puppet Theater, 1999.

Lloyd, Robin. *Columbus and the New World Order*. Green Valley Media, 1992.

———. *The Convention of the Gods*. Pageant, 1993. Green Valley Media, 1993.

———. *Men with Teeth*. Pageant, 1994. Green Valley Media, 1994.

Lloyd, Robin, and DeeDee Halleck. *Broken Off Letter: A Yugoslav Journal*. Green Valley Media, no date.

Lloyd, Robin, and Michael Sacca. *Gates of Hell*. Green Valley Media, 1998.

CONTRIBUTORS

ROGER BABB was the Artistic Director for Otrabanda Company. He worked as an actor and writer for Joseph Chaikin's Winter Project, Ping Chong's Fiji Company, and many other New York experimental theater artists including Julie Taymor, Talking Band, and Meredith Monk. He taught at Princeton University and Swarthmore College for many years and is currently Professor of Theatre at Mount Holyoke College.

ANNEMARIE BEAN is Assistant Professor of Theatre at Williams College. She is the editor of *A Sourcebook of African-American Performance: Plays, People, Movements* (Routledge, 1999); and coeditor with James V. Hatch and Brooks McNamara of *Inside the Minstrel Mask: Readings in Nineteenth-Century Blackface Minstrelsy* (Wesleyan University Press, 1996). Her articles include "Black Minstrelsy and Double Inversion, Circa 1890," in *African American Performance and Theatre History*, edited by Harry J. Elam Jr. and David Krasner (Oxford, 2001); "Presenting the Prima Donna: Black Femininity and Performance," *Performance Research* 1, no. 3 (1996); "The Plantation Mama Tells Her Woes: Plays by African-American Women of the Harlem Renaissance," in *Blackstream: Select Conference Papers from the 1995 San Francisco Conference* (Black Theatre Association of the ATHE, 1996); and "Disclosures, Silences, Agency: African Female Genital Circumcision," *Women & Performance* 7, no. 2 & 8, no. 1 (1995).

JOHN BELL is Assistant Professor of Performing Arts at Emerson College. He is a theater historian and puppeteer whose interests focus on modern drama, avant-garde performance, popular theater, and puppet theater. In addition to his academic work he is a member of the Obie Award-winning Great Small Works theater company, with whom he performs and directs. He has worked with Bread and Puppet Theater since the 1970s. His recent books include *Puppets, Masks, and Performing Objects* (MIT Press, 2001); *Strings, Hands, Shadows: A Modern Puppet History* (Detroit Institute of the Arts, 2000); and *Landscape and Desire: Bread and Puppet Pageants in the 90s* (Bread and Puppet Press, 1997).

YOLANDA BROYLES-GONZÁLEZ is Professor and Head of Women Studies at the University of Arizona, Tucson. She is the author of *Lydia Mendoza's Life in Music/La Historia de Lydia Mendoza: Norteño Tejano Legacies* (Oxford University Press, 2001); *El*

Teatro Campesino: Theater in the Chicano Movement (University of Texas Press, 1994); and *The German Response to Latin American Literature and the Reception of Jorge Luis Borges and Pablo Neruda* (Carl Winter, 1981). She is the editor of *Re-Emerging Native Women of the Americas: Native Chicana Latina Women's Studies* (Kendall/Hunt, 2001). In addition to some forty scholarly articles, essays, and reviews, she wrote on Chicano culture and performance for the *San Antonio Light* during the 1980s.

CHARLOTTE CANNING is Associate Professor of Theatre History and Criticism at the University of Texas, Austin. She is the author of *The Most American Thing in America: Circuit Chautauqua as Performance* (University of Iowa Press, 2005) and *Feminist Theaters in the USA: Staging Women's Experience* (Routledge, 1996). She has served as the Book Review Editor for *Theatre Journal,* President of the Women and Theatre Program, and President of the American Society for Theatre Research.

JAN COHEN-CRUZ is Associate Professor of Drama at New York University. She is the editor of *Radical Street Performance: An International Anthology* (Routledge, 1998) and coeditor with Mady Schutzman of *Playing Boal: Theatre, Therapy, Activism* (Routledge, 1994). Her articles include "When Seeing is Not Believing: Community-Based Arts and Criticism" *American Theatre* (forthcoming); "When the Gown Goes to Town," *Theatre Topics* (2001); "Dancing Across Communities: The Liz Lerman Dance Exchange," in *Performing Community, Performing Democracy,* ed. Tobin Nellhaus and Susan Haedacke (University of Michigan Press, 2001); "Motion of the Ocean: Theatre for Social Change Since 'the Sixties,'" *Theatre* (2001); and "A Hyphenated Field: Community-Based Theatre in the U.S.," *New Theatre Quarterly* (2000).

LYNNE GREELEY is Associate Professor of Theatre History at the University of Vermont. Her research focuses on experimental theater, the history of women playwrights and directors, interdisciplinary approaches to theater, and theater pedagogy. Her publications have appeared in *Theatre History Studies, Theatre Survey, Text and Performance Quarterly,* and *Belles Lettres.* She has contributed chapters to *Theatre and Feminist Aesthetics* (Fairleigh Dickinson University Press, 1995) and *Teaching Theatre Today* (Palgrave Macmillan, 2004).

JAMES M. HARDING is Associate Professor of English at the University of Mary Washington. He is coeditor with John Rouse of *Not the Other Avant-Garde: On the Transnational Foundations of Avant-Garde Performance* (University of Michigan Press, 2006) and editor of *Contours of the Theatrical Avant-Garde: Performance and Textuality* (University of Michigan Press, 2000). He is a former editor of the journal *Theatre Survey* and is the author of *Adorno and a Writing of the Ruins: Essays on Anglo-American Literature and Culture* (SUNY Press, 1997).

JORGE HUERTA is Chancellor's Associate Professor of Theatre at the University of California, San Diego. He is the author of *Chicano Drama: Performance Society and Myth* (Cambridge University Press, 2001) and *Chicano Theatre: Themes and Forms* (Bi-lingual Press, 1982) and editor of *Nuevos Pasos* (Players Press, 1989), *Necessary Theatre* (Players Press, 1982) and *Zoot Suit and Other Plays* by Luis Valdez (Arte Press, 1982). He has written over seventy articles and reviews on Chicano theater.

SONJA KUFTINEC is Assistant Professor of Theatre at the University of Minnesota. She is the author of *Staging America: Cornerstone and Community-Based Theater* (Southern Illinois University Press, 2003). Her articles include "The Art of Bridge

Building in Mostar," in *Performing Democracy: International Perspectives on Urban Community-Based Performance,* ed. Susan Haedicke and Tobin Nelhaus (University of Michigan Press, 2001); "Fighting Fences: Theatrical Rule-Breaking in Former Yugoslavia," *Slavic and Eastern European Performances,* Summer 1999, 50–57; "Playing With the Borders: Dramaturging Ethnicity in Bosnia," *Journal of Dramatic Theory and Criticism,* Fall 1998, 143–56; "Ghost Town: Cultural *Hauntologie* in Mostar, Bosnia-Herzegovina," *Text and Performance Quarterly,* Spring 1998, 81–95; "*Odakle Ste?* (Where Are You From?) Active Learning and Community Based Theater in Former Yugoslavia and the US," *Theatre Topics,* September 1997, 171–86; "Cornerstone's Community *Chalk Circle,*" *Brecht Yearbook* 22 (1997): 239–51; and "A Cornerstone for Rethinking Community Theater," *Theater Topics,* March 1996, 91–104.

CAROL MARTIN is Associate Professor of Drama at New York University. She is the author of *Dance Marathons: Performing American Culture of the 1920s and 1930s* (University Press of Mississippi, 1994), editor of *A Sourcebook of Feminist Theatre: On and Beyond the Stage* (Routledge, 1996), and coeditor with Henry Bial of *The Brecht Sourcebook* (Routledge, 2000).

SUSAN VANETA MASON is Professor of Theatre Arts at California State University, Los Angeles. She has edited *The San Francisco Mime Troupe Reader* (University of Michigan Press, 2005). She coauthored *Edgy Storytellers: A Film Companion & Liberation Theatre Workbook,* with Eugene van Erven (Houghten, Netherlands: Atalanta, 1997). Her numerous articles include "The Golden Arches and the Ivory Tower: Creating an *Acto* about the Corporate University," (*TDR,* forthcoming); "Finding the Edge: Multiple Community Goals," in *Performing Community, Performing Democracy: International Perspectives on Urban Community-Based Performance,* ed. Susan Haedicke and Tobin Nellhaus (University of Michigan Press, 2001); and "Conversation with Mame Hunt," in *Dramaturgy in American Theater: A Source Book* (Harcourt Brace, 1997).

ERIKA MUNK is an independent writer in New York City. From 1992 to 2004 she was the editor of *Theatre,* a triquarterly journal published by Duke University for Yale, where she was Professor of Dramaturgy and Dramatic Criticism at the Drama School. From 1978 to 1990 she was Senior Editor and a staff writer at *The Village Voice.* Earlier she was the editor of *Performance* (a quarterly), Scripts (a monthly), and *TDR.* She has published hundreds of critical and political articles, essays and reviews in magazines and journals including *The Nation,* the *New York Times,* the *Village Voice, Brecht Yearbook, American Theatre, TDR,* and *Performing Arts Journal.*

CLAUDIA ORENSTEIN is Associate Professor of Theatre at Hunter College. She is the author of *Festive Revolutions: The Politics of Popular Theatre and the San Francisco Mime Troupe* (University Press of Mississippi, 1999). Her articles include "A Taste of Tibet: The Nuns of Khachoe Ghakyil Ling Nunnery and the Theatre du Soleil," *Asian Theatre Journal* 19, no. 1 (2002): 212–30; "Agitational Performance, Now and Then," *Theater* 31, no. 3 (2001): 139–51; "Dance and Drama: An Overview," in *The Encyclopedia of Women and World Religion,* ed, Serenity Young (Macmillan, 1999), 232–34; and "Dancing on Shifting Ground: The Balinese Kecak in Cross-Cultural Perspective," *Theatre Symposium* 6 (August 1998): 116–24.

MARTIN PUCHNER is the H. Gordon Garbedian Professor of English and Comparative Literature at Columbia University and the author of *Stage Fright: Modernism, Anti-Theatricality, and Drama* (Johns Hopkins University Press, 2002) as well as of *Poetry of the Revolution: Marx, Manifestos, and the Avant-Gardes* (Princeton University Press, 2006). His edited books and introductions include *Six Plays by Henrik Ibsen* (Barnes and Noble, 2003), Lionel Abel's *Tragedy and Metatheatre* (Holmes and Meier, 2003), *The Communist Manifesto and Other Writings* (Barnes and Noble, 2005), and *Modern Drama: Critical Concepts* (Routledge, forthcoming). He is coeditor of *Against Theatre: Creative Destructions on the Modernist Stage* (Palgrave, 2006), and the forthcoming *Norton Anthology of Drama*. He will be editor of *Theatre Survey* from 2007 to 2009.

CINDY ROSENTHAL is Associate Professor of Drama and Dance at Hofstra University. She has published essays and reviews in *Radical Street Performance* (Routledge, 1998), *Theatre Survey, Theatre Journal, Women and Performance,* the *New York Times,* and *TDR;* her *TDR* essay on the community garden movement in New York City won Hofstra's Stessin Prize for Outstanding Scholarship. Her *TDR* cover story on Ellen Stewart and La Mama (Summer 2006) was translated into Italian (2006) and presented at the opening ceremonies of the 2006 Venice Biennale. As a founding member of the Bread Loaf Acting Ensemble, since 1986 she has conceived, directed, produced, and performed original work in Middlebury, Vermont, and Juneau, Alaska.

ALISA SOLOMON is the Director of the Arts and Culture Concentration in the new MA program at Columbia University's Graduate School of Journalism. She moved to Columbia after almost twenty years at the City University of New York—as Professor of English and Journalism at Baruch College as well as Professor of English and Theatre at CUNY Graduate Center. She is the author of *Re-Dressing the Canon: Essays on Theatre and Gender* (Routledge, 1997), which won the George Jean Nathan Award for Dramatic Criticism, and was Guest Editor for a special issue of *Theater,* "Theater and Social Change" (fall 2001). She is coeditor (with Framji Minwalla) of *The Queerest Art: Essays on Lesbian and Gay Theater* (NYU Press, 2002), and, with Tony Kushner, of *Wrestling with Zion: Progressive Jewish-American Responses to the Israeli-Palestinian Conflict* (Grove, 2003). Solomon was a staff writer and contributor at the *Village Voice* for more than two decades, writing theater criticism as well as covering immigration policy, queer culture and politics, Israel-Palestine, and women's sports, among other subjects, and she has freelanced for a wide range of newspapers and magazines. Her dramaturgy credits include projects with directors Anne Bogart, Lee Breuer, Anna Deavere Smith, and Lois Weaver.

MICHAEL VANDEN HEUVEL is Associate Professor of Theatre and Drama at the University of Wisconsin, Madison. He is the author of *Performing Drama/Dramatizing Performance: Alternative Theatre and the Dramatic Text* (University of Michigan Press, 1991, reprinted 1993) and *Elmer Rice: A Research and Production Source Book* (Greenwood, 1996). His articles include "'The Gray Line Tour': From Philosophy to Critical Theory in Theatre Studies," *Journal of Dramatic Theory and Criticism,* Spring 2002; "'Is Postmodernism?': Stoppard Among/Against the Postmoderns," in *The Cambridge Companion to Tom Stoppard* (2001); "'Mais je dis le chaos positif': Leaky Tests, Parasited Performances and Maxwellian Academons," in *Contours of the Avant-Garde: Performance and Textuality* (University of Michigan Press, 2000); "Waking the Text: Intertextuality and Dissipative Structure in the Wooster Group's Route 1 & 9," *Journal of Dramatic Theory and Criticism,* Fall 1995; and "Complementary Spaces: Realism, Performance, and a New Dialogics of Theatre," *Theatre Journal* 44, no. 11 (1992).

INDEX

Abdoh, Reza, 360, 373n6, 404
ACT I, 286, 296
ACT I Theater and Festival, 295
acting: American realist acting, 36,
122; community-based, 18, 203,
239, 250, 255, 266, 288, 292, 294,
295, 298, 299, 301, 336, 338, 359,
379; "jamming," 118; method acting, 116; "My House Is Burning" exercise, 118; nonnaturalistic approach to, 79; process, 75; Sound
and Movement exercises, 62, 76,
115, 116, 117, 122; Stanislavski
method, 15, 116, 121; training, 16,
29, 121, 205, 213, 228, 231, 232,
234, 314, 335, 336, 340, 341, 346,
396 (see also Open Theatre); "Viewpoints," 121
Actor's Workshop Encore Theater,
198
Adams, Franklin, 307
Adams, John, Nixon in China, 388
Addams, Charlie, 354; Shoestring Theater, 400
addiction, 37, 38, 39, 136–37
Adler, Stella, 116
Adorno, Pedro, Agua, Sol y Sereno,
399
Adorno, Theodor, Aesthetic Theory, 19,
20, 22
Aeschylus, Children of Herakles, 388,
389

African-American culture. See culture:
African-American
African-American poetry, Free South-
ern Theater performance of, 265,
281
African-Americans: and community
building, 282; and sacrifices of lives
and livelihoods in struggle for civil
rights, 273. See also Black Arts Move-
ment; civil rights movement;
DuBois, W. E. B.; Free Southern
Theater; Gilbert, Moses; Junebug;
Lovelace, Alice; San Francisco Mime
Troupe: The Mozamgola Caper; Sulli-
van, Michael
Agua, Sol y Sereno; Una de Cal y una de
Arena, 399; workshops, 399
"Ain't Gonna Study War No More," 287
Akalatis, JoAnne, 120
Alabama, 265, 270, 284n21, 304n4
Alexander, Robert, 191
Algeria, 229
Alive and Trucking Theatre, 130
All Species Day, 392, 394
Alternate ROOTS (Regional Organiza-
tion of Theaters South), 297, 301;
Community/Artist Partnership Pro-
gram, 297
American Civil Liberties Union
(ACLU), 170, 200
American Festival Project (AFP), 297,
298, 300, 302; workshops, 299